AUTISM

CLINICAL AND RESEARCH ISSUES

AUTISM

CLINICAL AND RESEARCH ISSUES

Edited by Pasquale J. Accardo, M.D.
Christy Magnusen, M.S., M.Ed. and
Arnold J. Capute, M.D., M.P.H.

Baltimore

This book was manufactured in the United States of America.
Typography by Type Shoppe II Productions, Ltd.
Printing and binding by Data Reproductions, Inc.
Cover design by Joseph Dieter, Jr.

Library of Congress Cataloging-In-Publication Data

Autism : clinical and research issues / edited by Pasquale J. Accardo, Christy Magnusen, and Arnold J. Capute.

p. ; cm.

Includes bibliographical references and index.

ISBN 0-912752-48-3

1. Autism. 2. Autism in children. I. Accardo, Pasquale J. II. Magnusen, Christy. III. Capute, Arnold J., 1923-

[DNLM: 1. Autistic Disorder. WM 203.5 A93695 2000]

RC553.A88 A845 2000

616.89'82--dc21

00-043235

Contents

Contributors

Pasquale Accardo, M.D.
Westchester Institute for Human Development
Cedarwood Hall
New York Medical College
Valhalla, New York 10595

Brian Bonfardin, M.D.
Director of Psychiatric Services
Greene Valley Developmental Center
Greeneville, Tennessee

Arnold J. Capute, M.D., M.P.H.
Kennedy Krieger Institute
707 North Broadway
Baltimore, Maryland 21205

Michelle A Dunn, Ph.D.
Albert Einstein College of Medicine
Yeshiva University
Jack and Pearl Resnick Campus
1300 Morris Park Avenue
Kennedy Building, Room 808
Bronx, New York 10461

Jeremy Goldberg, M.D.
Box 2000
Hamilton, Ontario
Canada L8N 3Z5

Barry Gordon, M.D., Ph.D.
The Johns Hopkins Hospital
Department of Neurology
600 North Wolfe Street
Baltimore, Maryland 21287-7222

Marco A. Grados, M.D.
Kennedy Krieger Institute
1750 East Fairmount Avenue
Baltimore, Maryland 21231

Martin Kozloff, Ph.D.
The University of North Carolina at Wilmington
Donald R. Watson School of Education
Department of Specialty Studies
601 South College Road
Wilmington, North Carolina 28403-3297

Rebecca J. Landa, Ph.D., CCC-SLP
Kennedy Krieger Institute
Pierce Building, 3rd Floor
3825 Greenspring Avenue
Baltimore, Maryland 21211-1398

O. Ivar Lovaas, Ph.D.
University of California, Los Angeles
UCLA Clinic for the Behavioral Treatment of Children
Department of Psychology
1282 A Franz Hall
Box 95163
Los Angeles, California 90095-1563

Christy Magnusen, M.S., M.Ed.
Belleville Area, Special Services Cooperative
2411 Pathways Crossing
Belleville, Illinois 62221

John F. Mantovani, M.D.
St. Louis Child Neurology Services, P.C.
621 South New Ballas Road, Suite 5009
St. Louis, Missouri 63141

Daria A. McCarthy, M.S.W., LCSW-C
The Coordinating Center
8258 Veterans Highway
Suite 13
Millersville, Maryland 21108

Scott M. Meyers, M.D.
Neurodevelopmental Pediatrics
Geisinger Medical Center
100 North Academy Avenue
Danville, Pennsylvania 17822-3102

Donna M. Noyes-Grosser, Ph.D.
New York State Department of Health
Bureau of Childhood and Adolescent Health
Room 208, Corning Towers Building
Empire State Plaza
Albany, New York 12237-0618

Joseph Piven, M.D.
Department of Psychiatry
Seventh Floor Neurosciences, CB#7250
University of North Carolina at Chapel Hill
Chapel Hill, North Carolina 27599-7250

John S. Rice, Ph.D.
The University of North Carolina at Wilmington
Donald R. Watson School of Education
Department of Specialty Studies
601 South College Road
Wilmington, North Carolina 28403-3297

Mary Joan Sebastian
Saul R. Korey Department of Neurology
Rose F. Kennedy Center for Research
In Mental Retardation and Human Development
Albert Einstein College of Medicine
Bronx, New York 10461

Peter Szatmari, M.D.
Chedoke-McMaster Hospital
Chedoke Division
Patterson Building
1280 Main Street, West
Hamilton L8N 3Z5
Canada

Darold Treffert, M.D.
St. Agnes Hospital Behavioral Health Services
430 East Division Street
Fond du Lac, Wisconsin 54935

Brooke R. Whitted, Esq.
Foran and Schultz, Attorneys at Law
30 North La Salle Street, Suite 3000
Chicago, Illinois 60602

Andrew W. Zimmerman, M.D.
Johns Hopkins Medical Institutions
Kennedy Krieger Institute
707 North Broadway
Baltimore, Maryland 21205

Preface

On October 10th and 11th, 1997, the Illinois Center for Autism celebrated its twentieth anniversary of service to the community by holding an "International Symposium on Autism" in Fairview Heights, Illinois. The program director for this seminar was Christy Magnusen, then Assistant Director of the Center.

On March 30th through April 1st, 1998, the Kennedy Fellows Association sponsored the twentieth Spectrum of Developmental Disabilities course at the Johns Hopkins Medical Institutions in Baltimore, Maryland. The course director for this and for the previous nineteen programs was Arnold J. Capute, M.D. In addition to this being the twentieth anniversary of the Spectrum course, it also marked the twentieth anniversary of the founding of the Kennedy Fellows Association.

Having presented at these two conferences, I noted that both programs were comprehensive while maintaining different but relatively complementary emphases. Previous Spectrum conference proceedings had been published and well-received.[1] It was considered appropriate to select some of the best papers from the two programs to combine into a single volume. The present collection is the result. The contributors have succeeded in maintaining much of the excitement of the original oral presentations while adding the research scholarship appropriate to a published text. It is offered in celebration of all three anniversaries.

Pasquale J. Accardo, M.D.

In accordance with the theme *Celebrating Dedication, Research, and Progress*, we were honored with the distinction of bringing together 17

[1]Capute, A. J., Accardo, P. J., Shapiro, B. K. (editors) *Attention Deficit Disorders and Learning Disabilities* (Parkton, Maryland: York Press, 1994); Accardo, P. J., Shapiro, B. K., Capute, A. J. (editors) *Behavior Belongs in the Brain* (Parkton, Maryland: York Press, 1997); Accardo, P. J., Capute, A. J. (editors) *Mental Retardation. Mental Retardation and Developmental Disabilities Research Reviews* (number 1, 1998) 4:1–58; Shapiro, B. K., Capute, A. J., Accardo, P. J. (editors) *Specific Reading Disability* (Timonium, Maryland: York Press, 1998).

internationally recognized experts in the field of autism and related spectrum disorders. Merging the best minds in education, law, medicine, psychology, and first-hand experience with the challenging disability of autism, this forum of experts generated enthusiasm, inquiry, and synergy in participants and presenters alike. I extend my heartfelt gratitude to all of you who were so gracious to join us in celebrating the 20-year anniversary of the Illinois Center for Autism.

Since the early 1970s, I have passionately followed a personal quest to help children with autism. It has been a wonderful career, and I am thankful to the families of these special children who had faith in my efforts to help their children. No small task, it has been challenging but never discouraging! Always a source of hope and inspiration, the parents have continually been a font of knowledge and support to me all along the way. I admire each and every one of them for their tireless energy and dedication.

A special note of recognition must also go to McKendree College in Lebanon, Illinois, the site of our International Symposium. Because of their graciousness, we were afforded a comfortable site for our conference, as well as a collegial and creative team with whom to bring about this much-needed forum.

This preface would be noticeably incomplete without applauding the hard work and dedicated efforts of the many teachers, aides, speech pathologists, and other wonderful individuals who have helped to bring services to the children and families who have attended the Illinois Center for Autism. They are the ones who truly deserve the highest degree of honor and recognition, for without them, our cause would have certainly floundered. These gifted individuals are a testimony to the human spirit as they reach out to those less fortunate. I would also like to thank the Board of Directors of the Illinois Center for Autism who had faith in this project, who helped to forward our cause, and who so generously supported our efforts in bringing about this symposium.

Finally, I hope that the readers of this text can appreciate the brilliance and hard work of the presenters who so graciously agreed to share their knowledge and dreams with us on October 10th and 11th, 1997. As first-degree experts, they individually and collectively inspired us to celebrate this joyous occasion. They truly helped us to appreciate the past, to analyze the present, and to anticipate the future as we all come together on behalf of all persons with autism and related spectrum disabilities.

Christy Magnusen, M.S., M.Ed.

The Kennedy Fellows Association (KFA) was incorporated in the state of Maryland in 1978. This academic organization consists of board certified pediatricians who completed a two- to three-year post-pediatric residency training program (fellowship) in Neurodevelopmental Disabilities at the Kennedy Krieger Institute (formerly the John F. Kennedy Institute for Handicapped Children) and the Johns Hopkins University School of Medicine's Department of Pediatrics in Baltimore, Maryland. The organization presently has 109 members, the majority holding academic positions at various medical centers throughout the nation and in several foreign countries.

The Kennedy Fellows Association serves as both an academic and service advocate for people with neurodevelopmental disabilities: these disorders include the chronic neurological spectrum such as mental retardation and cerebral palsy, the learning disability continuum, autistic spectrum disorders, and impairment of vision and hearing.

As part of its national advocacy mission, the Kennedy Fellows Association sponsors an annual multi-disciplinary three-day course held in the Turner Auditorium of the Johns Hopkins Medical Institutions. Although it shares its annual presentation with the Society for Developmental Pediatrics, Kennedy Krieger Institute and the Division of Child Development of the Johns Hopkins University School of Medicine's Department of Pediatrics, the Kennedy Fellows Association retains the fiscal and planning responsibility for the presentation of this course. The organization has also assisted with financial awards to several academic centers for similar course presentations in regions distant from Baltimore.

The constitution and bylaws of the Kennedy Fellows Association includes the above and also highlights its support for subspecialty recognition for neurodevelopmental disabilities in pediatrics. The "venture to board recognition" (subspecialty certification) was politically and financially subsidized by this organization.

Since its inception, the other accomplishments of the Kennedy Fellows Association include the following:

1. During the 1970s the Kennedy Fellows Association made possible visits by its officers to the chairpersons of Departments of Pediatrics at various major academic medical centers throughout the country. The purpose of these visits was to familiarize those chairpersons with what a developmental pediatrician contributes to academic pediatrics and to the care of children with neurodevelopmental disabilities. A further purpose was to attempt to increase support for subspecialty recognition in the field. Approximately thirty visits occurred over a three-year period.

2. The Kennedy Fellows Association assisted with the formation of a Section on Children with Disabilities within the American Academy of Pediatrics.
3. The Kennedy Fellows Association was instrumental in the establishment of the Society for Developmental Pediatrics, a national academic organization consisting of board certified pediatricians who either have formal training in neurodevelopmental disabilities or devote a majority of their practice time to this subspecialty area.
4. The Kennedy Fellows Association continues to support the American Academy for Developmental Medicine and Cerebral Palsy with its annual course presentations, as well as with other academic and service matters related to persons with neurodevelopmental disabilities.
5. The Kennedy Fellows Association provided significant funding for a Chair in Neurodevelopmental Disabilities named the Arnold J. Capute, M.D., M.P.H. Professorship in Developmental Disabilities at the Hopkins/Kennedy Krieger Institutions.
6. The Kennedy Fellows Association is presently funding a multi-site study to standardize infant milestones in a screening/assessment tool called the "CAT/CLAMS." The "CLAMS" is an acronym for "Clinical Linguistic and Auditory Milestones," and the "CAT" for "Clinical Adaptive Tests." (This instrument is also referred to as the *Capute Scales*.) This test is used to screen/assess the neurodevelopmental progress of infants and children under the age of three.

The annual Kennedy Fellows Association Spectrum course will continue to emphasize the clinical and basic neurosciences to enable pediatricians, neurodevelopmental pediatricians, child neurologists, child psychiatrists, pediatric psychiatrists, and professionals in associated disciplines to keep abreast of the rapid escalating discoveries relating to diagnosis and management in this field.

The celebration of their twentieth anniversaries by both the Kennedy Fellows Association and the Illinois Center for Autism with courses on autism stimulated the production of this collaborative volume.

Arnold J. Capute, M.D., M.P.H.

Chapter • 1

Neural Mechanisms in Autism

Andrew W. Zimmerman and Barry Gordon

This chapter is a commentary on what might be the neural bases for the disorders that occur in the autistic spectrum. Our overall objective is to begin to bridge the gap between behavioral definitions and possible underlying neurobiologic mechanisms in these conditions. A related objective is to lay the groundwork for more informed investigations of these mechanisms in the future. Ultimately, the goals of all these efforts are to determine the best strategies for prevention, diagnosis, and treatment of individuals afflicted with autism.

There have been a number of recent, extensive reviews of the neuropsychology and neurology of autism (Bailey, Phillips, and Rutter 1996; Ciaranello and Ciaranello 1995; Happé and Frith 1996; Rapin 1997; Rumsey 1996; Waterhouse, Fein, and Modahl 1996), and several older but still valuable overviews of the deficits in the disorder (Damasio and Maurer 1978; Litrownik and McInnis 1982; Prior 1987). Our intentions, and hence the nature of these comments, appear to be somewhat different from those which motivated those reviews. We start with the admission that there is currently no reliable evidence for the neural basis (or bases) for autism. As of this writing, there are no accepted genetic markers, even though there are several candidates (Bailey et al. 1998; Folstein et al. 1998; Szatmari et al. 1998). It has also become increasingly clear that autism is a heterogeneous disorder, even if it is genetic. The presentation of autism may differ within families (Piven et al. 1997), and even between identical twins (Kates et al. 1998). In addition, no objective tests *in vivo* are specific for the condition. There have been no structural, metabolic, or neuropathologic abnormalities reliably linked to autistic features, even though there have been a number of studies trying to do so, as depicted in figure 1 (Lewin 1995). There is no accepted animal model of the condition, although infant monkeys with selective brain lesions (Bachevalier 1991; Bachevalier and Merjanian 1994) and rats infected intracerebrally with Borna virus during the neonatal period show behavioral features suggestive of autism (Pletnikov et al. 1999).

Since prior efforts have not yielded answers, we feel it is appropriate to reconsider the problem of determining the neural bases for autism. We suggest that it may be a productive strategy to: (1) Consider autism as, at least, several different syndromes with some possible commonalities of mechanism or outcome; (2) Continue the current trend of interpreting the overt behavioral features of the different autisms in terms of their underlying, internal mental operations and functions; and (3) Analyze both the strengths and weaknesses in the different autisms as clues to their neurobiologic etiology, in light of current understanding of how complex cognitive functions are based in neural mechanisms, and how normal and abnormal functions might occur in the course of development. These suggestions are necessarily tentative, and our examples fragmentary. However, they may provide new avenues for investigation.

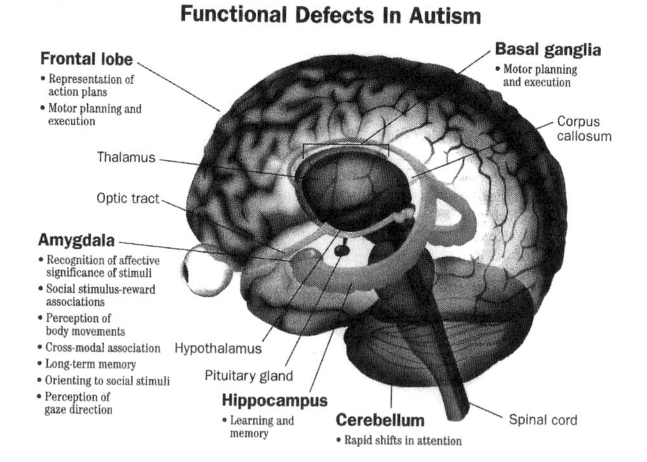

Figure 1. Brain structures and their functions as they relate to autism. Involvement of each structure has been postulated from pathological and neuroimaging studies, or from cognitive functions attributed to it. From Lewin, 1995; Adapted and reprinted with permission from F. Bloom and A. Lazerson, *Brain, Mind and Behavior* (W. H. Freeman and Co., New York, 1988, p. 25) and *Journal of NIH Research* (Medical Economics, Montvale, NJ).

Before beginning attempts at recombination and synthesis, we will first consider some specific issues in the neurobiology of autism and their possible implications.

NEUROBIOLOGIC STUDIES

While no neuropathologic features have yet been found to be characteristic of autism, a number of abnormalities have been reported. Bauman and Kemper (1994) found consistent neuronal changes ("too many, too small") in the hippocampus, amygdala, and other areas of the limbic system, as well as decreased Purkinje cells in the lateral cerebellum. More recently, Bailey, Luthert, and colleagues (1998) reported cerebellar, neocortical, and olivary (but not limbic) changes. These findings may reflect "developmental curtailment" of the cellular connections in the developing cortex (neuropil) that affects information processing and representational memory (in the hippocampal complex); recognition of facial gestures and cross-modal memory (amygdala); and shifting attention, language processing, and motor function (cerebellum). In spite of the limitations of traditional methods inherent in light microscopic studies of autism so far (Rapin and Katzman 1998), and the paucity of postmortem tissue available for study, these studies have fostered a new era in neurobiological research in autism by other investigators who are using recently developed genetic, neurochemical, and morphological techniques. Reduced dendritic branching in the hippocampus was demonstrated by means of Golgi analysis in two cases of autism by Raymond, Bauman, and Kemper (1996; see figure 2). Although this technique did not allow for the counting of synapses, the curtailment of dendritic development and synaptogenesis (or perhaps, excessive pruning) represents abnormal development of the neuropil, which is the substrate of complex neuronal networks and higher order processing (Minshew, Goldstein, and Siegel 1997).

In addition to neuropathological studies, there have been a number of reports of structural neuroimaging (CT and MRI), global and regional metabolic abnormalities, either glucose metabolism or blood flow (Rumsey 1996), and neurochemistry using PET (Chugani et al. 1997). Either no correlations have been found within studies, or subsequent studies have failed to confirm others' initial reports. There are many possible reasons why no consistent picture has emerged from all of these efforts. The populations studied may have been too heterogeneous. The neuroimaging studies, for example, typically rely on high-functioning autistics; the neuropathologic studies typically rely on low-functioning ones who have often had seizures and uncontrollable behaviors (which may have contributed to their deaths). There is

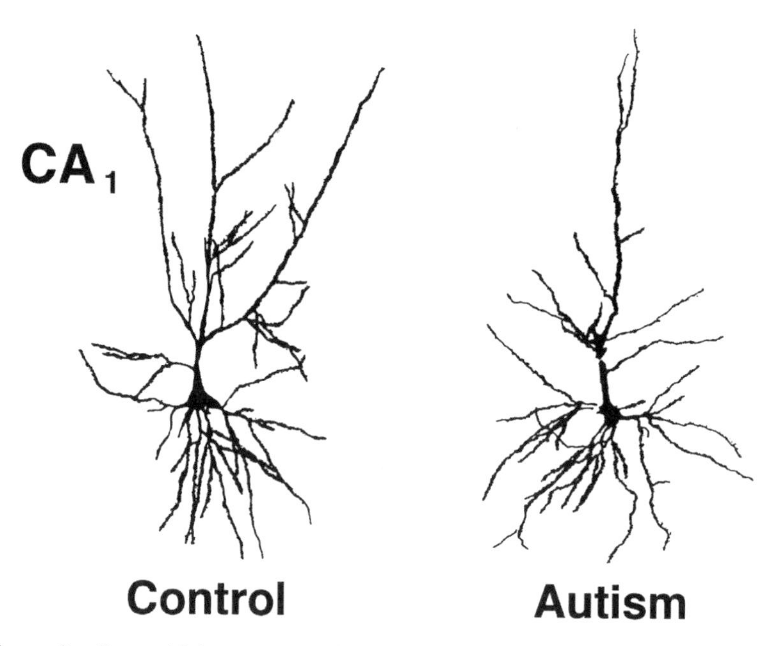

Figure 2. Pyramidal neurons in hippocampus (CA1 field) from autistic and age-matched patient and age-matched control; Golgi-stained section. Note decreased branching of dendrites in autism compared to control tissue; findings were similar for cells in CA4. Cell bodies of neurons of the autistic patients were similar in size in CA1, but smaller in CA4, compared to controls. From Raymond, Bauman, and Kemper (1996); reprinted with permission from *Acta Neuropathologica* (Springer-Verlag, Heidelberg, Germany).

more variability in putative normals than had been thought (This is not just a possibility; it is almost certainly true.). The measures that have been used may simply be too insensitive to the real neurobiologic disorders in autism. For example, if autism were due to subtle irregularities in cell-to cell connections, it could be beyond the resolving power of techniques currently available (figure 2).

Diverse causes for similar defects of *higher cortical functions*

Another explanation for the host of individual abnormalities is that the autistic condition can be caused by a number of different insults and etiologies. These causes may be as diverse as viral infections, dysmorphic syndromes, or genetic abnormalities of intracellular metabolism. In any individual, these would produce a fairly unique pattern at the neural level, even though behavioral outcomes are similar. This latter possibility is in keeping with current views on the complexity of relating behavior to neurobiology, particularly in developmental impairments such as autism. There are some aspects of function in which it is possible to make fairly direct correlations to neuroanatomy, particularly in the fully-developed organism. The elementary sensory and motor systems are the best examples. However, higher cognitive abilities, by their very nature, are the products of different underlying mental functions. Each of these functions may have very complex relationships to neural structures. These mental functions may not even be products of structures per se, so much as internal dynamics or the dynamics of multiple systems and structures. The cerebellum, which has recently been recognized as taking part in a number of non-motoric functions, is a case in point. Moreover, many of the functions we consider to be *higher* abilities are actually *chains* of abilities, unfolding over time. An additional perspective is that the higher functions we consider to be most important are unlikely to have sprung up full-blown in phylogeny. More likely, they have been cobbled together out of refined and rearranged combinations of other functions. Therefore, we should not expect such functions to have very direct brain correlations.

The situation is even more complicated in the case of developmental disorders. Normal mental development proceeds through a cascade of many different processes, which tend to bootstrap each other. An interruption or just simple delay in any part of this sequence can, and often does, have major effects on the final components and their assembly into a functional whole. Development is an even greater reason why the relationship between malfunction and the brain would not be expected to be transparent.

Given these challenges, where should we look for the neural basis of disorders in autism? We should not be surprised if any or all of several different possibilities prove to be true. The genetic deficits of autism may be expressed in peculiar patterns that can be related to neurobiologic organization, but not to the functional organization of the nervous system. Some of the mitochondrial diseases may be examples. The genetic deficits in autism may be expressed at different times in the developing nervous system. Some of these effects may be visible at the time they occur, while some may take a longer period of subsequent development to be expressed. It is still a reasonable strategy to look at development as early as possible for clues to neurobiologic problems. A recent example is the study by Teitelbaum et al. (1998), which showed that movememt disorders could be retrospectively detected in autistic children as early as ages 4 to 6 months. (Of particular relevance to the issues we have raised, it should be noted that the movement disorders were expressed in different movements and in different ways among the children. It should also be noted that this study did not examine other developmentally-impaired children, so the specificity of this finding is still unknown.)

We cannot completely discount the disorders that typically accompany autism but which are not critical to its definition, such as the attentional deficits and the speech and language delays. The precursors to these problems may be reflections of the primary deficits in autism, even if the deficits themselves cannot be the necessary and sufficient causes. What may be even more informative is to consider what the patterns of these accompanying disorders and areas of preserved functions may reveal about the neural basis for the disorders that occur in autism. Clearly, the behavioral and neural disorders we are discussing may not be central to the deficits in autism, if there is such a pure, separable entity, but they are very much part of the disorders that occur in individuals with autism.

NEURAL NETWORKS

In autism, varied neuropathological findings in the limbic system, cerebellum, and frontal cortex suggest that these structures may be the affected important components of relevant neural networks. Variations in clinical expression among autistic spectrum disorders may relate to different types of effects, as well as to their distribution in related structures such as the basal ganglia (important for motor planning) and prefrontal cortex (motivation, executive functions; see figure 3). These regions may be dysfunctional in themselves (e.g., following closed head injury, stroke, or encephalitis) or may become disconnected from their interactive partners within networks due to their failure to develop, modify, or prune their connections during development of the neuropil (Zilbovicius et al. 1995). For example, the basal ganglia (caudate and globus pallidus) and thalamus are essential subcortical integrating waystations in networks with prefrontal and anterior cingulate cortex. Abnormalities in subcortical neurotransmission to or from the prefrontal cortex are likely to contribute to executive dysfunction, disinhibition, irritability, apathy, and inertia (Denckla and Reiss 1997).

The anatomical sites that have been postulated to be involved in autism (figure 1) are likely to be critical waystations in neural networks that may fail to modulate interactions among multiple types of connections in persons with autism (or in other related neurodevelopmental and neuropsychiatric disorders, such as ADHD, Tourette's syndrome, obsessive-compulsive disorder, and schizophrenia). We are beginning to appreciate the brain's network complexities through functional imaging studies in vivo during neuropsychological evaluations (Minshew and Dombrowski 1994). For example, with the use of positron emission tomography (PET), Heckers and colleagues (1998) found impaired hippocampal recruitment despite robust activation of

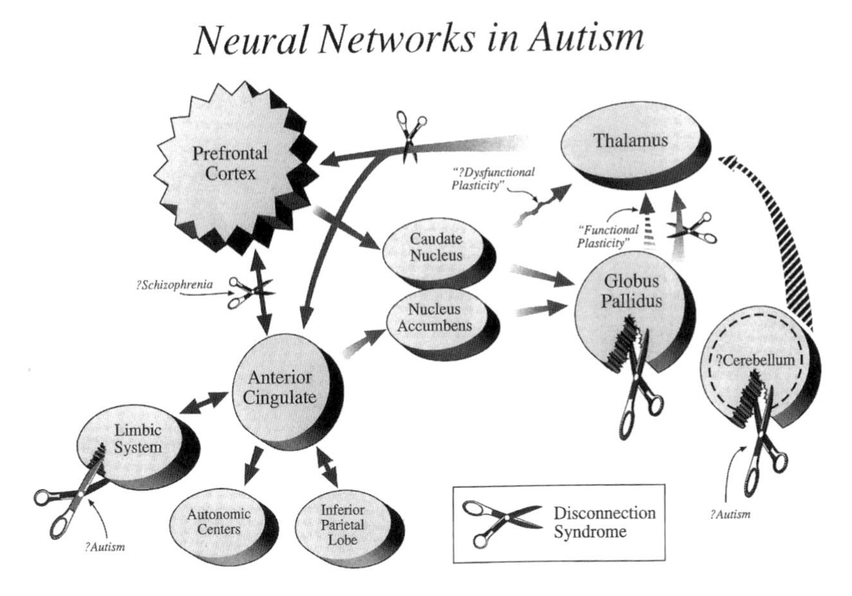

Figure 3. Putative neural networks in autism. Solid arrows indicate direction of neural transmission, based on current information; large striped arrow depicts uncertain cerebellar effects. Large scissors depict cellular "lesions" in important structures that might contribute to network dysfunction or a "disconnection syndrome." Small scissors show potential sites for disconnection within networks and an example of "functional" (correct: globus pallidus to thalamus) or "dysfunctional" (aberrant) repair that might occur from bypassing the globus pallidus. In schizophrenia, a disconnection is thought to occur between the dorsolateral prefrontal area and the anterior cingulate cortex (Benes, F. M. 1993. Relationship of cingulate cortex to schizophrenia. In *The Neurobiology of Cingulate Cortex and Limbic Thalamus*, eds. B. A. Vogt and M. Gabriel. Boston: Birkhauser.).

the dorsolateral prefrontal cortex during memory retrieval tasks in adult males with schizophrenia. This and other types of imaging studies are likely to lead to new understandings of the interactive pathology within networks. Such studies may be applied best to cooperative and unanesthetized high-functioning subjects, using PET or functional MRI (fMRI). Many of the subjects of previous neuropathological and imaging studies have had associated features (e.g., mental retardation, epilepsy) that complicate interpretation of the findings. Unfortunately, these imaging approaches cannot focus yet on young children with autism during critical stages in their early brain development. After we find specific *target* areas and techniques for use with older subjects, it may be possible to apply them to younger subjects using protocols with sedation.

NETWORK REPAIRS

The capacity for repair of or compensation for brain lesions (plasticity) is maximal during the early years of development (Jacobson 1991). Therapeutic programs in autism take advantage of this potential for repair (Lovaas 1987; Greenspan and Wieder 1997). Although its biological basis is poorly understood, clinically effective repair may depend on the regulation of multiple neurotransmitters, growth, and other trophic factors in the brain while training is taking place (and may occur to some degree with or without training). Compensation for defective waystation processes (e.g., hippocampal or cerebellar) or disconnection within networks probably depends on correct forms of rerouting (functional plasticity; figure 3). *Plasticity* is functional if it compensates for a disconnection between waystations (e.g., between globus pallidus and thalamus). *Dysfunctional plasticity* (e.g., from caudate to thalamus) may reduce the efficiency of the repair or even negate its effects if the new route bypasses critical parts of the network (e.g, globus pallidus; figure 3). Functional neuroimaging studies in autistic subjects may eventually help to define the factors (e.g., training techniques, drug effects, diets) that enhance (or inhibit) *functional plasticity* in response to clinical interventions.

COMPUTATIONAL APPROACHES

Artificial neural networks offer computational approaches to the question: "Are there too many or too few cells and connections in autism?" Cohen (1994) demonstrated that too many (as opposed to too few) connections in a model system differentiated hypothetical children with autism from those with mental retardation. In one group of autistic children, "overdetermined networks" provide a strong ability to recognize and discriminate stimulus patterns, but a weak ability to generalize from them due to excessive attention to details. A second group may have difficulty with stimulus discrimination (and, therefore, also generalization) due to too few neurons or neural connections.

Regression in the autistic child's ability to generalize (which typically appears between 18 and 30 months of age) could occur in either group. Those with excessive connections would have relatively normal early concept formation, but would develop overlearning and decreased generalization coincident with regression. The second group (with insufficient cells or connections) would have early delays but still show regression due to increasingly incorrect generalization. Patterns of connectivity may be defective due to an inability either to strengthen or prune out weak connections within (or between) critical waystations (Rakic 1991). Ultimately, each child's pattern of network connectivity may uniquely correspond to his or her own clinical symptoms.

Genes, critical periods, and susceptibility factors

It may be difficult to correlate biological *causes* (once known) directly to clinical symptoms in autism. Recent pathological findings in autism might reflect the tail of a spectrum of defects, or they could be late effects of other, more crucial abnormalities that develop early in gestation. In autism, single genes probably do not affect specific cells in defined brain areas. Rather, several interacting gene loci are likely to act during critical periods for the development of the neural networks discussed above (Rutter, Bailey, and Simonoff 1997). In addition, there may also be individual susceptibility factors (e.g., genetically determined immune dysfunction, increased susceptibility to viral infections, or other infectious causes) that contribute to autism (Zimmerman, Frye, and Potter 1993).

Effects on development of the neuropil in autism, therefore, may represent a summation of developmental variants or a critical accumulation of errors. Possible contributors include neurotransmitters and their receptors, not only serotonin and dopamine, but also acetylcholine, glutamate, and opiates (Anderson and Hoshino 1997). For example, dysfunctional glutamate receptors could result in endogenous excitotoxicity and selective neuronal vulnerability (especially limbic and cerebellar; see chapter on neuropharmacology). Insufficient growth factors (e.g., nerve growth factor, [NGF]), cell adhesion molecules (neural cell adhesion molecule, [NCAM]), DNA transcription factors, intracellular signaling molecules, cytoskeletal proteins, peptides (secretin, vasointestinal peptide or VIP) and programmed cell death (apoptosis) are all important areas for study in model systems. The development of pertinent animal models with behavioral correlates to autism and cell cultures from autistic subjects and controls, such as olfactory neuroblasts (Naidu, Leopold, and Ronnet 1997) will engender further research, from genes to cellular growth regulation.

What are the fundamental behavioral deficits in autism?

A number of attempts have been made to tease apart the cognitive and behavioral deficits that occur in autism, and, hopefully, identify some as more fundamental than others (For reviews see Bailey, Phillips, and Rutter 1996; Happé and Frith 1996; Litrownik and McInnis 1982; Rapin 1997; Rumsey 1996). A recent example has been attention to the lack of a theory of mind in autism. Theory of mind was the term used by Premak & Woodruff (1978) to describe an individual's understanding of the motives, knowledge, and beliefs of others. Frith and Happe (1994), Baron-Cohen (1995), and Baron-Cohen and Swettenham (1997) have noted that autistic individuals do not seem to have such understanding, nor are they able to develop it.

They have, accordingly, posited that a deficit in the primitive functions that form the basis for having a theory of mind could be a major cause of the difficulties in autism. However, just what constitutes a theory of mind, who has it, and whether it is truly impaired in autism has been much debated (see, for example, Povinelli and Preuss 1995).

We suggest that a different, perhaps more fundamental deficit should be entertained as being present in many autistics—low-functioning autistics in particular, and that is a deficit in the ability to manipulate selective thoughts and sensory experiences, independent of the thoughts and experiences themselves. In basic terms, this is a problem with the *ability to imagine*. However, it is not a deficit in simple visual imagery; there is evidence based on self-reports that suggests high-functioning autistics not only have visual imaginations, but rely upon them (Grandin 1997). Instead, what we are referring to is the ability to select elements of mental states and manipulate them or to manipulate the mental state itself (without necessarily permanently affecting it). Normally, humans are able to focus on different aspects of an object or experience, and appear able to separate aspects from the original experience and manipulate them separately. We can see a red cup and separate out its redness from its shape. But autistic persons are notorious for not being able to do this and for, apparently, focusing on the *wrong* features of everyday objects.

There is some evidence that, in normal individuals, this ability to select features from otherwise unitary representations is dependent upon the prefrontal cortex (Thompson-Schill et al. 1997). A deficit in such functions would certainly fit with many of the other behavioral characterstics of autistic persons, e.g., rigidity, repetitive behavior, perseveration, lack of symbolic play, and, more elaborately, a theory of mind. Deacon (1997) and others have suggested that this type of mental manipulation, which is essentially symbolic, is one of the important mental prerequisites of humanness. If so, the lack of this ability would go a long way toward explaining why many autistic persons have the patterns of deficits that they do.

These varied issues in the psychology and neurobiology of autism suggest two more global strategies for future efforts. One is to reconsider how the autistic spectrum of disorders is categorized. The other is to explain the puzzling clinical and neurobiologic heterogeneity in autism.

SUBGROUPS OF AUTISM

Autism is currently diagnosed by a variable combination of three defining characteristics: (1) "Qualitative impairments in social interaction;" (2) "Impairments in communication;" and (3) "Restricted, repetitive, and stereotyped patterns of behavior" (DSM-IV 1994). Searches for a neurobiology of autism have typically been based on cases that meet these criteria. There are several problems with this approach. The best example is, perhaps, the "Impairments in communication." Most individuals fitting this diagnosis have "delayed or absent development of spoken language . . . without attempts to communicate through alternative modes (e.g., signing)." Other individuals can meet this criterion by having speech, but with *abnormal use of language* because of impaired pragmatics or abnormally repetitive speech. It is very likely that the neurobiologic basis for absent speech and language is different when speech and language are present, but not used in social situations.

A second problem with these criteria is that they do not have a single underlying cause. No theory yet links them. Empirical studies have, if anything, suggested that all of these are independent factors. A related problem is that their defining features may not be causative or explanatory features. The characteristics that separate out populations are not necessarily direct markers of the causes of those differences. An analogy to autism in neurology may include the frequently similar, yet diverse, presentations of seizures, coma, and encephalitis. Seizures and coma can result from encephalitis, yet each of these three has its own defining features and causes that may not be relevant to the others. Furthermore, their ultimate causes may remain unknown in some patients despite the best diagnostic efforts.

The major problem with these criteria is that they have not produced a coherent picture of the neural basis for autism. Therefore, it seems reasonable to ask if there may be other grounds for separating out subtypes of autism. We suggest the following four-part grouping as providing what may be better defined subgroups for investigation: (1) High-functioning autism; (2) Developmentally low-functioning autism; (3) Low-functioning autism that begins after a period of normal development (secondary regression); and (4) Autism occurring in the context of other defined conditions. The characteristics and rationale for these subgroups are as follows. Some of these features are already known from epidemiologic and clinical studies; some will necessarily have to await further refinements in diagnosis.

1. High-functioning autistics are those whose only appreciable deficits are in social awareness and sensitivity. Their speech, language, and general intellectual functions are within expected normal limits. These are, of course, the individuals now commonly labeled as Asperger's syndrome (Volkmar, Klin, and Pauls 1998). Since these are the individuals with the fewest functional disabilities, they are the ones who represent the purest form of the *autistic* deficit (if there is a *pure* form of autism). Therefore, studies of these individuals are most likely to reveal basic neurobiologic problem(s) of autism.

This is not to say that this definition is completely without problems. It is arguable whether any given function is impaired or not, given that normal individuals have appreciable cognitive heterogeneity (Selnes and Gordon, in press). Lack of social awareness and sensitivity undoubtedly can cause various kinds of intellectual deficits in their own right, particularly in the intensely social milieu of modern human society. Nevertheless, a category of individuals with just deficits in social intelligence (including the use of language for social reasons) and no other cognitive or behavioral deficits, can be viewed as a prototype for the most specific, least complicated presentation of one form of autism. Since these are the individuals with the fewest other brain malfunctions, they are the most likely to reveal the neurobiology of their own particular form of autism.

2. Developmentally low-functioning autistics. These individuals make up the majority (~50%) of those diagnosed with autism. Abnormalities in motoric functioning, speech and language, and cognitive abilities will have been present from the earliest possible assessment dates. In addition to the classic triad of impairments, these individuals, typically, have a wide range of deficts, spanning a large number of domains: attention (particularly in shifting attention); intent to communicate; elementary intellectual capabilties; speech perception and production; oromotor praxis; learning in simple paradigms; lack of generalization (overspecificity and concreteness); and what seems to be abnormally rapid forgetting.

One reason to make a distinction between the high-functioning persons with autism and those who are lower functioning is that the causal mechanisms in the two are likely to be very different. If there is any rationality behind a neurodevelopmental model of autism, then deficits in the developmental, low-functioning persons with autism would have necessarily occurred earlier in the developmental process, and be far more pervasive and severe in their effects. For the high-functioning persons with autism, whatever the deficit(s), they are necessarily far more constrained. In this multifactorial and multigenic *spectrum* disorder, limiting the number of features that define each subgroup under study should decrease the number of possible underlying variables.

3. Autism due to regression, without discernable cause. The following clinical picture has been described in about 30% of those diagnosed with autism: normal development up to the age of 18 to 30 months, including normal development of language and social skills up to age-appropriate levels. However, these children then fail to develop further skills and lose the language and social skills that they did have. The literature suggests that these children become low-functioning persons with autism, otherwise indistinguishable from the group described above. Our own clinical experience suggests that a wide range of functioning may occur following regression, and various degrees of improvement can take place over the ensuing months and years. (At least, it has not been established in the literature that any individuals who are ultimately described as high-functioning start out in this category, or that specific treatment programs affect their rates of improvement.)

It seems almost certain from clinical experience that autistic regression exists (Rapin 1997). However, it has proven difficult to validate the alleged regression in many cases. Parental reports of regression do not always correlate with videotaped evidence or with the data from contemporaneous evaluations, and vice versa. Nonetheless, there seems to be fairly good evidence that such a pattern exists, even though it may be difficult to determine whether some children fit this pattern or not. Granting the existence of this pattern, its causes are likely to be somewhat different from those in the first two forms of autism. If it is neurodevelopmental, it suggests a somewhat later and different sequence is being followed than in those individuals whose development was never normal. For example, it may be that there are normally two overlapping developmental sequences for social skills and language: an initial one that is the basis for abilities such as single-word comprehension and production, and a later one that forms the basis for complex, multiword comprehension and production. (Bickerton [1990] has suggested that these mechanisms are separable, and that, normally, multiword, grammatical language replaces single-word language at about age 30 months.) In this scenario, the initial developmental sequence normally would be completely replaced by the later one, somewhat akin to the way fetal hemoglobin is replaced by the adult forms. However, in the neurodevelopmental model of this subtype, something prevents the normal expression of full social skills and language; the earlier ones eventually atrophy and are not replaced as they normally would be. Alternatively, but not exclusively, this may be the subgroup in whom secondary, possibly neurochemical or immunological causes for autistic regression may be found. The underlying etiology in these children might, therefore, be more related to those of some cases of Landau-Kleffner syndrome or to Rasmussen's syndrome (Rapin and Katzman 1998).

4. Autism occuring in the context of other conditions, such as Fragile X or tuberous sclerosis (Bregman, Leckman, and Ort 1988; Rutter et al. 1994; Rapin 1997). These individuals are relatively rare, but at least three possibilities exist: (a) The other condition has nothing to do with autism; these were independent conditions. (b) The Fragile X disease or tuberous sclerosis is directly responsible for the autistic picture in these individuals through neuropathologic mechanisms. This would imply that what we know to be shotgun-like effects can, by chance, affect systems and structures that can cause the autistic syndrome. (c) The underlying genetic deficit in these conditions causes the autistic condition through neurodevelopmental mechanisms, not through neuropathologic ones. None of these possibilities (or any others) can be differentiated with the information currently available. While these individuals may ultimately illuminate the neurobiology of autism, currently they should probably be in their own category, and kept distinct in any biologic studies.

There is one clear example of this category at the present time: Rett syndrome. Rett syndrome has several clinical differences from autism, but it also has a number of similarities in clinical course, with early regression, stereotypic movements, and seizures (Naidu 1997). Moreover, the neuropathology of Rett syndrome, unlike that of autism, seems to be more definable, with diffuse abnormalities in development of the neuropil. Therefore, it is plausible that studies of Rett syndrome (which is clinically homogeneous) will lead to important findings relevant to autism (which is clinically heterogeneous). Recent findings from studies of receptor autoradiography in Rett syndrome suggest that deficient cholinergic innervation of cortex may lead to deficient serotonergic activity, along with reactive increases in glutamatergic innervation (Blue, Naidu, and Johnston 1999a, 1999b). More importantly, these changes appear to be dynamic and change with age, so that one can begin to hypothesize relationships to patterns of clinical regression, stability, or improvement during a lifespan. The recent identification of mutations in an X-linked methyl-CpG-binding protein 2 (MeCP2) gene in Rett syndrome by Amir et al. (1999) also provides a novel mechanism whereby these multiple abnormalities can result from failure of MeCP2 to normally repress gene transcription during brain development.

Unifying hypotheses for the behavioral and neuropathologic features

Within these proposed categories of autism, much still needs to be explained. Each of the categories described above (with the possible exceptions of autism occurring in the context of other conditions and Rett syndrome) are known to be associated with at least two paradoxes. One is that autistic individuals often have disproportionate mental abilities and skills, in addition to their obvious disabilities. The other paradox is that, despite the clear cognitive and behavioral abnormalities in each of the autistic categories, the underlying neural pathology still seems to resist a consistent description. Going back and reclassifying the pathology of autism into the categories we propose above does not result in any more coherent picture. From what we can tell from published studies, even within the categories we have described, reported abnormalities may be present in some individuals, and absent or different in others.

Earlier, we suggested that some of this apparent inconsistency was due to inconsistencies in the way autistic disorders have been categorized, and we suggested a different categorization that might reduce the etiologic and neuropathologic heterogeneity. Our inability to find the expected benefits of our categorization scheme may simply reflect the conflation of categories in reported studies and the impossibility of reconstructing the studies from published accounts. But it is also possible that some heterogeneity in mental functions as well as in neuropathology will prove to be a fundamental characteristic of each category of autism. This is the possibility we will discuss now.

BEHAVIORAL HETEROGENEITY

One of the most striking features of autism is that it is often accompanied by relative strengths in some areas of cognition and by disabilities in others (Happé and Frith 1996; O'Connor and Hermelin 1989). Such a pattern is not completely unknown in developmental disorders. In Williams sydrome, speech, surface language abilities, and, at times, musical ability are typically far superior to visuospatial abilities and general cognitive abilities (Capirci, Sabbadini, and Volterra 1996; Tager-Flusberg, Boshart, and Baron-Cohen 1998). Many of the developmental syndromes of mental retardation have relative preservation of visual perceptual ability (Pulsifer 1996). However, supranormal islands of ability are much rarer in other conditions compared to autistic spectrum disorders (Happé and Frith 1996). It has been claimed that 10% of the autistic population has *special abilities* (Rimland and Fein 1988). The supranormal skills that have been described (in both autistics and in individuals with other diagnoses) have included: lightning calculation; calender skills; list learning (Mottron et al. 1998); visual memory; hyperlexia; puzzles; drawing ability; musical memory; and playing by ear and improvisation (for more complete lists, see Happé and Frith 1996; O'Connor and Hermelin 1989). Regardless of the exact number of those having such abilities, the overabundance of such abilities demands some explanation, and might even shed some light on the nature and neurobiology of autism itself, as Frith (1989), O'Connor and Hermelin (1989), and others have suggested.

Not all of the apparently superior skills that have been reported are difficult to explain. Restricted attentional focus, repetitiveness, and lack of competing thoughts or abilities (Frith 1989) can certainly account for many apparent abilities. A recent study of atypical memory abilities in one individual (Mottron et al. 1998) is, perhaps, an example of how superior performance in one area may be accounted for, in some instances, by actual cognitive deficiencies in other areas.

However, other examples of apparently superior ability which seem to arise spontaneously (e.g., Selfe 1977), and which do not seem to be easily explained by the absence of normal mental impediments, also exist. These often seem to involve implicit learning of rules and patterns (Hermelin and O'Connor 1986). Often, they seem to be remarkably circumscribed. An individual who can do lightning calculations of dates may not even be able to multiply numbers (Happé and Frith 1996). It may not be unreasonable to ask that any unified account of the neural basis for autism account for these abilities as well as disabilities.

NEUROPATHOLOGIC HETEROGENEITY

We simply note again a point made previously, and by many commentators: While a host of abnormalities have been described in autistic individuals, none has been generalizable to autism as a whole. Most—if not all—of the explanations for this may be trivial.

It may simply be that the real neuropathology in autism is below the resolving power of current instruments. It may also be that no previous studies have used proper subjects, proper controls, or proper techniques to delineate the neural and neuropathologic disorders that are actually present. Or, perhaps, these studies have been accurate, at least up to a point. Perhaps individuals with autism really do have abnormalities that can be appreciated by current techniques, but are too diverse across individuals.

It may be possible to unify both the behavioral heterogeneity—the abnormalities and the supernormalities—as well as the possible neural heterogeneity. To do so requires a digression into neural network theories. (It should be noted that Cohen [1994] raised many of the same hypotheses proposed here.)

Neural network theories of cognitive processes posit that many mental operations are carried out through successive sets (layers) of neuronal processing elements (for a brief overview, see Gordon 1997, and "Computational approaches" above). With the proper input and training criteria, and the proper learning rules, such networks have proven to be extremely adept at embodying rules and patterns that are implicit in the data presented to them. However, the accuracy of this extraction is very dependent upon the number of processing elements in the active learning layer (Baum and Hausler 1989). If there are too few elements, then the network does not learn with very good accuracy. It, in fact, overgeneralizes. If there are too many elements, then the network learns each specific situation presented to it and doesn't generalize enough. If some number of working elements leads to adequate performance, a somewhat greater number can result in truly superior performance in learning implicit rules and patterns, so long as it avoids becoming too specific.

This obervation might be tied into normal development and to the abnormal development(s) that occur in autism, in the following way: It is thought that the normal development of higher cerebral functions in a child's cortex is driven by at least two major influences. One is predetermined connections. The other is activity and use. It has often been noted that the number of genes coding for the brain and neural tissue (~50,000) are insufficient to specify all the connections of the mature brain. The development of these connections must be guided in part by experience. Edelman and his colleagues (Edelman 1987; Intrator and Edelman 1997) have suggested that whether an uncommitted area develops connections with one region or another is based on the outcome of a competition for use. The developing child's brain normally has several primary sensory inputs (including vision, audition, and touch). These are hardwired and fairly compelling. Such sensory inputs will do all they can to recruit whatever upstream neuronal processing resources are not yet committed. Normally, the multiple influences on a child lead to a balance of forces, with the normal balance of lower- and higher-processing abilities (and neuroanatomic maps) as a result. The amount of neural tissue that is devoted to each higher function, therefore, represents trade-offs among several forces: an attempt to optimize processing; the practical limits on optimization (because of lack of enough experience and training time); and competition with other functions for those same neuronal processing elements.

What if a developing brain had all those same forces at work, but for some reason some processing systems were impaired or delayed in their development? What if the systems in question were those involved in speech perception and speech production? Specific genetic deficits in speech production have been tentatively identified; it is conceivable that there are other deficits or combinations of deficits with more widespread effects, on both speech production and speech perception. If the systems related to speech perception and speech production were developmentally impaired, then many higher abilities dependent upon appropriate auditory input and output would never develop properly. And whatever cerebral tissue would have been devoted to those higher functions would be free to be incorporated into other processes (assuming the tissue itself was not too badly affected by the same defects).

If vision were intact, then visual-related abilities would be expected to appropriate the extra cerebral tissue. The result would be a child's brain that was not capable of all of the normal functions of a child, but which could do some functions superlatively well. It would not be capable of those abilities which are related to speech and language capability, such as a long-term component of working memory (the part normally dependent upon an articulatory loop), and perhaps even such higher functions as the *inner voice* aspects of consciousness. It would, however, be extraordinarily good at wordless visual perception and analysis. Neuropathologically, such a brain might have only a few, apparently nonspecific abnormalities. It would not have to have fewer neurons than normal. Autistic brains are, if anything, average or larger-than-average in size (Lainhart et al. 1997; Courchesne, Muller, and Saitoh 1999). It might be possible to detect additional territory devoted to visual-related functions, but perhaps not with current behavioral tasks and instrumentation. Autism may, therefore, represent disorders of activity-dependent plasticity during brain development, occurring at several different levels: gene, synapse, neuron, network, and neuronal group.

In broader outline, the hypothesis is this: Either because of genetics or external influences, several regions or neuronal networks of the developing brain are damaged or delayed in their development. Regions involved in social connection, and those involved in speech and language seem to be particularly susceptible. (It is not too speculative to imagine that they have a functional linkage, and perhaps a genetic one as well.) There are two consequences of this primary pathology. Functions that require these inputs cannot develop fully. Functions that are not dependent on impaired routes can develop normally, and might well develop supranormally. They would develop supranormally if these functions were normally kept constrained by a competition for neural resources from the functions that were now impaired (with the competition either in functional space, or, perhaps, just through simple anatomic proximity).

This hypothesis has several testable consequences. There will be *forme frustes* of autistic disorder—in speech and language, and in socialization—representing less extreme forms of the autistic pathology. These types of deficits should be familial. The domino effect on functions should be predictable once we have a better understanding of what functions depend upon other functions in both development and in operation. Finally, it should be possible to identify some *in vivo* correlates of the extra neural tissue that has been adopted for processing, for example, vision in these individuals.

This hypothesis does not explain the primary cause or causes of the deficits. It would, however, help to explain why persons with autism tend to have the patterns of disabilities and abilities that they do. It might also suggest ways in which functional retraining can try to ameliorate some of their disabilities or take advantage of particular strengths.

CONCLUSIONS

While we do not yet know the neural mechanisms in autism, we have some important clues about the search. The next stages of investigation of neural mechanisms in autistic spectrum disorders should focus on the selection of subjects and the clinical definition of subsets. Although well-studied animal models are desirable, high-functioning subjects with autism are more likely to reveal the essential abnormalities in this very *human* disorder. Multiple investigative techniques, from cellular and neurochemical to cognitive neurophysiology, quantitative and functional neuroimaging, will help us to define the neural networks that contribute to autism.

CHAPTER SUMMARY

1. Autism is not a single entity, but rather a collection of syndromes with possible commonalities of etiological mechanism or outcome.
2. The different patterns of strengths and weaknesses in autism may represent behavioral clues as to the underlying neurobiology.
3. There are no consistent neuropathologic or neuroimaging abnormalities in autism.
4. Higher cortical functioning is the end product of a number of underlying brain functions which may themselves be impaired in different ways to yield the same or similar neurobehavioral deficit patterns.
5. The genetic defects underlying autism may be expressed at different times during the development of the nervous system, so that several interacting genes affect the development of specific neural networks at critical periods.
6. Regression can be explained by several different types of neural dysfunctions.
7. Functional plasticity may compensate for disconnection among the different layers or components of the neural networks that underlie cognitive processes.
8. Theory of mind describes an individual's awareness of the motives, knowledge, and beliefs of others; a prefrontal cortical deficit to select and manipulate elements of mental states may help explain the absence of such a theory of mind in autism.

9. An alternative grouping of the subtypes of autism can be based on clinical and epidemiological studies:
   a. high-functioning autism (Asperger's syndrome)
   b. developmentally low-functioning autism (autism with mental retardation)
   c. low-functioning autism that begins after a period of normal development (secondary regression)
   d. autism occurring in the context of other defined conditions (e.g., Fragile X, tuberous sclerosis, or Rett syndrome)
10. Relative strengths, supranormal, or savant skills are more common in individuals with autism than in those with other developmental disorders; any effective neural explanatory basis for autism will need to address this phenomenon.

Acknowledgements: Preparation of this chapter by A.W. Z. was supported, in part, by the National Alliance for Autism Research and the East Tennessee Chapter, Autism Society of America; B. G. was supported in part by the New York Community Trust — Hodgson Fund, by the Hodgson Family, by the Benjamin A. Miller Family Fund, and by gifts made in memory of Bernard Gordon. We thank Martha Bridge Denckla, MD, for helpful discussions regarding neural pathways in autism. James Marcum contributed to the artwork (figure 3).

REFERENCES

American Psychiatric Association. 1994. *Diagnostic and Statistical Manual of Mental Disorders* (4th ed.). Washington, D.C.: Author.

Amir, R. E., Van den Veyver, I. B., Wan, M., Tran, C. Q., Francke, U., and Zoghbi, H. Y. 1999. Rett syndrome is caused by mutations in X-linked MeCP2, encoding methyl-CpG-binding protein 2. *Nature Genetics* 23:185–8.

Anderson, G. M., and Hoshino, Y. 1997. Neurochemical studies of autism. In *Handbook of Autism and Pervasive Developmental Disorders*, eds. D. J. Cohen and F. R. Volkmar. New York: John Wiley and Sons.

Bachevalier, J. 1991. An animal model for childhood autism: Memory loss and socioemotional disturbances following neonatal damage to the limbic system in monkeys. In *Advances in Neuropsychiatry and Psychopharmacology*, eds. C. A. Tamminga and S. C. Schulz. New York: Raven Press.

Bachevalier, J., and Merjanian, P. 1994. The contribution of medial temporal lobe structures in infantile autism: A neurobehavioral study in primates. In *The Neurobiology of Autism*, eds. M. L. Bauman and T. L. Kemper. Baltimore: Johns Hopkins University Press.

Bailey, A., Phillips, W., and Rutter M. 1996. Autism: Towards an integration of clinical, genetic, neuropsychological, and neurobiological perspectives. *Journal of Child Psychology and Psychiatry* 37:89–126.

Bailey, A., Palferman, S., Heavey, L., and Le Couteur, A. 1998. Autism: The phenotype in relatives. *Journal of Autism and Developmental Disorders* 28(5):369–92.

Bailey, A., Luthert, P., Dean, A., Harding, B., Janota, I., Montgomery, M., Rutter, M., and Lantos, P. 1998. A clinicopathological study of autism. *Brain* 121:889–905.

Bailey, C. H., Bartsch, D., and Kandel E. R. 1996. Toward a molecular definition of long-term memory storage. Proceedings of the National Academy of Sciences of the United States of America 93(24):13445–52.

Baron-Cohen, S., and Swettenham, J. 1997. Theory of mind in autism: Its relationship to executive function and central coherence. In *Handbook of Autism and Pervasive Developmental Disorders*, eds. D. J. Cohen and F. R. Volkmar. New York: John Wiley & Sons.

Baum, E. B., and Hausler, D. 1989. What sized net gives valid generalization? *Neural Computation* 1:151–60.

Bauman, M. L., and Kemper, T. L. 1994. Neuroanatomic observations of the brain in autism. In *The Neurobiology of Autism*, eds. M. L. Bauman and T. L. Kemper. Baltimore, MD: Johns Hopkins University Press.

Benes, F. M. 1993. Relationship of cingulate cortex to schizophrenia. In *The Neurobiology of Cingulate Cortex and Limbic Thalamus*, eds. B. A. Vogt and M. Gabriel. Boston: Birkhauser.

Bickerton, D. 1990. *Language and Species*. Chicago: University of Chicago Press.

Blue, M. E., Naidu, S., and Johnston, M. V. 1999a. Development of amino acid receptors in frontal cortex from girls with Rett syndrome. *Annals of Neurology* 45:541–45.

Blue, M. E., Naidu, S., and Johnston, M. V. 1999b. Altered development of glutamate and GABA receptors in the basal ganglia of girls with Rett syndrome. *Experimental Neurology* 156:345–52.

Bregman, J. D., Leckman, J. F., and Ort, S. I. 1988. Fragile X syndrome: Genetic predisposition to psychopathology. *Journal of Autism and Developmental Disorders* 18:343–54.

Capirci, O., Sabbadini, L., and Volterra, V. 1996. Language development in Williams syndrome: A case study. *Cognitive Neuropsychology* 13:1017–40.

Chugani, D. C., Muzik, O., Rothermel, R., Behen, M., Chakraborty, P., Mangner, T., da Silva, E. A., and Chugani, H. T. 1997. Altered serotonin synthesis in the dentatothalamocortical pathway in autistic boys. *Annals of Neurology* 42:666–69.

Ciaranello, A. L., and Ciaranello, R. D. 1995. The neurobiology of infantile autism. *Annual Review of Neuroscience* 18:101–28.

Cohen, I. L. 1994. An artificial neural network analogue of learning in autism. *Biological Psychiatry* 36:5–20.

Courchesne, E., Muller, R. A., and Saitoh, O. 1999. Brain weight in autism: Normal in the majority of cases, megalencephalic in rare cases. *Neurology* 52:1057–59.

Damasio, A. R., and Maurer, R. G. 1978. A neurological model for childhood autism. *Archives of Neurology* 35:777–86.

Deacon, T. 1997. *The Symbolic Species: The Co-evolution of Language and the Brain*. New York: W. W. Norton and Company.

Denckla, M. B., and Reiss, A. L. 1997. Prefrontal-subcortical circuits in developmental disorders. In *Development of the Prefrontal Cortex: Evolution, Neurobiology and Behavior*, eds. N. A. Krasnegor, G. R. Lyon, and P. S. Goldman-Rakic. Baltimore, MD: Paul H. Brookes.

Edelman, G. M. 1987. *Neural Darwinism: The Theory of Neuronal Group Selection*. New York: Basic Books.

Folstein, S. E., Bisson E., Santangelo, S. L., and Piven, J. 1998. Finding specific genes that cause autism: A combination of approaches will be needed to maximize power. *Journal of Autism and Developmental Disorders* 28:439–45.

Frith, U. 1989. *Autism: Explaining the Enigma*. Oxford: Blackwell.

Frith, U., and Happé, F. 1994. Autism: Beyond "theory of mind." *Cognition* 50:115–32.

Gordon, B. 1997. Models of naming. In *Anomia*, eds. H. Goodglass and A. Wingfield. San Diego, CA: Academic Press.

Grandin, T. 1997. A personal perspective on autism. In *Handbook of Autism and Pervasive Developmental Disorders*, eds. D. J. Cohen and F. R. Volkmar. New York: John Wiley and Sons.

Greenspan, S. I., and Wieder, S. 1997. Developmental patterns and outcomes in infants and children with disorders of relating and communicating: A chart review of 200 cases of children with autistic spectrum diagnoses. *The Journal of Developmental and Learning Disorders* 1:87–141.

Happé, F., and Frith, U. 1996. The neuropsychology of autism. *Brain* 119: 1377–1400.

Heckers, S., Rauch, S. L., Goff, D., Savage, C. R., Schacter, D. L., Fischman, A. J., and Alpert, N. M. 1998. Impaired recruitment of the hippocampus during conscious recollection in schizophrenia. *Nature Neuroscience* 1:318–23.

Hermelin, B., and O'Connor, N. 1986. Idiot savant calendrical calculators: Rules and regularities. *Psychological Medicine* 16:885–93.

Intrator, N., and Edelman, S. 1997. Competitive learning in biological and artificial neural computation. *Trends in Cognitive Sciences* 1:268–72.

Jacobson, M. 1991. *Developmental Neurobiology*, 3rd Edition. New York: Plenum Press.

Kates, W. R., Mostofsky, S. H., Zimmerman, A. W., Mazzocco, M. M. M., Landa, R., Warsofsky, I. S., Kaufmann, W. E., and Reiss, A. L. 1998. Neuroanatomical and neurocognitive differences in a pair of monozygous twins discordant for strictly defined autism. *Annals of Neurology* 43:782–91.

Lainhart, J. E., Piven, J., Wzorek, M., Landa, R., Santangelo, S. L., Coon, H., and Folstein, S. E. 1997. Macrocephaly in children and adults with autism. *Journal of the American Academy of Child and Adolescent Psychiatry* 36:282–90.

Lewin, D. I. 1995. From mind to molecule, researchers try to unravel the complexity of autism. *Journal of National Institute of Health (NIH) Research* 7:44–8.

Litrownik, A. J., and McInnis, E. T. 1982. Cognitive and perceptual deficits in autistic children: A model of information processing, critical review, and suggestions for the future. In *Advances in Child Behavioral Analysis and Therapy*, eds. J. J. Steffen and P. Karoly. Lexington, KY: Lexington Books.

Lovaas, O. I. 1987. Behavioral treatment and normal educational and intellectual functioning in young autistic children. *Journal of Autism and Developmental Disorders* 9:315–23.

Minshew, N. J., and Dombrowski, S. M. 1994. In vivo neuroanatomy of autism: Neuroimaging studies. In *The Neurobiology of Autism*, eds. M. L. Bauman and T. L. Kemper. Baltimore, MD: Johns Hopkins University Press.

Minshew, N. J., Goldstein, G., and Siegel, D. J. 1997. Neuropsychologic functioning in autism: Profile of a complex information processing disorder. *Journal of the International Neuropsychological Society* 3:303–16.

Mottron, L., Belleville, S., Stip, E., and Morasse, K. 1998. Atypical memory performance in an autistic savant. *Memory* 6:593–607.

Naidu, S. 1997. Rett syndrome: A disorder affecting early brain growth. *Annals of Neurology* 42:3–17.

Naidu, S., Leopold, D. A., and Ronnet, G. V. 1997. Abnormal olfactory receptor neuronal development in Rett syndrome. *Annals of Neurology* 42:513.

O'Connor, N., and Hermelin, B. 1989. The memory structure of autistic idiot-savant mnemonists. *British Journal of Psychology* 80:97–111.

Piven, J., Palmer, P., Jacobi, D., Childress, D., and Arndt, S. 1997. Broader autism phenotype: Evidence from a family history study of multiple-incidence autism families. *American Journal of Psychiatry* 154:185–90.

Pletnikov, M. V., Rubin, S. A., Vasudevan, K., Moran, T. H., and Carbone, K. M. 1999. Developmental brain injury associated with abnormal play behavior in neonatally Borna disease virus-infected Lewis rats: A model of autism. *Behavioural Brain Research* 100:42–50.

Povinelli, D., and Preuss, T. 1995. Theory of Mind: Evolutionary history of a cognitive specialization. *Trends in Neurosciences* 18:418–24.

Premack, D., and Woodruff, G. 1978. Does the chimpanzee have a theory of mind? *Behavioral Brain Sciences* 4:515–26.

Prior, M. R. 1987. Biological and neuropsychological approaches to childhood autism. *British Journal of Psychiatry* 150:8–17.

Pulsifer, M. B. 1996. The neuropsychology of mental retardation. *Journal of the International Neuropsychological Society* 2:159–76.

Rakic, P. 1991. Plasticity of cortical development. In *Plasticity of Development*, eds. S. E. Brauth, W. S. Hall, and R. J. Dooling. Cambridge, MA: MIT Press.

Rapin, I. 1997. Autism. *New England Journal of Medicine* 337:97–104.

Rapin, I., and Katzman, R. 1998. Neurobiology of autism. *Annals of Neurology* 43:7–14.

Raymond, G. V., Bauman, M. L., and Kemper, T. L. 1996. Hippocampus in autism: A Golgi analysis. *Acta Neuropathologica* 91:117–19.

Rimland, B., and Fein, D. 1988. Special talents of autistic savants. In *The Exceptional Brain: Neuropsychology of Talent and Special Abilities*, eds. L. Obler and D. Fein. New York: Guilford Publications.

Rumsey, J. M. 1996. Neuroimaging studies of autism. In *Neuroimaging: A Window to the Neurological Foundations of Learning and Behavior in Children*, eds. G. R. Lyon and J. M. Rumsey. Baltimore, MD: Paul H. Brookes.

Rutter, M., Bailey A., Bolton, P., and Le Couteur, A. 1994. Autism and known medical conditions: Myth and substance. *Journal of Child Psychology and Psychiatry* 35(2):311–22.

Rutter, M., Bailey, A., Simonoff, E., and Pickles, A. 1997. Genetic influences and autism. In *Handbook of Autism and Pervasive Developmental Disorders*, eds. D. J. Cohen and F. R. Volkmar. New York: John Wiley and Sons.

Selfe, L. 1977. *Nadia*. New York: Harcourt Brace Jovanovich.

Selnes, O. A., and Gordon, B. (in press). Neuropsychological testing. In *Diagnostic Testing in Neurology*, ed. R. Evans. Philadelphia, PA: W. B. Saunders.

Szatmari, P., Jones, M. B., Zwaigenbaum, L., and MacLean J. E. 1998. Genetics of autism: Overview and new directions. *Journal of Autism and Developmental Disorders* 28:351–68.

Tager-Flusberg, H., Boshart, J. and Baron-Cohen, S. 1998. Reading the windows to the soul: Evidence of domain-specific sparing in Williams syndrome. *Journal of Cognitive Neuroscience* 10:631–39.

Teitelbaum, P., Teitelbaum, O., Nye, J., Fryman, J., and Maurer, R. G. 1998. Movement analysis in infancy may be useful for early diagnosis of autism. Proceedings of the National Academy of Sciences of the United States of America 95(23):13982–87.

Thompson-Schill, S., D'Esposito, M., Aguirre, G. K., and Farrah, M. J. 1997. Role of the left inferior prefrontal cortex in retrieval of semantic knowledge: A reevaluation. Proceedings of the National Academy of Sciences of the United States of America 94:14792–97.

Volkmar, F. R., Klin, A., and Pauls, D. 1998. Nosological and genetic aspects of Asperger's syndrome. *Journal of Autism and Developmental Disorders* 28:457–63.

Waterhouse, L., Fein, D., and Modahl, C. 1996. Neurofunctional mechanisms in autism. *Psychological Review* 103:457–89.
Zilbovicius, M., Garreau, B., Samson, Y., Remy, P., Barthélémy, C., Syrota, A., and Lelord, G. 1995. Delayed maturation of the frontal cortex in childhood autism. *American Journal of Psychiatry* 152:248–52.
Zimmerman, A. W., Frye, V. H., and Potter, N. T. 1993. Immunological aspects of autism. *International Pediatrics* 8:199–204.

Chapter • 2

Epidemiology of Autism and Other Pervasive Developmental Disorders: *Current Controversies*

Peter Szatmari
Jeremy Goldberg

"Autism is a rare disorder occurring in about 4 per 10,000 children." This is probably an accurate reflection of the current consensus of the prevalence of autism. The estimate is based on over twenty years of community surveys of autism and has been quoted many times in authoritative reviews (Zahner and Pauls 1987; Wing 1993; Fombonne 1996). However, this figure does not coincide with the impression of many clinicians and service providers who feel that the number of children diagnosed with autism is much higher than commonly thought. In fact, some experts in the field who have done epidemiologic work support an alternative view that autistic spectrum disorders may occur in up to 1% of the general population (Wing 1997; Arvidsson et al. 1997).

The purpose of this chapter is to try to understand the reasons for this substantial discrepancy in current thinking about the prevalence of autism. This chapter will address four questions: (1) Is there a true difference in prevalence estimates or is this variation due simply to sampling? (2) What methodologic factors might account for these differences? (3) Do the biases increase or decrease the reported prevalence estimates? and (4) Given the available information, what would be a reasonable estimate of the prevalence of autism and other pervasive developmental disorders?

This is not simply an academic debate. Prevalence estimates are important and are used by policy makers to assess the match between the numbers of children with a disorder and available services. If autism is seen as a rare disorder, it will have a significant impact on the financial resources available for diagnosis and treatment.

IS THERE A TRUE DIFFERENCE IN PREVALENCE ESTIMATES OR IS THE VARIATION DUE SIMPLY TO SAMPLING VARIATION?

One obvious explanation for the 25-fold difference quoted above is that the first figure refers only to autism, whereas the second estimate includes children with other types of pervasive developmental disorder; that is, all the autism spectrum disorders. The latter category includes Asperger's syndrome, atypical autism, childhood disintegrative syndrome, and Rett syndrome (Wing 1997). Other terms, such as non-Kanner autism, or pervasive developmental disorder not otherwise specified (PDD-NOS), have also been used to describe such children in several prevalence studies (Lotter 1966; Burd, Fischer, and Kerbeshian 1987). Although there are few epidemiologic studies of these non-autistic forms of pervasive developmental disorder, none suggests that they are 25 times more common than autism (Ehlers and Gillberg 1993; Gillberg and Gillberg 1989). Even excluding the other PDDs, there is considerable variation in the reported prevalence estimates of autism alone. Three recent authoritative reviews have systematically identified all available prevalence estimates of autism and summarized the results (Wing 1993; Fombonne 1996; Gillberg 1995). These reviews show that prevalence estimates of autism have varied widely from 2 to 16 per 10,000 since the earliest study by Lotter (1966) to the more recent estimates by Gillberg (1991) and Fombonne (1996). Although meta-analytic techniques allow one to assess statistically whether there is true heterogeneity in prevalence estimates or whether these differences represent sample variation, such techniques were not used. Even a brief perusal of the data suggests that the differences are too large, given the sample sizes, to be explained by sampling variation. Moreover, one alternative explanation (that is, that there has been a true increase in prevalence) is unlikely, given what is known about the etiology of autism. It now seems clear that genetic factors account for the largest part of the variance in etiology (Szatmari et al. 1998), and for the disorder to become more prevalent, an increase in the frequency of susceptibility genes would have to occur. This is very unlikely given the short time span over which the increase has been noticed and given the fact that most people with autism do not reproduce. To conclude, it seems clear that differences in methods must account for the different prevalence estimates of autism reported in the literature.

WHAT METHODOLOGIC FACTORS MIGHT ACCOUNT FOR THESE DIFFERENCES?

Boyle (1998) has identified key methodologic features with respect to sampling and measurement that aid in interpreting the quality of epidemiologic studies. These can also be used to decide whether methodologic factors account for the differences in prevalence estimates. With respect to sampling, Boyle identifies four main questions: (1) Does the survey design yield a sample of respondents representative of a defined target population? (2) Is the target population clearly defined; that is, who is in the denominator? (3) Was probability sampling used to identify potential respondents; what is the chance of an individual being included in the sample? and (4) Do the characteristics of the respondents match the target population; that is, is the sample representative, and what was the non-response or refusal rate?

It is difficult to carry out epidemiologic studies of rare disorders in view of the cost involved and the careful attention that must be paid to sampling and measurement. For rare disorders, a two-stage design is often employed; this has been the case for all the prevalence studies of autism. First, a brief screening of the target population is carried out to identify those individuals who might possibly have autism, and then a more intensive diagnostic work up is conducted to confirm the diagnosis. This type of design, while efficient, can also lead to several methodologic biases that affect prevalence estimates.

Most epidemiologic studies of autism used non-probability sampling methods and incomplete ascertainment procedures. In other words, it was impossible to calculate the probability of an individual's being selected from the general population and unclear as to whether representative samples of a defined target population were included in the studies. For example, many studies initially screened potential cases from clinics or administrative files (Brask 1970; Treffert 1970; Steinhausen et al. 1986; Fombonne and du Mazaubrun 1992; Fombonne 1996). These studies sampled autistic/PDD individuals already identified by a clinic, who were correctly diagnosed. In these and other two-stage screening studies, no estimates of the size of the target population, usually taken from census data, were calculated. Comparisons of administrative and epidemiological surveys of the same community have shown that administrative surveys miss those individuals with minimal disabilities attending schools for normal children (Wing et al. 1976). Children with mild autism often have not been referred to relevant clinics or assessment centers for diagnosis and, therefore, do not appear in the local authorities' lists of autistic children. Even if referral to an appropriate diagnostic or assessment service had occurred, no guarantee exists that the diagnosis of autism would form part of the administrative label given to the child (Wing et al. 1976). Rantakallio and van Wendt (1986) have shown that when following an entire birth cohort, even the best case registers are not perfect (Bryson, Clarke, and Smith 1988). Case registers tend to miss those who are very young, mildly affected, and those who are older, because it is unlikely that these individuals would have come to clinical attention and, thus, been captured by screening methods. More extensive two-stage epidemiological surveys that attempted to capture all potential individuals, including hitherto unidentified cases currently in the community, were carried out by Bryson, Clarke, and Smith (1988), Lotter (1966), and, to some extent, Wing et al. (1976) and Gillberg, Steffenberg, and Schaumann (1991). These studies reported higher prevalence estimates than studies using clinic or administrative files.

With respect to measurement, Boyle (1998) identified another four questions: (1) Do the survey instruments yield reliable and valid measures of psychiatric disorder and other key concepts? (2) Are the data collection methods standardized? (i.e., Are they understandable and reproducible?) (3) Are the survey instruments reliable with respect to their test-retest and inter-rater reliability? and (4) Are the survey instruments valid? (i.e., Do they accurately measure what they are supposed to measure?)

In this context, the sensitivity and specificity of the screening instruments become crucial features. Issues of sensitivity and specificity are also important when one discusses the accuracy of the diagnostic criteria and the measurement tool employed to capture those diagnostic criteria. Figure 1 illustrates the calculation of sensitivity and specificity and their meaning. Sensitivity (a ÷ a + c) refers to the proportion of individuals who truly have the disorder that were so identified by the screening tool. In contrast, specificity refers to the proportion of individuals who truly do not have the disorder that are so identified by the screening tool (d ÷ b + d). The false negative error rate (1- sensitivity) refers to the rate at which individuals are under-diagnosed (i.e., the rate

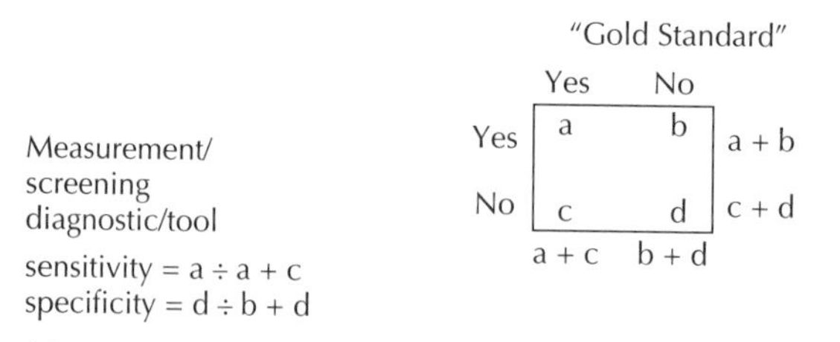

Figure 1. Sensitivity and specificity.

at which true cases of autism/PDD are missed). Similarly, the false positive error rate (1- specificity) refers to the rate of over-diagnosis, of missing true non-cases.

Applying these criteria to the epidemiologic studies quoted by Fombonne (1996) and Wing et al. (1976), we can identify several issues (see table I). First, no study has specifically estimated the sensitivity and specificity of the screening methods used. Individuals who might have autism were most often identified by screening instruments administered by physicians and/or teachers (Lotter 1966; Wing et al. 1976; Bryson, Clarke, and Smith 1988; Cialdella and Mamelle 1989; Ritvo et al. 1989; Gillberg, Steffenberg, and Schaumann 1991). Screening methods differed significantly among studies as to how much information teachers and other professionals received about the target population. While some studies distributed simple letters with clinical descriptions of autism to teachers and other potential informants, others provided a more comprehensive and systematic screening method, including educational lectures and opportunities for dialogue with more informed professionals within targeted communities.

Second, studies differed according to how decisions about population samples were made. In some instances, the decision as to whom to include or exclude from the study was left entirely to the teacher or another appropriate professional; while in other studies, the community professionals provided completed questionnaires on all children under their care, but did not make the final decisions as to which children should be included in the study (Bryson, Clarke, and Smith 1988; Gillberg, Steffenberg, and Schaumann 1991). These differences could have a significant influence on the numbers of cases included for further assessment, particularly for high functioning and PDD-spectrum cases, which are more atypical in their presentations and less likely to be identified by less experienced professionals. Bryson, Clarke, and Smith (1988) have shown that, in screening a total population, when the judgement resides more with the investigators and less with the teachers, the subsequent return rate for further assessment is significantly better (i.e., 12% vs. 2.5%). It is likely, therefore, that some of the

Table I. Critical Issues

1. Sensitivity of screening methods
2. Representativeness of exclusions; non-probability sampling
3. Low sensitivity of Kanner/Rutter/DSM-III criteria (70%)
4. Low specificity of DSM-III-R criteria (70% to 80%)
5. Sensitivity and specificity of measurement tools

screening methods employed are missing a substantial proportion of individuals with PDD, particularly those higher functioning children with autism, older children with autism, and those with atypical autism.

Third, studies have used different diagnostic criteria to identify children with autism (Kanner 1943; Rutter 1978; DSM-III criteria 1980; Treffert 1970; Hoshino et al. 1982; Bohman et al. 1983; McCarthy, Fitzgerald, and Smith 1984; Steinhausen et al. 1986; Burd, Fisher, and Kerbeshan 1987; Matsuishi et al. 1987; Sugiyama and Abe 1989; Cialdella and Mamelle 1989; and Ritvo et al. 1989). We know from other studies that the sensitivity of these criteria are low (around 70%), missing roughly 30% of individuals with true autism (Volkmar, Bregman, and Cohen 1988). The psychometric properties of these criteria are best for younger children and those who are severely impaired (Volkmar, Stier, and Cohen 1985; Volkmar, Bregman, and Cohen 1988). Bryson, Clarke, and Smith (1988) have suggested that the higher prevalence for autism in their study, as compared to that of Lotter (1966) or Wing et al. (1976), may reflect the use of broader diagnostic criteria (Denckla 1986) that emphasize areas of dysfunction rather than specific maladaptive behaviors.

Fourth, the DSM-III-R (1987) criteria were also used in a few studies (Gillberg, Steffenberg, and Schaumann 1991). While previous reviews have suggested that these criteria have very high sensitivity, their specificity is approximately 70% to 80% (Szatmari 1992). In other words, these criteria are over-diagnosing children with autism, particularly those who are severely developmentally disabled.

Fifth, the sensitivity and specificity of the measurement tools used to capture the diagnostic criteria have not been systematically estimated. For several studies, the use of standardized data collection methods, test-retest, or inter-rater reliability of survey instruments, and the extent to which the survey instruments were able to capture the diagnostic criteria were unclear. Just because a diagnostic instrument might have been designed to measure DSM-III or DSM-III-R criteria, it does not mean that the diagnostic algorithm, or the way the data were used to arrive at a diagnosis is accurate, i.e., has good sensitivity and specificity. In several studies (Wignyosumarto, Mukhlas, and Shirataki 1992; Gillberg, Steffenberg, and Schaumann 1991; Ritvo et al. 1989; Cialdella and Mamelle 1988; Bryson, Clarke, and Smith 1988; Burd, Fisher, and Kerbeshan 1987; Hoshino et al. 1982), expert clinicians conducted the intensive work ups, so one might expect that instruments were used in reliable and valid ways. However, this is a key issue, particularly in studies from other cultures where vocabulary and translations of concepts become extremely important.

DO THE BIASES INCREASE OR DECREASE REPORTED PREVALENCE ESTIMATES?

Table II is a summary of the impact that these methodologic features might have on the reported prevalence rates:

1. Non-systematic screening methods used in several prevalence studies of autism are likely to have poor sensitivity, and so negatively bias, that is, reduce the observed prevalence estimates away from the true value. Studies using more comprehensive screening methods for ascertaining potential cases of autism have reported higher prevalence rates for autism (Bryson, Clarke, and Smith 1988; Gillberg, Steffenberg, and Schaumann 1991).
2. Non-systematic sampling is likely to exclude higher functioning autistic children, those who are older, and those with milder forms of PDD to, again, bias prevalence estimates negatively. In general, studies that have relied on case registers and administrative records have under-reported prevalence rates for autism.
3. It is likely that the low sensitivity of the Kanner (1943), Rutter (1978), and DSM-III criteria (1980) will also decrease prevalence estimates.
4. The low specificity of the DSM-III-R (1987) criteria increases estimates.
5. The last issue, the sensitivity, specificity, and reliability of the measurement tools, will have unknown effects depending on the relative imbalance between specificity and sensitivity, and upon whether the measurement error was systematic or random.

   Therefore, given the available data, of the five identified methodologic features, three will tend to decrease reported prevalence estimates; one will increase it; and the effect of the other will be unknown. The overall effect of the known biases is probably to *underestimate* the true prevalence rate of autism.

Table II. Impact of Biases

		Bias
1.	Non-systematic screening methods—poor sensitivity	↓
2.	Exclusions miss HFA and other PDD	↓
3.	Low sensitivity of Kanner/Rutter/DSM-III criteria	↓
4.	Low specificity of DSM-III-R criteria	↑
5.	Sensitivity/specificity and reliability of measurement tools	?

WHAT WOULD BE A REASONABLE ESTIMATE OF THE PREVALENCE OF AUTISM AND OTHER PERVASIVE DEVELOPMENTAL DISORDERS?

It is difficult to arrive at precise prevalence estimates of autism. Given that the biases in most studies tend to decrease reported rates, it is probably safe to conclude that 4 per 10,000 is too low, but 1% is too high. It may not be unreasonable to suggest that the prevalence rate of autism from the best studies is between 5 and 10 per 10,000. Two recent studies that have used both community- and clinic-based samples, an extensive two-stage screening procedure, and structured diagnostic criteria to minimize potential methodological shortcomings have suggested that the prevalence of autism is in the order of 10 in 10,000 (Bryson, Clarke, and Smith 1988; Gillberg, Steffenberg, and Schaumann 1991). The diagnostic criteria in these studies were, perhaps, broader than the current DSM-IV criteria, so 10 per 10,000 may be the upper limit for the prevalence of autism.

For service planning, it is important that data on the prevalence of other PDDs be included as well. As far as we currently know, children with other forms of PDD require the same treatment and diagnostic services, and have similar etiologic risk factors and outcomes. In addition, the boundaries between autism and other PDDs are fluid and subject to change, so that in future versions of DSM, some of these may become included in the autism category. Unfortunately, only a few studies of the prevalence of non-autistic forms of pervasive developmental disorder exist. These studies were recently summarized by Fombonne (1996). The reported prevalence rates go from a low of 1.9 per 10,000 to a high of 16.3 per 10,000. These estimates need to be seen in the context of the complementary prevalence estimates of autism obtained from the same study population using the same diagnostic methods. For the most part, the prevalence of other forms of PDD is either the same as that of autism or roughly twice as much. The prevalence study by Wing and Gould (1979) gives an estimate of other forms of PDD to be roughly three times more common than autism.

There is only one prevalence study of Asperger's syndrome (Ehlers and Gillberg 1993). The sample included 1519 children, 7 to 16 years old. The prevalence rate of definite Asperger's syndrome was 36 per 10,000 (95% confidence interval 11-84). For suspected Asperger's syndrome, the prevalence estimate was 64 per 10,000, and using the ICD-10 criteria, an estimate of 29 per 10,000 was obtained. It is important to remember that this study identified only 14 out of roughly 15,000 children, accounting for the very wide confidence intervals around the estimates.

From some of the best studies, the rates of other forms of PDD are considered to be 2 to 15 per 10,000, but the rates of Asperger's syndrome vary widely, estimated between 2 and 35 per 10,000 depending on the diagnostic criteria used. If one were to add the upper and lower boundaries for these "best evidence" prevalence rates, one might surmise that the prevalence of all the pervasive developmental disorders is at least 10 per 10,000 and as high as 60 per 10,000. This suggests that as many as one out of every 200 children might have some form of pervasive developmental disorder; at the very least, one in a thousand.

CONCLUSION

Three conclusions can be drawn from this literature review. The first is that most of the methodological biases tend to *underestimate* the reported prevalence estimates. But the quality of the evidence is very uneven, and there is a critical need for new prevalence surveys of autism, atypical autism, and Asperger's syndrome, using systematic ascertainment methods and current diagnostic criteria. More attention also needs to be paid to assessing the sensitivity of the screening methods, the representativeness of excluded samples, and the accuracy and reliability of measurement tools.

The second conclusion is that despite these methodologic issues, it is clear that autism/PDD is not a rare disorder. The impressions of front line clinicians and service providers in the community seem to be accurate, at least to some extent. It is not so common as hyperactivity or uncomplicated speech delay, but, as a severe developmental disability with a morbidity equal to, or perhaps even greater than Down syndrome and cerebral palsy, clinicians and policy makers need to be aware of its prevalence. Third, it is also clear that given how common the disorder is, a substantial mismatch between prevalence estimates and available services exists in most communities, particularly for preschoolers and for those who are higher functioning. It appears as if many communities are not equipped to deal with the needs of children and families with PDD. Policy makers and many service providers are unaware that the disorder is not uncommon and carries a very high burden of suffering. Perhaps a new generation of epidemiologic studies will correct many of these misconceptions.

Table III. "Best-Evidence" Prevalence Rates per 10,000

	Lower	Upper
Autism	5	10
Other PDD	2	15
Asperger's syndrome	2	35
Total PDD	10	60

CHAPTER SUMMARY

1. Autism is not an uncommon disorder and probably occurs in up to 1 per 1,000 children.
2. Autistic spectrum disorders can occur in up to 0.5% of the population.
3. Incomplete ascertainment of cases results in missing children with milder symptoms of autism.
4. Sensitivity and specificity are not usually reported for the methods used to screen for autism, and when reported, tend to be weak.
5. The overall impact of different methodological biases will be to underestimate the true prevalence of autism.
6. School systems and other service delivery systems do not appear to be using realistic estimates to plan and meet adequately the needs of persons with autism in the community.

REFERENCES

American Psychiatric Association: *Diagnostic and Statistical Manual of Mental Disorders*, 3rd edition. 1980. Washington, D.C.: American Psychiatric Association.

American Psychiatric Association: *Diagnostic and Statistical Manual of Mental Disorders*, Revised 3rd edition. 1987. Washington, D.C.: American Psychiatric Association.

American Psychiatric Association: *Diagnostic and Statistical Manual of Mental Disorders*, 4th edition. 1994. Washington, D.C.: American Psychiatric Association.

Aravidsson, T., Danielsson, B., Forseberg, P., Gillberg, C., Mohansson, M., and Kjellgren, G. 1997. Autism in 3–6-year-old children in a suburb of Goteborg, Sweden. *Autism* 1(2):162–73.

Bohman, M., Bohman, I. L., Bjork, P. O., and Sjoholm, E. 1983. Childhood psychosis in a northern Swedish county: Some preliminary findings from an epidemiological survey. In *Epidemiological Approaches in Child Psychiatry*, eds. M. H. Schmidt and H. Remschmidt. Verlag, Stuttgart: George Thieme.

Boyle, M. H. 1998. Guidelines for evaluating prevalence studies. *Evidence Based Mental Health*. 1(2):37–39.

Brask, B. H. 1970. A prevalence investigation of childhood psychosis. In *Nordic Symposium on the Care of Psychotic Children*, Oslo: Barnepsychiatrist Forening.

Bryson, S. E., Clarke, B. S., and Smith, I. M. 1988. First report of a Canadian epidemiological study of autistic syndromes. *Journal of Child Psychology and Psychiatry* 4:433–45.

Burd, L., Fisher, W., and Kerbeshan, J. 1987. A prevalence study of pervasive developmental disorders in North Dakota. *Journal of American Academy of Child and Adolescent Psychiatry* 26:5,700–3.

Cialdella, P. H., and Mamelle, N. 1989. An epidemiological study of infantile autism in a French department. *Journal of Child Psychology and Psychiatry* 30(1):165–75.

Denckla, M. B. 1986. New diagnostic criteria for autism and related behavioural disorders: Guidelines for research protocols. *Journal of American Academy of Child and Adolescent Psychiatry* 25:221–24.

Ehlers, S., and Gillberg, C. 1993. The epidemiology of Asperger's syndrome: A total population study. *Journal of Child Psychology and Psychiatry* 34:1327–50.

Fombonne, E. 1996. Epidemiological surveys of autism. In *C.U.P. Monograph on Autism*, ed. F. Volkmar, Cambridge, UK: Cambridge University Press.

Fombonne, E., and du Mazaubrun, C. 1992. Prevalence of infantile autism in 4 French regions. *Social Psychiatry and Epidemiology* 27:203–10.

Gillberg, C. 1984. Infantile autism and other childhood psychoses in a Swedish urban region: Epidemiological aspects. *Journal of Child Psychology and Psychiatry* 25:35–43.

Gillberg, C. 1995. The prevalence of autism and autism spectrum disorders. In *The Epidemiology of Child and Adolescent Psychopathology*, eds. F. C. Verhulst and H. M. Koot. England: Oxford University Press.

Gillberg, I. C., and Gillberg, C. 1989. Asperger's syndrome: Some epidemiological considerations: A research note. *Journal of Child Psychology and Psychiatry* 30(4):631–8.

Gillberg, C., Steffenberg, S., and Schaumann, H. 1991. Is autism more common than ten years ago? *British Journal of Psychiatry* 158:403–09.

Hoshino, Y., Yashima, Y., Ishige, K., Tachibana, R., and Watenabe, M. 1982. The epidemiological study of autism in Fukushima-Ken. *Folia Psychiatrica et Neurologica Japonica* 36:115–24.

Kanner, L. 1943. Austic disturbances of affective contact. *Nervous Child* 2:217–50.

Lotter, V. 1966. Epidemiology of autistic conditions in children: Prevalence. *Social Psychiatry* 1:124–37.

Matsuishi, T., Shiosuki, M., Yoshimura, K., Shoji, H., and Imuta, F. 1987. High prevalence of infantile autism in Kurume City, Japan. *Journal of Child Neurology* 2:268–71.

McCarthy, P., Fitzgerald, M., and Smith, M. A. 1984. Prevalence of childhood autism in Ireland. *Irish Medical Journal* 77(5):129–30.

Rantakallio, P., and van Wendt, L. 1986. Mental retardation and subnormalities in a birth cohort of 12,000 children in Northern Finland. *Journal of American Association of Mental Deficiency* 90:380–87.

Ritvo, E. R., Freeman, B. J., Pingree, C., Mason-Brothers, A., Jorde, L., and Jenson, W. R. 1989. The UCLA-University of Utah epidemiological survey of autism: Prevalence. *American Journal of Psychiatry* 146(2):194–99.

Rutter, M. 1978. Diagnosis and definition of childhood autism. *Journal of Autism and Childhood Schizophrenia* 8:139–61.

Steinhausen, H. C., Gobel, D., Breinlinger, M., and Wohlloben, B. 1986. A community survey of infantile autism. *Journal of American Academy of Child and Adolescent Psychiatry* 25(2):186–89.

Sugiyama, T., and Abe, T. 1989. The prevalence of autism in Nagoya, Japan: A total population study. *Journal of Autism and Developmental Disorders* 19(1):87–96.

Szatmari, P. 1992. A literature review on the DSM-III-R criteria for autistic disorder. *Journal of Autism and Developmental Disorders* 22:507–25.

Szatmari, P., Jones, M. B., Zwaigenbaum, L., and MacLean, J. E. 1998. Genetics of autism: Overview and new directions. *Journal of Autism and Developmental Disorders* 28(5):363–80.

Treffert, L. 1970. Epidemiology of infantile autism. *Archives of General Psychiatry* 22:431–38.

Volkmar, F., Stier, D. M., and Cohen, D. J. 1985. Age of recognition of pervasive developmental disorder. *American Journal of Psychiatry* 142:1450–52.
Volkmar, F. R., Bregman, J., and Cohen, D. J. 1988. DSM III and DSM III-R diagnoses of autism. *American Journal of Psychiatry* 145:1404–8.
Wignyosumarto, S., Mukhlas, M., and Shirataki, S. 1992. Epidemiological and clinical study of autistic children in Yogyakarta Indonesia. *Kobe Journal of Medical Science* 38:1–19.
Wing, L. 1993. The definition and prevalence of autism: A review. *European Journal of Child and Adolescent Psychiatry* 2:61–74.
Wing, L. 1997. The autistic spectrum. *The Lancet* 350:13,1761–66.
Wing, L., and Gould, J. 1979. Severe impairments of social interaction and associated abnormalities in children: Epidemiology and classification. *Journal of Autism and Developmental Disorders* 9:11–29.
Wing, L., Yeats, S. R., Brierly, L. M., and Gould, J. 1976. The prevalence of early infantile autism: Comparison of administrative and epidemiological studies. *Psychological Medicine* 6:89–100.
Zahner, G. E. P., and Pauls, D. L. 1987. Epidemiological surveys of infantile autism. In *Handbook of Autism and Pervasive Developmental Disorders*, eds. D. J. Cohen, A. M. Donnellan, and R. Paul. New York: Wiley and Sons.

Chapter • 3

Clinical Practice Guidelines: *The New York State Experience*

Donna M. Noyes-Grosser

Assuring the delivery of high-quality, cost-effective services for children with disabilities (ages birth to three years) and their families is one of the most significant challenges for states and territories across the nation in implementing early intervention programs under the *Individuals with Disabilities Education Act* (IDEA). Ensuring that all children and families have access to the programs and services appropriate for their needs, regardless of where they reside, is an equally daunting task. Currently, there is wide variation in identification, assessment, and intervention practices across early intervention programs nationwide. As a result, a number of states, including New York State, have begun to consider the need for *service guidelines* in offering assistance to public officials, families, and service providers regarding referrals, assessments, and interventions with children eligible for early intervention programs.

In March, 1999, New York State released its first two clinical practice guidelines: *Clinical Practice Guideline: Autism/Pervasive Developmental Disorders—Assessment and Intervention for Young Children (ages 0-3 Years)* and *Clinical Practice Guideline: Communication Disorders—Assessment and Intervention for Young Children (ages 0-3)*. This chapter describes the New York State experience in the development of clinical practice guidelines for children with autism/-pervasive developmental disorders using the evidence-based approach developed by the Agency for Health Care Policy and Research (AHCPR).

AN OVERVIEW OF THE NATIONAL EARLY INTERVENTION PROGRAM

The National Early Intervention Program for infants and toddlers with disabilities and their families is established at the federal level in Part C (formerly Part H) of the *Individuals With Disabilities Education Act* (IDEA). The National Early Intervention Program, created by Congress as part of the 1986 reauthorization of IDEA, is a discretionary program to assist states in the implementation of statewide systems of early intervention services for children with developmental delays or disabilities (birth to three years of age) and their families (Brown 1994). The federal requirements necessary for implementation of state early intervention programs include:

1. A governor-designated lead agency responsible for state-level administration and oversight of the state's Early Intervention Program.
2. A comprehensive Child Find and public awareness program to ensure that potentially eligible children are identified and referred for early intervention services as early as possible.
3. State policies of eligibility for children with diagnosed physical or mental conditions with a high probability of developmental delay in their eligibility policies (Autism/pervasive developmental disorders are included in such conditions.). States must also establish a "state definition of developmental delay" to include as eligible those children without a diagnosed condition who are experiencing a developmental delay in one or more areas of development (physical development, communication development, cognitive development, social-emotional development, and adaptive development).
4. Service coordination services to assist families in obtaining a multidisciplinary evaluation to determine their child's eligibility for services; facilitate the development of Individualized Family Service Plans; assure the delivery of early intervention services included in the Individualized Family Service Plans; and, coordinate the delivery of early intervention services with other services needed by the child and family.
5. Provision of multidisciplinary evaluations to determine whether a child is eligible for early intervention services. States have the option of including children at risk for disabilities as eligible for early intervention services. These services

include: assistive technology services and devices; audiology; family training; counseling; home visits and parent support groups; medical services for diagnostic and evaluation purposes; nursing; nutrition; psychological, occupational therapy; physical therapy; service coordination; social work; special instruction; speech-language pathology; vision; health; transportation; and related costs.

6. Individualized Family Service Plans for all eligible children and their families, that specify the type, frequency, intensity, and duration of services and the outcomes to be achieved by early intervention services.

Under federal requirements, all early intervention services included in Individualized Family Service Plans must be provided at no cost to families unless state law provides for the use of a system of parent payments (such as a sliding fee scale). Services that are necessary to assist families in accessing their state's early intervention programs, including Child Find, service coordination, multidisciplinary evaluations, and Individualized Family Service Plans must always be provided at no cost to families.

States participating in the federal Part C program under IDEA are also required to establish an interagency coordinating council to advise and assist the lead agency in implementing the state's early intervention program. Members of the interagency coordinating council must be appointed by the Governor and must include parents; public and private providers of early intervention services; representatives from state agencies that provide services to infants and toddlers with disabilities; a representative of the state agency responsible for child care programs; and Head Start representatives.

NEW YORK STATE'S EARLY INTERVENTION PROGRAM

New York State joined the federal Early Intervention Program in 1987, with the Department of Health as the governor-designated lead agency. Legislation establishing a statewide program of early intervention services consistent with federal early intervention program requirements was enacted by the New York State Legislature on July 1, 1992 (Chapter 428 of the Laws of 1992, as amended by Chapter 231 of the Laws of 1993) and codified at Title II-A of Article 25 of the New York State Public Health Law.

The New York State Early Intervention Program has been in full implementation since 1993. As the lead agency for the Early Intervention Program, the New York State Department of Health is responsible for overall statewide administration and operation of the

Program. The governor-appointed Early Intervention Coordinating Council (EICC) meets on a regular basis to provide advice and assistance to the Department of Health in administering the Program. The mission of the Early Intervention Program is to identify and evaluate, as early as possible, those infants and toddlers whose healthy development is compromised and provide for appropriate intervention to improve child and family development. The goals for the Program are to:

- **Support parents** in meeting their responsibilities to nurture and enhance their children's development.
- **Create opportunities for full participation** of children with disabilities and their families by ensuring that services are delivered in natural environments to the maximum extent appropriate.
- **Ensure that early intervention services** are coordinated with the full array of early childhood, health and mental health, educational, social, and other community-based services needed by, and provided to children and their families.
- **Enhance child development, functional outcomes, and improve family life** through delivery of effective, outcome-based high quality early intervention services.
- **Ensure that services complement** the child's medical home by involving primary and specialty health care providers in supporting family participation.
- **Assure equity of access, quality, consistency, and accountability** in the service system by ensuring clear lines of public supervision, responsibility, and authority.

The New York State Early Intervention Program is a partnership of the state and local governments, families, and providers of early intervention services. As required by State Public Health Law, the chief elected officials of the fifty-seven counties and the City of New York have designated an Early Intervention official to be responsible for the local administration of the Program. Early Intervention officials are responsible for:

1. Finding eligible children.
2. Ensuring that children referred as potentially eligible receive a multidisciplinary evaluation.
3. Appointing an initial service coordinator to assist families with their children's multidisciplinary evaluations and Individualized Family Service Plan (IFSP).
4. Ensuring that children and families receive the early intervention services included in their IFSPs.

5. Protecting children and family rights under the Early Intervention Program.

The Individualized Family Service Plan (IFSP) is an agreement between the Early Intervention official (or his or her designee) and the child's parent(s) on: (a) the types of early intervention services to be provided; (b) frequency, intensity, and duration of those services; and (c) the outcomes to be achieved through the provision of early intervention services. The IFSP is developed through a team planning process that includes the child's parent(s); the service coordinator; the child's evaluators (or a designated representative of the evaluation team); and, other participants invited by the child's parent or service coordinator (with the consent of the parents). Individualized Family Service Plans must be reviewed every six months and evaluated on an annual basis.

WHY DEVELOP CLINICAL PRACTICE GUIDELINES ON AUTISM/PERVASIVE DEVELOPMENTAL DISORDERS?

Clinical practice guidelines can be powerful tools in assisting parents and professionals make the best possible decisions about early intervention services that are consistent with a child's and family's concerns, priorities, needs, and resources. As the state and nation move towards the development of managed care systems as a primary mechanism for financing health care, clinical practice guidelines will also be needed to help assure that children with special health care and developmental needs—including children with autism/ pervasive developmental disorders—are receiving the services they need to become productive, contributing members of their communities.

Although children with autism/PDD represent a relatively small proportion of all children receiving services in the New York State Early Intervention Program, these children and their families frequently require an intensive approach to early intervention to achieve improvements in child outcomes. Autism, particularly when defined as a spectrum disorder, may also be more common than previously thought. Earlier studies suggest that about three to four children in 10,000 have autism. More recent studies suggest as many as 20 or more children in 10,000 have autism. A range of 10 to 15 children per 10,000 is commonly accepted as a "middle range" estimate (see Autism/Pervasive Developmental Disorders Guideline Panel 1999).

The emphasis on applied behavioral therapies—especially the use of these types of interventions with very young children—has created a demand for information about known interventions and their effectiveness for children with autism. In addition to questions about what types of interventions are most successful for children with autism/pervasive developmental disorders, parents and professionals are faced with difficult decisions about the frequency, duration, and intensity of interventions necessary to achieve improved child and family outcomes.

The New York State Early Intervention Program Clinical Practice Guidelines on autism/pervasive developmental disorders were developed to help families, early intervention officials, and service providers improve the quality of care for young children with autism. They offer recommendations on sound practices based on scientific evidence and expert clinical opinion for:

1. Identifying children with potential autism/pervasive developmental disorder through routine developmental surveillance and screening included as part of children's primary health care.
2. Providing quality multidisciplinary evaluations and assessments that result in reliable information about a child's developmental strengths and needs, and, when possible, a diagnosis.
3. Determining effective intervention strategies and reaching agreement on the frequency, intensity, and duration of early intervention services that will lead to positive outcomes for children and families.
4. Measuring whether positive outcomes are being achieved through ongoing assessment of children's progress and modification of early intervention services and strategies, as needed, to achieve positive outcomes.

When used as part of the individualized family service planning process, clinical practice guidelines should also assist parents, evaluators, service providers, and public officials in:

- Agreeing on reasonable outcomes and expectations of early intervention services for the child and family.
- Selecting the type of service model or models that are appropriate to achieve those outcomes.
- Identifying the appropriate early intervention services for the child and family.
- Reaching agreement on the frequency, intensity, and duration of early intervention services appropriate for the child and family.
- Identifying the measures to be used in determining whether outcomes are being achieved.

- Distinguishing between early intervention services and medical services.
- Assessing the appropriateness of "emerging" therapeutic approaches being developed and promoted for specific types of disabilities.

Clinical practice guidelines will also facilitate state-level program evaluation efforts by establishing standards of quality care for young children with autism/pervasive developmental disorders that can be used to measure the effectiveness of the Early Intervention Program. As such, it is expected that clinical practice guidelines will also lead to a shift from emphasis on process measures in current state-level data collection and analyses to outcome measurements and performance indicators.

THE AGENCY FOR HEALTH CARE POLICY AND RESEARCH (AHCPR) APPROACH

The Clinical Practice Guideline—Autism/Pervasive Developmental Disorders: Assessment and Intervention for Young Children (Ages 0-3 years) is part of a series of clinical practice guidelines planned by the New York State Early Intervention Program on developmental problems in young children. The impact of these clinical practice guidelines will depend upon their credibility with families, service providers, and public officials. To ensure a credible product, the Department of Health has chosen to use the same methodology and guideline formats as those used in recent years by the Agency for Health Care Policy and Research (AHCPR), a part of the United States Public Health Service.

The AHCPR has sponsored several multidisciplinary consensus panels of topic experts and generalists who developed a series of evidence-based clinical practice guidelines for a variety of clinical conditions. A key goal of this effort by AHCPR was to establish a standard methodology for developing clinical practice guidelines useful to both consumers and providers of care.

The AHCPR methodology was derived from the work of many experts in health services research and incorporated the principles for developing high quality practice guidelines promulgated by the U.S. Institute of Medicine (1992). This methodology is now considered by many in health services research to be the standard for developing evidence-based clinical practice guidelines.

Key elements of the AHCPR approach include the following:

1. *A standard methodology* for screening and systematically evaluating scientific literature relevant to the guideline topic.

2. *Use of multidisciplinary consensus panels*, comprised of topic experts and consumers, to review available scientific evidence about clinical efficacy, information about potential benefits and harms, and quality and applicability of the evidence to the guideline topic.
3. *Recommendations based on panel opinion* when scientific evidence is lacking about a specific clinical question.
4. *Inclusion of methods used, evidence examined, and panel's rationale* for each guideline recommendation in the final guideline report, including the strength of evidence used as the basis for that recommendation.

The use of a multidisciplinary panel to review all available scientific evidence on the guideline topic and scope, and then develop *consensus* recommendations based on the evidence is a defining feature of the AHCPR methodology. Specific studies to be reviewed by the panel during their deliberations are selected through systematic screening and evaluation of the *quality* and *clinical applicability* of all available scientific literature pertaining to the scope of the guideline. *Quality* criteria relate to the study design and control for biases, while *clinical applicability* criteria relate to the extent to which the study's results would also be expected to occur in the particular clinical situation of interest. For example, the clinical applicability criteria used for our guideline were: High = all children under three years old; Moderately High = all children under four years old; Moderate = some children under three years old, all children under six years old; Moderately Low = all children from four to six years old; Low = some children under six and some children over six years old; Unacceptable = no children under six years old.

Studies that meet both the quality and clinical applicability criteria are then abstracted into evidence tables used by the panelists to derive consensus recommendations. An example of an evidence table used for the *Clinical Practice Guideline—Autism/Pervasive Developmental Disorders: Assessment and Intervention for Young Children (Ages 0-3 years)* is found in Appendix A.

The methodology used to develop the AHCPR clinical practice guidelines has been described in numerous publications (Eddy 1994; Holland 1995; Schriger 1995; Woolf 1991; and Woolf 1994). The New York State Early Intervention Program's *Clinical Practice Guideline—Autism/Pervasive Developmental Disorders: Assessment and Intervention for Young Children (Ages 0-3 years)* was developed by a multidisciplinary panel of topic experts, clinicians, and parents. Panel members were selected from individuals who responded to an announcement about the guideline initiative. A standardized instrument designed to rate their experience with young children with autism was used in the selection. In addition, an effort was made to ensure reasonable representation from the various professional disciplines who care for children with autism. The guideline development was facilitated by a panel methodologist and project staff, all of whom had been involved in the development of the AHCPR clinical practice guidelines.

The Guideline was developed through a series of panel meetings. Initial meetings entailed reaching agreement on the defined scope, as well as structuring the research and review of scientific literature available on the topic. The general approach was to search the relevant computer bibliographic databases from 1980 through the present. Databases searched included MEDLINE, psycINFO, and ERIC. At later meetings, panel members reviewed and weighed the evidence as the basis for making guideline recommendations.

The charge made to the panel from the Department of Health was to focus specifically on clinical practices related to the identification, assessment, and interventions for children with autism/pervasive developmental disorders from birth to three years of age. Panelists were explicitly asked not to consider the policies, procedures, and regulations governing New York State's Early Intervention Program in the development of guideline recommendations. Rather, the intent of the guideline initiative was to develop comprehensive recommended practices based on available scientific evidence and expert opinion. As a result, the *Clinical Practice Guideline—Autism/Pervasive Developmental Disorders: Assessment and Intervention for Young Children (Ages 0-3 years)* includes recommendations that go beyond the scope of services funded and provided for by the Early Intervention Program (for example, health and medical services and interventions).

The initial draft of the Guideline was extensively reviewed by national peer reviewers identified by the panel members and by key constituencies for the Early Intervention Program, including members of the Early Intervention Coordinating Council. Subsequent to this review process, panel members worked with the methodologists and project staff to finalize the recommendations and background information included in the final *Clinical Practice Guideline—Autism/Pervasive Developmental Disorders: Assessment and Intervention for Young Children (Ages 0-3 years)*.

All three versions of the Guideline, published by the New York State Department of Health, contain the same basic recommendations specific to the assessment and intervention methods evaluated by the panel, but with differing levels of detail describing the methods and evidence that support the recommendations. The three versions are:

1. *Guideline Technical Report* (includes the full text of the recommendations, background information, and a full report of the research process and evidence reviewed.
2. *The Clinical Practice Guideline: Report of the Recommendations* (includes full text of the recommendations, background information, and summary of the supporting evidence).
3. *The Quick Reference Guide for Parents and Professionals* (a summary of the major recommendations and background information).

A complete description of the guideline methodology, including the general criteria for selecting studies for in-depth review, can be found in the *Technical Report*.

AN OVERVIEW OF THE GUIDELINE RECOMMENDATIONS

The Guideline includes more than 250 evidence-based recommendations for effective practices in the identification, assessment, and intervention with young children with autism/pervasive developmental disorders. Each of the Guideline recommendations is rated for the strength of its supporting evidence. The strength of evidence rating provides an indication of the amount, general quality, and clinic applicability of the scientific evidence used as the basis for the recommendation. Table I provides the evidence ratings used for the Guideline.

The Guideline provides a comprehensive set of recommended practices related to the care of and early intervention with young chil-

Table I Evidence Ratings

Rating	Definition
[A]	**Strong Evidence:** evidence from two or more studies that met criteria for adequate evidence about efficacy and had at least moderate applicability to the topic; where the evidence consistently and strongly supports the recommendation.
[B]	**Moderate Evidence:** evidence from at least one study that met criteria for adequate evidence about efficacy and had at least moderate applicability to the topic; where the evidence supports the recommendation.
[C]	**Limited evidence**—evidence from at least one study that met criteria for adequate evidence about efficacy and had at least minimally acceptable applicability to the topic; where the evidence supports the recommendation.
[D1]	**Panel Consensus Opinion**—recommendations based on information not meeting criteria for adequate evidence about efficacy, on topics where a systematic review of the literature was done.
[D2]	**Panel Consensus Opinion**—recommendations on topics where a systematic review of the literature was not conducted.

dren with autism/pervasive developmental disorders. Clinical areas addressed include: (a) clinical clues of autism; (b) assessment techniques and instruments (e.g., behavioral, communication, cognition, environmental, family, food allergy or diet, immune status, organic acid metabolites, screening tests, social interactions/relationships, and parent concerns); (c) comprehensive health assessment; and (d) intervention approaches (including behavioral and educational approaches, effective program elements, medical therapies, developmental interrelatedness model, sensory integration, and parent training). In addition, the Guideline includes practical tables that summarize information for easy use by clinicians. Table II is an example of the types of tables included in the Guideline as a quick reference for clinicians and parents on clinical clues of autism.

Table III provides a sample of selected recommendations on linking early identification and diagnosis with early intervention, abstracted from chapter IV, Intervention Methods for Young Children with Autism, of the *Clinical Practice Guideline—Report of the Recommendations—Autism/Pervasive Developmental Disorders: Assessment and Intervention for Young Children (Ages 0-3 years).*

Table II Clinical Clues for Possible Autism

The clinical clues listed in this table represent delayed or abnormal behaviors that are often seen in children with autism. Some of these findings may also be seen in children who do not have autism but who may have other developmental problems.

If any of these clinical clues are present, further assessment may be needed to evaluate the possibility of autism or other developmental problems.

- Delay or absence of spoken language
- Looks through people; not aware of others
- Not responsive to other people's facial expressions/feelings
- Lack of pretend play; little or no imagination
- Does not show typical interest in, or play near peers purposefully
- Lack of turn taking
- Unable to share pleasure
- Qualitative impairment in nonverbal communication
- Not pointing at an object to direct another person to look at it
- Lack of gaze monitoring
- Lack of initiation of activity or social play

Source: This table is derived from Table III-5, which shows clinical clues found in articles that met criteria for in-depth review.

Table III Guideline Recommendations on Linking Early Identification and Diagnosis with Early Intervention

1.	It is important to identify children with autism and begin appropriate interventions as soon as possible since such early intervention may help speed the child's overall development, reduce inappropriate behaviors, and lead to better long-term functional outcomes [D1]
2.	It is recommended that appropriate interventions be provided as soon as possible after a diagnosis of autism has been made. [D1]
3.	Although early intervention is recommended, it is important for parents to understand that children who receive intervention at a later age can still benefit from intervention. [D1]
4.	When making decisions about interventions for a child with autism, it is recommended that parents seek guidance from qualified professionals with experience in treating children with autism. [D2]
5.	It is important to recognize that children with autism differ in terms of their strengths and needs, as well as their responses to specific intervention methods or techniques. Furthermore, children have different family situations. [D1]
6.	It is recommended that the use of any intervention for a child with autism be based upon an assessment of the specified strengths and needs of the child and family. [D1]
7.	If a child has identified developmental delays and autism is suspected but not confirmed, it is still important to initiate appropriate early intervention services to address identified developmental delays as soon as possible. [D2]
8.	It is recommended that target behaviors for each child be clearly identified and defined with developmentally appropriate measurable criteria for mastery. [A]

INVOLVING KEY CONSTITUENTS IN THE DEVELOPMENT OF CLINICAL PRACTICE GUIDELINES

The development of clinical practice guidelines and other types of "service guidelines" by state early intervention programs has been controversial. Concerns have been voiced by parents, advocacy organizations, and professionals that clinical practice guidelines are contrary to the concept of individualized services tailored to meet the unique needs of a given child and family. Other concerns include: (a) fear that clinical practice guidelines could be incorporated into law or regulation, potentially restricting options or reducing the availability of early intervention services for children and families; and (b) the perception that the state of the art of research on the effectiveness of early intervention services cannot support the development of evidence-based clinical practice guidelines (Feinberg and Beyer 1998).

The involvement of key constituents in all aspects of the development of the *Clinical Practice Guidelines on Autism/Pervasive Developmental Disorders* has been essential to the success of the New York State Early Intervention Program's efforts. The Department of Health worked closely with the Early Intervention Coordinating Council from the initial planning phases through implementation of this initiative. In addition, a state-level steering committee, comprised of early intervention officials, representatives of service providers, and parents, was also established to advise the department on the process used for Guideline development. The steering committee made important contributions related to the multidisciplinary composition of the consensus panel, recruitment of panelists, and design of a community education approach to assist parents and professionals in using the *Clinical Practice Guidelines* in the context of the New York State Early Intervention Program. All of the consensus panel members who were selected to participate in the development of guideline recommendations were expert researchers, clinicians, and parents of children with autism residing within New York State. A national advisory group of experts in early intervention has also been available to the department to review and provide feedback on the use of the AHCPR methodology and Guidelines.

The participation of the Early Intervention Coordinating Council and state steering committee members in the key constituent review process helped to develop confidence in the guideline approach and shaped the final guideline products in ways that will ensure their usefulness to parents and professionals in the New York State Early Intervention Program. For example, based on recommendations of these reviewers, the *Clinical Practice Guideline* has been annotated with key references to policies and procedures under the Early Intervention Program that relate to specific guideline recommendations.

NEXT STEPS: EDUCATING THE COMMUNITY AND EVALUATING THE IMPACT OF CLINICAL PRACTICE GUIDELINES

The New York State Early Intervention Program's *Clinical Practice Guideline—Autism/Pervasive Developmental Disorders: Assessment and Intervention for Young Children (Ages 0-3 years)* was released in Spring, 1999, in the context of a community education program to assist parents and professionals in using the Guideline recommendations to improve the quality of care for young children with autism and their families. Our initial community education approach involved a series of statewide and regional meetings with parents, providers, and early intervention officials across the state. These sessions focused on: (a) an overview of the AHCPR methodology used to develop the Guidelines;

(b) an overview of the Guideline recommendations; and (c) practical strategies for use of the Guideline recommendations in the New York State Early Intervention Program.

In addition, the New York State Early Intervention Program plans to make the *Clinical Practice Guideline—Autism/Pervasive Developmental Disorders: Assessment and Intervention for Young Children (Ages 0-3 years)* available on the New York State Department of Health website and through mail order (see Appendix B). Preliminary plans to evaluate the impact of the *Clinical Practice Guideline* on the quality of care for young children with autism include:

1. Development of state-level performance indicators that can be examined using data available from the Early Intervention Program's data management system (for example, age at referral and diagnosis).
2. Incorporation of measures related to the use (and usefulness) of the Guideline in program monitoring protocols (for example, reviewing child records to determine whether the Guideline improved the quality of evaluation, assessment, and intervention practices).
3. Surveys of parents and professionals to gain their perspectives on the effectiveness of the Guideline in improving the quality of care for young children with autism.

The *Clinical Practice Guideline* has the potential to be a valuable resource for other states across the nation implementing early intervention services under Part C of the *Individuals with Disabilities Education Act*. Since the Guideline is a set of practice recommendations based on scientific evidence and expert clinical opinion—and not regulations, policies, or procedures—families and professionals nationwide should find it helpful in making good decisions about providing high quality care to young children with autism.

The quality and credibility of any clinical practice guideline depend upon the use of current scientific evidence to support its practice recommendations. The New York State Early Intervention Program plans to re-evaluate and revise the Guideline as new evidence emerges on effective practices for assessment and intervention of young children with autism.

CHAPTER SUMMARY

1. Recent advances in the therapy of autism emphasize the importance of early intervention and, therefore, early identification.

2. The lack of uniformity in screening techniques and diagnostic procedures contributes to late identification of autism in infants and young children. At a sufficiently early age they would presumably show the most benefit from early intervention.
3. *Clinical Practice Guidelines* for the screening, diagnosis, and treatment of autism in infants and young children need to be based predominantly on critical reviews of the available scientific evidence.
4. The development of such *Clinical Practice Guidelines* can be used to educate both professionals and parents, improve the assessment and treatment of children, and crystallize the research needs.
5. The Agency for Health Care Policy and Research (AHCPR) experience has provided a model for the development of *Clinical Practice Guidelines* in a broad array of medical and medically related conditions, disabilities, and developmental disabilities.
6. The AHCPR method offers an effective approach to achieving consensus on recommendations and for objectively defending the appropriateness of such recommendations in a service delivery environment that increasingly demands proof of efficacy beyond the individual judgments of clinical professionals.

APPENDIX A

This evidence table is an abstraction of the article by Baron-Cohen, S., Allen, J., and Gillberg, C. 1992. "Can autism be detected at 18 months? The needle, the haystack, and the CHAT." *British Journal of Psychiatry* 168:158-63. It can be found in *Clinical Practice Guideline—Technical Report—Autism/Pervasive Developmental Disorders: Assessment and Intervention for Young Children (ages 0-3 years).*

Assessment Evidence—Checklist for Autism in Toddlers (CHAT)

Study Design Factors		Subject Characteristics			Statistics Used/Results
Citation/purpose of study/ setting/inclusion– exclusion criteria	Diagnostic tests/ reference standard/ other evaluation	Demographics/ clinical/ description/ social factors	Groups		Statistics Used/results
Author Baron-Cohen, Allen, and Gillberg 1992 **Purpose of study** To evaluate the effectiveness of the Checklist for Autism in Toddlers (CHAT) to detect autism in a high-risk population at 18 months.	**Tests evaluated** Checklist for Autism in Toddlers (CHAT) includes 9 questions for parents and 7 items scored based on interactions with the child. This test has 3 key items: 1) proto-declarative pointing (PDP), 2) gaze-monitoring (GM), and 3) pretend play (PP).	**Group**	**Group 1**	**Group 2**	**Statistics used** **Results**
		Demographics Number of subjects	50	41	
		Age (months) Range Mean	 17–20 18.3	 17–21 19.3	***Test reliability:*** Consistency in answering similar items was said to be good, but statistical reliability testing was not done.
Setting Community setting. UK and Sweden	***Administered by:*** The children's general practitioner (GP) or health visitor in a clinic setting.	% of males	56%	NR	***Test validity:*** Ability of the CHAT to predict a diagnosis of autism at 30 months, where positive test is ≥ 2 — Sensitivity / Specificity
		Developmental profile	NR	NR	
Study inclusion criteria Children met the criteria		**Clinical factors**	NR	NR	

Study Design Factors		Subject Characteristics			Statistics Used/Results		
Citation/purpose of study/ setting/inclusion– exclusion criteria	Diagnostic tests/ reference standard/ other evaluation	Demographics/ clinical/ description/ social factors	Groups		Statistics Used/results		
for Group 1 or Group 2 below. **Study exclusion criteria** Not reported **Subject groups** ***Group 1:*** General population sample: randomly selected 18-month-olds from the general population, who attended a health center for their routine 18-month-check-up. ***Group 2:*** High-risk group: younger siblings of children with a diagnosis of autism using accepted criteria. It was predicted that 2% to 3%	***Recording/scoring methods:*** Recorded which items were passed and which ones were failed. Key behaviors tested include pointing, pretend play, using index finger to point, interest in other children, peek-a-boo or hide and seek, and asking the child to bring something to you. **Reference standard** DSM-III-R ***Administered by:*** At follow-up when the child was 30 months old, a letter was sent to the parents (for Group 2) or the GP (for Group 1) asking if the child had developed psychiatric problems. If letters	**Social/family factors**	NR	NR	of the 5 key types of behavior **Other findings** Of the 4 children in Group 2 who failed at 2 or more key behaviors, all had a diagnosis of autism by 30 months. The other 37 children in Group 2 had no psychiatric diagnosis at 30 months.	100%	100%

Study Design Factors		Subject Characteristics		Statistics Used/Results
Citation/purpose of study/ setting/inclusion–exclusion criteria	Diagnostic tests/ reference standard/ other evaluation	Demographics/ clinical/ description/ social factors	Groups	Statistics Used/results
of this group would develop autism. Thirty-seven of 41 were free from a psychiatric diagnosis of autism.	reported problems, the child was evaluated by 2 psychiatrists to establish a diagnosis. ***Recording/scoring methods:*** 1) Report of whether child was free of psychiatric problems or had been diagnosed with autism. 2) Diagnosis of autism was confirmed by 2 independent psychiatrists using DSM-III-R criteria. **Blinding/controls for bias** Not reported **Other evaluation** Not reported			

APPENDIX B

Guidelines Ordering Information

The Clinical Practice Guideline—Autism/Pervasive Developmental Disorders: Assessment and Intervention with Young Children (Ages 0–3 years) may be ordered as follows:

Single copies of the Guideline publications are available free of charge to residents of New York State. To order, contact:

Publications
NYS Department of Health
Box 2000
Albany, NY 12220

A small fee will be charged to cover printing and administrative costs for non-residents of New York State.

To order, contact:
Health Education Services
P. O. Box 7126
Albany, NY 12224.
MasterCard and VISA accepted: (518) 439-7286.

Please specify the publication number when ordering:
Clinical Practice Guideline—Report of the Recommendations: Publication No. 4215
Clinical Practice Guideline—Quick Reference Guide: Publication No. 4216
Clinical Practice Guideline—Technical Report: Publication No. 4217

REFERENCES

Autism/Pervasive Developmental Disorders Guideline Panel. 1999. *Clinical Practice Guideline—Autism/Pervasive Developmental Disorders: Assessment and Intervention for Young Children (Ages 0–3 years). Clinical Practice Guideline No. 1*, NYDOH Pub. Nos. 4215, 4216, 4217. Albany, NY: New York State Department of Health, Early Intervention Program.

Baron-Cohen, S., Allen, J., and Gillberg, C. 1992. Can autism be detected at 18 months? The needle, the haystack, and the CHAT. *British Journal of Psychiatry* 168:158–63.

Brown, W. 1994. *Early Intervention Regulation—Annotation and Analysis.* Horsham, PA: LPR Publications.

Eddy, D. M., and Hasselbland, V. 1994. Analyzing evidence by the confidence and profile method. In *Clinical Practice Guideline Development: Methodology Perspectives*, eds. K. A. Moore, S. R. Siegel, and R. A. Siegel. Rockville, MD: U. S. Department of Health and Human Services.

Feinberg, E., and Beyer, J. 1998. Creating public policy in a climate of clinical indeterminancy: Lovaas as the case example du jour. *Infants and Young Children* 10(3):54–66.
Holland, J. P. 1995. Development of a clinical practice guideline for acute low back pain. *Current Opinion in Orthopedics* 6:63–9.
Institute of Medicine, Committee on Clinical Practice Guidelines. 1992. In *Guidelines for Clinical Practice*, eds. M. J. Field and K. N. Lohr. Washington, DC: National Academy Press.
Schriger, D. L. 1995. Training panels in methodology. In *Clinical Practice Guideline Development: Methodology Perspectives*, eds. K. A. McCormick, S. R. Moore, and R. A. Siegel. Rockville, MD: U. S. Department of Health and Human Services.
Woolf, S. H. 1994. An organized analytic framework for practice guideline development: Using analytic logic as a guide for reviewing evidence, developing recommendations, and explaining the rationale. In *Clinical Practice Guideline Development: Methodology Perspectives*, eds. K. A. McCormick, S. R. Moore, and R. A. Siegel. Rockville, MD: U. S. Department of Health and Human Services.

Chapter • 4

A Neuropsychological Approach to Language Intervention in Autistic Children

Michelle Dunn
Mary Joan Sebastian

Language impairment is a cardinal feature of autism in that autistic children manifest specific neuropsychologic profiles of cognitive and linguistic strengths and weaknesses. The focus of this chapter, therefore, will be to present two neuropsychologically based approaches to language intervention with the goal of remediating semantic deficits.

LANGUAGE IN AUTISM

All young children on the autistic spectrum have expressive and receptive language deficits at one or more language levels including phonology, syntax, semantics, and pragmatics (see Dunn and Rapin 1997 for summary of language levels). Children with Asperger's syndrome do not speak late, although the majority of autistic children do. With regard to severity of language disorder, autistic children range from completely nonverbal to hyperverbal with an extensive vocabulary. Some lower functioning children have little or no expressive or receptive language; some may have a number of words that appear and then disappear throughout the course of development; and some may only produce words under duress (when a desired object is withheld) or in a highly routine context such as a song or classroom routine. A lack of motivation to communicate may be present. In minimally verbal or nonverbal autistic children, there is little compensation through gesture;

and in higher functioning children, gesture is not well coordinated with the content of speech. Abnormal features in the language of verbal autistic children include immediate and delayed echolalia, pronoun reversal, aberrant prosody, and verbal perseveration. The speech of young lower functioning autistic children is marked by immediate echolalia. This distinguishes them from non-autistic children with developmental language disorders (Fein et al. 1996).

Language Profiles in Autism

Profiles of language impairment in autistic children differ across the spectrum. It is difficult to determine language disorder subtype in autistic children who speak little or not at all. However, as language develops, two major profiles emerge (Rapin and Dunn 1997). One involves persistent deficits at all levels of language (phonology, syntax, semantics, pragmatics); the other involves semantic and pragmatic deficits in the absence of abnormalities in the structural aspects (phonology and syntax) of language. All children on the autistic spectrum, including those with Asperger's syndrome, have comprehension deficits at some level. These may or may not involve deficient receptive processing of phonology and syntax. Comprehension may be affected at the single word or sentence level. Higher order comprehension (e.g., ability to identify the main point of the language, draw inferences, interpret figurative language) may be exclusively involved in some higher functioning individuals. Purely expressive deficits are not typically seen (Allen and Rapin 1992).

All children on the autistic spectrum have deficits in semantics and pragmatics. Also, it is not unusual to see structural (syntactic and phonologic) errors in the spontaneous speech of young, verbal autistic children, but perfect structure in their echoes (repetition of language). These autistic children may have delays in phonology and syntax when they are young, but then rapidly improve as they mature. For some children on the autistic spectrum, however, problems in phonology and syntax are not merely delays.

Pervasive language impairment. Some autistic children have frank deficits in syntax and phonology, along with significant deficits in semantics and pragmatics. This pattern is seen, not only in autistic children of low intelligence, but also in those with average to above average non-verbal intelligence. The language generated is typically dysfluent and sparse unless prompted. For children with lower level deficits, the goal is to establish meaningful, communicative language, and to build vocabulary and syntactically appropriate connected speech.

Impairment restricted to semantics and pragmatics. The majority of verbal autistic children show a developmental discrepancy between the structural and semantic aspects of language. They do not have fundamental problems in phonology and syntax, but are, invariably, deficient in semantics and pragmatics (Tager-Flusberg 1994). Their language impairment has been termed semantic-pragmatic language disorder (Rapin and Allen 1983; Bishop and Adams 1989). They are often fluent except for dysfluencies related to word retrieval and formulation/organization deficits. The language generated ranges from sparse to excessive.

The speech of high functioning, verbal autistic children is usually marked by organization/formulation deficits, evident in a poor ability to put language together in an organized way. Stories based on pictures are shorter and lack explanations of causal relationships between events, when compared with normal or mentally retarded children matched on verbal mental ages (Tager-Flusberg 1995). Narratives of verbal autistic children lack complexity and cohesive structure (Loveland et al. 1990). Expressive formulation deficits can prohibit children from saying or articulating all of what they know, or from using, in connected speech, syntactic forms that they possess. These children may frequently use formulaic language (delayed echoes) instead of formulating novel utterances. The hierarchic structure of the language is not understood. Speech is not organized according to overall topic, subtopics, and lower level details, but rather is over-focused on details, giving single details more importance than the topic itself. These children have difficulty maintaining a topic unless it is one of their preoccupations; and when they shift topics in conversation, they do not signal the shifts (Fay and Schuler 1980; Tager-Flusberg 1982). They may learn to adhere to a topic when it is identified for them, but they may not be able to identify the topic on their own. A focus of intervention must be identification of topic. Another must be development of types of speech acts used to maintain the topic under discussion, such as asking questions, adding information, or commenting.

Organizational issues are evident in autistic children's comprehension as well as in their expression. There may be an overemphasis on less relevant details with failure to integrate details into an overall concept for meaning. The children appear to memorize what they read or hear, but do not reorganize the information according to meaning and make it their own. Such problems may be related to pervasive cognitive deficits in organization, concept formation, or attention in some children; in others, the problems may be specific to language. High functioning verbal autistic children also make semantic errors at the single word level. They may sometimes simply fail to retrieve the words. Their speech often contains irrelevant words in which conventional meaning is ignored (Kanner 1946) or they may use high level vocabulary that they do not understand. In comprehending words in discourse, the meaning of a word is sometimes understood without respect for context.

It is interesting to consider these children's sense of the meaning of words. When they are asked to memorize word lists, they attempt to repeat the words in the exact order of presentation. Although they have normal ability to sort items by superordinate category, and their recall is improved by semantic category cuing, they do not actively reorganize the material by semantic category on their own to facilitate learning (Hermelin and O'Connor 1970; Tager-Flusberg 1991). While knowledge of superordinate categories is intact (Tager-Flusberg 1989), they have poor ability to decide which words within a category are most closely related to each other (Wolff and Barlow 1979) or most closely related to the category label. Performance on a word fluency task indicated that autistic children can rapidly retrieve exemplars of a superordinate category just as quickly as language matched normal children, but they retrieve less frequent and less prototypic exemplars (Dunn, Gomes, and Sebastian 1996). It appears that the meanings of words are organized categorically, but that organization within categories may be different from normal. It has been proposed that autistic children have a fundamental cognitive deficit in the ability to interrelate new and existing concepts and experiences (DeLong 1992) in order to develop "a complex, useful and flexible structure of meaning." This view could account for disruption in lexical organization and misuse of semantic knowledge. For verbal autistic children, a major goal of language intervention is to help the child organize meaning.

Language acquisition style. Autistic children appear to have an unusual language acquisition style. The verbal autistic child's reliance on immediate echolalia and formulaic speech suggests a gestalt style of language acquisition (Prizant 1983; Schuler and Prizant 1985). These children often memorize and repeat entire sentences verbatim. Echolalia may indicate that the echoed language is incompletely processed for meaning; thus, it is reasonable to suspect that the children use words that they do not completely or even partially understand. They are better at processing and memorizing the surface structure than at understanding the meaning of what they hear and say. It is also important to keep in mind that the severity of their comprehension deficit is easily overlooked because they can produce higher level vocabulary and more complex language in scripts (delayed echoes) than they can understand. Whereas normally developing children comprehend more than they can say, autistic children's expression precedes comprehension (Rapin, Allen, and Dunn 1992; Fein et al. 1996). Autistic children may also be precocious readers. Acquisition of

Figure 1. Two examples of symbols, "sun" and "water," used to teach autistic children to read.

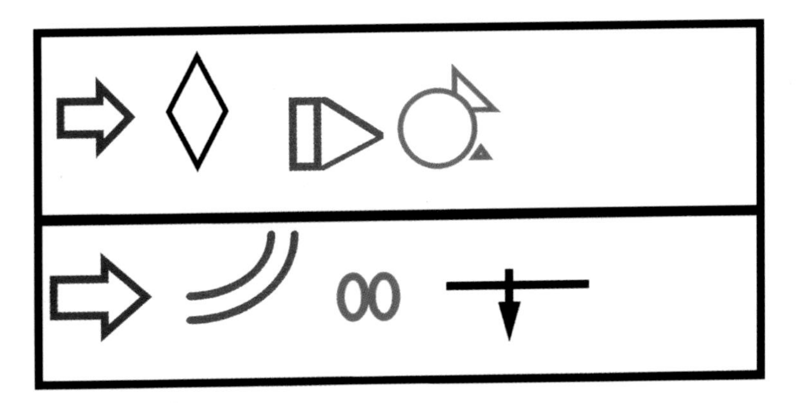

Figure 2. Sample symbol sentences color coded according to parts of speech.

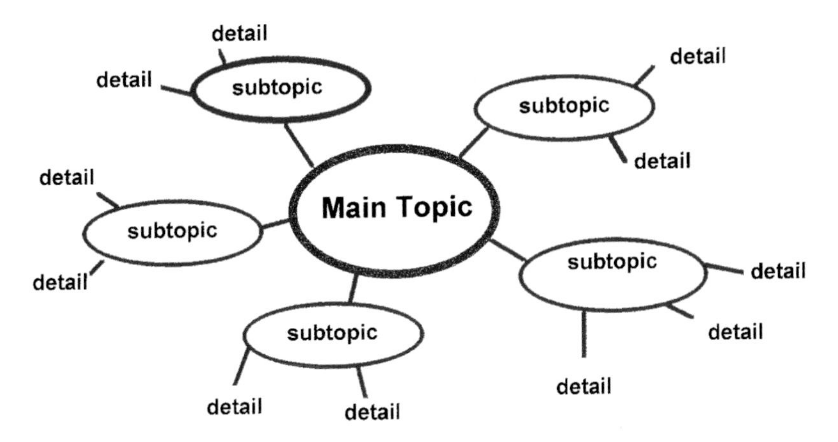

Figure 3. Description Organizer: Basic model.

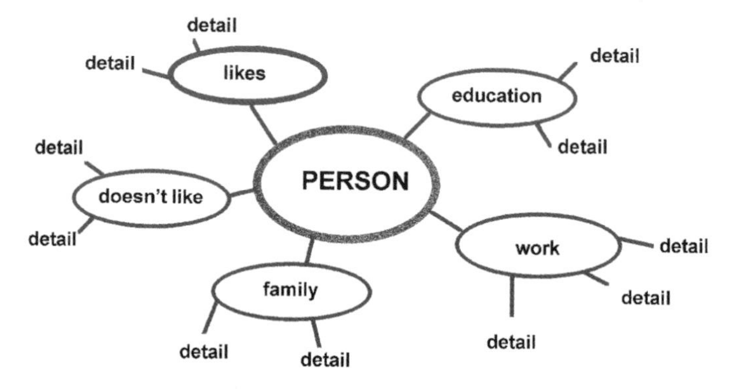

Figure 4. Description Organizer: Sample web used for describing a person.

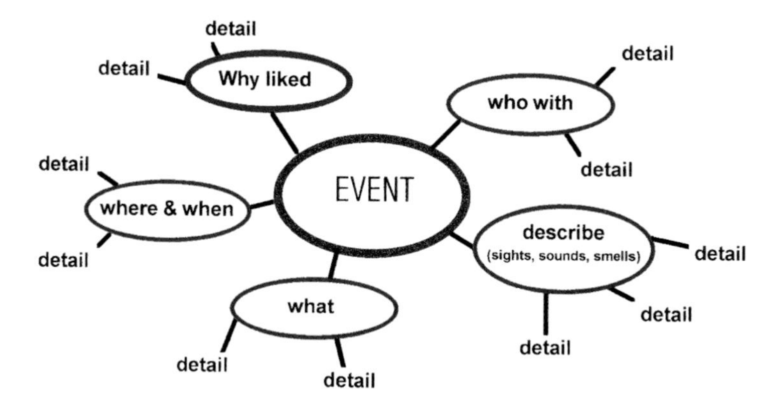

Figure 5. Description Organizer: Sample web for generating a simple description of an event.

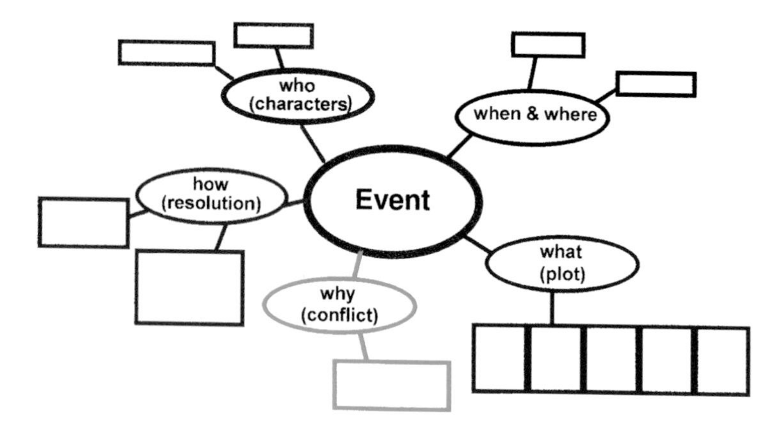

Figure 6. Description Organizer: Sample web for generating a complex description of an event.

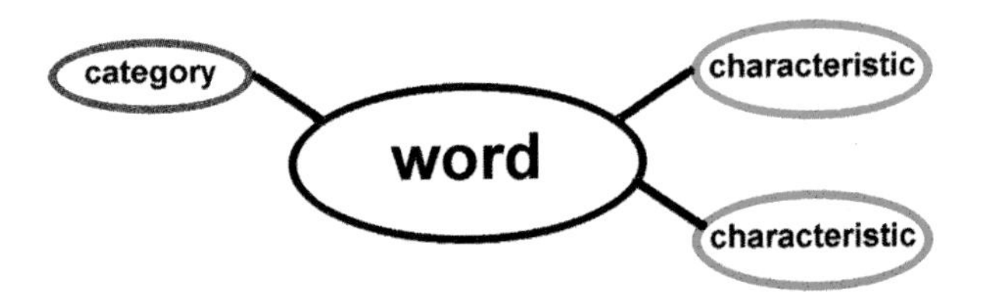

Figure 7. Description Organizer: Sample description web for generating a definition of a word.

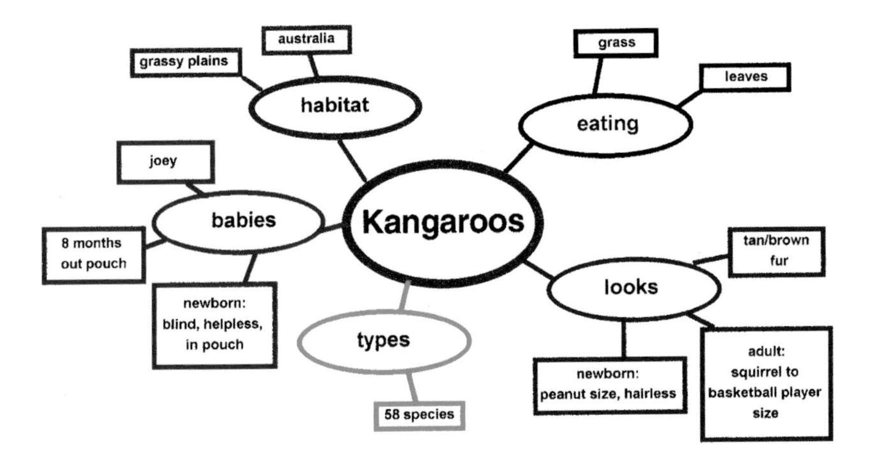

Figure 8. Description Organizer: Sample web generated based on a factual written description used for expression and comprehension.

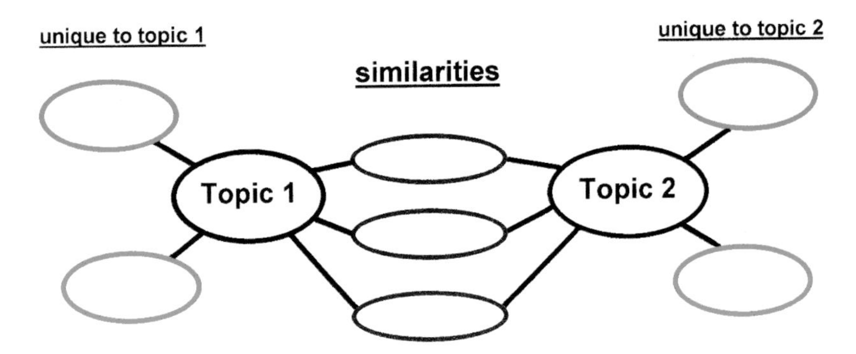

Figure 9. Comparison Organizer: Basic model for simple comparison.

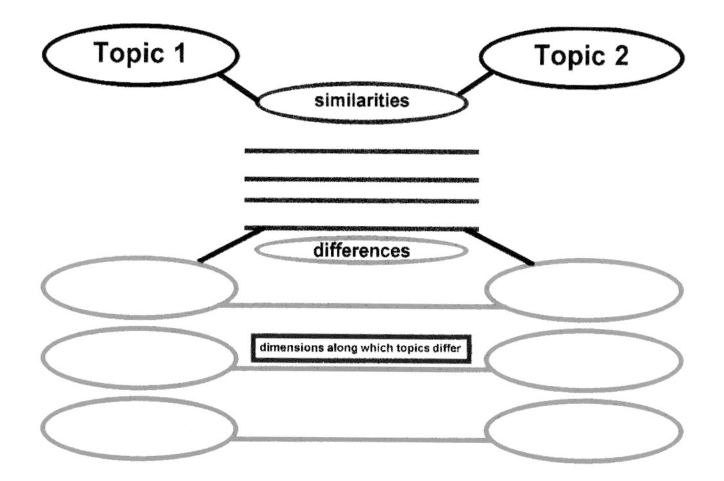

Figure 10. Comparison Organizer: Basic model for complex comparison.

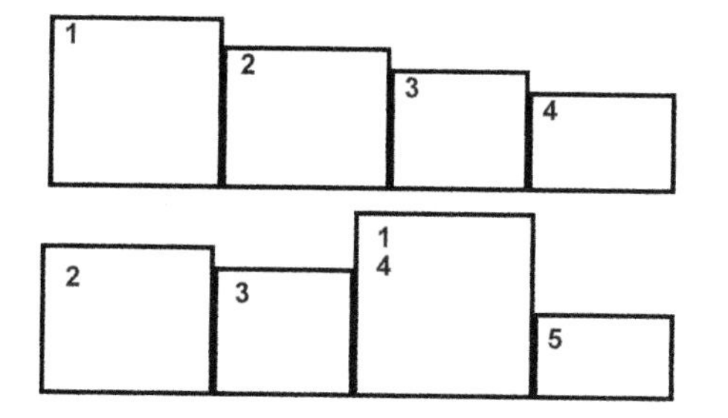

Figure 11. Time-line Organizer: Two models (top and bottom).

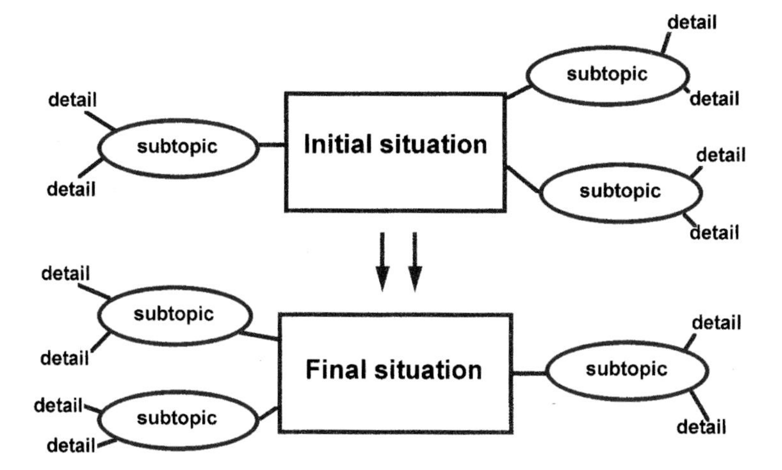

Figure 12. Cause and Effect Organizer: Basic model

written language may precede the development of oral language. Of course, precocious decoding of written language does not necessarily denote comprehension of what is read, although a proportion of autistic children have better comprehension of written or visually represented language than they do of oral language.

NEUROPSYCHOLOGICAL PROFILES IN AUTISM

Overall cognition in children on the autistic spectrum ranges from severely deficient to very superior, with approximately two thirds of children having IQs in the mentally deficient range. The neuropsychologic profile of these children indicates significant discrepancies among cognitive abilities. Visual spatial abilities are typically stronger than verbal abilities (Prior 1979; Lincoln et al. 1988; Smalley and Asarnow 1990; Fein et al. 1996), with the notable exception of Asperger's syndrome, where the reversed pattern or lack of a difference between verbal and nonverbal abilities is often in evidence (Szatmari et al. 1989). The majority of people with autism process information better when it is presented in a concrete, visual format than when it is presented verbally. High functioning autistic individuals demonstrate strengths in focused and sustained attention, simple memory, simple language, and visual spatial abilities. Rote memorization is a strength.

Deficits are seen in cognitive processing of complex information (Minshew et al. 1992) where a requirement of the task is an ability to plan an approach or discern or generate an organized scheme. Therefore, short-term memory is not improved by increasing semantic content of material (Fein et al. 1996). These children attempt to memorize the material by rote. Inherent organization is often not recognized spontaneously or used to aid processing, although cuing regarding the semantic structure of the material may be helpful (Tager-Flusberg 1991).

LANGUAGE INTERVENTION IN AUTISM

Neuropsychological Model

Neuropsychologically driven remediation uses a child's cognitive and linguistic strengths to improve or compensate for his or her weaknesses. The basic notion is that processing via an intact system takes the place of or supports processing via the deficient system. If teaching materials emphasize processing via relatively intact neural systems in concert with processing via impaired systems, accurate processing through the intact modality will support and develop the impaired one. For many children on the autistic spectrum, simple, visually presented information that can be memorized by rote can be used to support language development. Pictures or a combination of pictures and written language can be used effectively to foster language (Hodgdon 1995). If the child has a strength in rote auditory verbal memory, this can also be emphasized. However, teaching through the auditory modality often requires supporting visual information and, perhaps, more repetition than when a child is taught through the visual modality. Auditory information is fleeting and the child may have impaired auditory attention, impaired auditory discrimination, or slowed auditory processing. The general goal is to develop meaningful communication by way of the strongest modality or modalities available to the child.

General Considerations

Before one can start with specific training of language skills, certain basic skills must be established. These include joint attention, imitation on demand, at least rudimentary reciprocal interaction, and a basic understanding that one object or action can symbolize another.

Personal Characteristics. Decisions about the general format of intervention are driven by knowledge of the child's personal characteristics:

1. *IQ.* The overall approach to intervention appears to be strongly related to general intelligence. Children with lower IQs make better gains in more structured, direct teaching situations, although children with higher IQs benefit more from discourse-based situations, as well as through direct teaching (Friedman and Friedman 1980).
2. *Learning Style.* It is important to keep a child's learning style in mind when developing a treatment plan. Many autistic children appear to have a gestalt learning style—information is memorized in chunks and, perhaps, at a later time, analyzed. These children benefit from the paired presentation of auditory and visual information. Instead of discouraging echolalia and the use of scripts, the therapist can take advantage of an excellent rote memory for chunks of information, later encouraging the analysis of information. It is important always to associate language (including memorized chunks/scripts) with meaning.
3. *Sequence of language acquisition.* The optimal method for addressing language deficits should take advantage of the autistic child's natural order of language acquisition. For example, since expression often precedes comprehension, the child may be taught expressive scripts with meaningful associations. If the ability to decode the written word precedes or proceeds in concert with the development of expression, reading should be

encouraged and used to support the development of receptive language.

4. *Temperament.* Rigid temperament is the rule in autistic children, making consistency and predictability important considerations in developing any method of intervention. If information is presented one way at one time, and then the same information is presented in a different way at another time, the child will probably not understand that the same concept is being presented. Information should be presented repeatedly in exactly the same way until acquired, and then generalization should be encouraged. Predictability also appears to decrease anxiety and promote more rapid learning.

Long-term as well as short-term goals. Other major factors contributing to decisions about neuropsychological intervention with an individual child are long- and short-term environmental demands. Although short-term language goals in the early stages of language development may be focused on developing more basic language skills (e.g., receptive vocabulary, syntax), deficits in language organization, including topic identification and maintenance, persist. Early work on language organization can establish strategies for organizing and interpreting complex information that will be encountered in the future, specifically, expressing ideas and comprehending oral language and written text. Language intervention clearly needs to focus on all of those aspects of language that are deficient in the individual child with autism. In all autistic children, even when other symptoms abate, semantic and pragmatic deficits persist. Although the following approaches address pragmatics, syntax, and even phonology to some extent, the main focus of these neuropsychologically driven methods is semantics to help the child develop an abililty to understand and convey meaning.

Reading as an Avenue to Oral Language Development (Comprehension and Production)

Nonverbal autistic preschoolers who possess relative strengths in visually based processing can benefit from a focus on visually based language, such as communication boards. Older non-verbal autistic children may have acquired language through the use of sign language or reading (Bonvillian, Nelson, and Rhyne 1981). The development of language comprehension may be aided through the consistent pairing of oral language with sign and gestures by the teacher. Hyperlexia forms a subset of both low and high functioning autistic children. Hyperlexic children have a precocious ability to decode the written word, usually with poor written and aural language comprehension. This may first be evident in an obsession with shapes, letters, and numbers from a very young age. Decoding written language may precede the development of oral language. Rather than seeking to extinguish these preoccupations, this strength can be used as a particularly important skill for developing language. In a child with this profile, many therapists nurture and develop reading and use it to improve the child's language comprehension and production by consistently associating the written word with meaning, using written words and sentences to teach oral expression and comprehension.

In lower functioning children with hyperlexia, concrete objects and actions are first labeled with written words to develop a power vocabulary. In children who have difficulty producing oral language but who can read, written words, once understood, can become part of a communication board. Children with more language can read words, phrases, and sentences aloud, which, in turn, are associated with pictures or activities depicting the meaning of the written language. Sentences and phrases should be chosen based on specific language comprehension goals. Parts of speech can be color coded differently. Once the child gives evidence of having acquired the meaning of a group of sentences, a number of instructional activities can be carried out. The child can be given a variety of sentences and asked to match the written sentence to a drawing in an array that depicts its meaning. To encourage generalization, it is important that the picture depicting the meaning of the sentence not be the same picture every time the activity is presented. Another activity involves having the child enact a sentence. In another, a child is given a sentence composed of word cards and is then provided with "slot fillers" (words that can be substituted for words in the same grammatical class [and color]). These substitutions maintain the overall form of the sentence but change its content. An emphasis is on teaching sentence frames that serve a variety of pragmatic functions.

Next, the child can be given a series of word cards to construct sentences. In the beginning, these should only be the words in a given sentence, scrambled. The child's job is to place them in order. Later, the child can be given cards to formulate spontaneously his or her own sentences about pictures or situations. This approach works well with autistic children who are natural readers. But what about those children who are not reading?

Teaching Reading to Autistic Children Who Are Not Learning According to Traditional Approaches

Nearly all autistic children demonstrate relative strengths in their ability to process concrete, visual information. Autistic children who do not demonstrate a precocious ability to read may still sometimes benefit from visually presented language. Communication boards and sign language are frequently used. In addition, some autistic children may benefit from early teaching of written language, even if they are not hyperlexic. This is likely to be the case if the child has some interest in the written word, has a relative strength in processing concrete, visual material, and has strong visual and auditory memory.

Autistic children with significant deficits in both comprehension and production of language may have both auditory processing and visual analytic deficits. Or even though their visual analysis may be strong on standardized testing, in the context of reading, it is poor. In a standardized test such as block design, attention is focused exclusively on analyzing the material visually; however, success does not necessarily imply that visual analysis is an automatic skill. In some children, strong visual analysis breaks down during activities that require "multi-tasking," such as reading. For most of these children, efforts to teach reading in school through a phonics or sight word approach (despite a strength in visual memory) are fruitless. However, a concrete visual approach to teaching language comprehension and expression still appears to be the best approach because the children have strengths in visual memory, organization, and problem solving. Beginning with a sight word approach appears best, but the visual complexity of individual words needs to be reduced.

We have adopted an approach in which, instead of written words, the child is first taught to read a large number of visual, semi-representational symbols for words. Words written in traditional orthography are then taught through association with these symbols. A number of symbol systems have been used to improve communication in impaired children. These include Rebus, Picsyms, Pictogram Ideogram Communication Symbols (PIC), Picture Communication Symbols (PCS), and Blissymbols (Bloomberg, Karlan, and Lloyd 1990). However, the symbols we use to teach reading are different in that the words the symbols represent are not immediately apparent. The majority of Rebus symbols are pictures of objects and actions. The set of symbols we use are somewhat more like Bliss symbols and can differ from child to child. Different children need symbols to be more or less transparent, referring to the ease with which the label for the symbol could be construed from the form of the symbol itself. For example, Rebus symbols are completely transparent. Bliss symbols are not. There is some evidence that symbols such as Rebus are learned faster than Bliss symbols by autistic children (Kozleski 1991), but there may be more improvement in communication through the teaching of less transparent symbols (Burroughs et al. 1990). To help a child understand the symbolic nature of the written word, it is most helpful to use symbols that are not transparent, if possible. Symbols for sun and water are found in figure 1, p. 60a. The symbol for sun is more transparent than that for water. A therapist can use symbols from already established systems or make them up.

As with words written in traditional orthography, these symbols are associated with concrete actions and objects with the purpose of building vocabulary. Attaching index cards with symbols to objects around the house that a child can name helps the child learn labels for the symbols. Attaching the cards to new objects helps the child learn the labels for the objects. Symbols are read individually, and in sentences with appropriate punctuation. Reading this type of material stresses neither the phonetic system nor visual analysis. Our experience is that these symbols are learned very rapidly by autistic children with documented strength in visual memory. These symbols can be used just as written words can be used with hyperlexic children (described in the immediately preceding section), as an aid in language intervention.

A child is asked to read symbol sentences, add slot fillers to sentences created by the therapist, and, later, produce sentences with appropriate syntax using these symbols. Again, different classes of words (nouns, verbs, descriptive words) are color coded differently. Sample symbol sentences can be found in figure 2, p. 60a. The first sentence says, "The big dog barks." The second sentence says, "The water is deep." To teach traditional orthography, individual symbols are paired with written words on flash cards. The symbols are written in pencil and the words color coded. As the child practices reading these, over time, the symbols are slowly faded by erasing. Words with traditional orthography are then combined and read in sentences with new symbols. In this way, a sight word reading vocabulary is rapidly acquired.

Reading continues to provide the child with a tool by which to acquire language. As the child is ready, phonics skills are introduced by teaching the child to classify already acquired sight words according to their phonetic characteristics (initial and final consonant sounds and vowel sounds). This intervention takes into account the autistic child's gestalt learning style. Whole words and sentences are taught first and later analyzed. Using knowledge of the child's neuropsychological profile, a method of intervention can be adopted to teach a skill that could not be learned through more conventional methods.

As stated earlier, this approach is useful for developing language in autistic children, particularly in those with some ability to produce oral language, but who are not yet producing syntactically appropriate connected speech. In addition, reading can be used to support organization in many settings. Classroom instructions can be written. Daily routines in the home can be represented by pictures accompanied by single written words or briefly written instructions.

Remediation of Deficits in Language Organization

Because most verbal autistic children have abnormal language organization in the presence of relatively strong visual/nonverbal problem solving and visual memory, graphic organizers become an appropriate intervention method. A graphic organizer is a concrete visual representation of the organization of language (Pehrsson and Robinson 1985; Pehrsson and Robinson 1988; Parks and Black 1990; Parks and Black 1992). Issues that can be addressed through this method include identification of topic, topic maintenance, and ability to organize a coherent oral account or understanding of a concept. Autistic children benefit from being taught a plan or set of rules for how to organize verbal material hierarchically—teaching them to give the main topic more weight than secondary themes or details.

Deficient language organization is evident from a young age in verbal autistic children. As the child develops, even when other lower level language issues improve, language disorganization persists, showing up in poor oral and written language expression, as well as in poor auditory and reading comprehension. Based on long-term environmental demands, it is important to intervene as early as when the child is four years of age. We use four graphic organizers to represent the organization of language and other thematic material, such as using pictures that tell a story or some social situation observed by the child.

The four graphic organizers. There are numerous graphic organizers in the literature with different visual formats that represent the same semantic structure (Parks and Black 1990). The variety of graphic organizers is confusing for children, especially for those with language based learning issues. Therefore, graphic organizers were reviewed and distilled to four that cover the majority of language situations. These are (1) the description organizer, (2) the comparison organizer, (3) the sequential organizer, and (4) the cause and effect organizer. The four organizers help to improve language comprehension, as well as expression, and to improve verbal and social reasoning. They are used to structure oral and written expression (including stories, essays, current events, summaries, and term papers) and to guide listening for the hierarchic structure of thematic material. In the same way, they are used to improve reading comprehension for both factual and fictional material. Graphic organizers force autistic children to reorganize material and make it their own. The organizers can be used to integrate information from a number of sources and aid ability to draw inferences. Organizing material according to hierarchic structure not only aids meaning but also memory. Graphic organizers can also aid topic maintenance and the ability to answer questions in conversation. A description of each is presented below:

1. *Description Organizer.* The description organizer (see figures 3–8 on pp. 60a–c), also known as a web, can be used to define words, and to describe as well as understand accounts of people, places, objects, and simple and complex events. This organizer visually represents a main topic, subtopics, and lower level details (see figure 3 on p. ??a). The central node is the main topic and nodes connected to this central node represent subtopics. Each subtopic has lower level details attached to it. The main topic is weighted more heavily than subtopics and lower level details. The relative weights are signified by the size of the node.

Expression. Figure 4 on p. 60b presents an example of a web for describing a person. The child generates this web by brainstorming with an adult—first deciding on a main topic, then subtopics, and then adding details. Each branch of the web contains one subtopic and its corresponding details. The child should be encouraged to provide details in such a way that no subtopic is emphasized more than the others. Sometimes an autistic child with a particular preoccupation may emphasize one subtopic to the exclusion of others. For example, in describing a trip, a child might talk exclusively about the form of transportation used. When the child talks from a web, he decides the order in which he will talk about the branches; and then he talks out one branch at a time, never jumping from one branch to another, but always coming back to center, the main topic, before beginning discussion of a new subtopic. It is important that the child follow the web in his retelling and not be allowed to digress. For the simplest webs, he should provide one sentence about each branch. As the child progresses, each part of a tree can be used to cue more complex utterances.

Description organizers are also used to describe places, things, and events. Figures 5 and 6 (see p. 60b) provide examples of description webs for events, differing in levels of complexity. The simpler one (figure 5, p. 60b) is for younger children or those newer to the process. Description organizers can also be used to help children formulate definitions (see figure 7 on p. 60c). Each definition involves identification of the category to which a word belongs and the word's characteristics (e.g., form and function for nouns). Verb organizers and noun organizers (Pehrsson and Robinson 1988) can be used to determine the meanings of individual words. This activity can help children reorganize aberrantly organized meanings at the level of the lexicon.

Comprehension. Description organizers can be used to map the hierarchic structure of the meaning of thematic material. Producing a graphic organizer from oral language or written text fosters the ability to organize information one reads or hears hierarchically. First, the child is encouraged to identify the overall topic and then the subtopics. It is important that the child be taught to identify subtopics, as this is probably the most difficult part of organizing thematic material. In teaching a child to identify subtopics, it often helps to list all of the details on a piece of paper or index cards, then group these into common categories and label the category or subtopic. The child should first be taught to map factual material. Figure 8 on p. 60c is the web generated based on the following passage:

> In September, at springtime on the grassy plains of Australia, many female kangaroos are ready to give birth. A newborn kangaroo, called a joey, is about the size of a peanut. It is blind and hairless and will not be ready for life outside its mother's pouch until it is 8 months old. Adult kangaroos generally eat grass and leaves. There are 58 species of kangaroo. Most have brown or tan fur. The smallest type is about the size of a squirrel and the largest the size of a professional basketball player.

Graphic organizers can be used to develop a child's ability to answer wh-questions. While looking at a graphic organizer, a child is asked wh-questions regarding details on each subtopic. The adult asking the question helps the child answer by pointing to the part of the web containing information required to answer the question. Once the child has a sense of how to map factual material, work with fictional material should be undertaken. The event organizer in figure 6 on p. 60b can be used to map short stories, single chapters, or full books. The *who* branch refers to characters, the *when* and *where* branches to setting, *why* to the central conflict, *how* to the resolution, and *what* to the plot. It is not necessary to have the child describe the entire sequence of events, but rather to identify the three or four pivotal events in the piece. A description organizer for a book can be generated to aid in the writing of a book report. It can be used "as is" to write a summary, or a new organizer can be generated to address a specific question (e.g., a comparison organizer can be used to answer a question such as ("How would you compare the main character in the book to yourself?").

A special use of a description organizer involves topic maintenance in conversation. A group of children can be given a topic to talk about, with each generating a description organizer about the topic. They may keep their organizers within view as they practice conversations. They are told that they may comment, add information, or ask questions about the specified topic in response to what other children say.

2. *Comparison Organizer.* Comparison organizers are used to teach a child to articulate the similarities and differences between two topics. For younger, less experienced students, a simpler form of the comparison organizer is used (see figure 9

on p. 60c). The comparison organizer for older or more advanced students is more complex in that it involves identification of common dimensions along which differences between the two topics exist (see figure 10 on p. 60d) (adapted from Parks and Black 1990).

3. *Time-line Organizer.* Two examples of sequential organizers are presented in figure 11 on p. 60d. In each, the size of the box signifies the order in which the events in a sequence are related. The top row of figure 11 shows a sequence of events from the earliest to the most recent. The bottom row in figure 11 sequences events starting at one time, flashing back, and then working forward to the point at which the story started, and then continuing to the end.
4. *Cause and Effect Organizer.* A cause and effect organizer (see figure 12 on p. 60d) helps a child identify what, in an initial situation, produced the final situation. At the top of the page, the child builds a description organizer, often composed of the topic of the initial situation and corresponding details. At the bottom of the page, a description organizer for the final or resulting situation is constructed. Once the child has represented the information visually and concretely, he is asked to look at the initial situation and identify the event(s) in the initial situation that produced the final situation. This type of organizer is helpful for understanding cause and effect in social interactions and in academic subjects, such as science and social studies.

Considerations in teaching the use of graphic organizers to children. Graphic organizers can be used with children who function at a variety of levels. They are not only for very high functioning children, but can be used with any autistic child who can generate phrases based on visual material. Graphic organizers can include pictures as well as words, making it possible to use them with young non-readers. Graphic organizers can be used for the simplest tasks, such as giving a basic oral description of an object, as well as for complex tasks that involve organizing information from multiple sources, as is done in writing essays and lengthy reports on a topic. They can also be used to guide note taking from a text or to synthesize main concepts after taking notes from a lecture.

A child is first taught to use graphic organizers as an aid for expressive language. It is helpful to write out each of the child's stories (including special stories about the child's life) and to compile them in a book, along with the graphic organizers. Rehearsal of stories will be carried out differently for each child, since each child has different strengths. If the child has a particularly strong visual memory, he can be taught to imagine the organizers in his head and speak from them. If the child has a strength in rote verbal memory, stories can be rehearsed aloud. Adults can capitalize on children's use of scripts to teach them to produce more appropriate and flexible expressive language. The child should then be encouraged to tell these stories to others.

Once the child can use the description organizer for expression, work can begin to focus on the use of organizers for comprehension as well. Prior to this, however, it is important that the child be given practice in identifying the topic in auditory or written language (e.g., identifying categories to which words belong, the topic of a picture, the topic [main message, author's intent] of a paragraph), and in listing details. Once the child can do these tasks, graphic organizers are introduced to map main topic and details. Later, work using the organizers to represent the hierarchic structure of auditory or written language, including the main topic, subtopics, and lower level details can begin. Generally speaking, the most difficult activity for most communication impaired children is identifying subtopics and shifts in subtopics. Once the child has some experience with graphic organizers, he is given repeated practice in mapping written or oral material and in producing summaries.

Each of the four graphic organizers is taught in turn. After multiple graphic organizers have been introduced, giving the child practice identifying the appropriate graphic organizer for any auditory, written, or pictured thematic material becomes an important goal. The graphic organizers used with a given child depend on the child's neuropsychological profile of strengths and weaknesses. For example, if a child has problems with visual sequencing, the sequential organizer would not be used. The way in which the graphic organizers are implemented also depends on the individual child's neuropsychological profile. They can be color coded to focus the child's attention. If a child is having difficulty with topic maintenance, coloring each subtopic and its corresponding details a different color (as in figures 6 and 8) can help the child focus on each subtopic. If a child is having difficulty with the hierarchy of language, such as emphasizing a single detail over central ideas, the main topic can be one color, subtopics another color, and details a third color (as in figure 3). If a child is distracted by color, the organizers can be presented in black and white.

From the very beginning of instruction, the child is engaged in the process of generating organizers. Even if the child needs to be walked through the process and led to discover the structure, he or she should begin with a blank sheet of paper on which to draw the organizer. Children learn better and understand and recall linguistic material better if they produce the organizers themselves, as opposed to the organizers being created for them. A child should not be restricted to a set number of subtopics or details unless the child is hyperverbal and perseverative. The ultimate goal is for the child to generate graphic organizers independently.

CONCLUSION

Autistic children have unusual profiles of cognitive and linguistic strengths and weaknesses. They are usually deficient in processing complex information, but possess strengths in rote visual and auditory memory. The majority of autistic children (save those with Asperger's syndrome) have strengths in visual perception, analysis and synthesis, visual spatial skills, and concrete visual problem solving. Children on the autistic spectrum have impairments in both receptive and expressive language in which expression can be stronger than comprehension, and written language may develop more rapidly than oral language.

There are two major language disorder profiles in this group. The typical language profile in verbal autistic children is one of impaired semantics and pragmatics without deficits in the structural aspects of language; the other involves frank deficits in phonology and syntax as well. Even highly verbal children with Asperger's syndrome display verbal disorganization. Neuropsychologically driven remediation uses children's strengths to compensate for or support their weaknesses. For autistic children, a visually based approach to language accomplishes this. Young or lower functioning autistic children may acquire a visually based language system prior to an aural system. A proportion of these children are hyperlexic. Through linking written language with meaning, the development of oral language can be fostered. Even in lower functioning children, who have somewhat limited visual analysis but strong visual memory, a visual symbol system can be taught and used to enhance language development. Higher functioning verbal autistic children can be taught visually based strategies to organize verbal output and improve comprehension.

CHAPTER SUMMARY

1. All children with autism have deficits in spoken language.
2. There are two main patterns of language deficit in autism: 1) pervasive language involvement and 2) deficits in semantics and pragmatics.
3. In the first type, pervasive language impairment has an impact on all aspects of language: syntax (grammar), phonology (articulation), semantics (word usage), and pragmatics (conversational/social speech).

4. In the second type, semantic-pragmatic language disorder, there are no deficits in phonology and syntax.
5. Autistic children appear to have a gestalt style of language acquisition in which they say more than they actually understand.
6. Echolalia and hyperlexia can be used as substrates for neuropsychological intervention in autistic language. It is not a matter of simply encouraging these behaviors, but rather of progressively linking them with meaning.
7. Rigidity of temperament needs to be taken into account in the way information is represented.
8. Persons with autism can better process information when it is presented in a concrete visual format rather than in an auditory verbal format. Thus, a visually based approach to language remediation will use the autistic child's strengths by pairing meaning with a visual representation of auditory language (written symbols, words, or graphic organizers).
9. Visually based strategies (graphic organizers) can also be used to remediate organizational deficits in language.

REFERENCES

Allen, D.A., and Rapin, I. 1992. Autistic children are also dysphasia. In *Neurobiology of Infantile Autism*, eds. H. Naruse and E. M. Ornitz. Amsterdam: Excerpta Medica.

Bishop, D. V. M., and Adams, C. 1989. Conversational characteristics of children with semantic-pragmatic disorder I. What features lead to a judgement of inappropriacy? *British Journal of Disorders of Communication* 24:241–63.

Bloomberg, K., Karlan, G. R., and Lloyd, L. L. 1990. The comparative translucency of initial lexical items represented in five graphic symbol systems and sets. *Journal of Speech and Hearing Research* 33(4):717–25.

Bonvillian, J. D., Nelson, K. E., and Rhyne, J. M. 1981. Sign language and autism. *Journal of Autism and Developmental Disorders* 11:125–37.

Burroughs, J. A., Albritton, E. G., Eaton, B. B., and Montague, J. 1990. A comparative study of language delayed preschool children's ability to recall symbols from two symbol systems. *Aac: Augmentative and Alternative Communication* 6(3):202–06.

DeLong, G. R. 1992. Autism, amnesia, hippocampus and learning. *Neuroscience and Behavioral Reviews* 16:63–70.

Dunn, M., and Rapin, I. 1997. Communication in autistic children. In *Behavior Belongs in the Brain*, eds. P. J. Accardo, B. K. Shapiro, and A. J. Capute. Baltimore: York Press.

Dunn, M., Gomes, H., and Sebastian, M. 1996. Prototypicality of responses in autistic, language disordered and normal children in a verbal fluency task. *Child Neuropsychology* 2(2):99–108.

Fay, W., and Schuler, A. L. 1980. *Emerging Language in Autistic Children*. Baltimore: University Park Press.

Fein, D., Dunn, M., Allen, D., Hall, N., Morris, R., and Wilson, B. 1996. Neuropsychological and language findings. In *Preschool Children with*

Inadequate Communication: Developmental Language Disorder, Autism, Low IQ, Clinics in Developmental Medicine #139, ed. I. Rapin. London: MacKeith Press.

Friedman, P., and Friedman, K. 1980. Accounting for individual differences when comparing effectiveness of remedial language teaching methods. *Applied Psycholinguistics* 1:151–170.

Hermelin, B., and O'Connor, N., 1970. *Psychological Experiments with Autistic Children.* Oxford: Peragamon Press.

Hodgdon, L. A. 1995. *Visual Strategies for Improving Communication.* Troy, Michigan: Quirk Roberts Publishing.

Kanner, L. 1946. Irrelevant and metaphorical language in early infantile autism. *American Journal of Psychiatry* 103:242–46.

Kozleski, E. B. 1991. Visual symbol acquisition by students with autism. *Exceptionality* 2(4):173–94.

Loveland, K., McEvoy, R., Tunali, B., and Kelley, M. L. 1990. Narrative storytelling in autism and Down syndrome. *British Journal of Developmental Psychiatry* 8:9–23.

Lincoln, A. J., Courchesne, E., Kilman, B., Elmasian, R., Allen, M. 1988. A study of intellectual abilities in high functioning people with autism. *Journal of Autism and Developmental Disorders* 18:505–24.

Minshew, N. J., Goldstein, G., Meunz, L. R., and Payton, J. B. 1992. Neuropsychological functioning in nonmentally retarded autistic individuals. *Journal of Clinical and Experimental Neuropsychology* 14:749–61.

Parks, S., and Black, H. 1990. *Organizing thinking* (Book 2). Pacific Grove, California: Critical Thinking Press and Software.

Parks, S., and Black, H. 1992. *Organizing thinking* (Book 1). Pacific Grove, California: Critical Thinking Press and Software.

Pehrsson, R. S., and Robinson, H. A. 1985. *The Semantic Organizer Approach to Reading and Writing Instruction.* Rockville, MD: Aspen.

Pehrsson, R. S., and Robinson, H. A. 1988. Semantic organizers. *Topics in Language Disorders* 8(3):24–37.

Prior, M. 1979. Cognitive abilities and disabilities in infantile autism: A review. *Journal of Abnormal Child Psychology* 7(4):357–80.

Prizant, B. M. 1983. Language acquisition and communicative behavior in autism: Toward an understanding of the "whole" of it. *Journal of Speech and Hearing Disorders* 48:296–307.

Rapin, I., and Dunn, M. 1997. *Language Disorders in Children With Autism: Seminars in Pediatric Neurology,* ed. J. B. Bodensteiner. Philadelphia, PA: W. B. Saunders Company.

Rapin, I., Allen, D. A., and Dunn M. A. 1992. Developmental language disorders. In *Handbook of Neuropsychology* Vol. 7. Child Neuropsychology, eds. S. J. Segalowitz and I. Rapin. Amsterdam: Elsevier Science.

Rapin, I., and Allen, D. A. 1983. Developmental language disorders: Neurologic considerations. In *Neuropsychology of Language, Reading, and Spelling,* ed. U. Kirk. New York: Academic Press.

Schuler, A. L., and Prizant, B. M. 1985. Echolalia. In *Communication Problems in Autism,* eds. E. Schopler and G. Mesibov. New York: Plenum.

Smalley, S., and Asarnow, R. 1990. Cognitive subclinical markers in autism. *Journal of Autism and Developmental Disorders* 20:271–78.

Szatmari, P., Bartollucci, R., Bremner, R., Bond, S., and Rich, S. 1989. A follow-up study of high functioning autistic children. *Journal of Autism and Developmental Disorders* 19(2):213–25.

Tager-Flusberg, H. 1982. Pragmatic development and its implication for social interaction in autistic children. In *Proceedings of the International Symposium for Research in Autism*, ed. D. Park. Washington, DC: National Society for Autistic Children.

Tager-Flusberg, H. 1989. A psycholinguistic perspective on language development in the autistic child. In *Autism: Nature, Diagnosis, and Treatment*, ed. G. Dawson. New York: Guilford Press.

Tager-Flusberg, H. 1991. Semantic processing in the free recall of autistic children: Further evidence for a cognitive deficit. *British Journal of Developmental Psychology* 9:417–30.

Tager-Flusberg, H. 1994. Dissociation in form and function in the acquisition of language by autistic children. In *Constraints on Language Acquisition: Studies of Atypical Children*, ed. H. Tager-Flusberg. Hillsdale, NJ: Lawrence Erlbaum Associates.

Tager-Flusberg, H. 1995. "Once upon a ribbit": Stories narrated by autistic children. *British Journal of Developmental Psychology* 13(1):45–59.

Wolff, S., and Barlow, A. 1979. Schizoid personality in childhood: A comparative study of schizoid, autistic, and normal children. *Journal Of Child Psychology and Psychiatry* 20:29–46.

Chapter • 5

Stereotypies and Repetitive Behaviors in Autism

Marco A. Grados
Daria McCarthy

CLINICAL DOMAINS IN AUTISM: A UNITARY VIEW?

Children with autism, as defined by the *Diagnostic and Statistical Manual-IV* (DSM-IV) (APA, 1994), have significant impairment in communication, abnormal social development, and clinically significant odd behaviors/stereotypies. These three phenomenological areas appear to coexist in children with autism in a parallel, albeit segregated arrangement. Thus, although a child with autism must have the three clinical manifestations, these are seemingly uninfluenced by each other if viewed from a pathophysiological perspective. From the standpoint of studying a specific disorder, it is entirely plausible that these three clinical areas of autism have brain and/or somatic pathophysiologic interdependencies. If these interdependencies exist, they have not yet been explained or thoroughly explored.

The distinction as to whether or not the three clinical domains are interconnected or relatively independent, or whether one supercedes others to represent a core feature of autism, undoubtedly, has critical implications for autism research. We propose that a closer relationship exists among these domains than previously recognized and that the search for a core feature of autism may not be the most fruitful theoretical question. Previously, many research efforts have focused on isolated aspects of autism rather than on the interconnections among the three clinical domains. Family studies, imaging studies, basic pathophysiologic studies, or any other research modality that investigates the etiology or pathogenic mechanisms in autism, implicitly or explicitly, needs to consider the question of interrelationships of these areas, as well as the issue of the core feature. Only then can we give consideration to a unitary or interdependent concept of autism, based on the presence of three balanced, necessary, and sufficient clinical features.

Family-genetic data points to a broader phenotype of autism, with the coexistence of multiple features in the lesser affected family members. Previous considerations of the genetic basis of autism have postulated a *multiple hits* genetic model, whereby an affected individual would have to have three or four of the susceptibility genes in order to express the disorder. In family studies of first-degree relatives, higher rates of social and communication deficits, as well as stereotyped behaviors, were found in the relatives and parents of multiple-incidence autism families (Piven, Palmer, Landa et al. 1997). Learning disabilities and affective/anxiety disorders were also found more frequently in these first-degree relatives. Parents of children with autism had higher rates of rigid, aloof, anxious, and interpersonally sensitive personality characteristics, such as pragmatic language deficits. These parents also had more limited friendships than those found in parents of the Down syndrome comparison group (Piven, Palmer, Landa et al. 1997; Piven, Palmer, Jacobi et al. 1997). Thus, the heritability of autism (i.e., the genetically transmitted characteristics) may be represented by the three components, as expressed in the probands, and through parents' personalities—not just by a single core feature. We may now speculate on a physiological interrelationship among the three phenomenological domains of autism.

What is the pathogenetic mechanism that includes three separate clinical domains in the unitary nosologic entity of autism? One clue can be directly derived from the observation that multiple brain areas are affected in autism. The most parsimonious explanation of this phenomenon is the presence of a programmed sequence of deviant developmental events that progress temporally to produce abnormal neural networks in multiple brain systems, starting very early in fetal life. Deviant development, then, leaves traces throughout the neuraxis—in frontal, temporal, and parietal areas—as well as in the basal ganglia, limbic circuits, brainstem, and cerebellum, all areas known to be affected in autism (Courchesne et al. 1994; Courchesne, Press, and Yeung-Courchesne 1993; Baron-Cohen et al. 1994). A larger brain volume, relative to controls, may also be part of developmental deviancy (Piven et al. 1995), although this feature may not be specific to autism (Ghaziuddin, Tsai, and Zaccagnini 1998).

Therefore, it is the conjunction of multiple brain deficits, affecting multiple neuronal networks, and not a single core area deficiency that seems to underlie brain mechanism abnormalities in autism. In this chapter, starting from an exploration of the phenomenon of stereotypies and repetitive behaviors in autism, we propose a theoretical model that incorporates these phenomena as central features of the autistic condition; that is, we explore how stereotypies may be intrinsically linked to autism, rather than represent an epiphenomenon of the disorder. We then link these ideas to other studies in the broader field of repetitive behaviors, such as obsessive-compulsive disorder (OCD), and, finally, propose some directions for the future study of stereotypies in autism.

PHENOMENOLOGY: THE SPECTRUM OF REPETITIVE BEHAVIORS AND STEREOTYPIES IN AUTISM

The spectrum of repetitive behaviors includes motor stereotypies, repetitive behaviors (e.g., compulsions, rituals, restrictive interests), and obsessions. Specific characteristics and interrelationships of these behaviors, as applied to autism, are described here.

Since Leo Kanner first described the syndrome of infantile autism in 1943, the observation that children with autism have an obsessive need for sameness has prevailed. All subsequent descriptive surveys of the phenomenology of autism have concurred with this original observation: children with autism have stereotyped, restrictive motor movements and repetitive, rigid behaviors. In contrast to the rich descriptive literature on repetitive behaviors and stereotypies in autism, there has been, comparatively, little effort expended by clinical researchers to explain, or even explore, the phenomenon of stereotypies and repetitive behaviors from a pathogenetic perspective in autism. For example, a MEDLINE search of the past 5 years using the key words *autism* or *infantile autism* produced over 1200 articles. The relevant articles combined with the keywords *stereotyped behavior* or *stereotypy* produced only 54 articles, making up less than 0.5% of the total. Of these publications, only a handful addressed the clinical phenomenon of stereotypies in autism as the salient research question. In contrast, during those same years, there were over 5,000 articles on mental retardation and over 1,000 of these referred to stereotypies. The increasing trend in stereotypies research in mental retardation has been observed and maintained since the 1980s, but has not been reflected in autism research.

The paucity of research of stereotypies in autism is more evident vis-à-vis the amount of literature that has emerged in the last two decades regarding the other aspect of autism that Kanner described—*the autistic aloneness*. Multiple theoretical and empirical investigations have explored aspects of social deficits in autism from communicative theories to cognitive-symbolic approaches and theory of mind perspectives (Baron-Cohen and Frith 1985; Baron-Cohen 1990). This slant in research may have been due to the assumption that autism is essentially a neurocognitive deficit disorder rather than a more complex bio-behavioral disorder with neurocognitive correlates. Partly due to this research approach, no comparable theoretical or empirical corpus has emerged regarding stereotypies and repetitive behaviors in autism.

A *stereotype* is a plate made by molding a matrix of a printing surface and from this making a cast in type metal. A stereotypy is the act or process of making or printing from stereotype plates; thus, repetitious, cast-like movements and behaviors are implied. Clinical stereotypies were first described by Emil Kraepelin in patients with schizophrenia. These patients often displayed tics, spasms, mannerisms, and complex ritualistic behaviors. Other stereotypical manifestations in schizophrenics include spontaneous abnormal movements, catatonia, perseverative language, perseverative responses on the *Wisconsin Card Sorting Task* (WCST) (Abbruzzese et al. 1995), stereotyped responses in a two-choice responding task (Frith and Done 1983), and an inability to suppress habitual responses by the use of new context (Servan-Schreiber, Cohen, and Steingard 1996). While it is clear that autism and schizophrenia are distinct clinical conditions, the relationship between similar clinical phenomena (i.e., stereotypies) remains an intriguing question from a pathophysiological perspective. For example, in both schizophrenia and autism there is intense "stimulus-bound" processing and responding: concrete, here-and-now interpretations of sensory, language, and cognitive data. This cognitive processing style produces the capture of salient features that are often unintegrated into the social context.

Descriptively speaking, stereotypies are not "a behavior," but rather the categorization of a range of behaviors. Stereotypies can appear in normal children as part of a normative developmental sequence. Ritualistic and repetitive behaviors including "just right" behaviors, concerns with order, symmetry, and rules peak between 2 and 4 years of age (Zohar and Bruno 1997). As children mature and gain more awareness of causality, temporal relationships, reversible operations, and the perception of the self and others as agents, they rely less on repetitive and rule-driven behaviors (Piaget 1950). The attainment of cognitive flexibility in normative development may parallel the gradual *loosening* of motor sequences and more advanced executive motor possibilities in the developing child. Along this line, the persistence of stereotypies may be a pathological non-adaptive response to an environment that requires change and adaptation from the organism for the optimization of responses. Other pathological states that include repetitive behaviors are perseverative states of frontal lobe injury, hoarding behaviors of children with reactive attachment disorder, and repetitive movements due to the use of certain psychotropics.

While the spectrum of repetitive behaviors is broad, we have attempted to synthesize this broad band of phenomenology by subdividing it into (a) motor stereotypies, (b) repetitive behaviors, and (c) repetitive ideations. These three categories grossly capture the span of manifestations across diagnostic categories and, more importantly, bring together clinical features that may have a common underlying pathophysiology.

Motor Stereotypies

In the pathological range of functioning, motor stereotypies are iterative, non-goal directed motor movements with a rhythmic and topographically invariant quality. These movements have no obvious eliciting stimuli and no clearly established function for the organism (Ridley and Baker 1982). The latter part of the definition has generated controversy, since some investigators have proposed functions for stereotypical behavior based on physiological and psychological data. These functions would include self-stimulation (Berkson and Gallagher 1986); modulation of stress (Dantzer 1986); the signaling of an altered arousal state (Dantzer and Mormede 1983); maintenance of homeostatic arousal states (Brett and Levine 1979); promotion of neuronal development (Clark, Kreutzberg, and Chee 1977); or optimization of functioning through displacement behaviors (Dawkins 1986). For example, pathological stereotyped movements may be self-reinforcing in humans and the blocking of stereotypies in animals has been associated with increased pituitary-adrenal axis activity in a *stress reaction* (Vestergaard, Skadhauge, and Lawson 1997).

Motor stereotypies are often pervasive in children with autism and can appear under various guises. Repetitive movements include simple iterative motor movements, sequential movements with finality, and complex ritualistic or rigid motor scripts. Interspersed with these broad categories are movements that are more difficult to typify, including repetitive dyskinesias, tic-like repetitive bursts of movement, self-injurious behaviors, mannerisms, gesticulations, and complex sequences such as hoarding. Twenty years after Kanner's description, Hermelin and O'Connor (1963) showed that for the same degree of mental retardation, children with autism had more stereotypies, suggesting that stereotypies may be a distinctive feature of this disorder. Moreover, while enriched environments decrease stereotypies in non-autistic mentally retarded children (LaGrow and Repp 1984), this may not be the case for stereotypies in children with autism (Hutt and Hutt 1965).

Tics and motor stereotypies may be difficult to differentiate. Tics are involuntary, repetitive, stereotyped movements that are exacerbated with stress. *The Diagnostic and Statistical Manual-IV* (DSM-IV) defines tics as "sudden, rapid, recurrent, nonrhythmic, stereotyped motor movements or vocalizations." There are varieties of tics, with transient tics being more orofacial and varying while chronic tics tend to be fixed. Complex motor tics may blur boundaries with simple compulsions, such as those regarding symmetry, as in "evening up" movements. The topography of tics can be different from the topography of stereotypies. While tics tend to center on orofacial or truncal musculature, classic stereotypies may use more distal musculature and may not be as "involuntary."

Self-injurious behavior (SIB) has been described as "a class of behaviors, often highly repetitive and rhythmic, that result in physical harm to the individual" (Matson 1989). Self-injurious behavior topographies include head banging, head hitting, finger/hand biting, hair pulling, skin picking, eye gouging, and others. Empirical observation supports a continuum of behaviors between non-self-injurious stereotypies and SIB, often observed in the same individual. It is of interest that children (Davis 1940) and animals (Sackett 1968) reared in isolation and/or social deprivation show high rates of self-injury. As we shall see later, this observation may lead us to understand pathophysiological connections within the spectrum of stereotypies and repetitive behaviors.

Compulsions/Rituals

The characteristic "insistence on sameness" that was observed by Kanner in autistic children refers to a need for rigid adherence to routines and the maintenance of environmental sameness. A high level of anxiety and distress can result when this sameness is not maintained (e.g., when a different route is taken on the way to school or a piece of furniture is moved from its usual place in the room). This characteristic is almost pathognomonic of children with autism and is typically accompanied by the overfocusing tendencies of these children who direct attention to socially irrelevant but physically salient features of their environment.

Compulsive behaviors refer to behaviors that an individual feels compelled to perform in response to an internally perceived anxiety state: to a fear, or lacking a clear precedent, to an internal drive. The compulsive behavior is often repeated until a feeling of "just right" is attained in some instances. In other instances, accompanying anxiety caused by an obsessional ideation may exist. The anxiety must be allayed by performing a ritual such as repeated handwashing (e.g., fear of germs), checking (e.g., fear of harm), or counting (e.g., superstitious fear). Children with autism engage in behaviors that blur the boundaries between stereotypies and simple compulsive behaviors. Repeated touching and sniffing, ritualistic ordering, and collecting are common in children with autism and may be difficult to distinguish from simple repetitive motor sequences. For example, a child with autism had a complex repetitive motor sequence consisting of walking to a table, grasping at an invisible object, and dropping it to the floor, then dropping himself to the floor. This motor sequence would be repeated throughout the day, sometimes with little respite for him or his parents.

Exploratory behavior is an evolutionary product that facilitates the emergence of new behaviors. Repetitive behaviors stand on the opposite end of the spectrum to true exploratory behavior. The need for sameness and for engaging in stereotypies often interferes with true exploration and learning in children with autism. Other repetitive behaviors that may interfere with the learning process include motor sequences that are part of a larger motor script, such as pacing or lining up objects. The repetitive use of language is a frequent but poorly understood repetitive behavior. Ritualistic or rigid behaviors include rigid adherence to routines; sensory sensitivity constraints; persistence on execution of rigid schedules; maintenance of spatial object arrangements in the environment; and general insistence on the previously known or experienced (e.g., wearing the same clothes, or carrying the same object). In some children this characteristic is accompanied, or possibly driven, by sensitivities that are tactile, gustatory, visual, or auditory in nature. Thus, children with autism may need to wear the same clothes in a certain manner, eat the same foods, watch the same video, or hear the same song over and over.

Although similar to obsessive-compulsive behaviors, some authors contend that obsessions and compulsions in children with autism fail to satisfy the definitions of either obsessions or compulsions because essential subjective data relating to unwantedness, distress, resistance, senselessness, and ego-dystonia are not available. This observation is supported by the lack of a *theory of mind* in autistic children that makes them unable to contemplate or talk about their own mental states. The use of the terms *repetitive activities* or *repetitive behaviors* is suggested by the authors instead of *obsessions and compulsions* (Baron-Cohen 1989). In fact, ego-dystonic compulsions, (i.e., distress-inducing compulsions that the individual attempts to stop) have been a hallmark of obsessive-compulsive disorder (OCD). It has been repeatedly contended that repetitive behaviors in autism are *ego-syntonic*. But a careful reassessment of autistic phenomenology may not support this view. It has become more evident through clinical observations of multiple cases of high-functioning autism that some individuals with autism will express distress at having to perform repetitive behaviors. A recent observation of an individual with high-functioning autism, for example, revealed that he needed to engage in ritualistic measuring of himself against others. When asked about the reason, he stated that if he refrained, he would "be afraid of going crazy." He was able, eventually, to stop himself from engaging in this behavior. Thus, ego-dystonicity in autism may span a spectrum of possibilities rather than be an all-or-none phenomenon.

Similarities and differences between *ego-syntonic* and *ego-dystonic* compulsions have been used to distinguish autism and OCD phenomenology. The only study that has looked at the relation between these phenomenological manifestations in OCD and autism found that patients with autistic disorder could be distinguished from those with OCD on the basis of types of current repetitive thoughts and behaviors. McDougle et al. (1995) compared obsessions and compulsions in 50 adults with OCD and 50 adults with autism. The autistic patients were significantly less likely to experience thoughts with aggressive, contaminated, sexual, religious, symmetrical, and somatic content. Repetitive ordering, hoarding, telling or asking, touching, tapping or rubbing, and self-damaging or self-mutilating behaviors occurred with more frequency in adults with autism; whereas cleaning, checking, and counting behaviors were less common in this same group than in the patients with OCD. From what has been discussed, it appears that "autistic" OCD symptoms are more reminiscent of OCD symptoms seen in younger children with OCD; that is, symptoms predominantly based on sensory-motor components and at times tic-like in nature, but without autism.

Repetitive Ideations

Restrictive interests are characteristic of higher-functioning children with autism and Asperger's syndrome. These children may be consumed by unusual topics such as tornadoes, condensers, or telephone poles. Their narratives and cognitive excursions reliably return to familiar and well-known territory, as these children quickly become experts in their particular restricted area of interest. These topics are commonly experienced as ego-syntonic or are agreeable to the child, but distress is often observed if the child is impeded from playing, discussing, or engaging in the compulsory activity. Thus, we are again confronted with the possibility that ego-dystonicity may be an element that is only uncovered when the child is interrupted in the activity that seemingly provides pleasure or reduction of anxiety.

True obsessions are intrusive ego-dystonic thoughts, images, or impulses (i.e., that produce distress or anxiety). The intrusive quality

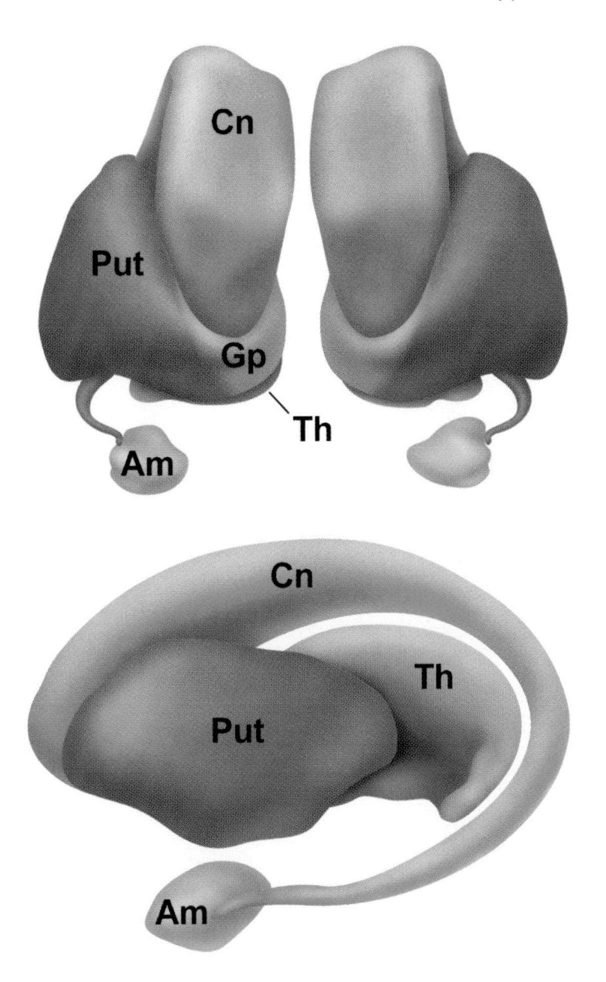

Figure 2. Brain Anatomy of Basal Ganglia. The basal ganglia of the brain appear early in the evolution of the central nervous system and regulate behaviors related to ritual, territory, and hierarchy throughout the animal kingdom. Cn = Caudate Nucleus; Put = Putamen; Gp = Globus Pallidus; Th = Thalamus; Am = Amygdaloid Body.

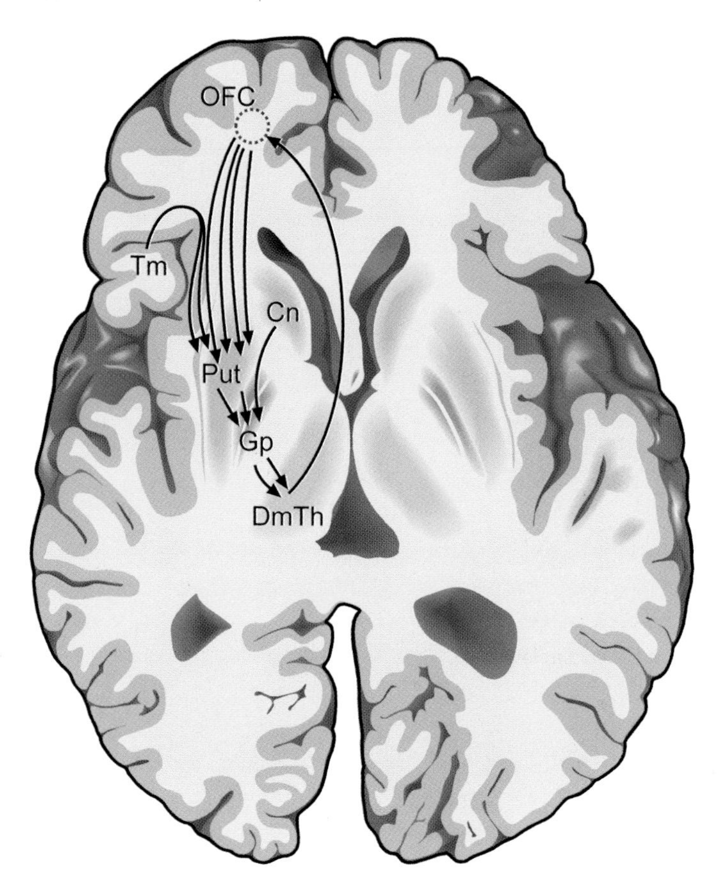

Figure 3. The Orbitofrontal Circuit. The orbitofrontal circuit conveys neural signals through a "loop" that initiates from extensive fronto-temporal areas, converges on striatal nuclei and the thalamus, and returns to specific areas of the orbitofrontal cortex. This loop functions aberrantly in OCD. OFC = orbitofrontal; Tm = Temporal Cortex; Cn = Caudate Nucleus; Put = Putamen; Gp = Globus Pallidus; DmTh = dorsomedial nuclei of Thalamus.

South Devon Coast, England, drawing by Richard Wawro #2121 wax-oil crayon.

of obsessions has caused some authors to describe them as *mental tics* or involuntary and disagreeable thoughts that intrude into mental space. It is a common nosological error to label thoughts that are egosyntonic and without distress or anxiety as obsessions. For example, a young child who perseverates on watching a certain video every day, several times a day, may be said to be *obsessed* with this activity, which clearly produces pleasure. Although appearing obsessive, this repetitive behavior does not meet the definitional criteria. Children with obsessions are distressed by having the intrusive thoughts and having to engage in rituals, repetitive behaviors, or compulsions in order to allay fears generated by the intrusive thoughts. While the causal sequence of obsessions to compulsions is commonly seen in adults with OCD, it is also occasionally observed in some children with OCD. However, many younger children with OCD, especially males, will have mostly sensory-motor compulsions with minimal accompanying obsessions (Grados et al. 1997). The developmental maturation of executive functions or narrative abilities may be required to produce the elaborate explanations for rituals seen in adults with OCD. That is, it is possible that the primary phenomenon is a compulsion to produce a stereotypical behavior, and then, as brain maturation progresses, more elaborate explanations (e.g., contamination fears) are overlaid on this behavior.

The need to structure mental content into a narrative or story is possibly an executive mental function made possible in humans through evolution. In an interesting split-brain experiment, an individual with no interhemispheric connections was provided with a frightening visual stimulus to the right brain, information to which the left side had no access. When asked to explain his reaction, the subject made up a story with a frightening content involving the experimenter. This drive to narrate has been used extensively in psychotherapy. It is possible that among other executive functions, the drive to construct a narrative (i.e., to produce obsessions from compulsions) is deficient in children with autism and in relatives of children with autism.

Phenomenologically, obsessions appear to belong in the same spectrum of manifestations as stereotypies, repetitive behaviors, compulsions, and restrictive interests. However, a higher degree of cognitive functional integration may be necessary for obsessions to be a primary clinical phenomenon. It is possible that patients who suffer predominantly from obsessions may be a subcategory of OCD that is distinct from the mixed obsessive-compulsive or the predominantly compulsive subgroups. This subgrouping is supported by a large epidemiological sample study in France (Hantouche and Lancrenon 1996) and is incorporated into the *International Classification of Disease-10*

(ICD-10). Repetitive behaviors in autism would then be more closely related to the predominantly compulsive or mixed presentation, more stimulus-bound and concrete, and less closely related to the predominantly obsessive subtype, which is more symbolic and cognitively elaborate. However, common pathophysiological mechanisms may still underlie all subtypes. The types of stereotypies, repetitive behaviors, and ideations discussed are summarized in table I. We note the type of behavioral reinforcement that appears to be related to each of the symptoms discussed. This behavioral underpinning highlights the differences in specificity between ego-syntonic and ego-dystonic features of symptoms and possible motivational components.

In the following section, we explore possible models of the pathophysiology of repetitive behaviors, encompassing the phenomenology previously described and using OCD as a model for exploring brain-behavior relationships.

OBSESSIVE-COMPULSIVE DISORDER: A MODEL FOR PATHOPHYSIOLOGY IN AUTISM?

Obsessive Compulsive Disorder (OCD) is defined as the occurrence of obsessions and/or compulsions with ensuing distress or impairment. Typical obsessions in children are contamination fears or thoughts of aggression. These are to be carefully distinguished from perseverative ruminations—as occur in depressive or anxiety states—and from ego-syntonic perseverative ideations. Perseverative ideations occur when

Table I Motor Stereotypies, Repetitive Behaviors, and Repetitive Ideations

	Example	Reinforcement
I. Motor Stereotypies	Mouthing Self-Injury Mannerism	Automatic Reinforcement
II. Repetitive Behaviors		
Perseveration	Lining up Objects Repetitive Language	Positive Reinforcement (enjoyment of activity) or Negative Reinforcement (averts fear or anxiety)
Rigidity	Adherence to Routine Need for Sameness Sensory Sensitivity	
Ritualistic	Counting Touching	
III. Repetitive Ideation		
Restrictive Interest	Tornadoes Telephone Poles Astronomy	Positive Reinforcement
Obsession	Contamination Fears	Automatic Reinforcement?

a child wants to have a preferred object or activity and is sometimes said to be *obsessed* with it. As discussed above, these ideations do not meet the criteria for obsessions. Typical compulsions in children with OCD are handwashing, symmetry compulsions, and repeating tendencies (Swedo et al. 1989). The question of subtypes in OCD is not fully resolved, nor is it a trivial issue. Tic-related or sensory-motor OCD, perhaps akin to the *predominantly compulsive* subtype of ICD-10, has been linked to a greater presence of sensory-motor rituals, with a younger age of onset, male predominance, and greater response to neuroleptic augmentation. All of these characteristics relate to traits present in the repetitive behaviors of children with autism. We will look for a common pathophysiological thread between the two disorders. As seen in figure 1, the overlap between OCD and autism occurs in this dimension of symptoms.

What do we know of the pathophysiology of OCD? In recent years, landmark findings have occurred in the area of brain mechanisms in OCD. Structural, and especially functional, imaging brain studies have consistently shown that basal ganglia and frontal cortical brain regions are implicated in OCD. These are the same regions that form the neural circuits first described by Alexander, DeLong, and Strick (1986), now called the cortico-basal ganglia (striatal)-thalamo-cortical loops (CSTC). (Figure 2 on p. 84a shows a schematic of the basal ganglia of the brain that includes the caudate nucleus, the putamen, the globus pallidus, and the thalamic nuclei.) These brain nuclei constitute relay stations forming several loop circuits including the (a) orbito-frontal loop, (b) anterior cingulate loop, and the (c) oculomotor loop. Morphologically, the component parts of these circuits include the caudate nucleus or *tail* that parallels the III ventricle and has an

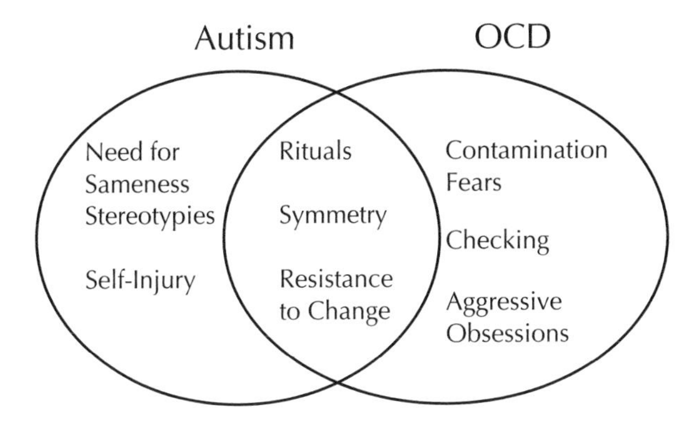

Figure 1. Phenomenological Similarities between Autism and OCD

enlarged head in the wall of the anterior horn. The caudate has a smaller body adjacent to the body of the ventricle and a still smaller tail adjacent to the inferior horn. The caudate and putamen merge anteriorly in the nucleus accumbens at the base of the septum pellucidum, an area that has been implicated in motivated and addictive behaviors. The putamen or *shell* fits its cone-like structure into the opening that the length of the caudate nucleus makes as it winds around the thalamus. The putamen is the external aspect of the lenticular nucleus, covering externally the globus pallidus, or internal portion of the lenticular nucleus. The striatum is composed of the caudate and putamen, structures that are grouped due to morphological neuronal similarities. The CSTC loops function as segregated basal ganglia- thalamo- cortical pathways with a downstream convergence that starts from wide cortical frontal areas. The pathways converge onto more restricted segments of basal ganglia, thalamic, and cortical areas, then begin their journey back to the starting point.

The orbitofrontal cortex (OFC) circuit is shown in figure 3 on p. 84b. In this loop, the lateral orbitofrontal cortex (Brodman 10) projects to the ventromedial caudate from the head to the tail, which also receives information from the auditory (superior temporal gyrus) and visual association areas (inferior temporal gyrus). The projections continue to the dorsomedial globus pallidus (pars interna) and to a rostromedial portion of the substantia nigra (pars reticularis). This nucleus then projects to the medial magnocellular anteroventral and dorsomedial thalamic nuclei before returning to the lateral orbitofrontal cortex. Lesions in the OFC can result in perseverative interference and an animal's capacity to make switches in behavioral settings, or can result in perseverative responses in humans (Abbruzzese et al. 1995). Initial wide neocortical inputs converge to specific areas of basal ganglia and thalamus, depending on whether the motor, orbito-frontal, or oculomotor circuits are involved and terminate in restricted portions of the frontal neocortex. This funneling effect occurs at progressive striatal, pallidal/nigral, and thalamic stations. At each station, particular neurotransmitters are involved in excitatory and inhibitory actions: cortical excitatory glutamatergic input, striatal inhibitory GABAergic input, and thalamic excitatory glutamatergic input. Sites of drug action are located in receptors in these brain areas. Serotonin and dopamine are the major neurotransmitters implicated and are present in structures such as the head of the caudate (serotonin) and the putamen (dopamine). While oversimplified, this model serves to illustrate the brain regions currently implicated in the pathophysiology of OCD.

Functional imaging studies such as positron emission tomography (PET) show how these circuits are operative in the production of OCD symptoms. A PET subtraction method detected differences within subjects for two states, a symptomatic OCD state and a resting state (Baxter et al. 1992). In this study, fludeoxyglucose F-18 PET scans of patients with OCD responded to behavior modification treatment before and after two months of therapy. Decreases in glucose metabolic rates after treatment were particularly striking on the right head of the caudate region. These same results were obtained with only behavior modification treatment of OCD, showing significant changes in right caudate glucose metabolic activity, normalized to the ipsilateral hemisphere. Such changes were not seen when treatment was not effective. A more recent follow-up study showed statistically significant pretreatment correlations among the right orbital gyri, head of the caudate nucleus, and thalamus that decreased after effective behavioral treatment. These correlations were not seen in normal controls or in patients with unipolar major depression. These findings and the fact that such effects can be demonstrated after behavior therapy alone suggest that *coupling* of activity among elements in this cortico-striato-thalamic circuit may be related to the expression of OCD symptoms (Schwartz et al. 1996). In another related study, Rauch et al. (1994) used oxygen 15-labeled carbon in a PET paradigm to explore regional cerebral blood flow (rCBF) on each of eight patients with OCD during resting and provoked symptomatic states. On successful provocation of symptoms, omnibus subtraction images demonstrated a statistically significant increase in relative rCBF during the OCD symptomatic state when compared to the resting state in the right caudate nucleus, left anterior cingulate cortex, and bilateral orbitofrontal cortex. There was also a non-significant increase of activity in the left thalamus. These findings were consistent with the CSTC loop model of OCD neurocircuitry. More recent observations from this research group have used functional imaging to show that subjects with OCD do not recruit the normal striatal structures used in performing a procedural learning task, but, instead, compensate by recruiting medial temporal areas, thereby supporting a role for abnormal striatal functioning in OCD (Rauch et al. 1997).

BRAIN ABNORMALITIES IN AUTISM

Compared to OCD, where the cortico-striato-thalamic circuits may play a central role in pathophysiology, practically no brain region of the human cerebrum is spared in autism. The extent of abnormalities in autism has led researchers to place this disorder within the group of neurodevelopmental disorders, ranging from schizophrenia to learning disorders. Underlying genetic factors and, as yet, unknown environmental ones probably figure into the final expression of abnormal neurodevelopment in autism. The environmental triggers in autism may occur as early as the third week of gestation and affect brainstem, cerebellum, and other brain centers. For example, Rodier et al. (1997) found that exposure to thalidomide in the early weeks of gestation appeared to induce the appearance of autism in exposed children (thalidomide babies), and this model has been replicated in the rat brain.

Brain areas implicated in autism include the brainstem (Ornitz and Ritvo 1968; Ornitz 1985), cerebellum (Courchesne et al. 1994), frontal lobes (Hughes, Russell, and Robbins 1994; Ozonoff et al. 1994; Zilbovicius et al. 1995), parietal lobes (Courchesne, Press, and Yeung-Courchesne 1993), and amygdaloid body (Bauman and Kemper 1985). A neuropathological case report has found numerous neurofibrillary tangles (NFTs) in the perirhinal and entorhinal cortex, grouped in nests or clusters. A few NFTs were observed in the amygdala and in the prepiriform and orbito-frontal cortex. In the cortex, NFTs are located in both layers II and III. The locations of these microscopic changes correspond to functional limbic areas, possibly including portions of orbito-frontal cortex that are of more primitive architectonic valence (Barbas 1993; Hof, Mufson, and Morrison 1998). Additional neuroanatomical findings include agenesis of the superior olive, dysgenesis of the facial nucleus, reduced numbers of Purkinje neurons, hypoplasia of the brainstem and posterior cerebellum, and increased neuron-packing density of the medial, cortical, and central nuclei of the amygdala and the medial septum (Bauman and Kemper 1985; Courchesne 1997).

In summary, brain changes described in autism affect multiple modular brain systems and may be related to early degenerative events (NFTs) in brain structures or to a delayed maturational sequence execution of neural development (i.e., increased cell packing density).

In figure 4, neural archaic structures, such as the brainstem and pons, are separated from more phylogenetically recent brain areas such as the cerebellum, basal ganglia, and limbic structures (hippocampus and amygdala). Isocortical components of the temporal, frontal, and parietal lobes are the most advanced brain areas from an evolutionary perspective. As described above, all of these regions have identifiable modular functional systems that may be impaired in autism. No single brain region has been identified, to date, as a primary or "lesion" area in autism, although several brain regions may be candidates. Rather than focusing on a candidate region, another approach would be to postulate that an early CNS insult may be a trigger for aberrant neurodevelopmental pathways in a susceptible embryo. In fact, a condition as pervasive as autism probably requires alteration of basic CNS developmental sequences, for example with

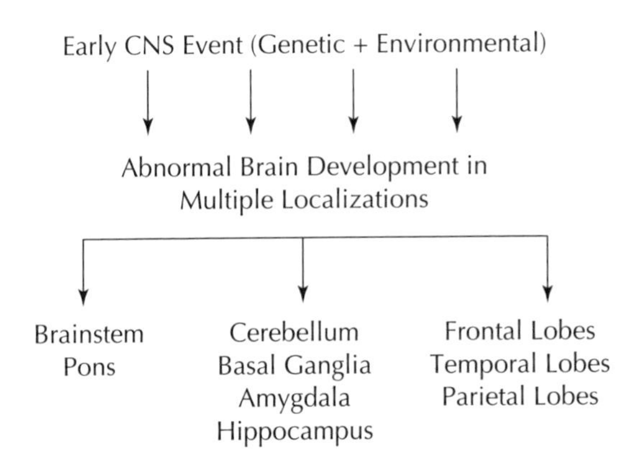

Figure 4. Brain Anomalies in Autism

the participation of neuronal growth factors or proto-oncogenes. Anecdotal evidence from individuals with autism and their families shows a possible increase in cancer rates in first-degree relatives (Grados, unpublished data), and an association of autism with HRAS proto-ongcogene markers has been documented (Herault et al. 1993; Herault et al. 1995; Waterhouse, 1997). These associations may reflect developmental abnormalities in cellular and receptor developmental pathways that affect neuronal pruning, receptor development, neuronal size, and number of neurons per unit area, resulting in the "retained fetal circuitry" observed by Baumann and Kemper (1985).

What evidence is there for dysfunction of basal ganglia circuits in autism? Preliminary clinical and biochemical evidence has confirmed that basal ganglia abnormalities result in stereotypical behaviors. For example, a 17-year-old boy acquired complex stereotyped movements of the hands and circling behaviors that interrupted his gait after a complicated repair of an aortic coarctation. An MRI scan showed a right putaminal infarct. The boy's behavior and stereotypies bore a close resemblance to those found in autism (Maraganore, Lees, and Marsden 1991). Behavioral stereotypies and SIB have also been localized preliminarily to the basal ganglia; this localization has been corroborated in animal models (Breese et al. 1995). If the same neural circuit that underlies repetitive thoughts and behaviors in OCD is related to SIB/stereotypical phenomena in autism and other disorders, then many of the findings in OCD research will be applicable to the study of stereotypies and repetitive behaviors in individuals with mental retardation. While morphological brain lesion localization is an important venue to determine basal ganglia involvement in the repetitive behaviors seen in autism, further understanding can be gained by an examination of neurotransmitter systems in this brain region as well.

THE DOPAMINE HYPOTHESIS

Multiple neurotransmitters are involved in neurochemical activity in the basal ganglia, including dopamine, acetylcholine, serotonin, GABA, substance P, dynorphin, neurotensin, and peptidases (Graybiel 1990). Neurotransmitter functions may be a link between the genetic basis of autism and the emergence of aberrant learning patterns and repetitive behaviors. Convergent lines of evidence now point to the dopamine system as the critical interface between neurochemical transmission in the basal ganglia and repetitive behaviors and stereotypies. Since the 1960s, it has been demonstrated that psychostimulants which enhance dopaminergic transmission, such as amphetamines, produce stereotyped sequenced behaviors in rodents (e.g., sniffing, licking, gnawing, grooming) (Randrup and Munkvad 1967; Randrup, Munkvad, and Usden 1963); primates (e.g., self-grooming, staring at hands, snatching in the air) (Ridley and Baker 1982); and humans (Rylander 1972).

As reviewed by Lewis et al. (1996) and Sprague and Newell (1996), stereotypies are induced in animals by L-dopa and apomorphine acting on dopamine receptors. L-dopa applied to the striatum in rats produces stereotypies; the same effect is obtained when GABA agonists are applied to the substantia nigra pars reticulata (SNpr). Lesions to the superior colliculus decrease the induction of stereotypies by dopamine agonists through descending nigral projections. Pharmacological manipulation, such as the dopamine antagonist (haloperidol) blockade of DA agonist actions induces stereotypies, an effect that is used as a screen for compounds with potential antipsychotic activity. Finally, inhibition of the production of dopamine in the CNS through the use of alpha-CH3-p-tyrosine or the destruction of the pre-synaptic DA terminals with 6-OH-dopamine also blocks the induction of stereotypies. From a developmental perspective, rat pups treated neonatally with 6-OH-dopamine show increased sensitivity to dopamine-induced stereotypies and SIB can be induced in them easily with apomorphine. Thus excitatory and inhibitory pathways, using several neurotransmitters, are possibly involved in the production of stereotypical behaviors.

Harlow macaque monkeys provide an in-vivo experience associating stereotypies and dopamine CNS pathways. When Harlow monkeys were reared in isolation during the first 6 to 9 months of life, the "isolate syndrome" was experimentally produced. The isolate syndrome is characterized by multiple stereotypies and repetitive behaviors with topographies that parallel those seen in clinical populations (Harlow, Dodsworth, and Harlow 1965). In a follow-up study with these macaque monkeys, Lewis et al. (1990) evaluated the monkeys at

20 years of age to investigate whether early social deprivation resulted in a loss of dopamine innervation to striatal areas. Isolate and control monkeys were challenged with the dopamine agonist apomorphine and spontaneous blink rates; stereotyped and self-injurious behaviors were measured. Isolate monkeys had increased sensitivity to the agonist agent for spontaneous blink rate, whole body stereotypies, and intensity of stereotyped behaviors. These observations were compatible with long-term or permanent dopamine receptor supersensitivity induced by social isolation at an early age (Lewis et al. 1990). These results were supported by immunocytochemical studies of the striatum of the socially deprived monkeys, indicating decreased dopamine innervation (Lewis et al. 1990).

When humans are exposed to high-dose stimulants, the equivalent of stimulating dopamine receptor sites, a phenomenon termed *punding* is observed. *Punding* consists of engagement in long, complex, and repetitive behaviors such as sorting collections of items or dismantling pieces of mechanical equipment while being cut off from interaction with others. The exposed subject also becomes distressed if interrupted from this behavior. The behavior can consist of shorter repetitive sequences that are carried out until exahustion ensues. If an additional psychostimulant is provided, a paranoid psychosis, resembling an acute schizophrenic episode, may ensue, perhaps signaling a common neurochemical pathway for stereotypies, schizophrenia, and possibly autism.

It is tempting to draw parallels between the neurodevelopment of socially isolated monkeys and the social development of children with autism. The similarities between the effects of dopamine agonists in animals and humans appear to support this view. In both socially isolated macaque monkeys and in children with autism, the co-regulation of behavior through social interaction is altered, and the consequent neural development that is mediated by this dynamic mother-child exchange at an early age may be consequently derailed. There are few studies of the parent-infant interaction of children with autism, but this is a promising area of study. Thus, in both socially isolated macaque monkeys and children with autism, the development of dopamine receptors may not occur along a normal developmental course. The consequence of this abnormal developmental sequence could be the production of stereotypies and a host of behaviors that correspond to the spectrum of repetitive behaviors. One should also consider that similar dopamine-mediated abnormalities, possibly developmental or genetic in origin as discussed above, may be present in OCD (Brambilla et al. 1997) and TS/tic disorders (Grice et al. 1996).

Dopamine receptor changes may thus underlie some manifestations of stereotypies, tic disorders, tic-related OCD, and autism.

Schizophrenic disorders may also be associated with dopamine receptor abnormalities, and the phenomenological overlap among schizophrenia, OCD, and autism would support this pathophysiology. Schizophrenic symptoms often include ritualistic tendencies and delusional systems with perseverative ideations. Schizophrenic hallucinations are experienced as intrusive voices and images; while in OCD, thoughts and visual images are intrusive, but not experienced as a part of a subjective reality. Obsessive and compulsive symptoms occur in up to 25% of schizophrenics and they have been shown to be markers of poor prognosis (Insel and Akiskal 1986). These considerations have been used to subtype OCD. A common dopamine-related abnormality may underlie the common association of sensory-motor-rituals, young age of onset, sensory hypersensitivity, and association with tics that has led to the postulation of tic-related and non-tic-related OCD subtypes. It is interesting to note that this specific subtype of childhood-onset OCD is closer to autism, as well as to a putative syndrome of *developmental basal ganglia disorder* that includes involuntary movements and other motor disturbances, including obsessive-compulsive behavior, attentional and executive dysfunction, and aggressive behavior (Palumbo, Maughan, and Kurlan 1997). Tactile defensiveness has been associated with the number of rigid or stereotyped behaviors in autism (Baranek, Foster, and Berkson 1997) and may constitute another marker of delayed development with a similar pathophysiology.

What roles, then, do serotonin, glutamate, opiates, somatostatin and other CNS neurotransmitters play in OCD and autism? Most of these neurotransmitters modulate the action of dopamine in the CNS and, therefore, mediate the symptom complexes discussed above. For example, dense concentrations of opioid peptides and their receptors are found in terminal fields receiving innervation by dopamine neurons in the striatum. Enkephalin projections also are afferent to substantia nigra and ventral tegmental areas. From a functional perspective, serotonergic agonists have been found to increase stereotyped behaviors such as head weaving and forepaw treading in animals (Curzon 1990). Serotonin has also been found to be abnormal in cerebrospinal (CSF) studies of Tourette's syndrome, but serotonergic agents such as fluoxetine (Prozac) have varying effects on tics. Glutamate upregulation may also be involved in some social aspects of autism and the interplay among various neurotransmitter systems needs to be further explored, for example, in the consolidation of memory (Johnston and Harum 1999). The importance of serotonin and its modulating role in the pathophysiology of autism is highlighted by recent advances in the treatment of stereotypies with serotonin-enhancing agents such as clomipramine, fluvoxamine, sertraline, and fluoxetine.

PHARMACOTHERAPY OF REPETITIVE BEHAVIORS

The use of medication to address the behavioral symptoms of autism is widely practiced and may promote the effectiveness of other therapeutic interventions. Among the behavioral symptoms commonly addressed with pharmacotherapy are stereotypies and repetitive behaviors. While current experience, as outlined below, generally demonstrates the effectiveness of pharmacotherapy in addressing these behaviors in select cases, it is evident that further studies of these agents are needed, particularly in their use with children.

In addition to being the best studied drug for OCD, clomipramine (Anafranil) is the most widely researched pharmacological agent used to address the obsessive-compulsive and stereotyped motor behaviors common in children with autism. A double-blind, controlled, crossover comparison of clomipramine versus desipramine found that clomipramine is superior on ratings of autistic symptoms including stereotypies, anger, and compulsive ritualized behaviors (Gordon et al. 1993). Another recent experience with adults indicates that clomipramine treatment is effective in 63% of adult subjects with autism, 33% of adult subjects with Asperger's syndrome, and 55% of adult subjects with Pervasive Developmental Disorder, Not Otherwise Specified (PDD-NOS). More specifically, it was demonstrated that clomipramine significantly reduced repetitive thoughts and behaviors, as well as aggression, and improved some aspects of social relatedness (e.g., eye contact, verbal responsiveness) (Brodkin et al. 1997). Additionally, an open pilot study on the effectiveness of clomipramine in young children with autism preliminarily suggested that clomipramine can be frequently associated with serious untoward effects in this age group (Sanchez et al. 1996).

Fluvoxamine (Luvox) has been used empirically to treat stereotypies in children with autism. A double-blind, placebo-controlled trial of fluvoxamine in adults with autism showed that fluvoxamine was effective in reducing repetitive thoughts and behaviors, as well as maladaptive behaviors and aggression. Further, it was demonstrated to improve some aspects of social relatedness, especially language use. This drug was well tolerated with no significant negative effects (McDougle et al. 1996). Fluvoxamine is now FDA approved for the treatment of OCD in children, but no controlled trials in children with autism are available.

Sertraline (Zoloft) was used in an open trial in adults with mental retardation presenting with target behaviors of self-injury and/or aggression. Sertraline led to improvements in Clinical Global Impressions (CGI) ratings of overall clinical severity. Side effects noted included agitation and worsening of self-picking, but were otherwise minimal (Hellings et al. 1996).

Fluoxetine (Prozac) was also used in the treatment of compulsions in individuals with mental retardation, demonstrating that fluoxetine was effective in decreasing aggression and self-injury only in those patients who also had compulsions (Bodfish and Madison 1993).

Thus, medications that enhance serotonin availability in CNS improve stereotypical manifestations in autism. Serotonin pathways may modulate dopamine effects in the CNS and regulate behaviors associated with autism and OCD.

FUTURE DIRECTIONS

How, then, do we propose to study stereotypies and repetitive behaviors in autism from an etiological or pathophysiological perspective? First, it is important to consider a unitary concept of the autism phenotype that includes a phenomenological-pathophysiological connection among the three symptom areas: communication deficits, social deficits, and repetitive behaviors. Autism symptom complexes may, thus, be considered phenomenological manifestations of neuronal network and neurochemical imbalances with a common underlying neurodevelopmental pathophysiology. Second, it is evident that multiple neurotransmitters and neuronal networks are aberrant in autism. An imbalance between excitatory and inhibitory neurotransmitter systems, with one set of phenomenological symptoms corresponding to neurotransmitter excitation or "overflow" (stereotypies) and another to neurotransmitter inhibition or deficiency (lack of social cognition) is a plausible hypothesis. Alterations in dopamine CNS function may provide a final common pathway for other transmitter imbalances. Third, a comprehensive view should also consider a genetic etiology of autism. A family study approach may yield information on subgroups by symptom complexes. It is of interest to investigate the hypothesis that the genes responsible for the autism phenotype could be pursued by studying lesser variants in relatives, possibly including medical disorders such as cancer (e.g., the p53 tumor-suppressor gene also plays a role in the regulation of apoptosis). The connection could be provided by mutations in certain growth factor genes that regulate cell apoptosis, pruning, reproduction, differentiation, and DNA self-repair, resulting in differential cell packing and neurofibrillary tangles (NFTs). Finally, brain regional dysfunction in cortico-basal ganglia circuits that subsumes the occurrence of stereotypies and repetitive behaviors may provide another clue to discovering the neural substrate of such behaviors, making it necessary to borrow from structural and functional imaging studies already carried out in other disorders such as OCD.

CHAPTER SUMMARY

1. The behaviors that comprise the three domains affected in autism (communication, socialization, and repetitive behaviors) may be interdependent without any one of them representing a presumed core of autism.
2. Repetitive behaviors include:
   (a) motor stereotypies (head banging and other self-injurious behaviors)
   (b) compulsions or rituals accompanied by severe anxiety at any change, such as tactile and olfactory exploration, or lining up toys, and
   (c) repetitive ideations relating to a restrictive, intrusive, and narrowly focused range of interests.
3. Stereotypies may appear in normal children between two and four years of age.
4. Stereotypies persist, or are intensively manifested, in several pathological conditions, such as frontal lobe injury, reactive attachment disorder, the use of certain psychotropic medications, and autism.
5. The neuroanatomic substrate for symptoms of obsessive compulsive disorder (OCD) has been localized to the cortico-basal ganglia (striatal)-thalamo-cortical loops (CSTC).
6. An early central nervous system insult to a susceptible brain may trigger aberrant neurodevelopmental pathways that, in turn, appear to involve many different regions of the brain in autism.
7. Serotonergic agents, such as clomipramine (Anafranil) and fluvoxamine (Luvox) have been effective in the treatment of repetitive and stereotypical behaviors in children with autism.

ACKNOWLEDGMENT

To Ms. Jennifer Winders for editing of the manuscript

REFERENCES

Abbruzzese, M., Bellodi, L., Ferri, S., and Scarone, S. 1995. Frontal lobe dysfunction in schizophrenia and obsessive-compulsive disorder: A neuropsychological study. *Brain and Cognition* 27(2):202–12.

Alexander, G. E., DeLong, M. R., and Strick, P. L. 1986. Parallel organization of functionally segregated circuits linking basal ganglia and cortex. *Annual Review of Neuroscience* 9:357–81.

American Psychiatric Association. 1994. *Diagnostic and Statistical Manual–IV*. Washington, D.C.: American Psychiatric Association.

Baranek, G. T., Foster, L. G., and Berkson, G. 1997. Tactile defensiveness and stereotyped behaviors. *American Journal of Occupational Therapy* 51(2):91–5.

Barbas, H. 1993. Organization of cortical afferent input to orbitofrontal areas in the rhesus monkey. *Neuroscience* 56(4):841–64.
Baron-Cohen, S. 1989. Do autistic children have obsessions and compulsions? *British Journal of Clinical Psychology* 28(Pt 3):193–200.
Baron-Cohen, S. 1990. Autism: A specific cognitive disorder of "mind-blindness." *International Review of Psychiatry* 2:81–90.
Baron-Cohen, S., and Frith, U. 1985. Does the autistic child have a theory of mind? *Cognition* 21:37–46.
Baron-Cohen, S., Ring, H., Moriarty, J., Schmitz, B., Costa, D., and Ell, P. 1994. Recognition of mental state terms. Clinical findings in children with autism and a functional neuroimaging study of normal adults. *British Journal of Psychiatry* 165(5):640–49.
Bauman, M., and Kemper, T. L. 1985. Histoanatomic observations of the brain in early infantile autism. *Neurology* 35 (6):866–74.
Baxter, L. R. J., Schwartz, J. M., Bergman, K. S., Szuba, M. P., Guze, B. H., Mazziotta, J. C., Alazraki, A., Selin, C. E., Ferng, H. K., and Munford, P. 1992. Caudate glucose metabolic rate changes with both drug and behavior therapy for obsessive-compulsive disorder. *Archives of General Psychiatry* 49(9):681–89.
Berkson, G., and Gallagher, R. J. 1986. Control of feedback from abnormal stereotyped behaviors. In *The Development of Coordination, Control and Skill in the Mentally Handicapped*, ed. M. G. Wade. Amsterdam: North Holland.
Bodfish, J. W., and Madison, J. T. 1993. Diagnosis and fluoxetine treatment of compulsive behavior disorder of adults with mental retardation. *American Journal of Mental Retardation* 98(3):360–67.
Brambilla, F., Bellodi, L., Perna, G., Arancio, C., and Bertani, A. 1997. Dopamine function in obsessive-compulsive disorder: Growth hormone response to apomorphine stimulation. *Biological Psychiatry* 42(10):889–97.
Breese, G. R., Criswell, H. E., Duncan, G. E., Moy, S. S., Johnson, K. B., Wong, D. F., and Mueller, R. A. 1995. Model for reduced brain dopamine in Lesch-Nyhan syndrome and the mentally retarded: Neurobiology of neonatal-6-OH-dopamine-lesioned rats. *Mental Retardation and Developmental Disabilities Research Reviews* 1:111–19.
Brett, L. P., and Levine, S. 1979. Schedule-induced polydypsia suppresses pituitary-adrenal activity in rats. *Journal of Comparative and Physiological Psychology* 93:946–56.
Brodkin, E. S., McDougle, C. J., Naylor, S. T., Cohen, D. J., and Price, L. H. 1997. Clomipramine in adults with pervasive developmental disorders: A prospective open-label investigation. *Journal of Child and Adolescent Psychopharmacology* 7(2):109–21.
Clark, D. L., Kreutzberg, J. R., and Chee, F. K. W. 1977. Vestibular stimulation influence on motor development in infants. *Science* 196:1228–9.
Courchesne, E. 1997. Brainstem, cerebellar and limbic neuroanatomical abnormalities in autism. *Current Opinion in Neurobiology* 7(2):269–78.
Courchesne, E., Press, G. A., and Yeung-Courchesne, R. 1993. Parietal lobe abnormalities detected with MR in patients with infantile autism. *American Journal of Roentgenology* 160(2):387–93.
Courchesne, E., Saitoh, O., Townsend, J. P., Yeung-Courchesne, R., Press, G. A., Lincoln, A. J., Haas, R. H., and Schriebman, L. 1994. Cerebellar hypoplasia and hyperplasia in infantile autism. *Lancet* 343(8888):63–4.
Curzon, G. 1990. Stereotyped and other motor responses to 5-hydroxytryptamine receptor activation. In *Neurobiology of Stereotyped Behaviour*, eds. S. J. Cooper and C. T. Dourish. Oxford, England: Oxford University Press.

Dantzer, R. 1986. Behavioral, physiological and functional aspects of stereotyped behavior: A review and reinterpretation. *Journal of Animal Science* 62:1776–86.
Dantzer, R., and Mormede, P. 1983. De-arousal properties of stereotyped behavior: Evidence from pituitary-adrenal correlates in pigs. *Applied Animal Ethology* 10:233.
Davis, K. 1940. Extreme isolation of a child. *American Journal of Sociology* 45:554–65.
Dawkins, M. S. 1986. *Unraveling Animal Behavior*. Avon: The Bath Press.
Frith, C. D., and Done, D. J. 1983. Stereotyped responding by schizophrenics patients on a two-choice guessing task. *Psychological Medicine* 13:779–86.
Ghaziuddin, M., Tsai L., Zaccagnini, M. S. 1998. Is macrocephaly specific to autism? Presented at the 45th annual meeting of the American Academy of Child and Adolescent Psychiatry in Anaheim, CA.
Gordon, C. T., State, R. C., Nelson, J. E., Hamburger, S. D., and Rapoport, J. L. 1993. A double-blind comparison of clomipramine, desipramine, and placebo in the treatment of autistic disorder. *Archives of General Psychiatry* 50(6):441–7.
Grados, M. A., Riddle, M. A., LaBuda, M., and Walkup, J. 1997. Obsessive-compulsive disorder in children and adolescents. *International Journal of Psychiatry* 9:83–97.
Graybiel, A. M. 1990. Neurotransmitters and neuromodulators in the basal ganglia. *Trends in the Neurosciences* 13(7):244–54.
Grice, D. E., Leckman, J. F., Pauls, D. L., Kurlan, R., Kidd, K. K., Pakstis, A. J., Chang, F. M., Buxbaum, J. D., Cohen, D. J., and Gelernter, J. 1996. Linkage disequilibrium between an allele at the dopamine D4 receptor locus and Tourette syndrome, by the transmission-disequilibrium test. *American Journal of Human Genetics* 59(3):644–52.
Hantouche, E. G., and Lancrenon, S. 1996. Modern typology of symptoms and obsessive-compulsive syndromes: Results of a large French study of 615 patients. *Encephale* 22(1):9–21.
Harlow, H. F., Dodsworth, R. O., and Harlow, M. K. 1965. Total social isolation in monkeys. Proceedings of the National Academy of Sciences 54:90–7.
Hellings, J. A., Kelley, L. A., Gabrielli, W. F., Kilgore, E., and Shah, P. 1996. Sertraline response in adults with mental retardation and autistic disorder. *Journal of Clinical Psychiatry* 57(8):333–36.
Herault, J., Perrot, A., Barthelemy, C., Buchler, M., Cherpi, C., Leboyer, M., Sauvage, D., Lelord, G., Mallet, J., and Muh, J. P. 1993. Possible association of c-Harvey-Ras-1 (HRAS-1) marker with autism. *Psychiatry Research* 46(3):261–7.
Herault, J., Petit, E., Martineau, J., Perrot, A., Lenoir, P., Cherpi, C., Barthelemy, C., Sauvage, D., Mallet, J., and Muh, J. P. 1995. Autism and genetics: Clinical approach and association study with two markers of HRAS gene. *American Journal of Medical Genetics* 60(4):276–81.
Hermelin, N., and O'Connor, N. 1963. The response and self-generated behaviour of severely disturbed children and severely sub-normal controls. *British Journal of Social and Clinical Psychology* 2:37–43.
Hof, P. R., Mufson, E. J., and Morrison, J. H. 1998. Human orbitofrontal cortex: Cytoarchitecture and quantitative immunohistochemical parcellation. *The Journal of Comparative Neurology* 359:48–68.
Hughes, C., Russell, J., and Robbins, T. W. 1994. Evidence for executive dysfunction in autism. *Neuropsychologia* 32(4):477–92.
Hutt, C., and Hutt, S. J. 1965. Effects of environmental complexity on stereotyped behaviour of children. *Animal Behavior* 13:1–4.

Insel, T. R., and Akiskal, H. S. 1986. Obsessive-compulsive disorder with psychotic features: A phenomenologic analysis. *American Journal of Psychiatry* 143(12):1527–33.

Johnston, M. V., and Harum, K. H. 1999. Recent progress in the neurology of learning: Memory molecules in the developing brain. *Journal of Developmental and Behavioral Pediatrics* 20(1):50–6.

Kanner, L. 1943. Autistic disturbances of affective contact. *Nervous Child* 2:217–50.

LaGrow, S. J., and Repp, A. C. 1984. Stereotypic responding: A review of intervention research. *American Journal of Mental Deficiency* 88:595–609.

Lewis, M. H., Gluck, J. P., Beachamp, A., Keresztury, M. F., and Mailman, R. B. 1990. Long-term effects of early social isolation in Macaca mulatta: In vivo evidence for changes in dopamine receptor function. *Brain Research* 513:67–73.

Lewis, M. H., Gluck, J. P., Bodfish, J. W., Beauchamp, A. J., and Mailman, R. B. 1996. Neurobiological basis of stereotyped movement disorder. In *Stereotyped Movements: Brain and Behavior Relationships*, eds. R. L. Sprague and K. M. Newell. Washington, D. C.: American Psychological Association.

Maraganore, D. M., Lees, A. J., and Marsden, C. D. 1991. Complex stereotypies after right putaminal infarction: A case report. *Movement Disorders* 6(4):358–61.

Matson, J. 1989. Self-injurious and stereotyped behavior. In *Handbook of Child Psychopathology*. New York: Plenum Press.

McDougle, C. J., Kresch, L. E., Goodman, W. K., Naylor, S. T., Volkmar, F. R., Cohen, D. J., and Price, L. H. 1995. A case-controlled study of repetitive thoughts and behavior in adults with autistic disorder and obsessive-compulsive disorder. *American Journal of Psychiatry* 152(5):772–7.

McDougle, C. J., Naylor, S. T., Cohen, D. J., Volkmar, F. R., Heninger, G. R., and Price, L. H. 1996. A double-blind, placebo-controlled study of fluvoxamine in adults with autistic disorder. *Archives of General Psychiatry* 53(11):1001–08.

Ornitz, E. M., and Ritvo, E. R. 1968. Neurophysiologic mechanisms underlying perceptual inconstancy in autistic and schizophrenic children. *Archives of General Psychiatry* 14:734–9.

Ornitz, E. M. 1985. Neurophysiology of infantile autism. *Journal of the American Academy of Child and Adolescent Psychiatry* 24:251–62.

Ozonoff, S., Strayer, D. L., McMahon, W. M., and Filloux, F. 1994. Executive function abilities in autism and Tourette syndrome: An information processing approach. *Journal of Child Psychology and Psychiatry and Allied Disciplines* 35(6):1015–32.

Palumbo, D., Maughan, A., and Kurlan, R. 1997. Hypothesis III. Tourette syndrome is only one of several causes of a developmental basal ganglia syndrome. *Archives of Neurology* 54(4):475–83.

Piaget, J. 1950. *The Psychology of Intelligence*. London: Routledge and Kegan Paul.

Piven, J., Arndt, S., Bailey, J., Havercamp, S., Andreasen, N. C., and Palmer, P. 1995. An MRI study of brain size in autism. *American Journal of Psychiatry* 152(8):1145–9.

Piven, J., Palmer, P., Jacobi, D., Childress, D., and Arndt, S. 1997. Broader autism phenotype: Evidence from a family history study of multiple-incidence autism families. *American Journal of Psychiatry* 154(2):185–90.

Piven, J., Palmer, P., Landa, R., Santangelo, S., Jacobi, D., and Childress, D. 1997. Personality and language characteristics in parents from multiple-incidence autism families. *American Journal of Medical Genetics* 74(4): 398–411.

Randrup, A., and Munkvad, I. 1967. Stereotyped activities produced by amphetamine in several animal species and man. *Psychopharmacologia* 11:300–10.

Randrup, A., Munkvad, I., and Usden, P. 1963. Adrenergic mechanisms and amphetamine induced abnormal behavior. *Acta Pharmacologica Toxicology* 20:145–57.

Rauch, S. L., Jenike, M. A., Alpert, N. M., Baer, L., Breiter, H. C., Savage, C. R., and Fischman, A. J. 1994. Regional cerebral blood flow measured during symptom provocation in obsessive-compulsive disorder using oxygen 15-labeled carbon dioxide and positron emission tomography (PET). *Archives of General Psychiatry* 51(1):62–70.

Rauch, S. L., Whalen, P. J., Savage, C. R., Curran, T., Kendrick, A., Brown, H. D., Bush, G., Breiter, H. C., and Rosen, B. R. 1997. Striatal recruitment during an implicit sequence learning task as measured by functional magnetic resonance imaging. *Human Brain Mapping* 5:124–32.

Ridley, R. M., and Baker, H. F. 1982. Stereotypy in monkeys and humans. *Psychological Medicine* 12:61–72.

Rodier, P. M., Ingram, J. L., Tisdale, B., and Croog, V. J. 1997. Linking etiologies in humans and animal models: Studies of autism. *Reproductive Toxicology* 11(2–3):417–22.

Rylander, G. 1972. Psychosis and the punding and choreiform syndromes in addiction to central stimulant drugs. *Folia Psychiatria Neurologica et Neurochirurgica Neerlandica*. 75:203–12.

Sackett, G. P. 1968. Abnormal behavior in laboratory reared rhesus monkey. In *Abnormal Behaviour in Animals*, ed. F. W. Fox. Philadelphia: W.B. Saunders.

Sanchez, L. E., Campbell, M., Small, A. M., Cueva, J. E., Armenteros, J. L., and Adams, P. B. 1996. A pilot study of clomipramine in young autistic children. *Journal of the American Academy of Child and Adolescent Psychiatry* 35(4):537–44.

Schwartz, J. M., Stoessel, P. W., Baxter, L. R. J., Martin, K. M., and Phelps, M. E. 1996. Systematic changes in cerebral glucose metabolic rate after successful behavior modification treatment of obsessive-compulsive disorder. *Archives of General Psychiatry* 53(2):109–13.

Servan-Schreiber, D., Cohen, J. D., and Steingard, S. 1996. Schizophrenic deficits in the processing of context. A test of a theoretical model. *Archives of General Psychiatry* 53(12):1105–12.

Sprague, R. L., and Newell, K. M. 1996. *Stereotyped Movements*. Washington, D.C.: American Psychological Association.

Swedo, S. E., Rapoport, J. L., Leonard, H., Lenane, M., and Cheslow, D. 1989. Obsessive-compulsive disorder in children and adolescents. Clinical phenomenology of 70 consecutive cases. *Archives of General Psychiatry* 46(4):335–41.

Vestergaard, K. S., Skadhauge, E., and Lawson, L. G. 1997. The stress of not being able to perform dustbathing in laying hens. *Physiology and Behavior* 62(2):413–19.

Waterhouse, L. 1997. Genes tPA, Fyn, and FAK in autism? *Journal of Autism and Developmental Disorders* 27(2):220–3.

Zilbovicius, M., Garreau, B., Samson, Y., Remy, P., Barthelemy, C., Syrota, A., and Lelord, G. 1995. Delayed maturation of the frontal cortex in childhood autism. *American Journal of Psychiatry* 152(2):248–52.

Zohar, A. H., and Bruno, R. 1997. Normative and pathological obsessive-compulsive behavior and ideation in childhood: A question of timing. *Journal of Child Psychology and Psychiatry and Allied Disciplines* 38(8):993–9.

Chapter • 6

Diagnostic Issues in Autism

Pasquale Accardo

HISTORICAL BACKGROUND

Autism was first described by Leo Kanner in 1943. Lorna Wing (1997) attempted to identify examples of autism prior to this, but the original documents remain fairly unconvincing. Although autism certainly existed before 1943, no one really saw the phenomenon. An attempt to perceive autistic features in literary characters such as Sherlock Holmes remains very unconvincing.[1]

In the last half century, autism has evolved from an emotional disorder to a neurodevelopmental disorder. Between 1943 and the early 1970s autism was considered an emotional condition, a withdrawal by the child into his own little world in response to the manner in which he was parented, or, more specifically, mothered. According to this earlier formulation, autism was related to cold, detached, humorless, rigid, perfectionistic, machine-like parents; it was the result of pathological and pathogenic mothering.

---

[1]Frith (1989) noted that Sherlock Holmes had many features of autism and argued that his fictional character was "reminiscent of very clever autistic people." Such a line of reasoning provides an excellent example of the fallacy inherent in over-reliance on symptom checklists to diagnose autism. Although Holmes does exhibit several characteristics that might be described as autistic, in context it represents a complete misinterpretation of his fictitious personality to describe him as a clinical case example. In balance, he also offers many behaviors that are diametrically opposed to what would be expected in autism. Frith goes on to indict almost all the fictional detectives in literature for their socially detached minds, odd personalities, obsessional characteristics, and "autistic intelligence." See Accardo (1987) for a different interpretation of the personality traits and eccentricities of Sherlock Holmes.

If autism were an emotional diagnosis, it is difficult to explain why tuberous sclerosis and phenylketonuria had been associated with it almost from the beginning. There was a further suggestion that autism might be something other than an emotionally caused condition when the last rubella epidemic in 1963 through 1965 produced 25,000 cases of congenital rubella syndrome (Alexander 1998). Apart from the striking physical defects produced by this viral embryopathy (deafness, cataracts, patent ductus arteriosus, other heart defects, growth deficiency with microcephaly, thrombocytopenia), there appeared to be an extremely high incidence of mental retardation and central auditory processing difficulties expressed as autism. Autism, or at least a reasonable facsimile of this complex and confusing behavioral syndrome, could obviously be produced by direct brain damage. But until the pioneering studies by Michael Rutter in England (Rutter and Bartak 1971) and Marianne K. DeMyer in Indianapolis (DeMyer, Hingtgen, and Jackson 1981) in the early 1970s, the concept of autism as a neurobehavioral disorder, a developmental disability rather than an emotional problem, made little headway. Among researchers, the tide turned in the early 1970s, but among the lay public and the majority of professionals in private practice, the older psychiatric and psychoanalytic conceptualizations persisted for another decade—or longer. Bruno Bettleheim, without a shred of scientific support, popularized a psychodynamic interpretation of autism through his many writings that still remain on library shelves (Pollack 1997; Sullivan 1994; Sutton 1996). And if one were to reference medical insurance claims adjusters, it would be clear that the acceptance of autism as a brain damage syndrome has not yet penetrated the professional imagination (Morowitz 1989).[2]

NEURODEVELOPMENTAL DIAGNOSIS

If autism is a brain disorder, we must first ask precisely what the brain does. The brain is the organ that provides human beings with the necessary organizing substrate for thinking, knowing, learning, moving,

[2]A somewhat similar depiction of parents (that is, mothers) as pathogenic to their children's well being remains in DMS-IV for the diagnosis of Reactive Attachment Disorder of Infancy, or what pediatricians refer to as Failure to Thrive. Since failure to thrive is, like autism, predominantly neurodevelopmental in origin (Accardo 1998; Reilly et al. 1999), this represents a current example of professional motherbashing. The persistence of such attitudes may result in part from the need for such professionals to presume parental incompetence in order to better validate their own roles. If no one but a professional (or a village of professionals and paraprofessionals) can successfully complete the complex tasks of child rearing, then whenever a child presents with a disorder of growth or development, it is a safe bet to "blame the mother."

sensing, and feeling. When the brain is damaged, depending on the degree of damage and the specific location of the damage, any and all of these functions may be left unimpaired, mildly involved, or severely disturbed. Chronic functional repercussions of brain damage (sometimes referred to as static encephalopathy) with a childhood onset are referred to as developmental disabilities. When cognition is seriously impaired, the child may be mentally retarded; when cognition is mildly impaired, the child may be a slow learner. When the motor system is severely impaired, the child may develop cerebral palsy; when the motor system is mildly involved, the child may exhibit a developmental coordination disorder (what used to be called the "clumsy child syndrome" and is sometimes referred to as apraxia or dyspraxia). Most people understand how brain damage can cause mental retardation and cerebral palsy, but many have difficulty in relating emotional, affective, or social-interactional behavior to brain damage.

Now brain damage does not necessarily refer to extraneous brain injury, either perinatal asphyxia or postnatal trauma (Accardo 1997). Most brain damage is prenatal—either genetic or the result of some very early adverse physical influence on the developing fetus. Such brain dysfunction is just becoming visible on sophisticated neuroimaging scans. In a revolution that started with autism and that still includes autistic behavior patterns as a major component of its field of study, the new area of behavioral phenotyping is demonstrating that even some of the strangest human behaviors may be uniquely preprogrammed by the human genome (see table I) (O'Brien and Yule 1995). For example, Smith-Magenis syndrome is caused by a deletion of the short arm of chromosome 17. In addition to being associated with a characteristic facies, mental retardation, and autism, this syndrome is characterized by several strikingly specific and possibly unique behaviors: (1) self hugging ("spasmodic upper-body squeeze"); (2) onychotillomania (pulling out of fingernails and toenails); and (3) polyembolokoilamania (insertion of foreign bodies into various bodily orifices).

Autism is a neurobehavioral syndrome, a condition caused by a central nervous system dysfunction, in which, according to DSM-IV, the child exhibits serious difficulty in each of three areas: (1) communication, (2) socialization, and (3) "strange" behaviors often characterized as restricted, repetitive, and stereotypic (see table II). The problems that the child has in the first two areas seem to contribute to the further development of the third. These three categories are not homogeneous: the first two refer to deficits in normal developmental processes; whereas, the third has no analogous normal developmental process.

Table I. Selected Behavioral Phenotypes in Genetic Syndromes

Five of these eight syndromes have strong associations with autism, and all eight are associated with mental retardation but not universally so.

SYNDROME	PHENOTYPE	ETIOLOGY
Down	developmental deceleration delayed expressive language relative strength in social skills sitting down, escaping visual spatial short-term memory (STM) better than auditory STM	Trisomy 21
Williams	inflated language/"cocktail party" speech auditory STM better than visual spatial STM	deletion 7q11
Smith-Magenis	self-hugging ("spasmodic upper-body squeeze"), onychotillomania (pulling out of fingernails and toenails), Polyembolokoilamania (insertion of foreign bodies into bodily orifices)	deletion 17p11.2
Rett	stereotypic "hand washing" or "hand wringing" midline repetitive movements	X q28 mutation
Prader-Willi	hyperphagia, obsessive compulsive traits, skin picking	deletion 15q11-13 (paternal)
Angelman	puppet-like gait, paroxysmal laughter	deletion 15q11-13 (maternal)
Lesch-Nyhan	severe self mutilation	X linked (Xq26-q27.2 mutation)
Fragile X	autistic features gaze avoidance (males) frontal deficits, emotional lability, deficits in social learning (including shyness, social anxiety), non-verbal learning disabilities, personality disorder (females)	mutation Xq27-q28

After screening, the diagnostic process for autism includes four distinct stages (see table III). Such a diagnosis cannot typically be achieved in one visit nor by a single professional. Indeed, it may take a considerable amount of prolonged observation and involve assessing long-term response to therapy to finally clarify some of the diagnostic issues. The critical component of developmental diagnoses is time—how the child performs over time and how the child responds to various interventions over time. While the identification of a specific etiology and the underlying neuropathology will be permanent, a developmental diagnosis such as autism may not be.

Table II. Diagnostic Features of Autism

qualitative impairment in social interaction	*qualitative impairment in communication*	*deviant behaviors*
poor eye contact	language delay	likes water play
no joint attention	echolalia, immediate and delayed	perseverative
no gaze monitoring	expressive language better than receptive language	preservation of sameness
doesn't read faces	hyperlexia (high decoding skills; reads without understanding)	stereotypies
treats people like furniture	equinus gait (toe walking)	rocking
in own little world	refers to self in third person	covers ears
laughs for no reason	pronominal reversal (between first and second persons)	spinning/twirling (self and objects)
no peer interaction	acts as if deaf	likes fans
no reciprocity or sharing	protoimperative but not protodeclarative pointing	stiff/non-cuddly baby
	good rote memory	splinter skills
	poor pragmatic language	savant behavior
	no imaginative play	inflexible routines/rituals
		obsessive-compulsive behaviors
		tone abnormalities
		blunted affect
		arching
		flapping
		lines up/groups toys
		inappropriate attachment to objects
		preoccupation with parts of objects
		insensitivity to pain
		olfactory (likes to sniff things)
		hyperactivity, impulsivity and inattentiveness (ADHD syndrome)

Mental retardation, for example, describes a person's present state of functioning and may not be of lifelong duration (Luckasson et al. 1992). Several decades ago, parents of children with mental retardation would sometimes desperately seek out a diagnosis of autism in preference to one of mental retardation; the former condition was considered treatable, the latter was incurable. Now it is well recognized that both are neurodevelopmental syndromes with similar etiologies and limited, but more optimistic, prognoses.

PEDIATRIC SCREENING FOR AUTISM

Assessment of growth and development is a routine component of well child visits, whether these are conducted by pediatricians, family practitioners, pediatric nurse practitioners, or other health care professionals.

Table III. A Staged Diagnostic Approach to Autism

Stage	Findings	Question	Instruments
Screening	delay, dissociation, and deviance in streams of development	Does this child present significant delay in one or more areas of development?	CAT/CLAMS and other pediatric assessment tools
Functional Diagnosis of Autism	the presence of the specific neuro-behavioral pattern for autism with significant deficits in each of the three requisite areas	Does this child have autism?	DSM-IV checklist or formal behavioral scale (e.g., CARS)
Functional Diagnosis of an Autistic Spectrum Disorder	the presence of an autistic variant	Does this child's neurobehavioral condition qualify as an autistic spectrum disorder?	DSM-IV checklist or formal behavioral scale (e.g., CARS)
Etiological Diagnosis	the identification of a specific etiology, if possible	Why does this child have autism or an autistic spectrum disorder?	Medical history, physical examination (including dysmorphology assessment), serology and chemistries, audiology, neuroimaging and chromosomes (including Fragile X DNA probe), as indicated by the history and physical examination
Associated Deficits	the presence of other neuro-developmental conditions	Does this child qualify for any neuro-developmental diagnoses other than autism? (such as mental retardation)	Neuro-developmental pediatric evaluation, neuro-psychological assessment, occupational therapy evaluation, physical therapy evaluation, as indicated

Although there exist standard curves on which to plot and interpret growth parameters such as height, weight, and head circumference, there are no comparable standarized routinely accepted measures of developmental status. Of the wide variety of standardized, non-standardized, and informal measures currently in use, almost none are especially sensitive to the early identification of the child with an autistic spectrum disorder. On typical measures, most children are rated as "passing" and only a small number as "failing." This latter group represents children who are so severely impaired that the use of any formal screening instrument is usually unnecessary. The large intermediate group scored "suspect" are often left in limbo, despite the fact that the large majority of children who will ultimately be eligible for a formal developmental diagnosis will fall into this category early on.

Difficulties with pediatric screening for developmental disabilities reflect a fundamental distortion in perspective. Development is viewed globally, and inquiry is made as to how well or how poorly a child is performing. It might be recommended, instead, that screenings be done according to a list of age specific developmental stages, with further assessment as indicated. For example, specific learning disabilities would not be addressed in infancy, although potential markers for learning disabilities (such as language delay) would be noted, as well as whether the children qualified for diagnosis and intervention.

Autism should be approached as just such an age specific diagnosis. Classically, autism is diagnosed at ages 24 to 30 months; it typically takes that long for most autistic children to demonstrate sufficient symptoms that come to professional attention. Although most children with autistic spectrum disorders should be identified before 30 months of age, one frequently encounters autistic children as old as 5 or 6 years without formal diagnoses of autism (Stone et al. 1994). With incomplete diagnoses, many of these children have been the subjects of professional intervention with placements in intervention programs providing early childhood special education and speech and language services.

Clinicians with responsibility for pediatric developmental surveillance should be closely monitoring all children from birth to three years for signs of developmental delay. Children with autism will exhibit delays in one or more areas of developmental skill acquisition at sometime during this period. Once any delay has been ascertained, one of the next questions that should be asked is whether this delay can be a presentation of autism. The clinician, with some degree of familiarity with the clinical features of autism, should simply observe the child at two years of age and try to obtain information from the parents to specifically rule out the possibility of autism.

Two steps can assist in screening for autism in young children. First, communication development should be a primary focus of developmental surveillance at every well child visit. By definition, children with autism will exhibit disordered communication. If one focuses on the critical age of two years, the expected expressive language milestones include a minimum 50 word vocabulary with the presence of several two word phrases. Children with autism, however, will present with one of three patterns of disordered language. Some childen with autism will be mute. If this is a chronic finding and was present at age 18 months, the child should have been referred for further assessment at that earlier age. If this is a new finding and the child's previous spoken language has regressed, immediate referral is warranted. Other children with autism will present with some spoken language, but at a level below the above cutoffs either because of a slow developmental rate or because of a similar but milder degree of regression. Referral is warranted.

Finally, some children with autism will seem to pass the above expressive language milestone cutoffs. It is for these children that the second step in the screening process needs to be applied. Those children with autism who do have at least 50 words in their expressive vocabulary, and who are putting two words together in short phrases and sentences will be found to have a significant percentage of their spoken language in the form of echolalia. That is, their speech will not be used to communicate with others spontaneously, but will only be used to express repetitions of words previously heard. Delayed echolalia (repetition that occurs a long time after the model being copied) is generally considered more severe than immediate echolalia. Whenever echolalia is observed spontaneously in the office setting, a language disorder should be considered a high probability even if autism is not present. Further, inquiry should be made about the child's communicative intent. Protodeclarative pointing (a sign of joint attention in which the child attempts to share his or her interest in something) should have come closer to 18 months of age; if this is still lacking by 24 months, autism can be suspected. It is also possible to utilize more formal screening tests at 18 months of age (Baron-Cohen and Gillberg 1992).

This approach to screening makes use of the three developmental phenomena of delay, dissociation, and deviance. Most children with autism will present with delay in expressive language milestone acquisition. There may, however, be a dissociation between the autistic child's expressive and receptive language skills. Because of echoing, the child's expressive language may appear to be at or above age level, while comprehension of spoken language will be delayed; this produces the anomalous and clearly impossible situation in which the child "says more than he or she understands." Delay and dissociation refer to milestones that are either absolutely or relatively out of sequence; but deviance refers to developmental phenomena that can occur in normal children, but which are more persistent and of greater intensity in certain conditions, such as echoing in autism and other communcation disorders.

FUNCTIONAL DIAGNOSIS OF AUTISM

The specific neurobehavioral pattern associated with autism is striking, but all developmental symptoms occur along a continuum of severity. It can sometimes be difficult to discriminate the presence of a specific behavior from the significant presence of that behavior. In this regard, the diagnosis of autism has made great strides from anecdotal clinical descriptions to the use of formal behavioral rating scales. Despite the development of several such instruments, the diagnosis of autism still presents serious challenges to clinicians. A scale is useless unless one knows when to use it and has the appropriate clinical experience to score and interpret it.

Kanner's (1943) original description of autism involved six key points (see table IV). The 14-item scale by Clancy et al. (1969) was one of the first attempts to objectify Kanner's six points (see table V). When used as a screening instrument, this scale mostly identified

Table IV. Kanner's Six Features of Autism

1) inability to relate to people
2) failure to use language to communicate
3) obsessive desire to maintain sameness
4) fascination with inanimate objects
5) good rote memory
6) intelligent, obsessive, and cold parents

Table V. The Clancy Scale for Autism

1. difficulty in mixing and playing with other children
2. acts as if deaf
3. resistance to learning
4. lack of fear about realistic dangers
5. resists change in routine
6. prefers to indicate needs by gestures
7. laughs for no apparent reason
8. not cuddly as a baby
9. hyperactivity
10. no eye contact
11. unusual attachment to objects
12. spins objects
13. repetitive and sustained odd play
14. standoffish

children with hearing problems (Capute et al. 1975). If we look closely at each of the items in the DSM-IV checklist or some of the typical autistic behaviors presented in table II, it readily becomes apparent that some degree of clinical discernment is required to apply such listings. It can even be difficult to determine in which column a given behavioral trait belongs. For example, hyperlexia might be listed under disordered communication or be considered a subtype of savant skills under deviant behaviors (see Treffert in this volume). One begins to have great respect for the clinicians who operated without the benefit of such instruments two decades ago and who used an unstructured observation period of 20 to 30 minutes duration.

Research on the development of behavior rating scales has had a great impact on refining the diagnostic sensitivity of clinicians who work with children with autism. But it is doubtful that quantification along a scale will ever become so scientific or objective as to allow one to dispense with clinical experience. Scaled scores can be helpful in quantifying marginal cases, but it may be precisely here that their limitations become most apparent. The decision that a specific child is mildly autistic versus nonautistic but with noticeable autistic features is something that most clinicians would not readily trust to the pseudo-objectivity of a scale.

All interview scales are inherently flawed, limited by the complex nature of the behavior pattern to be rated and the nature of the typically biased observer. (It is important to remember that bias can go in more than one direction.) Quantitative rating scales can be objective for clear and distinct behaviors, but many of the behaviors most characteristic of autism are outside the experience of many parents, teachers, and even professionals. Any behavior that is outside one's normal experience is very difficult to score.

Ambulation can provide a simple developmental example. When does a child walk? Well, that depends on what walking is. A mother once reported that her one-month-old baby was already walking. She was referring to the infantile reflexive pattern known as the "stepping response." In contrast, most developmental pediatrics referrals to evaluate children who are not walking turn out to be children whose gross motor locomotion is not significantly delayed; the referring professional was simply unfamiliar with exactly what the developmental sequence for normal "walking" was. If this is true of a relatively straightforward motor milestone, what can be expected regarding more complex behaviors that compose the autistic spectrum? Attention deficit hyperactivity disorder (ADHD) is considered the single most common neurobehavioral syndrome in children. Behavior rating scales, such as the Conners, are routinely used to quantify the behaviors of children with ADHD. Yet such scales can be fairly inaccurate for the diagnosis of this disorder. Their major usefulness is in measuring behavioral change in response to a specific intervention modality such as medication. In this common area of attentional deficits in children, rating scales tend to be more misused than appropriately used. This does not bode well for use of analogous scales in autism.

Allowing that behavioral checklists and rating scales may be helpful in research and in certain clinical situations, it becomes critical to know when one should suspect the possibility of autism, so as to utilize them or refer the child to a professional more familiar with autism. Several possible scenarios exemplify the different pathways and entrance points to diagnosis:

1. Children with autism may present with a variety of concerns. Sometimes parents note a general delay; more often they are concerned about specific deficits in communication skills. Occasionally, the atypical behavior, especially the poor social interaction, raises concern. Rarely is the frequently severe hyperactivity a primary complaint. One should not diagnose an infant or preschool child with developmental delay or a communication disorder without having considered the possibility of autism. Any professional who is evaluating young children for developmental problems should have sufficient familiarity with autism either to be comfortable with diagnosing it or to know when to refer a child for further assessment.
2. Whenever there is any suspicion of a developmental problem, a detailed family history should be taken. The presence of autism or communication disorders in relatives should raise the examiner's index of suspicion for the possibility of autism. Most persons, both lay and professional, presume that genetics influences skin, hair, eye color, height, weight, facial appearance, and body habits—and nothing else. When a child who has been struggling in school, and who has a parent and two siblings with diagnosed learning disabilities, is also diagnosed with a learning disability, it will typically come as a complete surprise to the family that the neurodevelopmental pattern can recur again.
3. In addition, the presence of a specific medical condition associated with autism (see table VI) should further focus the direction of the examiner's assessment toward considering autism as a possibility. If the incidence of autism among persons with Down syndrome, for example, were only 1.2 %, approximately 99 out of 100 persons with Down syndrome would not have autism. But the incidence of autism among persons with Down syndrome is 10 to 20 times greater than that found in the general population.

Table VI. Medical Conditions Associated with Autism

Angelman syndrome
Cornelia de Lange syndrome*
Central nervous system cysts
Congenital cytomegalovirus infection
Decreased cerebellar neuronal density*
Down syndrome*
Duchenne muscular dystrophy*
Familial [2% to 6% of siblings]
Fetal alcohol syndrome (FAS)
Fragile X*
Giles de la Tourette
Goldenhar syndrome
Histidinemia
H.I.V. infection
Hurler syndrome
Herpes simplex encephalitis
Hypomelanosis of Ito*
Hypothyroidism
Joubert syndrome
Lactic acidosis
Leber congenital amaurosis
Lujan-Fryns syndrome
Moebius syndrome
Mucopolysaccharidosis
Myotonic dystrophy
Neurofibromatosis
Noonan syndrome
Oculocutaneous albinism
Phenylketonuria
Plumbism
Prader-Willi syndrome
Purine overproduction
Rett syndrome*
Congenital rubella*
Smith-Magenis syndrome*
Sotos syndrome
Congenital syphilis
Tuberous sclerosis*
Turner syndrome
Williams syndrome

*suggests evidence to support more than a coincidental association (see Gillberg and Coleman 1992). Accardo et al. (1988) hypothesized a fairly non-specific relationship between lead poisoning and the intensifying of autistic patterns. A suggested association of Sotos syndrome with autism (Morrow, Whitman, and Accardo 1990) was not strengthened by a report on the psychological profiles of 16 individuals with that syndrome (Rutter and Cole 1991). There is an unreported case of autism associated with Turner syndrome with a ring chromosome that is of interest since the neurocognitive profile for Turner syndrome is the inverse of that seen in autism.

4. Certain specific behaviors such as toe walking, echolalia, spinning, and gaze aversion should, even in isolation, indicate

> that consideration be given to autism. Studies on toe walking (Accardo and Whitman 1989; Accardo et al. 1992; Shulman et al. 1997) support a non-specific relationship between toe walking and general developmental delay; a stronger and more specific association between toe walking and communication disorders; and a strong relationship between toe walking and autism.

It should be remembered that, in general, there are really no abnormal behaviors in children. In most developmental syndromes, diagnostic behaviors are normal but delayed in their appearance. This is typical for younger children. Many autistic features that do not, at first, strike the observer as normal, in fact, probably are. Two examples might suffice: both toe walking and echolalia discussed in the section on screening occur in normal infants. They occur, however, so transiently that they are usually missed. Thus, the deviant behaviors that characterize autism can be considered both delayed and prolonged, with an intensity not found in normally developing children. The child with autism falls back on an immature behavioral repertoire because his or her central nervous system impairment inhibits the development of more mature responses. A distinction remains between the diagnostic criteria for autism and the process by which these criteria are to be applied. Since no widely accepted guidelines exist as to how to diagnose autism in children, many clinicians have evolved their own approaches to this complex issue (see Noyes in this volume).

FUNCTIONAL DIAGNOSIS OF AUTISTIC SPECTRUM DISORDERS

It has been said that the beginning of all understanding is classification. It might be added that the end of all wisdom is correct classification. Within the autistic spectrum, there are four related conditions listed under the heading of Pervasive Developmental Disorders in DSM-IV that deserve consideration:

1. Asperger's syndrome appears to be identical with what is sometimes referred to as the "high functioning" child with autism. Often, these children are described as exhibiting deficits only in the social and behavioral areas, while their communication skills remain unimpaired. This is true only if one looks at the relatively unimpaired early language skills measured by objective tests. If one observes the "social" aspect of their communication, one can often identify significant deficits in what is called pragmatic language. Pennington's (1991) five group neuropsychological classification of learning

disabilities places autism and Asperger's syndrome in the category of impaired social cognition as distinct from phonological processing disorders that include developmental language disorders and dyslexia. If autism is interpreted as a profound disorder in communication, children with Asperger's syndrome are spared in selected aspects of this critical language functioning. Even some of the most severe cases of autism can exhibit isolated segments of language usage well above age level, well exemplified in the sometimes highly developed echolalia. Such fragments, however, are rarely useful for the purposes of communication. That commununciation crosses over into social behavior is most striking in much of the disordered non-verbal communication characteristic of autism in infancy: the arching, lack of cuddliness, gaze aversion, inability to read faces, and the isolation of being in one's own little world. All of these aspects reflect disordered communication, unrelated to specific language components, yet having an impact on social interactions. Asperger's syndrome or high functioning autism does, however, hold out the promise of a more positive long-term outcome.

2. Pervasive Developmental Disorder, Not Otherwise Specified (PDD-NOS) is characterized by severe problems in at least one of the three major functional areas (communication, socialization, and perseverative or deviant behaviors). If involvement in just one or two of the above areas is present or if involvement is of insufficient severity in a third area, a child is not diagnosed formally with autism. This is a child on the borderland of autism, a child who reminds the clinician of autism but who does not have the full classic neurobehavioral pattern. Many children with the diagnosis of PDD-NOS also have significant mental retardation. More recently, it has been argued that certain types of learning disabilities, especially those involving a social learning component, represent milder forms of this disorder. For example, the dyssemic child (right brain deficit pattern) who has difficulties with peer interactions might be considered to occupy the milder end of this PDD spectrum. The clinical and research utility of the Broad Autism Phenotype (BAP) appears promising (see Piven in this volume).
3. Childhood Disintegrative Disorder involves a major regression in development that begins after two years of age. From a neurologist's perspective, this term is synonymous with—or is simply the behavioral aspect of—the broad category of degenerative disorders with generally poor prognoses. Many children with the classical clinical presentation for autism will

also exhibit some degree of "autistic regression" late in the second year of life. Whenever the regression is restricted to language skills, Landau-Kleffner syndrome should be considered and a prolonged electroencephalogram (EEG) should be obtained (see Mantovani in this volume). Some degree of regression in both communication and social skills occurs in many cases of autism proper, but it should not be forgotten that a loss of limited acquired vocabulary during the second year of life is not infrequent in non-specific moderate mental retardation.

4. Rett syndrome is a rare and probably genetic disorder found only in girls. It is felt that the syndrome does occur in males, but that these are so severely affected that they die in utero. A girl with Rett syndrome will develop normally or with only mild delays until late in the first year or early in the second year of life. At that time, she will undergo a dramatic regression with complete loss of motor, language, cognitive, and social skills. Although the regression will be fairly rapid, it will not be so fast as to be confused with an acute encephalitic process. The head will stop growing leading to a deceleration in the head size (occipitofrontal circumference [OFC]) or acquired microcephaly. This syndrome is considered under the autistic or pervasive developmental disorder spectrum because of the striking gaze aversion and hand movement stereotypies that become prominent. The child will exhibit obsessive hand wringing or hand washing movements either spontaneously or on demand. The long-term prognosis for girls with Rett syndrome is one of profound generalized impairment and almost complete dependency. The microcephaly in this syndrome is in contrast to a tendency to observe macrocephaly/megalocephaly (large head size) in other autistic syndromes. There is no indication that therapies effective with autism have any specific impact on the outcome of Rett syndrome. Rett syndrome exemplifies the ease with which a child with significant mental retardation (and therefore severe deficits in communication and socialization) can qualify as autistic with the addition of only a few deviant behaviors.

It would not be unreasonable to change the heading Pervasive Developmental Disorders to Autistic Spectrum Disorders and for this new class to include: (1) Autism, (2) Asperger's syndrome, and (3) Pervasive Developmental Disorder, Not Otherwise Specified. Rett syndrome might be relegated to that group of specific etiologies sometimes associated with autism, and Childhood Disintegrative Disorders would be relocated to pediatric neuropathology textbooks. If Rett syndrome and Childhood Disintegrative Disorders are retained on the autistic spectrum, including the many cases of autism and PDD that also exhibit "autistic regression," most of the entries in this category of developmental diagnoses would be classified as developmental regression (see Zimmerman and Gordon in this volume).

ETIOLOGICAL DIAGNOSIS

A competent biomedical assessment of the child with a serious developmental problem is mandatory. The etiologies for autism are strikingly similar to the etiologies for mental retardation and other neurodevelopmental disabilities (see table V). Children diagnosed with autism should receive a comprehensive medical assessment from a professional familiar with the diverse etiologies associated with autism. Such professionals typically include developmental pediatricians, child neurologists, pediatric geneticists, and child psychiatrists. It may be true that a specific etiology may be identified in less than half to a third of children, but this percentage can be expected to increase over the next several years with the progress of the Human Genome Project. It can be of the utmost importance to the family to identify such a cause.

Fragile X syndrome is a genetic disorder characterized by the following features: hyperextensibility of joints, pectus excavatum, flat feet, a high arched palate, mitral valve prolapse, soft skin, dilated aortic arch, dyspraxic and dysfluent speech with litany-like phraseology, problems with word finding on demand, perseveration, sequential deficits, macrocephaly, macroorchidism (large testicles, but usually only after puberty), and large ears. Since not all the features are present in a given case, it is not completely clear when testing for Fragile X is indicated. Recently, Giangreco et al. (1996) developed a simplified six-item checklist that included: mental retardation, family history of mental retardation, large or prominent ears, elongated face, attention deficit hyperactivity disorder, and autistic-like behavior. Each of these items was rated 0 (absent), 1 (borderline), or 2 (present). Scores of 5 or more yielded a positive identification rate of 9.5 percent for Fragile X without missing any cases. Despite continued confusion, debate, and disagreement over the specific indications for Fragile X screening, it is generally accepted that children with autism and mental retardation and children with mental retardation with autistic features should receive a specific DNA probe for Fragile X. Children with autism, but without mental retardation, and not otherwise reaching the cutoff score of 5 on the above scale, would probably not benefit from Fragile X testing.

One of the most significant developments in the past two decades has been the recognition that many of the etiologies strongly associated with developmental diagnoses can run in families and not exhibit strikingly obvious developmental impairment. Most persons with fetal alcohol syndrome and many carriers of the Fragile X gene mutation are only mildly symptomatic.

Although it is extremely important to make a careful search for possible medical etiologies, there is no specific biomedical evaluation for autism. There is no test or procedure, no serological or neuroimaging test that should be routinely performed on all children with autism. For any given test, there need to be indications other than the presence of autism to warrant the investigation. The neurobehavioral syndrome of autism in and of itself does not require any specific test.

ASSOCIATED DEFICITS: THE SPECTRUM AND CONTINUUM OF DEVELOPMENTAL DISABILITIES

Neurodevelopmental disorders occupy a position on both the spectrum and the continuum of developmental disabilities. Typically, this is depicted by a triangle that is then interpreted in gestalt fashion as an iceberg, with the tip of the iceberg representing the spectrum and the part of the iceberg submerged representing the continuum.

The spectrum of developmental disabilities includes diagnostic categories that can answer such questions as "What sets this particular developmental diagnosis apart from other developmental diagnoses?" "What is the principal way in which it differs?" "How is this developmental disability distinct from other developmental disabilities?" This spectrum includes the broad categories of

- motor deficit (where the paradigmatic disorder is cerebral palsy) side one of the triangle
- cognitive deficit (where the paradigmatic disorder is mental retardation) side two of the triangle
- processing deficit (where the paradigmatic conditions include learning disabilities, attentional deficits, communication disorders, and probably autistic spectrum disorders) side three of the triangle

Thus, a disorder such as cerebral palsy is different from mental retardation because of the motor involvement; a learning disability is different from mental retardation and cerebral palsy because of the unimpaired general cognitive and motor functioning. The groupings that comprise the spectrum are functional, and, although they have an organic substrate in the brain, they do not follow any particular neuroanatomical localization pattern.

In contrast to the spectrum, the continuum of developmental disabilities is that grouping of signs and symptoms that can respond to questions such as: "What does this developmental disorder have in common with other developmental disorders?" "How does it overlap with other developmental disabilities?" "In what ways is this disorder similar to other developmental disabilities?" This continuum includes such items as:

- intelligence level
- motor incoordination or apraxia
- learning unevenness
- attentional deficits
- communication disorders
- socialization problems
- psychiatric conditions (oppositional defiant disorder, conduct disorder, anxiety disorder, and depression)
- oral motor difficulties (feeding or speech problems)
- seizure disorders
- dysmorphic features (minor malformations)
- hearing and visual impairments (including central processing deficits)
- orthopedic abnormalities.

Sometimes these are referred to as associated deficits. The more severe the primary disorder (the spectrum component), the greater the frequency of associated or secondary deficits (the continuum component). That is to say, the more severe the underlying brain involvement, the greater the chance that associated or contiguous areas of the brain (or for that matter, unassociated or non-contiguous areas of the brain) will be involved, and the greater the likelihood of other neurobehavioral manifestations of that involvement.

Neither the spectrum nor the continuum refer to co-morbidity. Co-morbidity implies the presence of two separate disease processes occurring simultaneously, whereas both the spectrum and continuum refer to a single central nervous system impairment with possible multiple neurobehavioral expressions. The spectrum and continuum serve an important unifying function. When a child qualifies for a long list of diagnostic conditions, one can explain to the parents that there are not a lot of different things wrong with the child, but rather brain involvement with many different ways of expressing itself. Thus, it is inadequate to describe the relationshp between autism and mental retardation as co-morbidity, a statistical coincidence. It is the same underlying brain involvement, often the same specific genetic etiology that is at the root of both. Autism and mental retardation represent two neurobehavioral continua that run parallel and frequently coincide, often running together over long stretches.

Recognizing the overlap between the spectrum and continuum can be extremely important to planning and assessing intervention strategies. When a baby is born with an obvious congenital organ system malformation, the rule is to look for others. The approach to functional brain lesions should be the same; having a single area impaired significantly raises the risk for other areas of impairment. The sides of the triangle are capable of increasing fragmentation or splitting; indeed, each side can be translated into its own triangle. Subdivisions on both the spectrum and continuum begin to take on the appearance of recursive fractal patterns. The spectrum and continuum obviously oversimplify an exceedingly complex reality. Nevertheless, they do stress a fundamental and very important homogeneity that underlies all the complex signs, symptoms, and syndromes of brain damage or central nervous system involvement.

The clinician first decides what discriminates the different neurodevelopmental disorders from one another, and then looks closely to see how much they resemble one another. Several examples from the motor side of the triangle might be used to illustrate this point: The more closely one examines a child with a specific type of cerebral palsy, the more one finds signs and symptoms of other types of cerebral palsy.

Although children with autism usually do not exhibit motor findings and, indeed, may appear quite agile, a quarter to a third of adolescents with autism will develop seizures. Their posture and gait will become "more obviously ill-coordinated and abnormal" as they enter adolescence (Wing and Atwood 1987). The child with a learning disability (even of the verbal deficit subtype) often exhibits some degree of fine or gross motor clumsiness, especially in the areas of handwriting and written expression.

Some associated disorders may represent either alternative diagnoses that need to be considered in the differential diagnosis or true associated diagnoses. In other words, it may be less a situation of either/or and more both/and. Mental retardation and hearing disorders are of paramount consideration. For autism and mental retardation there are several possible clinical scenarios:

1. children with mental retardation with some autistic features
2. children with autism who are also mentally retarded
3. children with mental retardation without autism
4. children with autism without mental retardation

Since both conditions under consideration (autism and mental retardation) are subject to degrees of severity, balancing the impact of one set of traits against the impact of the other set can be challenging.

AUTISM AS A COMMUNICATION DISORDER

Autism is both on the spectrum of developmental disabilities and simultaneously the creator of its own spectrum. But on which side of the triangle that describes the spectrum is autism to be located? Not that of cognitive or motor impairment, but rather that of communication disorders and learning disabilities. In children with various communication disorders (including hearing impairments), the further the child's communication abilities are below the child's general cognitive level, the more autistic features the child will exhibit. This relationship might be expressed by the formula:

$$AQ = f\,(IQ - CQ)$$

where the autism quotient (AQ) is directly related to (or a function of) the difference between the level of general intelligence (IQ) and the level of communication skills (CQ). This relationship will hold for all cognitive levels; it contributes to both the presence and the absence of autistic features in children with severe to profound mental retardation.

The presence of autistic features will not, however, always vary directly with the communication-cognition gap when communication is measured only by tests of spoken language. The impact of this gap will relate to the presence of autistic features only when a more global conceptualization of communication is employed. The communication skills important to the evolution of autistic features include more than verbal communication (expressive and receptive language). Prior to spoken language and underlying all the later usage of spoken language is gestural language, or more broadly, non-verbal communication. This includes such things as cuddling (the baby's adapting its body posture to the mother's cradling), imitation of gestures and body movements, and the reading of facial expressions and body postures of others. Much of the infant's social interaction is a component of such non-verbal communication. These same components will later evolve into what is called pragmatic language. Behaviors that relate to autism in infants under 12 months of age will probably neither be specific to autism nor discriminate among autism, language disorders, and other communication disorders.

Pennington's classification of learning disabilities (see table VII) has used Asperger's syndrome as an argument against communication as the primary behavioral deficit in autism. The existence of normal language skills in Asperger's syndrome suggests socialization to be the fundamental deficit in autism. If, however, one converses with a person with Asperger's syndrome, it becomes readily apparent that normal scores on tests of expressive and receptive language say little about pragmatics. One may interpret this weakness in pragmatics as

Table VII. Neuropsychological Classification of Learning Disabilities

Modular Function	Localization	Learning Disorder
Phonological processing	left perisylvian	left brain deficits dyslexia sequential processing deficits developmental language disorder
Executive functions	prefrontal	attention deficit hyperactivity disorder (ADHD)
Spatial cognition	posterior right hemisphere	right brain deficits dyscalculia dysgraphia developmental disorder of written language
Social cognition	limbic, orbital, right hemisphere	autistic spectrum disorder Asperger's syndrome
Long-term memory	hippocampus, amygdala	amnesia

After Pennington (1991)

an expression of his or her "social deficit," but it seems simpler to associate it with a fundamental communication disorder. Deficits in socialization can be understood as secondary to deficits in cognition and learning according to the formula:

$$SD = f\ (IQ, CQ, \text{experience})$$

in which social deficits (SD) are a function of intelligence (IQ), communication competence (CQ), and life experiences.

One other relevant finding that further links autism to communication problems is the high incidence of toe walking. A number of studies have documented that the same equinus gait that occurs with a very high incidence in autism is also quite common in a variety of communication disorders. Even though toe walking can occur in many different developmental disabilities, it tends to be more frequent in those with an associated communication deficit (Accardo and Whitman 1989; Schulman et al. 1997). In a broad population of children with developmental disabilities, the more prominent the toe walking, the more severely involved their communication skills, regardless of the primary (spectrum) developmental diagnosis. In typically developing children, toe walking was associated with lower, if normal, language achievement scores (Accardo et al. 1992). Pediatricians in practice should more carefully investigate language levels in any child who is observed to toe walk. For any child who presents with a language delay, the presence of toe walking should represent a red flag that the delay is more than "slow talking."

MENTAL RETARDATION

A quarter of a century ago mental retardation was clearly defined and categorized, while autism remained a puzzling and vaguely described behavioral syndrome of confusing origin. Today the situation is somewhat reversed. Autism has been subdivided into a spectrum of fairly distinct neurobehavioral syndromes, while the boundaries of mental retardation have become increasingly "soft." What is mental retardation? The classic definition included three requirements:

1. significantly subaverage intellectual ability (an intelligence quotient [IQ] in the retarded range; i.e., below 70)
2. onset during the developmental period (between birth and from 16 to 21 years of age)
3. concomitant adaptive behavior deficits

Generally, the older approach was problematical, since most examiners took little account of the second two criteria. The age criterion would, of course, be automatically met in the assessment of a child, but it was often assumed, without any specific attempt to measure, that any child with a significantly low IQ would also qualify for the adaptive deficit criterion. This would be a reasonably safe assumption only if: (1) the intelligence test used tapped a fairly broad array of cognitive abilities, and (2) the IQ was severely below average. If, on the other hand, the intelligence test was more narrowly focused, or if the results were interpreted globally, then a single IQ score might well mask a scatter of abilities and disabilities, strengths and weaknesses, that would have been better diagnosed as a communication disorder or a learning disability. The older *Stanford Binet Intelligence Scale* was liable to such misinterpretation, especially with less skilled examiners unfamiliar with how to adjust for its limitations, either by abstracting subscales or by supplementing it with other instruments with a complementary bias (e.g., tests of non-verbal intelligence).

The new American Association on Mental Retardation's (AAMR) definition of mental retardation has maintained the first two criteria (significantly low IQ and onset in the developmental period), but added the pseudo-quantitative requirement that the person exhibit significant deficits in at least two out of ten proposed adaptive skill areas:

- communication
- self-care
- home living
- social skills
- community use
- self-direction

- health and safety
- functional academics
- leisure
- work

Furthermore, these deficits are not defined so much by inability as by the level of support needed for the individual to function as independently as possible.

These recent developments in the concept of mental retardation are not necessarily a step backwards, but rather reflect the complexity of the changes that often accompany a dramatically increased knowledge base. The cognitive limitation that was previously the mainstay of the diagnosis of mental retardation is now replaced by more detailed neurobehavioral profiles of strengths and weaknesses. Unfortunately, the instruments to measure these patterns remain weak and, generally, unscientific. The non-IQ components of the current definition of mental retardation are not sufficiently objective for research studies. For scientific purposes, the term mental retardation should probably be discarded and replaced with the term cognitive limitation as defined exclusively by IQ scores. Such objective components will be better able to contribute to the delineation of complex syndrome identification.

In fact, a new mental retardation spectrum is currently evolving based on patterns of cognitive abilities as they relate to specific etiologies. In the area of behavioral phenotypes (see table I), one considers the spectrum of autistic syndromes and behaviors as one of the major groups of identifiers for behavioral subtyping. This preference seems to be a residual one of considering such autistic features as extremely atypical. The use of phenotypes more readily allows for identification of gene specific syndromes. As with the example of cerebral palsy noted earlier, the closer one looks for autistic features, the more one finds them. Behavioral phenotyping that lies more in the overall arrangement of a relatively small number of recurrent behaviors is not necessarily less specific than the identification of rare pathognomonic behaviors.

MENTAL RETARDATION AND AUTISM

Both mental retardation and autism are neurodevelopmental disabilities that share many common etiologies and many common neurobehavioral features. The incidence of Down syndrome is one to two per thousand; the incidence of autism is on the same order of magnitude (see Szatmari and Goldberg in this volume). The incidence of autism in Down syndrome may be one per hundred (Howlin, Wing, and Gould 1995) to as high as seven per hundred (Kent et al. 1999).

Lead poisoning has long been recognized as a contributor to the etiology of mental retardation, possibly increasing the incidence of autism in risk populations. In Fragile X syndrome (FRAXA), the primary association may be between FRAXA and mental retardation rather than between FRAXA and autism (Accardo and Shapiro 1998). The overlap between these two developmental disorders (autism and mental retardation), along with the tendency toward communication problems in Fragile X syndrome, has contributed to the obscuring of their true relationship in this genetic syndrome.

What is, then, the quantitative overlap between the two syndromes of autism and mental retardation? Knobloch and Pasamanick (1975) reported a figure of 85%; this estimate was limited by the fact that probably not all five categories of autistic spectrum disorder listed in the current DSM-IV were included in the study. Or possibly the study was limited by the fact that all five were included. Current diagnostic approaches assign a diagnosis of autism, autistic spectrum disorder, or pervasive developmental disorder to a much wider range of children.

Another limitation of past studies was the widespread reliance on the *Stanford Binet Intelligence Scale*. All of the editions prior to the most recent, the fourth, were heavily biased towards interpreting intelligence as verbal intelligence. Dependence on the *Stanford Binet* as the exclusive measure of intellectual capacity was, thus, always prone to underestimate cognitive abilities in children with communication disorders, language problems, and autistic spectrum disorders.

Now, some evaluators look down on the use of formal intelligence tests. This derives, in part, from the tests' history of misuse and misinterpretation. If they were used routinely, and if mental retardation (or cognitive limitation) was defined, as previously suggested, exclusively by IQ scores, then one would expect the incidence of mental retardation in a group of children with autism to be somewhere between 50% and 75% (for an average of, say, 67%), depending on the population under study.

If, instead of relying on IQ scores alone, we attempted to use the newer definition of mental retardation, we might get a different pattern. Taking into account the standard error of the mean, the upper IQ cutoff for mental retardation with the social supports definition is actually 80. Persons with autistic spectrum disorders who have intelligence quotients even in this borderline range might be expected to qualify as significantly limited in at least several of the social adaptive behavior skill areas, and, therefore, qualify as mentally retarded by the new definition, because of their need for increased levels of support. When it is reported that the coincidence of autism and mental retardation is decreasing, it is assumed that the newer spectrum approach to autistic disorders is being combined with the older definition of mental retardation.

Often when the diagnosis of autism is clear from the outset, there is a certain reluctance to perform a formal intelligence test. It is claimed that the resulting IQ scores are not very predictive in young children and can, therefore, be misleading. The behavioral characteristics of autism frequently militate against optimal test results at an age when most test results are already viewed with skepticism. Behaviors such as the attention deficit hyperactivity disorder (ADHD) symptoms, gaze avoidance, self stimulation, perseveration, lack of social reciprocity, obsessive compulsive behaviors, lack of joint attention, and echoing contribute to make intelligence testing challenging. The completion of a formal protocol may take several sessions. Nevertheless, an attempt to describe fully all the child's strengths and weaknesses by a psychological examiner familiar with autism can often discover useful information and provide a baseline for later estimates of progress. Although IQ scores should never be used to determine ceilings for expected progress, they may explain certain difficulties in attaining progress in selected areas of functioning. With time and intervention, most of the autistic features that inhibit testing will resolve, either spontaneously or as a result of diverse therapies. Ultimately, in long-term follow up, the most serious negative developmental outcome for autism is mental retardation, the underlying cognitive limitation so frequently associated with autism.

It is not urgent to make a decision on possible long-term cognitive outcomes in infancy. It is important, however, to assess from earliest childhood, continuing developmental progress even in those areas that may not be the primary focus of treatment. This is especially true when deficits in global cognition represent the major difficulty for adults who were diagnosed as autistic in childhood. In a noncategorical approach to developmental diagnosis, the differentiation and discrimination of mental retardation from autism is not imperative. From the perspective of medical diagnosis, the earliest detailed neurobehavioral profile can contribute to focusing the biomedical evaluation.

Researchers prefer to study pure forms of a disorder. This assumes that there is some pure form of autism that excludes certain features. If most children with autism are also mentally retarded, it makes about as much sense to investigate autism without mental retardation as it would to study cases of Down syndrome without simian creases. Perhaps the purest forms of Down syndrome (and of autism) are the ones with the most features rather than the least.

Much of the research and parental activism relating to autism is based on the distinctiveness and separateness of the syndrome. There have always been serious and valid concerns that interventions appropriate to children with mental retardation and general deveopmental delay might not be specific enough to maximize developmental progress in children with autism. Having established these points of difference, it remains important to recognize and understand the serious implications brought about by the large degree of overlap between these two conditions.

CONCLUSIONS

Primary health care providers and early intervention professionals need to become familiar with the early signs of autism in children. They need to recognize autism as a major category of developmental disorders requiring early identification. Diagnoses at ages three, four, and five years are very late, too late, and will probably have a negative impact on the child's future development. Knowing the classic picture of full-blown autism will allow professionals to begin to extend these symptoms downward to less obvious premanifestations of the disorder, so that even when a very early diagnosis may not be possible, a child's atypical development may still be closely monitored to permit the earliest possible diagnosis.

Autism is a rare disorder, but it is not that rare. Children appear to benefit from an intensive and highly specialized intervention program distinctly different from that for other developmental disorders (see Lovaas in this volume). It serves as a constant reminder that child development is not child's play. Autism teaches us to recognize, accept, and live with a complexity that we may never fully understand.

CHAPTER SUMMARY

1. Autism is a neurodevelopmental disorder that presents with qualitative impairments in social interaction and communication, and perseverative or stereotypic behaviors.
2. Autism causes, rather than is caused by, impairments in social relatedness.
3. The individual behaviors that make up the clinical features that define autism are themselves determined by specific structural impairments in the brain, which, in turn, may be controlled by specific genes.
4. Autism and autistic features represent a major focus of behavioral phenotyping in genetics.
5. Infants with autism will typically present with mild developmental delays before they exhibit the more characteristic behaviors of autism.
6. When infants and young children have any degree of delay in one or more areas of development, the clinician should consider the possibility of an early presentation of autism.

7. Physicians and health care professionals responsible for the well child should specifically address the question of whether a child of two years of age has autism.
8. Toe walking and echolalia are two incidental behaviors that can act as red flags for possible autism in the pediatric office setting.
9. A majority of children with autism will also be mentally retarded.
10. The diagnosis of autism hinges on the demonstration of a specific pattern of behaviors. There is no laboratory, biomedical, or neuroimaging test to confirm this diagnosis.
11. There is no routine medical evaluation for autism. Any tests to be performed should be in response to the presence of a sign or symptom other than autism; autism by itself is not an indicator for a specific procedure.
12. Behavioral questionnaires represent a useful adjunct to the diagnosis of autism but cannot replace direct observation of the child.
13. The diagnosis of autism should only be made by professionals with some degree of familiarity and experience with the condition.
14. Rett syndrome is a specific neurological disorder that presents with (a) dramatic and permanent regression in motor, cognitive, and language skills, (b) acquired microcephaly, and (c) stereotypic hand wringing and gaze aversion.
15. Fragile X testing should be considered in a child with autism when (a) that child is also mentally retarded or has a family history of mental retardation, or (b) there are other physical features of Fragile X syndrome such as large ears, macrocephaly, flat feet, pectus excavatum, hyperextensible joints, and macroorchidism.

REFERENCES

Accardo, P. J. 1987. *Diagnosis and Detection: The Medical Iconography of Sherlock Holmes.* Rutherford, New Jersey: Fairleigh Dickinson University Press.

Accardo, P. J. 1997. The "Expanded" Strauss syndrome. In *Behavior Belongs in the Brain: Neurobehavioral Syndromes*, eds. P. J. Accardo, B. K. Shapiro, and A. J. Capute. Baltimore: York Press.

Accardo, P. J. 1998. Failure to thrive: A reconceptualization. In *Child Maltreatment: A Clinical Guide and Reference*, ed. J. Monteleone. St. Louis, Missouri: G.W. Publishing Company.

Accardo, P. J., and Whitman, B. Y. 1989. Toe walking: A marker for language disorders in the developmentally disabled. *Clinical Pediatrics* 28:347–50.

Accardo, P. J., Whitman, B. Y., Caul, J., and Rolfe, U. 1988. Autism and plumbism: A possible etiological contribution. *Clinical Pediatrics* 27:41–4.

Accardo, P. J., Morrow, J., Heaney, M. S., Whitman, B. Y., and Tomazic, T. 1992. Toe walking and language development. *Clinical Pediatrics* 31:158–60.

Accardo, P. J., and Shapiro, L. R. 1998. FRAXA and FRAXE: Who to test or not to test. *Journal of Pediatrics* 132:762–4.

Alexander, D. 1998. Prevention of mental retardation: Four decades of research. *Mental Retardation and Developmental Disabilities Research Reviews* 4(1):50–8.

American Psychiatric Association. 1994. *Diagnostic and Statistical Manual of Mental Disorders*, Fourth Edition (DSM-IV). Washington, D.C.: American Psychiatric Association.

Baron-Cohen, S., and Gillberg, C. 1992. Can autism be detected at 18 months? The needle, the haystack, and the CHAT. *British Journal of Psychiatry* 161:839–43.

Capute, A. J., Derivan, A. T., Chauvel, P. J., and Rodiguez, A. 1975. Infantile autism I: A prospective study of the diagnosis. *Developmental Medicine and Child Neurology* 17:58–62.

Clancy, H., Dugdale, A., and Rendle-Short, J. 1969. The diagnosis of infantile autism. *Developmental Medicine and Child Neurology* 11:432–42.

DeMyer, M. K., Hingtgen, J. N., and Jackson, R. K. 1981. Infantile autism reviewed: A decade of research. *Schizophrenia Bulletin* 7:388–451.

Frith, U. 1989. *Autism: Explaining the Enigma*. Cambridge, MA: Basil Blackwell.

Giangreco, C. A., Steele, M. W., Aston, C. E., Cummings, J. H., and Wenger, S. L. 1996. A simplified six-item checklist for screening for fragile X syndrome in the pediatric population. *Journal of Pediatrics* 129:611–14.

Gillberg, C., and Coleman, M. 1992. *The Biology of the Autistic Syndromes. Clinics in Developmental Medicine*, No. 126. London: MacKeith Press.

Howlin, P., Wing, L., and Gould, J. 1995. The recognition of autism in children with Down syndrome: Implications for intervention and some speculations about pathology. *Developmental Medicine and Child Neurology* 37:406–14.

Kanner, L. 1943. Autistic disturbances of affective contact. *Nervous Child* 2:217–50.

Kent, L., Evans, J., Paul, M., and Sharp, M. 1999. Comorbidity of autistic spectrum disorders in children with Down syndrome. *Developmental Medicine and Child Neurology* 41:153–8.

Knobloch, H., and Pasamanick, B. 1975. Some etiological and prognostic factors in early infantile autism and psychosis. *Pediatrics* 55:182–91.

Luckasson, R., Coulter, D. L., Polloway, E. A., Reiss, S., Schalock, R. L., Snell, M. E., Spitalnik, D. M., and Stark, J. A. 1992. *Mental Retardation: Definition, Classification, and Systems of Supports*. Washington, DC: American Association on Mental Retardation.

Morowitz, H. J. 1989. Autism and authority. *Hospital Practice*, April.

Morrow, J. D., Whitman, B. Y., and Accardo, P. J. 1990. Autistic disorder in Sotos syndrome: A case report. *European Journal of Pediatrics* 149:567–9.

O'Brien, G., and Yule, W. 1995. *Behavioral Phenotypes. Clinics in Developmental Medicine*, No. 138. London: MacKeith Press.

Pennington, B. F. 1991. *Diagnosing Learning Disorders: A Neuropsychological Framework*. New York: Guilford Press.

Pollack, R. 1997. *The Creation of Dr. B: A Biography of Bruno Bettleheim*. New York: Simon & Schuster.

Reilly, S. M., Skuse, D. H., Wolke, D., and Stevenson, J. 1999. Oral-motor dysfunction in children who fail to thrive: Organic or non-organic? *Developmental Medicine and Child Neurology* 41:115–22.

Rutter, M., and Bartak, L. 1971. Causes of infantile autism: Some considerations from recent research. *Journal of Autism and Childhood Schizophrenia* 1:20–32.
Rutter, S. C., and Cole, T. R. P. 1991. Psychological characteristics of Sotos syndrome. *Developmental Medicine and Child Neurology* 33:898–902.
Shulman, L. H., Sala, D. A., Chu, M. L. Y., McCaul, P. R., and Sandler, B. J. 1997. Developmental implications of idiopathic toe walking. *Journal of Pediatrics* 130:541–6.
Stone, W. L., Hoffman, E. L., Lewis, S. E., and Ousley, O. Y. 1994. Early recognition of autism: Parental reports vs clinical observation. *Archives of Pediatric and Adolescent Medicine* 148:174–9.
Sullivan, R. C. 1994. Autism: Definitions past and present. *Journal of Vocational Rehabilitation* 4:4–9.
Sutton, N. 1996. *Bettleheim: A Life and a Legacy*. New York: Basic Books.
Wing, L. 1997. The history of ideas on autism. *Autism: The International Journal of Research and Practice* 1:13–23.
Wing, L., and Attwood, A. 1987. Syndromes of autism and atypical development. In *Handbook of Autism and Pervasive Developmental Disorders*, eds. D. J. Cohen, A. M. Donnellan, and R. Paul. Silver Spring, MD: V. H. Winston and Sons.

AUTHOR'S NOTE

This work was supported in part by Grant #MCJ-369029 from the Maternal and Child Health Bureau (Title V, Social Security Act), Health Resources and Services Administration, Department of Health and Human Services.

Chapter • 7

Experimental Design and Cumulative Research in Early Behavioral Intervention

O. Ivar Lovaas

For the last 30 years, empirical research on learning processes has shown behavioral treatments to be successful in helping children diagnosed with autism (DeMyer, Hingtgen, and Jackson 1981; Rutter 1985; Schreibman 1988; Smith 1993). This chapter attempts to describe the major research strategies employed in behavioral treatment research as contrasted with traditional approaches. The essential difference between the two is viewed as a difference in how to gain information, either by employing a theory-driven approach or a data-driven, inductive approach. The University of California, Los Angeles (UCLA) Young Autism Project will be used to illustrate behavioral treatment research.

BEHAVIORAL TREATMENT RESEARCH

Three significant steps were involved in the development of behavioral treatment research. First, the construct of autism was broken down into its separate behaviors to allow for accurate and sensitive measures of treatment outcomes. By directing the research on a behavior by behavior basis, the problem of the children's behavioral heterogeneity is avoided as well. Secondly, variables in the children's immediate environment were systematically manipulated (presented and withdrawn) to assess their effects on the various behaviors targeted for intervention. Thirdly, it was assumed that the laws of learning, which provide explicit and scientifically documented information about how typical organisms learn, could serve as a basis for the selection and testing of treatment variables. To approximate the learning opportunities available to typical individuals who appear to learn most of their waking hours, treatment was provided 40 hours per week in the children's homes and natural environments, and it was closely supervised by extensively trained staff and parents. The ways in which these three steps facilitated research and optimized treatment outcomes will be briefly discussed first.

MEASUREMENT

Measurement was facilitated because separate behaviors could be measured more reliably and precisely than the syndrome of autism as a whole. Ten developmental delays were identified: language, attention, motivation, imitation, toy play, peer play, social interaction, emotional expression, self-help skills, and cognitive functioning. Two behavioral excesses were also measured: aggression (including self-injury) and self-stimulatory behavior (repetitive or ritualistic behavior). Each of these behaviors provided opportunities to assess moment-to-moment fluctuations in the magnitude of a behavior in response to treatment variables, allowing the investigator immediate feedback regarding the effectiveness of a treatment variable. The use of precise and sensitive measures may be particularly important in the early stages of exploratory research, in part because smaller changes in behavior may be more frequently occurring than larger ones. Hence, they are more likely to be detected. Large changes in behavior may also represent the sum of smaller changes. Behaviorally oriented investigators have applied similar approaches to dividing other complex (hypothetical) structures into their separate behavioral components. For example, tests of cognitive ability (as indexed by IQ scores) have been analyzed as consisting of a collection of relatively separate behaviors (Bijou and Donitz-Johnson 1981; Greenwood et al. 1992; Goldfried and Kent 1972).

EXPERIMENTAL MANIPULATIONS

Once reliable, sensitive, and objective measures of the children's individual behaviors were obtained, variables in the immediate environment that might affect each of these behaviors were experimentally manipulated (systematically introduced and withdrawn) to determine which environmental interventions might help or hinder the development of these various behaviors. This kind of research differs from investigations that attempt to assess the effects of historical variables, such as early experience (including the effects of intra-uterine environment). An illustration of the importance and power of experimental manipulations in assessing the effects of treatments can be illustrated in the case of Gregg's self-injurious behavior.

Gregg was an 11-year-old boy diagnosed with severe retardation, whose self-injurious behavior started when he was 2 years old. He was hospitalized at the age of 3.5 years, having spent most of the preceding years in restraints, as in being tied from his legs and arms to the four corners of his bed.

The treatments of choice at the time of Gregg's hospitalization were derived from psychodynamic theories. According to these theories, the self-injurious behaviors were seen as the child's attempt to reduce guilt and/or punish a *hostile introject*, namely the parent. In an effort to alleviate the guilt or the power of the hostile introject, comfort and reassurance were provided whenever the client injured himself or herself. Many other theories about self-injury also existed (see Lovaas et al. 1965), none having been subjected to empirical tests. The effect of psychodynamic treatment on Gregg is depicted in figure 1. Data are recorded as cumulative curves, each self-injurious hit moving the pen upward in small incremental steps, yielding sensitive measures of behavior change. Sessions 1 and 2 represent base-rate and, except for a few self-injurious acts in the beginning of session 1, the rate is very low, Gregg being left to hit himself with the attending adult not responding. Treatment was introduced in session 3, as marked by the upward moving hatch-marks, accompanied by a sudden increase in self-injury. Treatment was withheld in session 4 and rate of self-injurious behaviors returned to baseline. Session 5 is a repeat of session 2, except that the treatment is introduced from the beginning. Within 10 minutes, Gregg hit himself about 200 times, only to recover in sessions 6 and 7 when treatment was again withdrawn.

More extensive descriptions of early experimental investigations in self-injury, including the very specific situational (Discriminative Stimulus) control over such behavior, can be found in Lovaas and Simmons (1969) and in Lovaas et al. (1965). Perhaps the most important contribution of this kind, within-subject replication design, centers on its effectiveness in isolating effective versus harmful treatment variables (Kazdin 1993). Furthermore, and contrary to what may be expected, the self-injurious behavior depicted in figure 1 is an example of the data that support the inference that such behavior is rational and lawful, obeying the laws of learning established on typical organisms.

PRIOR EMPIRICAL RESEARCH

There is considerable advantage (particularly in the initial search for effective treatment variables) to testing for treatment effects based on

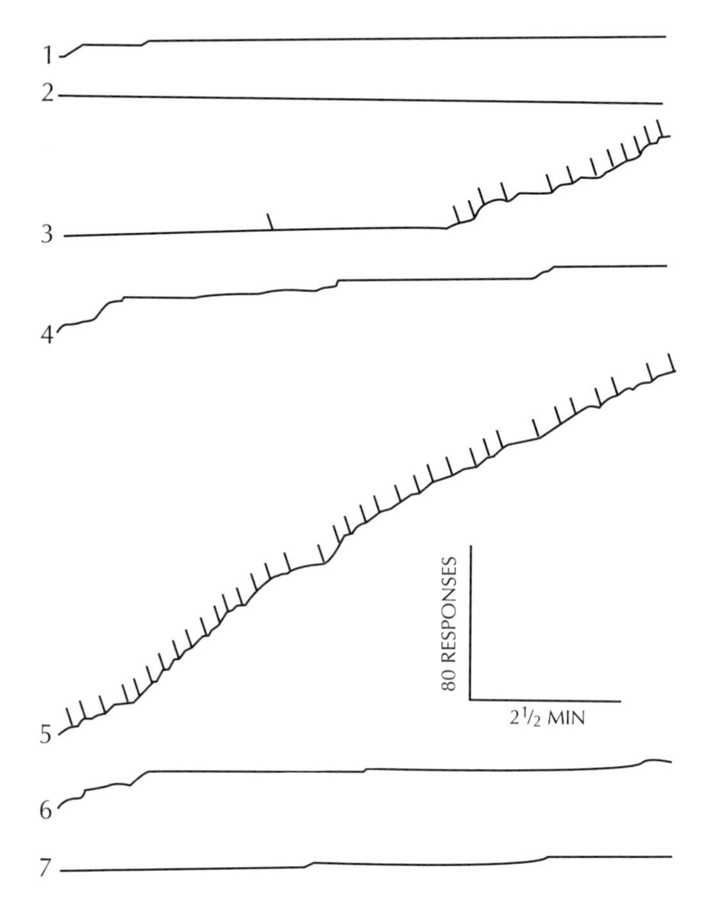

Figure 1. Gregg's self-injurious behaviors, plotted as cumulative curves, over successive 10-minute sessions (1 through 7). The upward moving hatchmarks in sessions 3 and 5 mark delivery of treatment consisting of sympathetic comments or expressions of concern contingent on self-injurious behavior.

what is already known from prior research. Treatment variables in the UCLA Young Autism Project were derived from what was already known about how organisms learn, especially regarding reinforcement, shaping, and discrimination learning (Lovaas and Smith 1988). There have been literally thousands of such studies published in peer-reviewed journals over the last 100 years. Comprehensive reviews of these data as they relate to individuals diagnosed with autism can be found in Newsom and Rincover (1989), and in Schreibman (1988).

Some general principles guiding research for effective treatment may now be described. To achieve a closer and more functional match between the child's nervous system and environment, processes and components of what is known about the learning process were systematically introduced, manipulated, and modified to identify which combinations would become functional for the child diagnosed with autism. Only essential changes were made; otherwise, the average environment served as model and was left intact with all or most significant adults in the child's home and neighborhood acting as teachers, typical of how most children learn. Perhaps the major benefit to clinical investigators has been the opportunity to build upon available research about how typical organisms learn. A brief and select review of behavioral research relevant to the treatment of the various behavioral excesses and delays in autism may help illustrate how behavioral treatment has been developed.

RESEARCH ON MODIFYING THE SEPARATE BEHAVIORS IN AUTISM

Self-injury

A large amount of experimental literature on the treatment of self-injury, a behavior which poses a major problem for many developmentally disabled clients, now exists. In addition to findings that self-injury can be increased by contingent social attention, Carr, Newsom, and Binkoff (1976) reported data showing instances of self-injurious behavior to be strengthened by the escape from environmental demands. Favell, McGimsey, and Schell (1982) found other instances of self-injurious behavior to be controlled by sensory reinforcers. In short, one behavioral topography apparently enjoys three different kinds of functional relationships to the environment. This implies that treatment providers must be competent in a functional analysis of self-injurious behavior to determine which of three different kinds of treatment to apply. A particular intervention that reduces one kind of self-injury may worsen another. To illustrate, placing clients in relative isolation, contingent on self-injury, is likely to reduce self-injury if based on positive reinforcement (such as delivery of attention). The same intervention may increase self-injury if based on negative reinforcement (escape-avoidance behavior) (Carr, Newsom, and Binkoff 1976). Self-injury based on sensory reinforcement would remain unaltered (Favell, McGimsey, and Schell 1982). Matson and Taras (1989) have provided a review of a variety of behavioral procedures for reducing self-injury, concluding that such interventions are successful in decreasing self-injury in the majority of cases.

Self-stimulatory Behavior

Persons with autism and other developmental disabilities exhibit high rates of self-stimulatory behavior, such as repetitive and stereotyped hand-flapping and body-rocking. Five of the major findings on self-stimulatory behavior can be summarized as follows:

1. Self-stimulatory behavior can be observed to occur across many diagnostic categories and, in transient form, among typical individuals, especially young children (Kravitz and Boehm 1971; Thelen 1979).
2. Self-stimulatory behavior varies inversely with the magnitude of socially appropriate behavior and appears to be maintained by the sensory reinforcement generated by such behavior (Lovaas, Newsom, and Hickman 1987).
3. Access to self-stimulatory behavior can be used to reinforce (reward and strengthen) socially appropriate behavior (Rincover and Newsom 1985).
4. Effective treatment may consist of changing low-level forms of self-stimulatory behavior to socially appropriate forms (Epstein, Taubman, and Lovaas 1985).
5. The sensory feedback generated by self-stimulation may fulfill a biological need serving to maintain the afferent nervous system from deterioration. Restricted visual and auditory stimulation have been reported to produce retarded neuronal development in the visual and temporal auditory cortex (Greenough, Volkmar, and Juraska 1973; Wiesel and Hubel 1965). If so, any treatment involving the direct suppression of such behaviors would be contraindicated.

Attention

Many individuals with autism exhibit apparent sensory deficits, acting as if they are blind and deaf. This may be evidenced by their failing to respond to their parents' calling their names, to people coming and going, and to other significant environmental events. By contrast, they may respond to other sounds such as a barely audible siren or the unwrapping of a candy bar. The UCLA Project's attempts to understand this phenomenon has been labeled *stimulus overselectivity* (overly narrow attention), referring to the experimental finding that only a small and restricted number of stimuli in a complex array control the behavior of a child diagnosed with autism (Lovaas, Koegel, and Schreibman 1979). The same authors proposed that overselective attention may be a significant cause in the development of autism;

that is, if a child is unable to concurrently process both visual and auditory stimuli (e.g., fail to attend to the parents' concurrent facial and verbal expressions), then social, emotional, and cognitive behavior will all be delayed. For example, ". . . much of the meaning in language involves associating multiple inputs, as in associating language cues to a variety of sensory inputs such as sight and feel. . . . If the child responds to only one or two of these dimensions, he or she will not understand what is said." The acquisition of emotional attachment was also proposed to be similarly affected, since such behaviors may necessitate "attention to two or more stimuli (the conditioned and unconditioned) as in classical conditioning" (p. 1241). While we are unable to support these hypotheses in all cases of autism, subsequent research indicates that overselective attention is greatly reduced and eventually disappears, in the best outcome group, as a function of early and intensive treatment (McEachin, Smith, and Lovaas 1993). A likely explanation for such reduction may be that the results of discrimination learning allows a child to identify and attend to various environmental stimuli that signal access to reinforcers. Joint-attention deficit findings in an hypothesis proposed by Mundy and Sigman (1989), appear similar to the findings on stimulus overselectivity, both in terms of a potential role in delaying development and in sensitivity to early intervention effects (Lewy and Dawson 1992). In cases where attentional behaviors do not improve with early and intensive treatment, many remedial interventions exist to reduce the effect of narrow attention and help the child attend to increasingly complex stimuli (Lovaas, Koegel, and Schreibman 1979).

Motivation

Most children diagnosed with autism appear to be indifferent to social and other symbolic rewards, such as verbal approval, being correct, and having the company of others. The apparent failure of social reinforcers was earlier postulated to be a likely reason for the autistic child's behavioral delays (Ferster 1961). Early attempts to establish social reinforcers for children with autism, although successful, were initially found to be short-lived (Lovaas et al. 1966; Lovaas Schaeffer, and Simmons 1965). However, subsequent research has identified a large range of effective reinforcers, such as sensory-perceptual reinforcers which help to normalize the child's motivational makeup (Lovaas, Newsom, and Hickman 1987). The acquisition of a varied behavioral repertoire that develops with treatment also increases the likelihood of exposure to new and varied reinforcers, a development that appears analogous to what happens to typically developing children.

Imitation

Typical children learn many new behaviors by imitating other children (Bandura 1969), while children with autism are delayed in this area. The children's failure to imitate has both practical and theoretical significance. Baer, Guess, and Sherman (1972) made initial and important progress toward identifying essential steps in teaching imitation through learning-based principles. Subsequently, discrete trial procedures were used to teach nonverbal imitation (Lovaas et al. 1967). The acquisition of nonverbal imitation through observations of others helps a child with autism establish a learning strategy for gaining a wide range of complex behaviors (Granpeesheh 1990). Subsequent programs for teaching verbal imitation became central in the establishment of language (Lovaas et al. 1966). It is important to note that generalized and clearly enunciated verbal imitation of adults' vocalizations was achieved by only 9 out of 19 children undergoing early and intensive behavioral intervention in a study by McEachin, Smith, and Lovaas (1993). These were the same (and only) children who reached best outcome in the Lovaas (1988) treatment study.

Language

The role of language delay as a contributor to autism has been advocated by Churchill (1978) who, like Chomsky (1965), questioned the efficacy of behavioral interventions in building language. Procedures for teaching communicative language can be derived from laboratory research on operant conditioning and discrimination learning through the use of discrete trials, prompting, fading, shaping, and chaining. Beginning steps in language training involve teaching mute clients to imitate simple sounds, followed by combining sounds into syllables, and then forming the syllables into words (Lovaas et al. 1966). Once clients are able to imitate words, they are taught to use these words to request favorite objects and activities, and then to label these events (Risley and Wolf 1967). Subsequently, clients are instructed to combine words into simple sentences such as "I want. . . ." and "This is a. . . ." (Risley, Hart, and Doke 1972).

There are substantial individual differences in rates of language acquisition. Clients who proceed at rapid rates are instructed on how to use abstract concepts including yes/no (Hung 1980); plurals (Baer, Guess, and Sherman 1972); adjectives (Risley, Hart, and Doke 1972); prepositions, pronouns, opposites such as big/little and hot/cold, and time relations such as first/last and before/after (Lovaas 1977). If they master these concepts, they are taught to ask questions (Hung 1977; Lovaas 1977) and engage in simple conversations (Gaylord-Ross et al. 1984; Lovaas 1977). Recent research has described procedures for facilitating conversational speech in children with autism and typically developing peers (Charlop and Milstein 1989; Gaylord-Ross et al. 1984; Haring et al. 1986). Thus, experimentally validated procedures exist for helping clients progress from being mute to possessing some or all of the language skills displayed by typical children and adults.

Despite difficulties in interpretation (Howlin 1981), several points are clear: Numerous investigations have documented that behavioral approaches help clients with autism acquire language. However, the extent to which gains are maintained over time and generalized across persons and situations is in doubt. Data from the McEachin, Smith, and Lovaas (1993) research give some indication of the strengths and weaknesses of a behavioral approach to teaching language. The best-outcome children (9 of 19) in the intensively treated experimental group scored within or above the normal range on the verbal subscales of the WISC-R, with peaks on the similarities and comprehension subscales (p. 366 table II). Such scores are inconsistent with what would be expected if these were high-functioning persons with autism. The scaled scores of subjects who did not reach normal functioning, but reached the basal level on the WISC-R are consistent with the diagnosis.

The studies reviewed above are examples of research that cumulatively form a basis for the design of comprehensive behavioral treatment. Hundreds of similar studies with interventions described in replicable detail have been published in peer-reviewed journals. Many studies have, in fact, been replicated. These smaller studies were combined into a comprehensive treatment program yielding the outcome data presented below.

TREATMENT OUTCOME RESEARCH

Treatment outcome research has investigated the long-term effects on clients receiving intensive and early behavioral treatment. Since the first outcome study in 1973, the number of smaller experimental studies has increased so that, at present, more than 400 separate treatment programs constitute the comprehensive intervention offered by UCLA and affiliated clinics. The earlier treatment outcome data will be reviewed first to illustrate how weaknesses were identified and solutions sought.

The 1973 Follow-up

The 1973 follow-up study published data evaluating the strengths and weaknesses of intensive and early behavioral intervention (Lovaas et al. 1973). A group of 20 children, 3-10 years of age at intake, received treatment between 1964 and 1970. Treatment consisted of 40 or more hours a week of one-to-one instruction for 12 to 14 months. Some children received treatment as inpatients, while others were outpatients in the psychology department's Autism Clinic. Some children were discharged to a psychiatric institution; the remainder were discharged to their parents who had been trained in behavioral teaching approaches.

The positive findings from the Lovaas et al. (1973) study were:

1. All children improved, though they evidenced marked individual differences in amounts of improvement.
2. The longer the treatment lasted, the greater was the improvement.
3. Complex behaviors, such as language and toy play, could be acquired.
4. The children showed gains on standardized tests of intelligence and adaptive functioning.
5. Maladaptive behaviors, such as self-stimulation and self-injury, could be decreased.

The negative findings from the same study were:

1. No child appeared to have achieved normal functioning.
2. No child developed social interactions or played with other children.
3. Treatment gains that were achieved in the clinic showed limited generalization to other environments and to behaviors that were not a focus of treatment.
4. Children who were discharged to psychiatric institutions lost all their treatment gains, although those who were discharged to their parents continued to improve as evidenced on follow-up measures taken two to three years after discharge.

The findings from the 1973 study are consistent with subsequent reports in the literature which showed that clients with autism made only small or temporary gains with behavioral treatment (Schreibman and Koegel 1975; Hemsley et al. 1978). However, the findings also suggested improvements in the treatment as described below.

The 1987 Follow-up Study

The negative findings in the 1973 study strongly influenced the design of the early intervention strategies that form the basis for the (Lovaas 1987) report. Numerous studies by other investigators also suggested refinements (Smith 1993). Four main changes were made: (1) The youngest children in the 1973 study had made the greatest progress. Treatment was, therefore, concentrated on very young children (mean chronological age of 34 months at intake). It was reasoned that the younger children would need less time to catch up with their typical peers because their maladaptive behaviors might be less excessive and disruptive. Their nervous systems might also be better able to assimilate new behaviors, such as language skills (Huttenlocher 1984). Once they caught up, their typical peers were likely to help increase behavioral growth and prevent relapses. (2) The 1987 study made specific attempts to teach children peer play and to mainstream them into normal pre-school environments. Programs to facilitate mainstreaming were not available in the 1960s; neither was the social or legal basis for such mainstreaming. (3) The 1973 study restricted the intensive treatment to one year. The 1987 study treated the clients intensively for two or more years, with 40 hours or more per week of one-to-one behavioral teaching combined with parent training. This amount of treatment more closely approximated the opportunities available to average children, who appear to learn from their environments most of their waking hours. (4) Because no solution to the limited response generalization (no pivotal or cardinal response) had been found, as many as possible of the children's behaviors were targeted. Failure to observe significant stimulus generalization necessitated that treatment be conducted in the children's everyday environments (home, school and neighborhood) rather than in offices or clinics.

The 1987 study contained three groups of children with autism: (a) an experimental (intensive treatment) group (n = 19); (b) a minimal treatment Control Group I (n = 19); and (c) a no-treatment Control Group II (n = 21). Subjects referred to the clinic were assigned to the experimental group or Control Group I based on therapist availability. If enough therapists were available, they entered the experimental group; otherwise, they entered Control Group I. Subjects in the experimental and Control Group I were similar on 19 out of 20 pretreatment variables that may have been predictive of outcome. These included IQ test scores, chronological age (CA) at diagnosis, toy play, peer play, presence of vocal speech, self-help skills, numbers of siblings, and socio-economic status of the family. Subjects in Control Group II were selected from another treatment agency based on the similarities of CA and IQ scores to children in the experimental group. (The same IQ tests were used.) Control Group II was included as a check on the representative sampling of children referred to the project. To be included in the study, subjects had to have a minimum ratio IQ of 37, because autism is difficult to distinguish from other diagnoses in children who obtain scores lower than 37 IQ (Wing 1981).

The 1987 follow-up study was conducted when the children were seven years old; that is, one to two years after discharge. Children in the experimental group had gained an average of 20 IQ points and had made major advances in educational achievement. Only one of 40 children in the two control groups achieved such a favorable outcome.

The 1993 Follow-up Study in Adolescence

The 1993 follow-up study was conducted when the children in the experimental group had reached an average age of 13 years. It showed that the experimental group as a whole had maintained its gains over the children in Control Group 1 (McEachin, Smith, and Lovaas 1993). Eight out of nine children who had been classified as best-outcome had remained in regular classes. Further, these eight children performed in the normal range on tests of intelligence, adaptive and emotional behavior, and personality, as well as in a clinical interview, when tested by examiners blind to who had originated the requests for assessment and blind as to the children's history of behavioral disturbance. The ninth subject maintained an IQ in the normal range and was not diagnosed with autism, but showed significant adjustment difficulties in other respects. (Control Group II children were not available for the 1993 follow-up).

The 1998 Follow-up Study in Adulthood

The 1998 follow-up study is in progress. It is comprised of a large range of assessments, including those designed to identify signs of subtle symptoms in individuals with high-level autism, such as abnormal social relationships, rigid thought processes, unusual ways of reasoning, lack of awareness of the thoughts and feelings of others, and impaired social and pragmatic language. Preliminary data on six out of the nine best outcome clients as adults show: (1) Mean IQ: 108 (compared to 107 at age 7 and 109 at age 12); (2) Superior performance on the *Wisconsin Card Sorting Task*; (3) *Normal Minnesota Multiphasic Personality Inventory* and *Rorschach* profiles; (4) Evidence of recognition of mental states of others; and (5) Independent functioning and relationships within the normal range on the *Socio-Emotional Functioning-II*. In summary, the children with best outcomes were able to maintain their gains into adulthood, showing normal intellectual and neuropsychological functioning without displaying clinically significant abnormal behavior on administered assessments, and achieving considerable independence and close relationships. A complete list and description of the various assessments and assessment protocol can be found in a grant entitled Long-Term Outcome of Early Intervention for Autism, #MH-51156.

EVIDENCE FOR GENERALIZATION ACROSS BEHAVIORS

The need to address all or most of the behaviors in autism is at variance with the position that major changes may occur by addressing one or two *pivotal* behaviors. Despite the failure to identify a pivotal behavior, there was evidence of therapeutic changes in a limited number of behaviors not specifically targeted for early intervention. This was the case in emotional behavior, social interactions, and cognitive functioning.

Emotions and Emotional Behaviors

Emotions and emotional behaviors such as happiness, attachment, fear, and sadness gradually emerged during the course of treatment. Many or most of these were attributed to the treatment that provided the child with control of and access to an increasingly larger and varied range of effective reinforcers. For example, the children evidenced happiness and joy as they achieved success and avoided failure; they became sad when their parents left.

Social Interactions

Social interactions increased in proportion to the children's acquiring a large range of related behaviors, such as tantrum control, self-help skills, like dressing and toileting, conversational skills, and appropriate toy play. Scores obtained from *Vineland Adaptive Behavior Scales* when the children reached 13 years of age showed a significant increase as well (McEachin, Smith, and Lovaas 1993).

Investigators from UCLA's Neuropsychiatric Institute (UCLA-NPI) and Treatment and Education of Autistic and Related Communication Handicapped Children (TEACCH) at the University of North Carolina have suggested that intensive behavioral treatment may not foster independence. A direct comparison of independence, as assessed by *Vineland Adaptive Behavior Scales*, exists and can be used to address this claim. Scores on the *Vineland* are analogous to those obtained on IQ tests (m = 100; SD = 16) and are presented in table I. The UCLA-NPI data were collected on children, originally seen at ages 2 to 3 years, who had reached an average age of 15 years (Freeman et al. 1991). The TEACCH data were collected only on high functioning autistic children at an average age of 14 years (Venter, Lord, and Schopler 1992). The *Vineland* subscale scores of means at

TABLE I. *Vineland* Subscale Scores Expressed as Means.

Vineland Scale	UCLA YAP	UCLA-NPI	TEACCH
Communication	75.1	56.6	47.6
Daily Living Skills	73.1	54.6	49.1
Socialization	75.5	51.6	38.1
Composite	71.6	50.3	41.6

UCLA Young Autism Project (YAP), UCLA-NPI, and TEACCH, expressed as standard scores, are presented in table I.

In looking at table I, intensively treated children at UCLA,YAP appeared to function substantially more independently and competently in all areas when compared to children at UCLA-NPI or TEACCH. The increase in *Vineland* scores is consistent with Waterhouse's position (1988) that competent social behavior is a function of prior acquisition of numerous "sub-skills."

Cognitive Functioning

Cognitive deficits have been proposed as a contributing cause in autism (Rutter 1983). Yet, some have expressed hopes that IQ gains could be possible (e.g., Bryant and Ramey 1987). Most have expressed doubts (Guralnick and Brickner 1987). Zigler and Trickett (1978) have suggested that "efforts to dramatically alter IQ scores are bound to fail" (p. 357) and Spitz (1986) characterized those who reported such increases as "fools, frauds, and charlatans." In any case, cognitive functioning increased by 20 IQ points in the group as a whole (McEachin, Smith, and Lovaas 1993), even though it was not specifically targeted for intervention; that is, the project did not specifically teach the tasks assessed in IQ tests. As in the case of increased social behavior, increases in IQ scores and educational achievement seemed to be consequences of the children's gaining competence across a large range of behaviors. Behavioral psychologists consider IQ scores as one measure of what a person has learned up to the time of testing (cf. Nelson 1993).

EXPERIMENTAL SAFEGUARDS

A large number of publications have questioned the adequacy of the reported findings. Such questions are important because they help define what constitutes requirements for adequate treatment research. A discussion of six areas of concern have been presented in some detail by McEachin, Smith, and Lovaas (1993) as well as in commentaries by Foxx (1993); Kazdin (1993); Mesibov (1993); and Mundy (1993). More detailed comments regarding questions about design and outcome data are provided in Smith and Lovaas (1997). Four important areas of concern are briefly described below.

1. Did Subject Selection Result in a Representative Sample of Autistic Children?
   All children were independently diagnosed with autism by M.D. or Ph.D. licensed clinicians, and there was consensus on the diagnosis among the independent examiners (see Lovaas 1987). Altogether, 20 pretreatment variables, considered to be descriptive of autism and/or related to outcome, were assessed. These variables did not favor high-functioning children who might have a favorable prognosis regardless of treatment (Schopler, Short, and Mesibov 1989). In two large-scale investigations of IQ scores in preschool children, higher-functioning children at intake showed the least improvement over time (Freeman et al. 1985; Lord and Schopler 1989).
2. Did Subject Assignment Result in Equivalent Groups?
   Assignment to the experimental or control group was made on the basis of therapist availability, determined prior to family contact with the clinic. This is a generally accepted procedure in clinical research (Kazdin 1980) and one that has been employed in several highly-regarded outcome studies on children with autism (e.g., Bartak and Rutter 1973; Howlin and Rutter 1987). The groups did not differ on 19 of the 20 pre-treatment variables (variables such as recognizable speech, IQ scores, CA at diagnosis, number of siblings, and socioeconomic status of family). Thus, the subject assignment procedure yielded groups comparable to each other prior to treatment on factors that could predict outcome, supporting the inference that the assignment had produced equivalent groups. Differences at follow-up can, therefore, be attributed to the treatment provided to the experimental group.
3. Are Treatment Effects Believable and Durable?
   The following observations are relevant: (a) In the McEachin, Smith, and Lovaas (1993) outcome study, conducted an average of six years after discharge, a wide range of assessment measures were administered to avoid over-reliance on intelligence tests which have limitations if used in isolation. (b) The follow-up evaluation used reliable, standardized tests and double-blind examination procedures (selection of examiners by professionals who were not associated with the Project and who did not reveal the UCLA YAP as the source of the request). Comparisons with normal children were included to prevent bias that could occur if examiners only

tested children with obvious signs of pathology. Such evaluations allowed for objective, detailed, and quantifiable assessments of treatment effectiveness.

4. Can Treatment be Replicated?

   Two major questions arise in all treatment research. One concerns replicability of the treatment protocol by different service providers. The other concerns replication of outcome data across children with the same diagnosis, but from different social and geographic environments. At present, some 13 replication sites across the United States and Europe have employed staff who have passed the academic background and required a nine-month full-time internship using the UCLA treatment model. The first reports on replicability were submitted to peer-reviewed journals in 1999. A more detailed description of this project is provided in a grant entitled Multi-site Young Autism Project, #MH48863.

Outcome data from investigators not associated with the UCLA multi-site project have reported major improvements in children's cognitive growth following early and intensive behavioral intervention with treatment programs similar to those employed by the UCLA YAP (Fenske et al. 1985; Harris et al. 1991). Although these projects support replicability, long-term follow-up studies of these children are needed, as are data on their emotional and social post-treatment adjustment. A comprehensive review of early and behavioral intervention is provided by Smith (1999). A teaching manual (Lovaas et al. 1981) and associated video-tapes (Lovaas and Leaf 1981) describe the treatment components in detail and include additional information for facilitating replication.

TRADITIONAL TREATMENT RESEARCH

It may be helpful to contrast traditional and behavioral approaches to research and treatment of children diagnosed with autism. By *traditional* assumptions we refer to Kanner's (1943) hypothesis that autism represents a distinct diagnostic category whereby behaviors (referred to as symptoms) are held together by a central dysfunction. Once this central dysfunction is located and treated, the various behavioral deviations can be normalized. Kanner's hypothesis is traditional in the sense that it represents the first attempt to define a separate diagnostic category.

Kanner's approach constitutes an example of theory-driven research. On the basis of relatively few observations (in Kanner's case, 11 children), an inferential leap is made in the form of a theory from which a large number of smaller hypotheses pertaining to causes and treatments are deduced. Various smaller-case experiments are then designed to test the theory. If confirmed, these smaller studies help validate the larger theoretical statement. Such an approach has yielded major discoveries in the physical and biological sciences.

Kanner's hypothesis has helped generate a large variety of treatments with a common assumption; that is, that by addressing one or a limited set of cardinal behaviors or processes for a limited time, and in a clinical or segregated setting, comprehensive improvements will occur across most or all of the clients' behaviors and generalize across all significant environments.

Examples of such treatments include Psychodynamic Therapy, Holding Therapy, *Fast ForWord*, Gentle Teaching, Facilitated Communication, Pet therapies, Doman-Delacato method, Auditory Integration, Joint Attention Hypothesis, Sensory Integration, Music Therapy, Floor Time method, and the Option method.

Since little is known about autism, almost anyone can propose a cause or treatment for it. The many behavioral deviations demonstrated by persons diagnosed with autism allow one to choose one or more deviations as the *cardinal symptom* or *pivotal response* which, once ameliorated, would help normalize the rest. In the history of treatment for autism, almost every behavioral deviation (language, attention, social, cognition, emotional) as well as combinations of behaviors (e.g., social/emotional, language/cognitive) have been proposed as the cause of autism. Given the large number of behavioral deviations and the large number of combinations and permutations of these, it is likely that an ever larger number of treatments will be proposed in the future.

Although it is beneficial to scientific progress that a problem be viewed from several perspectives, two major problems have beset most traditional approaches to date. One is the difficulty in providing empirical tests for the various hypothetical constructs and establishing causal relationships. For example, an investigator may present data showing that a particular brain structure is inadequately developed in a sample of autistic individuals and propose that the deviant brain structure (e.g., the cerebellum) may be the cause of autism (Courchesne et al. 1988). The difficulty is to rule out the reverse, namely, that the autistic behaviors caused the deviant brain structure in the first place; and, secondly, to decide if it is possible for individuals to possess such a deviant structure without becoming autistic.

Another investigator (Frith 1993) proposed that normal individuals possess *empathy*, hypothesized as basic in evaluating one's own thought processes and those of others. This ability is thought to be the product of an innate cognitive structure located somewhere in the frontal cortex. This structure is proposed to be lacking in autism because children who are autistic show deficits in reciprocal social interaction, failure to make friends, failure to engage in fantasy, and failure in all the other desirable and defining features of human beings.

Finally, because of innate origins, the deficits and resulting autism cannot be *cured*. The problems with such elaborate arrangements of hypothetical constructs lie in the many unobservable behaviors which render empirical testing of validity and causal relationships difficult or impossible. The same problems, of being outside scientific scrutiny, characterized Freud's theory of neurosis and several other theories in clinical psychology and psychiatry.

The second problem, regarding treatments for autism, involves failure to report outcome data. The absence of outcome data constitutes a major difficulty because it prolongs treatments that may ultimately be found ineffective or harmful (as in the case of psychodynamic interventions and certain drug treatments such as Phenfloramine). The difficulty in developing sensitive measures for autism may be due, in part, to the difficulty in manipulating complex independent variables such as cognition, attention, and emotional bonding. There are other risks which may not be readily apparent, such as attributing a *reduction in autism* to changes in one or two behaviors when these are conceptualized as *symptoms of autism*. Increase in eye contact and decrease in self-stimulatory behaviors may be used for that purpose; yet both behaviors fluctuate in response to a large range of environmental influences.

Inadequate information about treatment outcomes of traditional interventions is also likely to delay the search for effective treatment plans. Psychodynamic treatments are a case in point. Dominating the field for more than 40 years, psychodynamic treatments were stimulated by Kanner's publication in 1943 and are still being practiced in many parts of the world. Early on, Rimland (1964) provided much circumstantial evidence questioning the efficacy of psychodynamic therapy for autism and presented data supporting an organic etiology. Over the years, many others have objected to the treatment as well. Objective outcome data would have put an end to this harmful treatment at a much earlier time. Finally, without outcome data, there is no way of knowing which interventions should be discarded and which should be kept, so as to build a cumulative body of knowledge about autism. We have not learned how to build on the work of others.

As failures to demonstrate effective treatments accumulate, a concomitant increase in pessimism about finding a solution to the cause and treatment of autism has developed. DeMyer, Hingtgen, and Jackson (1981) expressed this as follows: "In the past, psychotic children were believed to be potentially capable of normal functioning in virtually all areas of development . . . during the decade of the 1970s, it was the rare investigator who gave even lip-service to such previously held notions . . . infantile autism is a type of developmental disorder accompanied by severe and, to a large extent, permanent intellectual/behavioral deficits" (p. 432). Concurrently, there is an increase in the use of terms denoting damage. Terms like *pathology, impaired, disordered, unable, deficient*, and *defective* are frequently used. The failures to raise IQ and develop language, referred to earlier in this chapter, have more often been attributed to organic damage than to inadequate interventions. At the same time, behaviors that could be considered evidence for strength are classified as symptoms of illness. Echolalia (imitation of speech) is a case in point. The presence of echolalia implies that the client's nervous system is capable of both processing a complex auditory stimulus and generating an auditory response which matches the stimulus, no minor achievement. Unusually good memory is classified as *autistic savant* features, despite their potential significance in retention of learned material. Finally, by conceptualizing the cause of autism as based on a central dysfunction, and normalization of behaviors as based on the removal of this cause, behavioral interventions seem to be precluded from offering anything but superficial *symptom* alleviation ". . . as a means of ameliorating some of the deficits and difficulties associated with autism, not as a cure for the fundamental disorder" (Howlin 1997, p. 60).

Some words of caution are in order. It is important to recognize that Kanner's diagnosis represents an hypothesis which may have hindered research as to causes and effective treatments for children so diagnosed. Helping these children may not be so difficult as many have implied. In this context Rutter (1978) cautions that "Kanner's use of the term autism was more than a simple label, and that is where the trouble really increases. It was also an hypothesis—a suggestion that behind the behavioral description lay a disease entity" (p. 3). Lovaas (1971) expressed his reservations as follows: "The diagnosis of autism may lead to premature decisions about what it is we are studying. An empirical and functional definition of 'autism,' or autistic behaviors, may become very different from what we have considered here. . . . Autistic children present a whole set of behaviors and these different behaviors have different properties. The problem behaviors may not hang together" (p. 109). To place the issue in sharper perspective: children diagnosed with autism may be described as children diagnosed with an hypothesis. Kraeplin's (1981) diagnosis of schizophrenia as a unique disorder (disease) is an example of such an hypothesis. Research on schizophrenia, like autism, has yet to identify the cause(s) or effective treatments for persons so diagnosed.

Both traditional and behavioral approaches would agree that the diagnosis of autism predicts the future of children so diagnosed, and provides the ultimate test of treatment efficacy. The diagnosis has also helped organize children's parents, such as establishing the Autism Society of America to provide information and emotional support for parents and help bring problems regarding autism to the attention of the public and granting agencies.

INDUCTIVE VERSUS THEORY-DRIVEN RESEARCH

Perhaps the question of who is right, behavioral or traditional, can be clarified by contrasting two different strategies for gathering information: theory-driven (hypothetico-deductive) research versus data-driven (inductive) research. Theory-driven research places its focus on generalizations about underlying causes of a phenomenon relatively early in the research process and based on relatively few data. Hypotheses are derived from these generalizations and subjected to empirical tests leading to rejection or support for the theory. If the theory turns out to be right, there may be a big pay-off. To illustrate, if the cause of autism were to be discovered and the cause removed, a large number of problems would be eliminated at once. But, if the data do not support the theory, there is no pay-off. Data-driven research is more inductive in that more data are collected before reaching a comprehensive theoretical formulation. The process is cumulative, new facts build upon, rather than replace older findings. Lovaas and Smith (1989) have provided a more detailed presentation of how the two approaches differ in research and treatment of autism.

AN EVOLUTIONARY PERSPECTIVE

It may be more parsimonious and productive to collectively consider the behavioral deviations in persons diagnosed with autism, not as those caused by a unique disease, but as variability across nervous systems caused by evolutionary forces. (Variability is inevitable because it is essential for survival.) The search for evolutionary causes may help us better understand and treat the autistic individual. Space allows for only a brief description of four observations that support such a proposal.

First, most behaviors of autistic individuals may occur with less frequency among typical individuals, including normal infants (Rutter 1978). The variability, which may include instances of mild autistic behavior (Landa et al. 1992), across and within the behaviors of autistic individuals (e.g., from low- 169to high-functioning) may differ from typical individuals in degree rather than in kind. The form of the learning curves generated by autistic persons is similar to those generated by typical individuals. This allows for autistic persons to be considered as belonging to the natural order of life.

Secondly, evolutionary forces may have favored some individuals who sought solitude and escape from what they experienced as the aversive properties of increasingly crowded social places. Our nervous systems were not selected for survival in crowded cities or other densely populated areas. Rather, our nervous systems evolved to match small groups with lesser demands on verbal and social interaction. Creating distance from others is likely to have freed some individuals from social conventions or other restrictions and enhanced the individual's expression of novel ideas in art and science. Painters like Edvard Munch and Vincent Van Gogh illustrate this phenomenon. Both painted obsessively, independent of social reinforcement, defining art for the future.

Thirdly, a Darwinian interpretation of autism is consistent with evidence that autism may be based on a genetic etiology (DeMyer, Hingtgen, and Jackson 1981; Rutter 1978; and Rutter et al. 1993). Several articles in this volume discuss genetic contributions to autism. Nesse and Williams (1996) have presented an extensive description of how evolutionary forces could be causing many medical diseases and mental health problems, including schizophrenia, depression, and panic disorders. Their discussion focuses on adaptations, including the cost of adaptations, mismatches between nervous systems and current environments, and the like.

Although there is strength in variability, nature overshot her mark in most cases of autism. As evolution selected for higher levels of solitary existence, some individuals ended up with extreme solitude, as in autism. Evolution is fraught with errors. Some genes cause "quirks" that are harmless in some environments, but may cause detrimental functioning in others. Autism may be the terrible price we pay for survival and progress.

Finally, in designing interventions for autistic individuals, one may assume that their failure to develop was based on mismatches between their nervous systems and the average environments, as often occurs in evolution. The average environment serves the average nervous system best, perhaps, because the average environment evolved (was shaped by) the average nervous system. That same environment, however, is unlikely to teach the unusual nervous system adequately, leaving the autistic person with severe delays and necessitating the discovery of new and functional learning environments. Behavioral treatment is based on the laws of learning, developed from research on how typical organisms learn, and modified to the extent of becoming functional for the autistic individual. The success of such treatments provide further support for the continuity in learning processes between typical and autistic individuals. An evolutionary perspective and a detailed design of learning-based treatments have been presented by Lovaas et al. (1981).

If a common underlying problem is not organizing and grouping behaviors observed in the diagnosis of autism, what then could be the reason for the similarities among the children that enables one to reach the diagnosis? Perhaps what is now called autism represents a random collection of behaviors, each behavior occurring with relatively low frequency in the typical population. The larger the number of behavioral deviations constituting the diagnosis, the lower the incidence of the diagnosis. Considering the possibility that autism consists of the largest number of deviant behaviors, it should be less frequently diagnosed (1/1000 births, Klinger and Dawson 1996) and be the most resistant to treatment. Attention Deficit Disorder (ADD) is likely to represent a smaller number of low-frequency behaviors and, hence, be more frequently diagnosed 4/100 (Davison and Neale 1974). Asperger's syndrome is reported as 3/1000 (Ozbayrak 1998) and schizophrenia at 1/100 (Davison and Neale 1974), both representing intermediate numbers of low-frequency behaviors. Treatment provided would address the various diagnostic entities on a behavior-by-behavior basis, but would not be unique to each diagnosis, except in extent.

PROBLEMS

The 40 hours per week of one-to-one treatment for an average of two years per child requires a major investment of time, expense, and commitment, both from staff and parents. Estimated cost of treatment can be placed at $5,000 per month or $120,000 for two years of treatment. This expense should be evaluated in contrast to the significant cost of life-long care and special services estimated at an average of $40,000 per year for a total of $2.4 million, given the normal life expectancy of persons diagnosed with autism. The educational background of service providers is demanding and includes an academic background in learning and behavior, as well as a nine-month full-time internship at UCLA or at one of the replication sites, if following the regimen of the UCLA Young Autism Project. After such training, the service provider will still need continuous supervision and consultation from qualified colleagues, given the enormous variability among clients necessitating a team approach, all of which restricts the application of the intervention. Replication of treatment outcome is critical; data from long-term follow-up studies may take several years to secure.

Furthermore, any body of prior research, including the research which provided the basis for the laws of learning, may obscure and restrict one's inquiry. It is, therefore, important for the investigator to keep an open mind for alternative treatment variables. The failure to improve, significantly, the functioning of more than one-half of the intensive treatment group reflects a major challenge in view of the likelihood that the project may have exhausted what is currently known about the laws of learning. Behavioral treatment appears to be ineffective in reducing problems associated with Rett syndrome (Smith, Klevstrand, and Lovaas 1995).

Various alternatives are open, such as awaiting discoveries of learning-based variables to enhance the effectiveness of behavioral treatments. Another alternative is to start treatment during the first year of life, when the nervous system is maximally redundant and, perhaps, more capable of correcting its deviations (Huttenlocher 1984). Designing a learning environment that relies on visual rather than on auditory forms of communication, as in reading and writing (Watthen, Lovaas, and Eikeseth in preparation) or sign language (Carr 1979) may also help. Neurobiological research may identify, and some day, help to modify the neurological deviations so that learning language and verbal imitation can be accelerated. Recent progress in identifying brain-behavior relationships through functional Magnetic Resonance Imagining (MRI) and Event-Related Brain Potential is likely to offer valuable aid in this search.

CONCLUDING COMMENTS

The contrast between traditional and newer behavioral approaches is substantial. The behavioral approach, described here, places its focus on a functional analysis of separate causes and treatments for separate behaviors, whether these variables are biological, environmental, or both. A functional (rather than the hitherto nominal) definition of these children's problem behaviors reveal extensive individual differences across children, as well as across behaviors of the same diagnosis or topography. No currently available theory of autism can account for such diversity.

Behaviorists do not *treat autism* and do not search for the *causes of autism*. Research generated within the traditional framework has not contributed data which would facilitate or guide behavioral treatment research. In a very real sense, behaviorists started from the beginning. The replacement of an older and established paradigm with a new orientation has been referred to as a paradigm shift (Kuhn 1970), a radical shift that is accomplished by many and that takes time to be actualized. Although the paradigm shift described here has vastly less impact than those described in Kuhn, millions of dollars may have been wasted on discovering the cause and treatment of autism without ever having relieved the burdens of the persons affected by this problem.

CHAPTER SUMMARY

1. Instead of focusing on a hypothetical construct of autism, the UCLA Young Autism Project measured twelve specific behaviors (ten delays and two excesses), and experimentally manipulated environmental variables to identify those treatments which increased behavioral delays and decreased behavioral excesses.
2. The behaviors which characterize the children diagnosed with autism can be observed in transient form in typical individuals and, particularly, in young children. Furthermore, these behaviors have shown themselves to be subject to the laws of learning that govern all organisms.
3. Learning-based approaches have demonstrated an increase in cognitive, social, emotional, attentional, and other significant delays in autism.
4. There is limited evidence for generalization across behaviors (few, if any, "pivotal responses") and limited generalization across environments and persons. Given this finding, treatment is provided for each behavioral delay and behavioral excess and is conducted across many environments with the participation of most significant adults.
5. Preliminary studies support that more intensive (40 hours a week, one-to-one, for two years duration) and earlier (starting at age 2 years) behavioral interventions offer the best promise for sustained improvements in autism.
6. Behavioral delays are considered a mismatch between the child's deviant nervous system and the average environment. It may be more parsimonious and consistent with available data to consider the behavioral delays collectively, as variability across nervous systems caused by evolutionary forces, not as that caused by a unique disease requiring a unique treatment. Genetic causation supports such a position.
7. There does not appear to be any bias in selection of study groups to restrict significantly the applicability of the research findings for early and intensive behavioral interventions.
8. Apart from research (some completed, some in progress) on the effectiveness of the UCLA Young Autism Project, comprehensive and long-term outcome studies on the effectiveness of treatment approaches for autism are seriously lacking.
9. A significant feature of behavioral intervention is its reliance on experimental research design which involves an experimental manipulation of the treatment variables and accurate and precise measures of treatment outcomes.

10. There is wide variability, a 47% to 53% split of best to non-best outcome, across children treated according to the UCLA protocol. Future discoveries in brain-behavior relationships are likely to be needed to help accelerate improvements with learning-based treatments.

AUTHOR'S NOTE

This study was supported by Grant MH-51156 from the National Institute of Mental Health. Special thanks to Tristram Smith, Ph.D., for his helpful comments during the preparation of this manuscript and to Kristin O'Hanlon for editorial assistance. Correspondence concerning this article should be addressed to: O. Ivar Lovaas, Department of Psychology, University of California, P.O. Box 951563, Los Angeles, California 90095-1563.

REFERENCES

Baer, D. M., Guess, D., and Sherman, J. 1972. Adventures in simplistic grammar. In *Language of the Mentally Retarded*, ed. R.L. Schiefelbusch. Baltimore, MD: University Park.

Bandura, A. 1969. Social learning theory of identificatory processes. In *Handbook of Socialization Theory and Research*, ed. D. A. Goslin. Chicago: Rand McNally.

Bartak, L., and Rutter, M. 1973. Special educational treatment of autistic children: A comparative study: Design of study and characteristics of units. *Journal of Child Psychology and Psychiatry* 14:161–79.

Bijou, S. W., and Donitz-Johnson, E. 1981. Interbehavioral analysis of developmental retardation. *Psychological Record* 31:305–29.

Bryant, D. M., and Ramey, C. T. 1987. An analysis of the effectiveness of early intervention for environmentally at-risk children. In *The Effectiveness of Early Intervention for At-risk and Handicapped Children*, eds. M. J. Guralnick and F. C. Bennett. New York: Academic Press.

Carr, E. G. 1979. Teaching autistic children to use sign language: Some research issues. *Journal of Autism and Developmental Disorders* 9:345–59.

Carr, E. G., Newsom, C. D., and Binkoff, J. A. 1976. Stimulus control of self-destructive behavior in a psychotic child. *Journal of Abnormal Child Psychology* 3:331–51.

Charlop, M. H., and Milstein, J. P. 1989. Teaching autistic children conversational speech using video modeling. *Journal of Applied Behavior Analysis* 22(3):275–85.

Chomsky, N. 1965. *Aspects of the Theory of Syntax*. Cambridge, MA: The M.I.T. Press.

Churchill, D. W. 1978. Language: The problem beyond conditioning. In *Autism: A Reappraisal of Concepts and Treatment*, eds. M. Rutter and E. Schopler. New York: Plenum.

Courchesne, E., Yeung-Courchesne, R., Press, G. A., Hesselink, J. R., and Jernign, T. L. 1988. Hypoplasia of cerebellar vermal lobules VI and VII in autism. *New England Journal of Medicine* 318(21):1349–54.

Davison, G. C., and Neale, J. M. 1974. *Abnormal Psychology*. New York: John Wiley and Sons, Inc.

DeMyer, M. K., Hingtgen, J. N., and Jackson, R. K. 1981. Infantile autism reviewed: A decade of research. *Schizophrenia Bulletin* 7:388–451.

Epstein, L., Taubman, M., and Lovaas, O. I. 1985. Changes in self-stimulatory behaviors with treatment. *Journal of Abnormal Child Psychology* 13:281–94.

Favell, J. E., McGimsey, J. F., and Schell, R. M. 1982. Treatment of self-injury by providing alternative sensory activities. *Analysis and Intervention in Developmental Disabilities* 2:83–104.

Fenske, E. C., Zalenski, S., Krantz, P. J., and McClannahan, L. E. 1985. Age at intervention and treatment outcome for autistic children in a comprehensive intervention program. *Analysis and Intervention in Developmental Disabilities* 5:49–58.

Ferster, C. B. 1961. Positive reinforcement and behavioral deficits of autistic children. *Child Development* 32:437–56.

Foxx, R. M. 1993. Sapid effects awaiting independent replication. *American Journal on Mental Retardation* 97:375–76.

Freeman, B. J., Rahbar, B., Ritvo, E., Bice, T. L., Yokota, A., and Ritvo, R. 1991. The stability of cognitive and behavioral parameters in autism: A twelve-year prospective study. *Journal of the American Academy of Child Psychiatry* 30:479–82.

Freeman, B. J., Ritvo, E. R., Needleman, R., and Yokota, A. 1985. The stability of cognitive and linguistic parameters in autism: A five-year prospective study. *Journal of the American Academy of Child Psychiatry* 24:459–64.

Frith, U. 1993. Autism. *Scientific American*, June, 108–14.

Gaylord-Ross, R. J., Haring, T. G., Breen, C., and Pitts-Conway, V. 1984. The training and generalization of social interaction skills with autistic youth. *Journal of Applied Behavior Analysis* 17:229–47.

Goldfried, M. R., and Kent, J. 1972. Traditional terms versus behavioral personality assessment: A comparison of methodological and theoretical assumptions. *Psychological Bulletin* 77:409–20.

Granpeesheh, D. 1990. Teaching common preschool games to autistic children to increase interaction with peers. Unpublished doctoral dissertation, University of California, Los Angeles.

Greenough, W. T., Volkmar, F. R., and Juraska, J. M. 1973. Effects of rearing complexity in dendritic branching in frontolateral and temporal cortex of the rat. *Experimental Neurology* 41:371–78.

Greenwood, C. R., Carta, J. J., Hart, B., Kamps, D., Terry, B., Arreaga-Mayer, C., Atwater, J., Walker, D., Risely, R., and Delquadri, J. C. 1992. Out of the laboratory and into the community: 26 years of applied behavior analysis at the Juniper Garderns Children's Project. *American Psychologist* 47:1464–74.

Guralnick, M. J., and Bricker, D. 1987. The effectiveness of early intervention for children with cognitive and general developmental delays. In *The Effectiveness of Early Intervention for At-risk and Handicapped Children*, eds. M. J. Guralnick and F. C. Bennett. New York: Academic Press.

Haring, T. G., Roger, B., Lee, M., Breen, C., and Gaylord-Ross, R. 1986. Teaching social language to moderately handicapped students. *Journal of Applied Behavior Analysis* 19:159–71.

Harris, S., Handleman, J., Gordon, R., Kristoff, B., and Fuentes, F. 1991. Changes in cognitive and language functioning of preschool children with autism. *Journal of Autism and Developmental Disorders* 21:281–90.

Hemsley, R., Howlin, P., Berger, M., Hersov, L., Holbrook, D., Rutter, M., and Yule, W. 1978. Treating autistic children in a family context. In *Autism: A Reappraisal of Concepts and Treatment*, eds. M. Rutter and E. Schopler. New York: Plenum.

Howlin, P. A. 1981. The effectiveness of operant language training with autistic children. *Journal of Autism and Developmental Disorders* 11:89–105.

Howlin, P. A. 1997. Prognosis in autism: Do specialist treatments affect long-term outcome? *European Child and Adolescent Psychiatry* 6:55–72.

Howlin, P. A., and Rutter, M. 1987. *Treatment of Autistic Children.* New York: Wiley.

Hung, D. W. 1977. Generalization of "curiosity" questioning behavior in autistic children. *Journal of Behavior Therapy and Experimental Psychiatry* 8:237–45.

Hung, D. W. 1980. Training and generalization of yes and no as mands in two autistic children. *Journal of Autism and Developmental Disorders* 10:139–52.

Huttenlocher, P. R. 1984. Synapse elimination and plasticity in developing human cerebral cortex. *American Journal of Mental Deficiency* 88:488–96.

Kanner, L. 1943. Autistic disturbances of affective contact. *The Nervous Child* 2:217–50.

Kazdin, A. E. 1980. *Research Design in Clinical Psychology.* New York: Harper and Row.

Kazdin, A. E. 1993. Replication and extension of behavioral treatment of autistic disorder. *American Journal on Mental Retardation* 97:377–79.

Klinger, L. G. and Dawson, G. 1996. Autistic disorder. In *Child Psychopathology*, eds. E. J. Mash and R. A. Barklay. New York: Guilford.

Kraeplin, E. 1981. *Clinical Psychiatry* (A. R. Diefendorf, trans.) Delmar, NY: Scholars' Facsimiles and Reprints (original work published in 1883).

Kravitz, H., and Boehm, J. J. 1971. Rhythmic habit patterns in infancy: Their sequence, age of onset, and frequency. *Child Development* 42:399–413.

Kuhn, T. S. 1970. *The Structure of Scientific Revolutions.* Chicago: University of Chicago Press.

Landa, R., Piven, J., Wzorek, M. M., Gayle, J. O., Chase, G. A., and Folstein, S. E. 1992. Social language use in parents of autistic individuals. *Psychological Medicine* 22:245–54.

Lewy, A. L., and Dawson, G. 1992. Social stimulation and joint attention in young autistic children. *Journal of Abnormal Child Psychology* 20(6):555–66.

Lord, C., and Schopler, E. 1989. The role of age at assessment, developmental level, and test in the stability of intelligence scores in young autistic children. *Journal of Autism and Developmental Disorder* 19:483–99.

Lovaas, O. I. 1971. Considerations in the development of a behavioral treatment program for psychotic children. In *Infantile Autism. Proceedings of the Indiana University Colloquium*, eds. D. W. Churchill., G. D. Alpern, and M. K. DeMyer. Springfield, IL: Charles C Thomas.

Lovaas, O. I. 1977. *The Autistic Child: Language Development Through Behavior Modification.* New York: Irvington.

Lovaas, O. I. 1987. Behavioral treatment and normal educational and intellectual functioning in young autistic children. *Journal of Consulting and Clinical Psychology* 55:3–9.

Lovaas, O. I., Ackerman, A., Alexander, D., Firestone, P., Perkins, J., and Young, D. 1981. *Teaching Developmentally Disabled Children: The ME Book.* Austin, Texas: PRO-ED.

Lovaas, O. I., Berberich, J. P., Perloff, B. F., and Schaeffer, B. 1966. Acquisition of imitative speech by schizophrenic children. *Science* 151:705–07.

Lovaas, O. I., Freitag, G., Gold, B. J., and Kassorla, I. C. 1965. Experimental studies in childhood schizophrenia: Analysis of self-destructive behavior. *Journal of Experimental Child Psychology* 2:67–84.

Lovaas, O. I., Freitas, L., Nelson, K., and Whalen, C. 1967. The establishment of imitation and its use for the development of complex behavior in schizophrenic children. *Behavior Research and Therapy* 5:171–81.

Lovaas, O. I., Koegel, R. L., and Schreibman, L. 1979. Stimulus overselectivity in autism: A review of research. *Psychological Bulletin* 86(6):1236–54.
Lovaas, O. I., Koegel, R. L., Simmons, J. Q., and Long, J. S. 1973. Some generalization and follow-up measures on autistic children in behavior therapy. *Journal of Applied Behavior Analysis* 6:131–66.
Lovaas, O. I., and Leaf, R. 1981. Five Video Tapes for Teaching Developmentally Disabled Children. Austin, Texas: PRO-ED.
Lovaas, O. I., Newsom, C., and Hickman, C. 1987. Self-stimulatory behavior and perceptual reinforcement. *Journal of Applied Behavior Analysis* 20:45–68.
Lovaas, O. I., Schaeffer, B., and Simmons, J. Q. 1965. Building social behaviors in autistic children by use of electric shock. *Journal of Experimental Research in Personality* 1:99–109.
Lovaas, O. I., and Simmons, J. Q. 1969. Manipulation of self-destruction in three retarded children. *Journal of Applied Behavior Analysis* 2:143–57.
Lovaas, O. I., and Smith, T. 1988. Intensive behavioral treatment with young autistic children. In *Advances in Clinical Child Psychology*, eds. B. B. Lahey and A. E. Kazdin. New York: Plenum.
Lovaas, O. I., and Smith, T. 1989. A comprehensive behavioral theory of autistic children. *Journal of Behavior Therapy and Experimental Psychiatry* 20:17–29.
Matson, J. L., and Taras, M. E. 1989. A 20-year review of punishment and alternative methods to treat problem behaviors in developmentally delayed persons. *Research in Developmental Disabilities* 10:85–104.
McEachin, J. J., Smith, T., and Lovaas, O. I. 1993. Long-term outcome for children with autism who received early intensive behavioral intervention. *American Journal of Mental Retardation* 97:359–72.
Mesibov, G. B. 1993. Treatment outcome is encouraging. *American Journal on Mental Retardation* 97:379–80.
Mundy, P. 1993. Normal versus high functioning status in children with autism. *American Journal on Mental Retardation* 97:381–84.
Mundy, P., and Sigman, M. 1989. The theoretical implications of joint-attention deficits in autism. *Development and Psychopathology* 1:173–83.
Nelson, R. O. 1993. Behavioral assessment: Past, present, and future. *Behavioral Assessment* 5:195–206.
Nesse, R. M., and Williams, G. C. 1996. *Why We Get Sick.* New York: Random House, Inc.
Newsom, C., and Rincover, A. 1989. Autism. In *Treatment of Childhood Disorders*, eds. E. J. Mash and R. A. Barkley. New York: The Guilford Press.
Ozbayrak, K. H. 1998. Asperger's Disorder Homepage. http://www.ummed.edu/pub/o/ozobayrak/asperger.html
Rincover, A., and Newsom, C. D. 1985. The relative motivational properties of sensory and edible reinforcers in teaching autistic children. *Journal of Applied Behavior Analysis* 18:237–48.
Rimland, B. 1964. *Infantile Autism.* New York: Appleton-Century-Crofts.
Risley, T., Hart, B., and Doke, L. 1972. Operant language development: The outline of a therapeutic technology. In *Language of the Mentally Retarded*, ed. R. L. Schiefelbusch. Baltimore, MD: University Park.
Risley, T., and Wolf, M. 1967. Establishing functional speech in autistic children. *Behaviour Research and Therapy* 5:73–88.
Rutter, M. 1978. Diagnosis and Definition. In *Autism: A Reappraisal of Concepts and Treatment*, eds. M. Rutter and E. Schopler. New York: Plenum Press.
Rutter, M. 1985. The treatment of autistic children. *Journal of Child Psychology and Psychiatry* 26:193–214.
Rutter, M. 1983. Cognitive deficit in the pathogenesis of autism. *Journal of Child Psychology and Psychiatry* 14:241–70.

Rutter, M., Bailey, A., Bolton, P., and LeCouteur, A. 1993. Autism: Syndrome definition and possible genetic mechanism. In *Nature, Nurture, and Psychology*, eds. R. Plomin and G. E. McClearn. Washington, D.C.: American Psychological Association.

Schopler, E., Short, A., and Mesibov, G. 1989. Relation of behavioral treatment to "normal functioning": Comment on Lovaas. *Journal of Consulting and Clinical Psychology* 57:162–64.

Schreibman, L. 1988. *Autism*. Beverly Hills, CA: Sage.

Schreibman, L., and Koegel, R. L. 1975. Autism: A defeatable horror. *Psychology Today*, March, 61–7.

Smith, T. 1993. Autism. In *Handbook of Effective Psychotherapy*, ed. T. R. Giles. New York: Plenum Press.

Smith, T. 1999. Outcome of early intervention for children with autism. *Clinical Psychology: Science and Practice* 6(1):33–49.

Smith, T., Klevstrand, M., and Lovaas, O. I. 1995. Behavioral treatment of Rett's Disorder: Ineffectiveness in three cases. *American Journal on Mental Retardation* 100(3):317–22.

Smith, T., and Lovaas, O. I. 1997. The UCLA Young Autism Project: A Reply to Gresham and MacMillan. *Behavioral Disorders* 22(4):202–18.

Spitz, H. H. 1986. *The Raising of Intelligence*. New Jersey: Lawrence Erlbaum Associates.

Thelen, E. 1979. Rhythmical stereotypes in normal human infants. *Animal Behaviour* 27:699–715.

Venter, A., Lord, C., and Schopler, E. 1992. A follow-up study of high-functioning autistic children. *Journal of Child Psychology and Psychiatry* 33:489–507.

Waterhouse, L. 1988. Aspects of the evolutionary history of human social behavior. In *The Biological Aspects of Autism*, ed. L. Wing. London: British Society for Psychiatry.

Watthen-Lovaas, N. W., and Eikeseth, S. *The Reading and Writing Program*. (in preparation).

Wiesel, T. W., and Hubel, D. H. 1965. Comparison of the effects of unilateral and bilateral eye closure on cortical unit responses in kittens. *Journal of Neurophysiology* 28:1029–40.

Wing, L. 1981. Language, social and cognitive impairments in autism and severe mental retardation. *Journal of Autism and Childhood Schizophrenia* 8:79–97.

Zigler, E., and Trickett, P. K. 1978. IQ, social competence, and evaluation of early childhood intervention programs. *American Psychologist* 33:789–98.

Chapter • 8

Pragmatic Language Intervention for Children with Autism Spectrum Disorders

Rebecca Landa

Autism spectrum disorders (Pervasive Developmental Disorder-Not Otherwise Specified, Autism, Asperger's syndrome) are heterogeneous in etiology, symptom presentation, severity, and comorbid disorders. Although the specific type and severity of speech, language, and communication impairments vary from child to child with autism, one thing is constant: social language functions are impaired in all individuals with autism spectrum disorders (ASD), even those with a high IQ (Baron-Cohen 1988). This social language abnormality, known to speech-language pathologists as pragmatic language disorder, is among the most stigmatizing aspects of ASD.

Pragmatics may be thought of as the symphonic blend of other aspects of the language system (e.g., paralinguistic, phonological, grammatical, semantic), along with input from other cognitive systems, such as social cognition, for the purpose of using and interpreting language within context. To be a successful communicator, one must be able to do more than use words and combine words into sentences. One must be able to use a form of communication (e.g., gesture, visual symbol, words, sentences) to express intended meaning relevant to the context. The successful communicator must also be an effective listener, using contextual cues, a fund of social and linguistic knowledge, and knowledge about the communicative partner to infer intended meaning. For individuals with ASD, pragmatic language therapy is required to maximize communication success, build relationships, avoid social-emotional challenges related to social isolation, and avoid anxiety related to communication impairment.

Pragmatics represents an attempt by the linguistic community to embrace an ecologically valid approach to the study of communication, and by the clinical community to guide efficacious treatment of communication disorders. Before pragmatics was recognized as a component of language functioning, students of child language development focused on isolated parts of the language system without regard to how the communication system functioned as a whole. For example, Chomsky (1968) focused on the rules of syntax, which govern how words are arranged into phrase and sentence structures. These rules tell us how to go from a declarative form such as "John is helping Bob" to an interrogative form such as "Is John helping Bob?" Intact syntactic ability, however, is insufficient to guarantee that the speaker will be able to provide well-organized accounts of experiences, generate appropriate background information for the listener, communicate in a manner appropriate for the social context, or use those sentences to create a reciprocal, meaningful conversational exchange. A knowledge of pragmatics assists in adapting the form and content of language to the informational needs of the listener, in maintaining the topic of conversation, and the degree of formality of the situation. It is only when people within a culture follow pragmatic rules, or systematically violate them that we understand when someone is being polite, humorous, sarcastic, or misleading (Grice 1975).

Development of a pragmatic language system follows a predictable course throughout childhood and adolescence, with specific rules differing from culture to culture. While most pragmatic rules are tacit, some are explicitly taught. For example, adults often teach their children to say *thank you* or *Don't say that in front of Aunt Sally*. This formally teaches a child something about the forms of language to use in certain contexts (e.g., politeness rules) and about contextual taboos. The acquisition of pragmatic rules relies heavily on other aspects of development, such as other language subsystems (discussed above), cognitive systems (including social cognition and the executive control functions such as set shifting or inhibiting prepotent responses), social-emotional knowledge, and visually based aspects of information processing. The growing normative pragmatic literature is enhancing clinicians' abilities to compare pragmatic development to other aspects of language, along with social, emotional, and cognitive growth.

One organizational framework for understanding pragmatic language involves three somewhat overlapping domains: the acts of expressing communicative intentions, presupposition, and discourse organization. The next segment of this chapter defines each of these domains, discusses normal development of pragmatic language within the domains, and reviews patterns of impairment in autism spectrum disorders (ASD). The review of impairment in ASD reflects general trends rather than an enumeration of well known facts because there are few empirical studies of pragmatic functioning in individuals with ASD and because each study focuses on a discrete set of pragmatic skills rather than on the whole pragmatic system. Furthermore, researchers approach the study of pragmatics in autism in different ways and focus on different groups (differing in age, severity of autistic symptoms, presence of mental retardation). This makes comparison of discrepancies across studies difficult.

COMMUNICATIVE INTENTIONS

Definition

Utterances produced by a speaker typically have an intended communicative function (Austin 1962) and, thereby, perform a speech act (Searle 1975) or action. While this is most obvious when we say things like "I promise to call." where the act of promising has occurred simply by producing the statement, it is also true of nearly every utterance we produce. According to Dore (1977), even the intentional communicative vocalizations and gestures of pre-verbal children (which begin at around 9 months of age) can be assigned a type of function (e.g., greeting, showing, commenting, rejecting, protesting). Speakers may communicate different intentions through the production of a single form and, conversely, may use a variety of forms to express a single intention. For example, the form "Can you walk the dog tonight?" may have intended functions of politely commanding, requesting information, or making a sarcastic comment. The intended communicative function of the sentence is made clear by the context, including shared information between the speakers (e.g., both parties knowing that the listener has tentative plans for the evening that might affect the dog walking routine), cues signalled through intonation (vocal pitch and loudness variations), facial and gestural expressions, and environmental cues.

The use of various forms to express one intention is illustrated by the options to use indirect, polite expressions such as "Do you have the time?" or a more direct expression such as "What time is it?" in less formal situations. For social success, it is important to develop the ability to recognize situations in which intentions should be expressed indirectly (e.g., develop presuppositional skills). It is also important to have the linguistic flexibility to select appropriate forms for expressing the intention. Failure to do so could have dire social consequences, including social isolation or decreased cooperation from others.

Normal Development

Before words are acquired, children express a variety of declarative (attention-getting, socially-oriented) and imperative (efforts to obtain an object or action) communicative intentions through gestures, including pointing and facial expressions. Very early in life, they establish joint attention with their partner, actively checking the partner's gaze patterns to determine whether their intent has been accurately recognized (Bates, O'Connell, and Shore 1987). During the preschool years, children develop increasing options for expressing their intentions and learn how to frame their messages indirectly. Yet, sometimes, to the embarrassment of their parents, they still express their thoughts very forthrightly. A variety of new intentions appear during the preschool years (e.g., teasing), but more complex communicative intentions (e.g., negotiation, introductions, clarification requests) are acquired in informal and formal polite forms at around 9 years of age (Wiig 1982). Throughout childhood, the means (grammatical, semantic, integration of paralinguistic signals) of expressing intentions and tailoring them to the context at hand increases.

In Autism Spectrum Disorders

Children with ASD, even those with high IQs, exhibit impairment in the development of communicative intentions. Retrospective studies indicate that some children with autism are impaired from infancy in their ability to send understandable signals about their needs and states to others. For example, one retrospective study reported that, unlike typically developing infants, infants later diagnosed with autism exhibit patterns of crying that are difficult to *read* for their caregivers and unfamiliar adults (Ricks and Wing 1975). Even after they enter the developmental stage wherein intentional communication is expected to have emerged, children with ASD may fail to consciously recognize that they intend to communicate with someone. When seeing something that they want, a child with ASD may prance around the object, reach for it, and even vocalize, but fail to signal to the person nearby that they desire the object. The failure to direct eye gaze toward the potential communicative partner, to call his or her name, or to use conventional gestures or words creates an ambiguous, faulty communicative situation that is difficult to interpret as either intentional or communicative.

Children with ASD also differ in the types of communicative intentions expressed; they exhibit a restricted repertoire of communicative intentions (Wetherby 1986; Wetherby, Prizant, and Hutchinson 1998). Notably, expression of social intentions (e.g., establishing joint attention for social communicative purposes, greeting, calling for attention) are greatly outnumbered by instrumental intentions, such as requesting a cookie or requesting to be spun) (Wetherby and Prutting 1984). This contrasts with the developmental pattern of typically developing children whose communicative acts for social interactive purposes may be more frequent than behavioral regulatory communicative acts during the early stages of language development, that is before 12 months of age (Snow et al. 1996).

Although children with ASD may use pointing for joint attention, most do so in acts of behavior regulation (requesting things or actions they desire) rather than in initiating social engagement and joint focus (social-declarative act), where gaze is shifted from the object or event of interest to the eyes of the partner and back to the object again (Mundy et al. 1986). Different cognitive skills may underlie the development of behavior regulation communicative acts and social-declarative communicative acts with shared attention (Camaioni 1996; Mundy and Gomes 1997; Carpenter, Nagell, and Tomasello 1998). One theory is that behavioral regulations require cause-effect understanding, that another person can cause something to happen. But initiation of joint attention for social communicative purposes requires the understanding that another person is an intentional agent (Carpenter, Nagell, and Tomasello 1998). Furthermore, initiating joint attention during acts of social engagement requires social intention on the part of the child, and the ability to shift attention from an object of focus to the communicative partner, and back to the object again. These three aspects of development (understanding that others are intentional agents, experiencing social intentional motivations, and shifting attention) are impaired in individuals with autism (Baron-Cohen 1989; Wetherby 1986; Courchesne et al. 1994). If language development is somehow critically tied to the development of joint attention and joint engagement (Carpenter, Nagell, and Tomasello 1998), and these social/neuropsychological abilities are required for joint attention/engagement to develop, the child with autism is at high risk for significant, longstanding language impairment, especially in the social (pragmatic) use of language.

When a child is conscious of wanting to communicate, the signals used may be idiosyncratic in form (e.g., saying "Bibbity Bobbity Boo" to request being tickled), or very concrete in nature (e.g., placing the partner's hand on the object of the child's desire or using the partner's hand as though it were a tool) (Landry and Loveland 1988). Children with ASD also may use idiosyncratic forms, including immediate or delayed echolalia, to express fear, request objects, and for other intentions. An illustration of this was one child's use of the phrase "Got a splinter" whenever she was upset or hurt (Prizant and Wetherby 1987). The child had originally heard the phrase during a painful experience, but then began to use it in contexts she associated with the original experience. Idiosyncratic expression of communicative intentions may appear as repetitive questions or statements, the function of which may be to sustain interactions in the absence of more creative ways of doing so (Caparulo and Cohen 1977; Turner 1995).

This contrasts with the purpose for which repetition is used by unimpaired children (e.g., to emphasize a point, express surprise, or acknowledge). The idiosyncratic communications of intended meaning are difficult for listeners to understand, especially if they do not share essential aspects of past experiences with the child. Caregivers' efforts to infer the intention being expressed may be unsuccessful, limiting their ability to soothe and fulfill the child, possibly leading to a cascade of socially unacceptable behavior from the child (e.g., tantrums or aggression) secondary to the child's communicative frustration. A complex, difficult dynamic may result, which may be partly alleviated through the development of an alternative communication system. Such a system may be developed by a speech-language pathologist, in conjunction with the family and educational professionals, to provide a conventional code (e.g., pictures, icons) of shared meaning between the child and his or her communicative partner.

When social intentions are expressed, inappropriateness or awkwardness is apt to be noted. For example, opinions may be expressed forthrightly rather than in more subtle, socially acceptable indirect ways. This may lead to impressions of impoliteness, rudeness, or insensitivity. This poses a particular problem for teen-aged and adult individuals who express their fondness or desire to be near someone of the opposite sex in an offensively direct way. Understanding the intended meaning of others may also pose a problem for the ASD individual, who may interpret indirect expressions literally (Ozonoff and Miller 1996; Rumsey and Hanahan 1990). This limits the ability to respond in the socially expected way and sets the stage for communication breakdown.

PRESUPPOSITION

Definition

Presupposition refers to the knowledge, expectations, and beliefs that a speaker assumes are shared with the conversational partner. When making a *presupposition*, a speaker assesses what information he or she shares with the communicative partner and uses this information to plan the content and form of the message to be communicated. Other aspects of the situation are also taken into consideration, including physical qualities (e.g., age), social status of the partner, setting (e.g., formal office setting versus a picnic), and contextual variables (e.g., presence or absence of referent), history of shared experiences, and previous content of the discourse. Accurate judgements about amount and type of shared knowledge may enable the speaker to communicate clearly with only one word (Bates 1976). An example of a presuppositional error is when a speaker uses informal words and speech patterns (e.g, "Wanna soda?") rather than more formal means (e.g., "Would you like something to drink?") when speaking to an authority figure. Another example would be omitting important background information or details that the partner needs to fully understand the message (e.g., giving too few details in directions to get to the airport when the listener has never driven in that part of town before).

Presuppositional ability requires intact attentional mechanisms, an awareness of social rules, the ability to consider the perspectives of others (Flavell et al. 1968), the ability to consider alternative ways for phrasing ideas, and having the language skills to do so. Presuppositional skills include knowing: (a) when and how to be polite, formal, or colloquial, (b) when to elaborate on an idea or to give a condensed version, (c) how much background information to provide, (d) how complex the words and sentence structures should be, (e) and what topics are taboo in what situations. These judgements will have an impact on how receptive, motivated, and successful a partner will be in continuing the conversational interaction. Communicative behavior resulting from these judgements will also leave an impression on the listener about the overall social appropriateness of the speaker and may have substantial consequences in situations such as job interviews.

Normal Development

Many skills that seem important for developing presuppositional abilities are acquired in the first two years of life. For example, an early form of joint referencing (looking in the direction that a partner is looking) is present by 18 months of age. Joint attention skills are needed to track the changes in referents during conversations, so that inferences about the speaker's intentions may be made successfully. Another example is young children's awareness of saliency in their environment. They pay attention to what is important; and this detection of saliency is reflected in children's first words, which typically represent an important person, place, thing, or action, such as *ball*, *kitty, cookie* rather than inanimate objects, which have little relevance in their lives. This seemingly innate detection of salience sets the stage for identifying referents of others' utterances, and for detecting salient social cues that guide interpretation of ambiguous linguistic input. Later, it helps in recognizing the main topic of someone's utterance or in text.

By four years of age, children recognize differences in listeners' abilities to process language input. Four-year-olds speak differently to younger children, age-peers, and adults, adjusting the complexity of their grammar to their audiences (Shatz and Gelman 1973). They also adjust their language according to the listener's role or occupation (Bates 1976; Ervin-Tripp 1977). They recognize the communicative significance of nonlinguistic cues and requests for them to clarify ambiguous messages. Strategies for clarifying misunderstood messages increase across the preschool years. While 12- to 24-month-old children clarify messages by repeating them more loudly and with more precise articulation, three-year-olds are able to substitute, delete, or add words in revising their messages (Gallagher 1977). Rules are acquired that pertain to certain manners of expression and types of topics that are taboo in certain contexts. Thus, the *openness* of the preschooler who bluntly comments on a stranger's personal features diminishes with age.

In Autism Spectrum Disorders

Individuals with ASD make errors of presupposition on a regular basis. Beginning early in life, the child fails to indicate clearly the referent of his or her communication, or to signal that he or she has received a message given by others. Older children with ASD have difficulty adjusting their language productions to ever-changing contextual cues. A classic example is their tendency to use a pedantic, formal speaking style when a more relaxed or colloquial speech register is more appropriate (Kanner 1943). In part, impaired presuppositional skills may result from impaired comprehension of non-verbal and verbal cues. For example, limited comprehension of affective (Sigman, Dissanayake, and Ruskin 1997) and linguistically based intonational (Fine et al. 1991; Baltaxe and Simmons 1985) cues may compromise an individual's ability to understand marked syntactic boundaries, judge others' degree of social engagement, judge speakers' attitudes, and recognize that an utterance is not meant to be taken literally (e.g., jokes, sarcasm).

Such difficulty, in addition to poor comprehension of implied meaning (as expressed in indirect speech acts), contributes to poor recognition that a request for clarification has been presented by a listener. Indeed, Loveland, and Tunali (1991) reported that autistic individuals failed to respond to general inquiries for additional information, thus, requiring specific prompts to clarify their ambiguous utterances. Even when the clarification request was comprehended, adolescents with ASD reportedly made fewer revisions in their messages compared to controls (Baltaxe 1977). Baltaxe further reported that when revisions were made, they reflected the developmentally immature strategy of repetition rather than changing the content of the message.

Abnormality was also observed in many autistic children's use of nonverbal and verbal forms to *point* things out. Children with ASD have particular difficulty using forms of language with no fixed referents, that is, language that depends on contextual variables (e.g., use of deictic markers such as personal pronouns and demonstratives such as *here, there*) for meaning (Fay and Schuler 1980). This difficulty creates a challenge for the communicative partner to determine the child's intended referent and intended meaning.

Impaired recognition of nonverbal and indirect verbal cues is also evident in high functioning ASD individuals' tendencies to initiate topics of their special interests without regard for the listener's interest in the topic (Wing and Attwood 1987). Socially inappropriate topics may also be initiated (e.g., asking a stranger his or her age) (Langdell 1980) and messages may be expressed in a blunt manner. In addition, individuals with ASD display poor awareness of contextual rules for discourse behavior. This is illustrated by the experience of a young woman who loudly answered her minister's questions during his sermon on Sundays. She did not appreciate the rule that individual members of an audience do not take the roles of responders. From her view, she was simply doing the expected by responding to the questions. Like other individuals with ASD, this young woman was puzzled at the irritated reactions she sometimes received in response to her social communicative behaviors. Once a discourse rule is explicitly stated, however, it is often followed successfully by individuals with ASD.

Making inferences about the intended meanings of others may also be disrupted by the autistic individual's difficulty in understanding nonliteral uses of language (e.g., jokes, metaphor) and of how meaning shifts with changes in context. The literature indicates that individuals with ASD have impaired non-literal language comprehension, but are not globally impaired in this domain. High-functioning autistic individuals do recognize general differences in different types of speech acts. For example, they understand the formal requirement that jokes end in a humorous way, but that stories may not (Ozonoff and Miller 1996). Furthermore, they are typically able to appreciate simple or slapstick humor (Van Bourgondien and Mesibov 1987).

Comprehension of more complex humor, however, is a challenge, even for high-functioning individuals. Ozonoff and Miller (1996) hypothesized that the problems many autistic individuals have in understanding more complex jokes lie in a cognitive rigidity that interferes with abandoning initial impressions and reinterpreting the initial information so that a humorous, semantically correct ending may be selected. An alternative explanation is that individuals with ASD fail to understand abstract language due to an overall deficit in complex information processing (Minshew et al. 1995).

Individuals with autism not only have problems appreciating socially relevant signals, but they often fail to provide signals that would permit their listeners to make appropriate presuppositions about them. The ability to signal intended meaning is partly compromised due to impaired use of intonational cues that express special or novel meanings (Fine et al. 1991; Rumsey, Andreasen, and Rappoport 1986). Listeners may not know how to *read* what has been said and are, then, unsure about how to react. Such challenges in the communicative interchange may cause the listener to perceive the autistic individual as odd or rude and avoid frequent contact with him or her.

DISCOURSE

Definition

Discourse refers to an ongoing series of utterances that create a *text* of sorts. It may have a hierarchy of topics and sub-topics (Bates and MacWhinney 1987) or a series of topics, with digressions from the main topic. Of the types of discourse, only social discourse (conversation), which has a predictable organizational structure and developmental sequence, is discussed here.

Social Discourse

Social discourse is guided by rules for topic management (topic initiation, maintenance, and termination) and conversational repair following communication breakdown. Information is presented in a predictable way, with speakers giving signals that they are about to speak, relinquish a turn, or change a topic. When tacit rules, such as contributing informative and relevant information in the discourse are broken (Grice 1975), coherence is likely to decrease.

The organization of information in discourse typically involves providing background information first. This principle is also followed at the sentence level, where old information precedes new information, providing a context for interpreting new information. Speakers use words (cohesive devices) to link current information to that presented earlier in the discourse (Halliday and Hassan 1976). Effective use of cohesion enables conversational partners to avoid confusion about referents. For example, in the two utterances "Tom broke the chair. He felt terrible about it." the cohesive devices *he* and *it* make sense because they refer to words previously presented in the discourse. Using pronouns enables the speaker to avoid redundancy, but if the rules for using cohesive devices are not followed properly, the referent for a pronoun may be difficult to determine and coherence will be compromised.

Cohesion and other strategies are used to maintain topics. Topic maintenance is a complex skill, requiring the ability to employ grammatical skills, understand and produce meaningful semantic relationships, recognize shared information with conversational partners, and notice and interpret the significance of changing contextual cues.

NORMAL DEVELOPMENT

The rudiments of discourse are seen early in infancy. Infants initiate social communicative interactions as well as respond to and maintain the interactions initiated by others. They engage in reciprocal gaze and affective exchanges (Stern 1974), setting the stage for later conversational turn-taking. The rules for reciprocal verbal turn-taking appear to be appreciated very early in development, with rare instances of turn overlap or *interruption* (Ninio and Bruner 1978). As early as 3 months of age, infants take a vocal turn after being spoken to by their caregivers (Bloom, Russell, and Wassenberg 1987). Effective verbal turn-taking continues once language forms are acquired as can be observed when one- and two-year-olds remain quiet during their mothers' conversational turns (Schaffer, Collis, and Parsons 1977). With increasing age, children attend to and recognize signals being sent by multiple conversational partners at once. They become capable of negotiating a three-way conversational exchange by four years of age.

Early forms of topic maintenance are observed when infants and their caregivers attend to the same thing at the same time (joint attention). Between 6 and 8 months of age, infants begin to follow their caregivers' lines of visual regard (Scaife and Bruner 1975), setting the stage for later topic maintenance. With the acquisition of words, children become increasingly adept at establishing topics pertaining to themselves and to objects or events outside of themselves. At first, adults shoulder the responsibility for developing and maintaining these topics by building a sort of scaffold (Bruner 1978) around what the child says. By referring to events, engaging in routines, and using words and sentence structures familiar to the child, adults foster children's development of mental scripts for events with socially and semantically appropriate language (Foster 1981,1986; Ervin-Tripp 1979). This both supports the likelihood that the child will maintain the topic and sets a foundation for later topic maintenance skills.

As the ability to integrate verbal (linguistic content) and non-verbal (including intonational cues, shared experiences, setting, body language) cues develops, children become increasingly capable of identifying others' topics. During the primary grades, children become facile at identifying the gist or topic of an entire discourse text, such as a conversation or story, and making inferences and predictions based on that idea. Recognizing topics is paramount to producing topically contingent responses and contributing to the discourse in a coherent and socially acceptable way.

Strategies for maintaining topics increase with development, from repeating part of the partner's utterance to adding new information. A repertoire of topic maintenance strategies is developed, enabling the speaker to select a strategy well suited to the context. One set of strategies involves the use of cohesive devices. Cohesive devices are used to tie segments of the discourse together and make smooth transitions to new topics. The sophistication of these devices increases with age. By kindergarten, children make semantic ties between current utterances and previous discourse using phrases (e.g., "Speaking of games, I learned a new game today.") and cohesive devices (e.g., substituting pronouns for nouns or using ellipsis). Competent use of cohesive devices is important for discourse to be coherent, but it is not sufficient. Coherent discourse also depends on factors such as well organized presentation of information and appropriate signalling for how messages are to be interpreted.

In Autism Spectrum Disorders

In autism, the early bases of discourse, joint attention, and reciprocal social play are impaired (Mundy and Sigman 1989; Ungerer and Sigman 1981). Deficits in joint attention are characterized by absent or decreased use and comprehension of pointing and showing gestures (Mundy et al. 1986) and of eye gaze patterns for engaging in social communicative acts (Loveland and Landry 1986; Mundy et al. 1986). Early deficits in reciprocal social communicative exchanges appear to linger throughout life, perhaps in more subtle form for the more able individuals with ASD. This will have an impact on abilities such as establishing co-reference with a partner (leading to topic maintenance difficulties), using eye contact to modulate turn length, and detecting signals (e.g., rolling the eyes) indicating non-literal language use.

Individuals with ASD exhibit difficulty using signals to modulate discourse. Some typical situations in which they use signals in discourse inconsistently or inappropriately include: (a) indicating that they are about to speak, (b) clearly identifying the intended recipient of their message, (c) indicating that they are about to relinquish a turn, (d) and indicating an intended transition in the course of the topic (Langdell 1980). One major consequence of poor signalling is confusion on the part of the listener. In some cases, an intended listener may not attend to the speaker at all, which the speaker may then interpret as being ignored.

Another difficulty involves maintaining topics that are of interest to the communicative partner. Individuals with ASD have a reputation for being associative, leading them to shift a topic abruptly when the current topic reminds them of something else. Poor maintenance of others' topics stands in stark contrast to their ability to sustain topics of their own interests for extended periods of time. The information shared within these special interest topics tends to be a series of detailed facts rather than a story that leads to a main point. Therefore, conversational partners tend to have difficulty building a reciprocal exchange of information with ASD individuals. The information imparted by the ASD individual may be new and interesting to a listener upon the first encounter, but repeated encounters often reveal that the information is stereotypical. Within a discourse event, individuals with ASD have difficulty using linguistic strategies, such as cohesion, for tying new information to previous discourse (Loveland et al. 1990; Baltaxe and D'Angiola 1992; Fine et al. 1994). This is likely to negatively impact the coherence of the discourse.

ASSESSMENT OF PRAGMATIC SKILLS

Any time there is a possible diagnosis of an autism spectrum disorder, assessment must include an examination of pragmatic language skills because of the substantial impact on daily living and academic success. Areas to be assessed will change as a child gets older and makes gains in communicative, cognitive, and social abilities. In general, the assessment will include analysis of the child's current means (and complexity of those means) of communicating with others (including idiosyncratic and conventional forms), types of communicative intentions expressed, types of meanings expressed (semantic categories and relationships) in social communicative exchanges, strategies for initiating and maintaining social communicative exchanges, topic or interaction maintenance skills, and perspective-taking abilities. In very young children, available forms for intentional communication must be assessed. These include gestures, non-specific vocalizations, idiosyncratic verbalizations such as echolalia, word imitation, turn-taking, reciprocity of affect during interactions, use of joint attention for social communicative purposes, eye contact to modulate communication, contingency of language or other communicative behavior, and responsiveness to the social bids of others. One excellent test that addresses many of these skills between 12 and 24 months of age is the *Communication and Symbolic Behavior Scales: A Developmental Profile* (Wetherby and Prizant 1998).

In older children, pragmatic skills, discussed earlier in this chapter, may be sampled through classroom observation, observation with a peer in play, language sampling in the assessment context, and administration of standardized tests such as the *Test of Problem Solving-Revised* (Zachman et al. 1994), *Test of Pragmatic Language* (Phelps-Terasaki and Phelps-Gunn 1992), *Test of Pragmatic Skills* (Shulman 1985), and *Test of Language Competence* (Wiig and Secord 1989). A structured coding system should be used to organize information obtained from the language sample and observation contexts (see Bishop 1998). Based on the assessment, an individualized intervention program should be designed.

INTERVENTION

All children with ASD will require intervention to address pragmatic language skills early in the treatment process, because language development appears to rely heavily on processes related to the development of social communicative intentionality (Rollins 1999). Having the opportunity to develop basic pragmatic awareness (e.g., that the child's behavior has communicative significance that can be *read* by others and can be used by the child for enjoyable social engagement) may be necessary for substantial growth in the early stages of language development. Since 50% of children with autism have been reported to be functionally nonverbal by age 5 (Rutter 1978), the importance of teaching pragmatics to children with ASD cannot be overemphasized. Setting pragmatic language goals will help a child improve social and adaptive skills, decrease maladaptive behaviors, and develop conceptual content relevant to communication and academic skills. Pre-requisite and basic communication skills are established first, and later, more pragmatic skills may be taught. The following is an overview of some aspects of pragmatic impairment in ASD, and a sample of how that aspect of impairment might be addressed in intervention.

Decreased communicative intentionality may be addressed in a therapeutic context. Using an activity preferred by the child, an adult gets down to the child's eye level and presents the object of interest to him or her. If the object is a jar of bubble liquid, the clinician may hold the bubble wand next to his or her eyes to direct the child's line of vision to the face and eye region. Once the child's attention is engaged, the child has entered a teachable moment. Now the clinician may reinforce the child for looking, acknowledge intent ("Want bubbles?"), model an effective requesting behavior (e.g., simplified speech model for "bubble"), and assist the child in producing some communicative form (e.g., word approximation, a pointing gesture, reach toward bubble). Repeated experience in such joint action routines enables children to learn that their movements and sound productions mean something to others and that they can intentionally produce those movements or sounds again to indicate what is desired.

As part of a treatment program designed to teach communicative intentionality, goals will include assisting a child in developing a consistent, conventional form of communication via gaze, vocalization, word production, gestures, and/or a non-verbal augmentative communication system, such as the *Picture Exchange Communication System* (Bondy and Frost 1994). The vocabulary taught to children in the early stages of language emergence must be chosen carefully so that the child may gain the maximum benefits from learned words for communicative, social, and control purposes. Learning a *functional* language (as opposed to rote, memorized vocabulary or sets of phrases learned in a drill, but not incorporated into daily life) is a painstaking process for most children with ASD.

Acquisition of each word is a monumental feat. The speech-language pathologist should work with parents and teachers to determine what words the child will have to comprehend or produce to cooperate more fully in the home and school setting and to make use of the curricular content presented at school. The goal of developing these words includes enabling the child to develop adaptive means of asserting control, integrate into the social world, use language for self-regulatory purposes, and use language as a learning tool. To maximize progress toward these goals, therapists may consider the following general guidelines for selecting the first vocabulary to teach to a child. They are:

- words that represent salient actions or objects associated with motivating activities or special interests;
- words that reflect concepts that emerge early in the developmental chronology (e.g., *in, up, no*);
- words that enable the child to exert adaptive control over his environment such as *all done, stop*, or *help*;
- labels for important people in the child's life (e.g., *mama, dad*);
- words that can be used to begin to develop a generative grammar (planning to introduce words from different semantic categories such as agents, actions, locations, so that these may be combined into agent + action phrases such as *me go* or *go outside*);

- words to reflect emotional states (such as *mad*) and labels for affection (such as *love you, hug*).

Many therapists teach an extensive vocabulary in drills (using pictures, printed words, and/or objects), but neglect to teach the child to use the words to communicate. This is a great disservice to the child, for the child must be taught to express a variety of communicative intentions, beginning with the most instrumental intents that would serve his or her immediate needs and wants (e.g., requesting actions and objects). Gradually, the child should be taught to communicate a greater range of intentions, branching out into more social types of intent such as greetings, calling for attention before communicating, commenting, regulating affect, and informing. A variety of means may be used to accomplish these goals.

In our preschool, we target a communicative function intensively for about two weeks at a time, with ongoing generalization opportunities thereafter. The children are given many opportunities in engineered and spontaneous interactions to observe functional models of language used for social purposes and to practice using language for the targeted purpose. The children are taught that they are not simply passive recipients of the language of others, but are expected to be active in giving to and sharing with peers within classroom events. In a unit on using language to regulate oneself and others' emotional states, two major events happened that illustrated the benefit of formally teaching children to use and understand language for these purposes.

Example 1: A boy with emerging language consistently expressed frustration and anger by biting and pulling hair. One morning, he dashed for some playdough and the teacher removed it, telling him "no playdough." He reached out to bite her but stopped himself, ran over to the lights, and turned them off as he said "night night" and then jumped into the ball pit and sang his bedtime song.

Example 2: A girl in the class was having a hard time with transitions. She cried as she moved from the morning preparation table to morning circle, and continued to cry well into the circle time. Another child watched the crying girl for a while, then approached her and said "It's okay." and hugged the crying girl, falling on top of her. After regaining her stance, the child offering the comfort tapped the crying child on the nose lightly and said "boop." The girl stopped crying. As the "boop" game was repeated, the girl who had been crying began to smile.

The concept of identifying our own and others' emotional states, and knowing that language and actions can be used to alter those emotional states was very powerful for the students described above.

It should be noted that learning to use language for social purposes is a challenge for students with ASD. We assist them through this process by teaching them to communicate using forms already taught in other facets of our program, using visual supports (see Dalrymple 1995; Hogdon 1995; Schopler, Mesibov, and Hersey 1995), engaging them in motivating learning contexts that meet their sensory motor needs (see Greenspan and Wieder 1997; Ayres 1974), adapting input so that it is appropriate for the child's conceptual level (including task analysis), providing an appropriate prompt hierarchy, using a reactive learning environment (see Rogers et al. 1986), using natural reinforcers wherever possible, and employing narratives and social stories (see Gray 1995).

Difficulty initiating and responding to joint attention bids is seen in the ASD child's failure to point to objects of desire or interest, and failure to understand the pointing gestures of others', gaze direction, and head orientation. The speech-language pathologist decides when a child is ready to learn these skills. In our program, we begin by teaching a child to comprehend the meaning of the finger pointing gesture and other gestures within concrete tasks that the child is able to complete. The child is also taught to reach or point to desired objects, and, later, to point out objects of interest. For children who are further along in their language development, we teach the use and meaning of pointing words such as *this*, *that*, *here*, and *there*.

The tendency to exhibit limited initiation and maintenance of communicative exchanges is addressed in pragmatic language therapy by creating highly motivating communicative contexts, wherein the child is shown an object or provided with an action that is very stimulating. The object or action is provided in very small doses, so that the child wants more. This creates a need for the child to initiate a communicative exchange, and the child is given models or prompts as needed to continue the exchange. Because a child's attention often wanders before he or she tires of the exchange, the clinician must learn how much demand for attention the child can tolerate in a given session. Breaks may be necessary to maximize the child's learning opportunities.

In preparing to address difficulties with maintaining communicative exchanges, children with ASD are taught turn-taking skills and social contingencies. Here again, sensory experiences or simple cause-effect games may be used for teaching turn-taking skills to very young children. Visual cues may be used to identify who is supposed to be taking the turn. Forms of social contingency are taught early in the therapeutic process. This may be done by teaching children that you are interested in their actions and by doing what they are doing.

It is important to imitate the children's movements, since these are within their action repertoires and they will have more success replicating these movements than novel ones. As time goes on, adults will do what the children do, but will vary some obvious aspect of the action. Most children take note of this and attempt to imitate the adult's behavior. This series of imitative interactions lend themselves to helping children understand social contingencies and set the stage for communicative contingencies.

Difficulty maintaining others' topics and using linguistic devices (cohesion) during topic maintenance or shifts can be addressed in a therapeutic setting. Intervention may begin with teaching children certain semantic skills, so that they are aware of how word meanings relate to one another. Understanding such semantic contingencies will better enable children to produce responses to others, using ideas that are meaningfully related, and, thereby, maintaining the topic. Students are given specific strategies presented in very concrete form for maintaining topics and for making topic shifts, such as "When you see someone you know, look into their eyes and say hello." Students practice scripts and role playing. These scripts provide the event representation, linguistic content, and social rules that a child may need to know to engage in a social situation successfully.

Once a child learns the script, the language or social nuances within the script may be systematically varied to build creativity and generalization. This teaches a child flexibility, but, in the meantime, provides him or her with pre-planned language if anxiety or contextual demands impair the ability to plan novel language constructs within an interaction. Scripts chosen for therapy may be based on an event a child has experienced, an action routine used in therapy, an event a child is about to experience, or a narrative used in the intervention process. Older, more linguistically capable children may also require that the form or grammar of events and narratives be laid out concretely (e.g., setting, problem encountered by the characters, action taken by the characters to deal with the problem, outcome of the action, and characters' responses to that outcome).

Another strategy for helping children with more complex language ability (spoken or nonverbal symbolic form of expression), is to have families create memory books about an event a child has experienced. Each book focuses on one major event. For each component of the event (or each day of a vacation), there are three pages: (1) Page one consists of about five specific questions that the child is to answer (in writing or having someone transcribe the answers given by the child) about a particular aspect of the event (or the day of the trip); (2) Page two consists of a drawing, photograph, or postcard representing a component of the event or day of the trip; and (3) Page three consists of the child's narrative about the event (written by the child or for the child based on his or her own words). This book is then used in pragmatic language therapy, along with the specific rules and strategies given to the child for initiating and maintaining conversations. The book serves as the functional, motivating content of the conversation. Being familiar with the content, the child is likely to be able to maintain a topic about the event.

These books help students expand their topic maintenance abilities beyond their topics of special interest, which often monopolize conversations and frustrate their partners. Self-monitoring strategies are taught so that students may identify when they have dropped the conversational ball and make the necessary repairs. Several good resources for teaching topic maintenance skills are: *Teach Me Language* (Freeman and Dake 1997); and various programs published by Thinking Publications.

Limited comprehension of others' communicative intents is common in children with ASD. Here, a child may understand the words being produced, but may not understand what outcome is intended from the production of the words. For example, when asked by a caller "Is your mother there?" the child answering the telephone may say "Yes" without understanding that the caller really intends for the child to call the mother to the phone. In intervention, narratives which contain the language structures being taught may be presented to a child. The child will be led in structured, supported role playing situations to use and understand the targeted language forms. She or he will be required to think flexibly, to recognize the contextual cues that signal one interpretation of the words, gestures, or written language as opposed to a different interpretation.

Difficulty comprehending non-literal language affects comprehension of words used in new and different ways, i.e., jokes, sarcasm, indirect speech acts, and more. Socially, this has the potential to isolate children with ASD from their peers because they will have difficulty getting the punchline of jokes and recognizing subtle innuendos. In the earliest stages of addressing this difficulty in treatment, the emphasis may be on expanding a child's comprehension of existing vocabulary words to new linguistic and communicative contexts. When the child is ready to work toward greater cognitive-linguistic flexibility and metalinguistic awareness, the clinician may use simple narratives, preferably ones with good pictures and appealing content. Visual representations of the pragmatic concepts to be taught is a powerful medium through which the child with ASD may cross a bridge to comprehension.

As the child and clinician read the story together, target words or phrases are identified and explained. For example, a child opening a book and reading the first sentence: "One day Sally arrived home and saw that Rover wasn't there" may need help inferring that the sentence implies that Rover is habitually in the place where Sally is looking right now. The clinician can help the student imagine where Rover is supposed to be by looking at the gaze direction of Sally. The child is then given the opportunity to interpret and use these precise targets within predictable environments, such as role playing, where other aspects of the conversational exchange may have been written out. Generalization opportunities are created so that the child learns to understand and use the words or phrases in new ways.

Abnormal prosody and other nonverbal communication skills in children with ASD often have a deleterious effect on how their communicative intentions are interpreted by others. When children become verbal, they may be taught to use appropriate loudness levels (speaking loudly enough to be heard) and to begin to monitor intonational contours and loudness levels. Explicitly, children may be taught to raise vocal pitch at the end of a sequence of words to request information (e.g., a question) and to lower their pitch at the end of a sentence that is intended to make a statement. Children with ASD will have greater communicative success if they are taught the intonational cues that signal others' communicative intent (e.g., for emphatic commands, questions, sarcasm) and affective state (loud voice may signal that the listener is too far away to hear a standard loudness level or that the speaker is experiencing a heightened emotional state such as happiness or anger).

Nonverbal skills that modulate social conversational exchanges are also addressed for many students with pragmatic language difficulties. Some students need to be taught to "look at me" (the speaker) at a very young age. Once mastered in a demand context, the student is then taught to look at their conversational partner during communicative events. The use of gesture, facial expression, and vocal tone also contribute in a major way to successful communicative exchanges, and may specifically need to be taught to the child with ASD.

One of the greatest challenges for children with ASD is being able to take others' perspectives. While children with ASD seem able to understand people as agents of action, they do not do well with understanding other people as agents of contemplation or as having perspectives that can be shared (Sigman, Dissanayake, and Ruskin 1997). Understanding that people differ from one another in how they see the world is the first step in teaching perspective-taking skills.

Very concrete situations are presented to the child using direct experiences and short stories that can be role played. One type of story that is helpful is known as "Social Stories"(Gray 1995; Gray and Garand 1993). These are created by parents or professionals, sometimes recruiting the assistance of the student. The story identifies and describes relevant social cues and target responses to a problem, tailored to a child's comprehension and visual processing abilities. They may be presented in picture or written format. The precise information given in the stories helps a student understand an event and the rules for behaving socially (including conversationally if that is the goal) in that context.

Building a file of information about the personal characteristics of others and the types of background information that others are likely to have also helps a child learn to anticipate or predict others' perspectives and to provide information that is appropriately detailed. Later, a child learns to adjust phrasing and word selection to be appropriate for the social context. This aspect of pragmatic language therapy helps reduce much of the mystery and complexity that may decrease a child's success and confidence during communicative exchanges.

There are many more skills to address in pragmatic language therapy. These include the ability to read social and emotional cues; to use language flexibly so that ideas are expressed in socially acceptable ways; and to develop social and linguistic inferencing skills, such as understanding social nuances.

PRAGMATIC LANGUAGE INTERVENTION: INSTRUCTIONAL METHODS

Pragmatic language skills are not often the focus of intervention programs in autism. However, pragmatic language and related social skills are key to the success of children with autism. To prepare a child for pragmatic language, communication, and social learning, our staff employs a multi-faceted approach to understand the strengths, vulnerabilities, and preferences of each child. Treatment goals and methods are then tailored to a specific child's learning style.

Developing pragmatic language skills will promote children's abilities to have positive experiences when they are with other people, and enable them to demonstrate some degree of reciprocity during their interactions. It is unlikely that any one of the popular methods for treating autism will, by itself, adequately address pragmatic language therapeutic needs of children with ASD. However, some principles should be used to guide intervention that addresses pragmatic and related skills. These include:

- Get child's attention. Just calling the child's name is usually insufficient to get his or her attention. After the child has had a warm-up time, approach the child and join in the activity. Call the child's name, and, if necessary, turn his or her face toward yours before delivering the teaching or discriminitive stimulus.

- Engage in activities that are interesting, pleasurable, and motivating to the child whenever possible. The key here is to get the child engaged. Gradually, the therapist introduces more adult-led activities.
- Provide success. If social engagement is desired, build on skills already in the child's repertoire. Remember not to overwhelm the child with too much novelty.
- Build relationship and trust.
- Show the child how much you enjoy him or her. Having fun will help to reduce the child's anxiety level and make him or her more receptive to the therapeutic stimulation.
- Create communicative need for meaningful use of language forms.
- Systematically increase interactions.
- Teach communication scripts or routines (Joint Action Routines).
- Create predictability through repetition. Do not introduce too many novel variables or demands at once.
- Conduct a task analysis of skills that will be taught, breaking them into specific tasks so that the student will experience success with them.
- Employ peers as interactive partners in the teaching process whenever possible. Typically developing peers will require some coaching to be good partners.
- Make the learning task as concrete and the rules as explicit as possible upon introduction.
- Provide visual parameters and examples whenever possible.
- Build in choices for the child. These choices may be about the nature of the activity to be completed, the reinforcer to be used, or the order of tasks to be completed. The number of choices should be set at two until the child demonstrates that he or she is capable of selecting from a larger number. Present choices using forms (objects, photographs, icons, written words) that the child is able to understand. The choices should reflect activities that are interesting for the child, but not to the point where the child becomes deeply preoccupied with them.
- Create a physical environment that is conducive to learning (decrease distractions, provide sensory feedback, and create clear physical boundaries for different types of activities) (see Dalrymple 1995).
- Define goals objectively for yourself. Know precisely what you are working on in every situation.
- Take data to monitor the student's progress toward the goals, but data taking must be done on a schedule, using a format

that will not interrupt the social exchange and child-focus of every session.

- Provide reinforcing feedback to the child, letting the child know when he or she has performed in the targeted manner.
- Incorporate parents' insights and goals.

These principles are present to a lesser or greater degree in treatment methods commonly employed with children having autism, including Applied Behavior Analysis and a sub-type of this known as Discrete Trial Teaching endorsed by Lovaas (1981) and Maurice (1996). Other treatment methods include the TEACCH program (Schopler, Mesibov, and Hersey 1995); Sensory Integration (Ayres 1974), and transactional models (Koegel, Odell and Koegel 1987; Koegel and Koegel 1996; Rogers et al. 1986; Warren and Kaiser 1986; Halle 1987). There is a debate about whether a behavioral or transactional/child-focused method should be employed in teaching children with autism. The debate is heightened when the focus of therapy is pragmatic language and related social skills.

The behavioral method is based on principles of operant conditioning. Behavioral therapy is designed to teach a discrete set of skills and subskills. One form in which principles of Applied Behavior Analysis are used is in Discrete Trial Teaching (DTT). This method has been widely acclaimed in the area of autism and has been endorsed by Lovaas (1981). In DTT, all aspects of the intervention are clearly defined, including stimuli, prompt hierarchy, and reinforcements (positive and negative). Numerous trials are presented with a restricted range of stimuli until the child has reached pre-set criterion for that goal. The child is often a passive recipient of instruction in an adult-led, tightly controlled interaction. This, combined with the highly predictable atmosphere created within behavioral therapy, places the learner at risk for difficulties with generalization, spontaneity, and generativity. Furthermore, the emerging evidence of the critical role played by social cognition in the language acquisition process (Rollins 1999; Carpenter et al. 1998) suggests that using an exclusively DTT approach to language intervention may actually serve to inhibit the full language developmental process for a child.

The transactional approach is in contrast to the behavioral approach. The transactional approach promotes a child-led, naturalistic interaction. Here, an adult, familiar with developmental sequences, serves as a facilitator of interactive exchanges, employing a greater variety of stimuli in teaching a child. Within the transactional approach, a child is permitted (and encouraged) to play with the stimuli and to appreciate its functional, pleasure-giving qualities. Reinforcers are naturally occurring (e.g., giving a child a ball after he has said *ball* rather than a piece of candy).

Clinicians should not feel that they have to decide between behavioral and transactional approaches. Both play important roles in pragmatic language intervention. It is important to remember that as a child matures cognitively, socially, and linguistically, a shift in the dominance of one instructional method for another (at least for certain goals) will have to occur if learning is to be maximized. Selection of instructional methods should not only be based on a child's learning style, but also on the nature of the goals. Some goals (e.g., social contingency versus learning to match objects) may be better addressed using one method or another.

Teaching initial skills in attending and cooperating within a structured learning environment, for example, is well addressed within a discrete trial format, as is teaching initial skills at some levels of pragmatic development. However, social, communicative engagement is best addressed within a more transactional approach. To craft an instructional method tailored to a child's learning style and goals, it is important for a clinician to be familiar with specific principles from different approaches, such as the ones mentioned above. In this way, rich, interactive instructional programs may be developed. Here is an example that blends principles from the transactional and behavioral approaches.

A two-year-old nonverbal child noticed his therapist sitting upon a bookshelf. When he looked toward her, she initiated an affectively rich game of peek-a-boo. The child leaned forward watching her and she provided a discriminitive stimulus of "boo" with exaggerated tone and mouth movement. The clinician paused, understanding the common motor planning difficulties experienced by children with autism, but did not break gaze with the child. When the child approximated a "boo" production, she initiated the routine again, hence reinforcing the child for his communicative attempt. This cycle was repeated at least five times, offering the child repeated opportunities to practice his newly developing communication skill in a functional, communicative atmosphere that was intrinsically interesting to him. In this treatment interaction, features of the transactional method included a naturalistic context, child-led and motivating activity in which the child was responsive (a natural interchange), and a natural reinforcer. Yet, there was also a discrete skill being taught using a consistent discriminitive stimulus and reinforcer, with a repeated series of trials, all features of the behavioral approach.

SUMMARY

Children with ASD consistently present pragmatic language challenges. Yet because of the complex, multi-dimensional, context-dependent nature of pragmatic language, the measurement and treatment of pragmatics is often neglected. In very high-functioning children, pragmatic deficits may be overlooked by adults due to their children's intact intellectual skills and given the complexity of assessing pragmatic language skills. In children with greater cognitive challenges, pragmatic language skills may be overlooked in the design of the educational/therapeutic program because a great emphasis is placed on teaching the child to attend and cooperate, along with teaching basic language, and pre-academic/academic skills. All children suspected of having ASD should have a pragmatic language assessment. Following the assessment, goals for pragmatic language intervention should be set, building on established linguistic, social, and cognitive skills.

There are many instructional methods and resources that may be adopted in designing a pragmatic intervention program. However, there is little empirical data available to clinicians to guide their decisions about which instructional methods to use for which children. Many experienced clinicians apply a variety of techniques in their treatment approaches, the success of which will differ for different children. Ultimately, children will benefit from pragmatic language intervention by learning that others in their environments value them as communicators, and by being provided with strategies for building social communicative relationships with others. This will do much to foster self confidence, reduce anxiety and related maladaptive behaviors, and promote the child's acceptance in the community.

Chapter Summary

1. Pragmatic language disorder (difficulty with the social aspects of language) is characteristic of all autistic spectrum disorders (ASDs).
2. Pragmatic aspects of language include both verbal (such as inflection and pauses) and non-verbal (such as gesture and facial expression) aspects of communication.
3. It is possible for an individual to perform well on tests that measure the individual components of language, such as vocabulary and sentence structure while still exhibiting significant difficulties in pragmatics and communication.
4. The development of pragmatics in normal children assumes a predictable course throughout childhood and involves the cooperation of several interrelated systems (language, cognition, social-emotional, and visual processing).
5. Pragmatic language can be considered under three domains: communicative intentions, presuppositions, and discourse organization.

6. Impairment in the development of joint attention in children with ASDs reflects a problem with expressing and understanding communicative intention. It is also an early diagnostic sign of autism.
7. Presupposition reflects a speaker's assumption of information shared with the communicative partner. Impaired presuppositional skills may be conceptually related to the theory of mind in autism.
8. Multiple aspects of communicative impairment may contribute to the difficulties that persons with autism have in maintaining the flow of discourse.
9. The assessment of pragmatic language is a necessary component of the evaluation of a child with an ASD; therapy directed at such deficits can contribute significantly to the success of overall intervention programs.
10. Pragmatic language disorders can occur without autism. It is important that clinicians be competent to screen for these sometimes subtle but potentially severely incapacitating impairments in communication.

REFERENCES

Austin, J. 1962. *How to do things with words.* Cambridge, MA: Harvard University Press.

Ayres, A. J. 1974. *The Development of Sensory Integrative Theory and Practice.* Dubuque, IA: Kendall/Hunt Publishing.

Baltaxe, C. A. M 1977. Pragmatic deficits in the language of autistic adolescents. *Journal of Pediatric Psychology* 2:176–80.

Baltaxe, C. A. M., and Simmons, J. Q. 1985. Prosodic development in normal and autistic children. In *Communication Problems in Autism,* eds. E. Schopler and G. B. Mesibov. New York: Plenum Press.

Baltaxe, C. A. M., and D'Angiola, N. 1992. Cohesion in the discourse interaction of autistic, specifically language-impaired, and normal children. *Journal of Autism and Developmental Disorders* 22:1–21.

Baron-Cohen, S. 1988. Social and pragmatic deficits in autism: Cognitive or affective? *Journal of Autism and Developmental Disorders* 18:379–402.

Baron-Cohen, S. 1989. The autistic child's theory of mind: A case of specific developmental delay. *Journal of Child Psychology and Psychiatry* 30:285–97.

Bates, E. 1976. *Language in context.* New York: Academic Press.

Bates, E., and MacWhinney, B. 1987. Competition, variation, and language learning. In *Mechanisms of Language Acquisition,* ed. B. MacWhinney. Hillsdale, NJ: Erlbaum.

Bates, E., O'Connell, B., and Shore, C. 1987. Language and communication in infancy. In *Handbook of Infant Development,* 2nd ed., ed. J. Osofsky. New York: Wiley.

Bishop, D. V. M. 1998. Development of children's communication checklist (CCC): A method for assessing qualitative aspects of communicative impairment in children. *Journal of Child Psychology and Psychiatry* 39:879–91.

Bloom, A., Russell, A., and Wassenberg, K. 1987. Turn-taking affects the quality of infant vocalizations. *Journal of Child Language* 14:211–27.

Bondy, A. S., and Frost, L. A. 1994. The picture exchange communication system. *Focus on Autistic Behavior* 9:1–19.

Bruner, J. 1978. The role of dialogue in language acquisition. In *The Child's Conception of Language*, eds. A. Sinclair, R. J. Jarvella, and W. J. M. Levelt. Berlin: Springer-Verlag.

Camaioni, L. 1996. The emergence of intentional communication in ontogeny, phylogeny, and pathology. In Edition du Centre National de Suresnes, *The Development of Communication: What's New?* (DeafBlind International Publication). Paris, France.

Caparulo, B., and Cohen, D. 1977. Cognitive structures, language, and emerging social competence in autistic and aphasic children. *Journal of the Academy of Child Psychiatry* 15:620–44.

Carpenter, M., Nagell, K., and Tomasello, M. 1998. Social cognition, joint attention, and communicative competence from 9 to 15 months of age. *Monographs of the Society for Research in Child Development* 6, Serial No. 255.

Chomsky, N. 1968. *Language and mind*. New York: Harcourt Brace Jovanovich.

Courchesne, E., Townsend, J. P., Askhoomoff, N. A., Saitoh, O., Yeung-Courchesne, R., Lincoln, A. J., James, H. E., Haas, R. H., Schreibman, L., and Lau, L. 1994. Impairment in shifting attention in autistic and cerebellar patients. *Behavioral Neuroscience* 108:848–65.

Dalrymple, N. J. 1995. Environmental supports to develop flexibility and independence. In *Teaching Children with Autism: Strategies to Enhance Communication and Socialization*, ed. K. A. Quill. New York: Delmar Publishers, Inc.

Dore, J. 1977. Children's illocutionary acts. In *Discourse Production and Comprehension*, ed. R. O. Freedle. Norwood, NJ: Ablex Publishing.

Ervin-Tripp, S. 1977. Wait for me, Roller Skate! In *Child Discourse*, eds. S. Ervin-Tripp and C. Mitchell-Kernan. New York: Academic Press.

Ervin-Tripp, S. 1979. Children's verbal turn-taking. In *Developmental Pragmatics*, eds. E. Ochs and B. B. Schieffelin. New York: Academic Press.

Fay, W. H., and Schuler, A. L. 1980. *Emerging Language in Autistic Children.* Baltimore: University Park Press.

Fine, J., Bartolucci, G., Ginsberg, G., and Szatmari, P. 1991. The use of intonation to communicate in subjects with pervasive developmental disorders. *Journal of Child Psychology and Psychiatry* 32:771–882.

Fine, J., Bartolucci, G., Szatmari, P., and Ginsberg, G. 1994. Cohesive discourse in pervasive developmental disorders. *Journal of Autism and Developmental Disorders* 24:315–29.

Flavell, J., Botkin, P. T., Fry, C. C., Wright, J. W., and Jarvis, P. E. 1968. *The Development of Role-taking and Communication Skills in Children.* New York: Wiley.

Foster, S. 1981. The emergence of topic type in children under 2: A chicken and egg problem. *Papers and Reports on Child Language Development* 20:52–60.

Foster, S. 1986. Learning discourse topic management in the preschool years. *Journal of Child Language* 13:231–50.

Freeman, S., and Dake, L. 1997. *Teach Me Language: A Language Manual for Children with Autism, Asperger's Syndrome, and Related Developmental Disorders.* Langley, British Columbia: SKF Books.

Gallagher, T. 1977. Revision behaviors in the speech of developing children. *Journal of Speech and Hearing Research* 20:303–18.
Gray, C., and Garand, J. 1993. Social stories: Improving responses of students with autism with accurate social information. *Focus on Autistic Behavior* 8:1–10.
Gray, C. 1995. Teaching children with autism to "read" social situations. In *Teaching Children with Autism: Strategies to Enhance Communication and Socialization*, ed. K. Quill. New York: Delmar Publishers, Inc.
Greenspan, S., and Wieder, S. 1997. *The Child with Special Needs: Encouraging Intellectual and Emotional Growth.* Reading, MA: Addison-Wesley.
Grice, H. P. 1975. Logic and conversation. In *Syntax and Semantics: Speech Acts*, eds. P. Cole and J. Morgan. New York: Academic Press.
Halle, J. 1987. Teaching language in the natural environment: An analysis of spontaneity. *Journal of the Association for Persons with Severe Handicaps* 12:28–37.
Halliday, M. A. K., and Hassan, R. 1976. *Cohesion in English.* London: Longman Group Limited.
Hogdon, L. A. 1995. *Visual Strategies for Improving Communication Volume 1: Practical Supports for School and Home.* Troy, MI: Robert Quirk Publishing.
Kanner, L. 1943. Autistic disturbances of affective content. *Nervous Child* 2:227–50.
Koegel, R. L., O'Dell, M. C., and Koegel, L. K. 1987. A natural language teaching program for nonverbal autistic children. *Journal of Autism and Developmental Disorders* 17:187–200.
Koegel, R. L., and Koegel, L. K. 1996. *Teaching Children with Autism.* Baltimore: Paul H. Brookes.
Landry, S. H., and Loveland, K. A. 1988. Communication behaviors in autism and developmental language delay. *Journal of Child Psychology and Psychiatry* 29:621–34.
Langdell, T. 1980. Pragmatic aspects of autism: Or why is "I" a normal word? Unpublished paper presented at the BPS Developmental Psychology Conference, Edinburgh.
Loveland, K. A., and Landry, S. H. 1986. Joint attention and communication in autism and language delay. *Journal of Autism and Developmental Disorders* 16:335–49.
Loveland, K. A., McEvoy, R. E., Kelley, M. L., and Tunali, B. 1990. Narrative story-telling in autism and Down's syndrome. *British Journal of Developmental Psychology* 8:9–23.
Loveland, K. A., and Tunali, B. 1991. Social scripts for conversational interactions in autism and Down's syndrome. *Journal of Autism and Developmental Disorders* 21:177–86.
Lovaas, O. I. 1981. *The Me Book.* Austin, TX: PRO-ED.
Maurice, C. 1996. *Behavioral Intervention for Young Children with Autism: A Manual for Parents and Professionals.* Austin, TX: PRO-ED.
Mundy, P., and Gomes, A. 1997. A skills approach to early language development. In *Communication and Language Acquisition*, eds. L. B. Adamson and M. A. Romski. Baltimore: Paul H. Brookes.
Mundy, P., Sigman, M., Ungerer, J. A., and Sherman, T. 1986. Defining the social deficits in autism: The contribution of non-verbal communication measures. *Journal of Child Psychology and Psychiatry* 27:658–69.
Mundy, P., and Sigman, M. 1989. The theoretical implications of joint attention deficits in autism. *Development and Psychopathology* 1:173–83.
Ninio, A., and Bruner, J. S. 1978. The achievement and antecedents of labelling. *Journal of Child Language* 5:1–15.

Ozonoff, S., and Miller, J. 1996. An exploration of right hemisphere contributions to the pragmatic impairments of autism. *Brain and Language* 52:411–34.

Phelps-Terasaki, D., and Phelps-Gunn, T. 1992. *Test of Pragmatic Language.* Austin, TX: PRO-ED.

Prizant, B. M., and Wetherby, A., M. 1987. Communicative intent: A framework for understanding social-communicative behavior in autism. *Journal of the American Academy of Child and Adolescent Psychiatry* 26:472–9.

Ricks, D., and Wing, L. 1975. Language, communication, and the use of symbols in normal and autistic children. *Journal of Autism and Childhood Schizophrenia* 5:191–221.

Rogers, S. J., Herbison, J. M., Lewis, H. C., Pantone, J., and Reis, K. 1986. An approach for enhancing the symbolic, communicative, and interpersonal functioning of young children with autism or severe emotional handicaps. *Journal of the Division for Early Childhood* 10:135–148.

Rollins, P. R. 1999. Early pragmatic accomplishments and vocabulary development in preschool children with autism. *American Journal of Speech-Language Pathology* 8:181–190.

Rumsey, J., Andreasen, N. C., and Rappoport, J. 1986. Thought, language, communication, and affective flattening in autistic adults. *Archives of General Psychiatry* 43:771–7.

Rumsey, J., and Hanahan, A. P. 1990. Getting it "right": Performance of high functioning autistic adults on a right hemisphere battery. *Journal of Clinical and Experimental Neuropsychology* 12:81.

Rutter, M. 1978. Diagnosis and definition of childhood autism. *Journal of Autism and Developmental Disorders* 8:139–161.

Schaffer, H. R., Collis, G. M., and Parsons, G. 1977. Vocal interchange and visual regard in verbal and preverbal children. In *Studies in Mother-Infant Interaction*, ed. H. R. Schaffer. New York: Academic Press.

Scaife, M., and Bruner, J. S. 1975. The capacity for joint visual attention. *Nature* 253:265–6.

Schopler, E., Mesibov, G. B., and Hersey, K. 1995. Structured teaching in the TEACCH system. In *Learning and Cognition in Autism*, eds. E. Schopler and G. Mesibov. New York: Plenum Press.

Searle, J. R. 1975. A taxonomy of illocutionary acts. In *Minnesota Studies in the Philosophy of Language*, ed. K. Gunderson. Minneapolis: University of Minnesota Press.

Shatz, M., and Gelman, R. 1973. The development of communication skills: Modifications in the speech of young children as a function of the listener. *Monographs of the Society for Research in Child Development*, No.38. SRCD: Chicago.

Shulman, B. 1985. *Test of Pragmatic Skills.* Tucson, AZ: Communication Skills Builders.

Sigman, M., Dissanayake, S. A., and Ruskin, E. 1997. Cognition and emotion in children and adolescents with autism. In *Handbook of Autism and Pervasive Developmental Disorder*, eds. D. J. Cohen and F. R. Volkmar. New York: John Wiley and Sons, Inc.

Snow, C. E., Pan, B., Imbens-Bailey, A., and Herman, J. 1996. Learning how to say what one means: A longitudinal study of children's speech act use. *Social Development* 5:56–84.

Stern, D. N. 1974. Mother and infant at play: The dyadic interaction involving facial, vocal, and gaze behaviors. In *The Effect of the Infant on its Caregiver*, eds. M. Lewis and L. A. Rosenblum. New York: Wiley.

Turner, M. 1995. Repetitive behavior and generation of ideas in high-functioning individuals with autism: Is there a link? Paper presented at the Society for Research in Child Development, Indianapolis, IN.

Ungerer, J., and Sigman, M. 1981. Symbolic play and language comprehension in autistic children. *Journal of the American Academy of Child and Adolescent Psychiatry* 20:318–37.

Van Bourgondien, M. E., and Mesibov, G. B. 1987. Humor in high-functioning autistic adults. *Journal of Autism and Developmental Disorders* 17:417–24.

Warren, S. F., and Kaiser, A. P. 1986. Incidental language teaching: A critical review. *Journal of Speech and Hearing Disorders* 51:291–99.

Wetherby, A., M., and Prutting, C., A. 1984. Profiles of communicative and cognitive-social abilities in autistic children. *Journal of Speech and Hearing Research* 27:364–77.

Wetherby, A. 1986. Ontogeny of communication functions in autism. *Journal of Autism and Developmental Disorders* 16:225–316.

Wetherby, A., and Prizant, B. 1998. *Communication and Symbolic Behavior Scales: A Developmental Profile.* Chicago, IL: Applied Symbolix.

Wetherby, A., Prizant, B., and Hutchinson, T. 1998. Communicative, social-affective, and symbolic profiles of young children with autism and pervasive developmental disorders. *American Journal of Speech-Language Pathology* 7:79–91.

Wiig, E. 1982. *Let's Talk: Developing Prosocial Communication Skills.* Columbus, OH: Charles E. Merrill.

Wiig, E., and Secord, W. 1989. *Test of Language Competence Expanded Edition.* The Psychological Corporation.

Wing, L., and Attwood, A. 1987. Syndromes of autism and atypical development. In *Handbook of Autism and Pervasive Developmental Disorders*, eds. D. J. Cohen and A. M. Donnellan. New York: John Wiley and Sons.

Zachman, L., Huisingh, R., Barrett, M., Orman, J., and LoGiudice, C. 1994. *Elementary Test of Problem Solving Revised.* East Moline, IL: LinguiSystems.

Chapter • 9

The Savant Syndrome in Autism

Darold A. Treffert

Savant syndrome is a rare, but spectacular, condition in which persons with various developmental disorders, including autistic disorder, have astonishing islands of ability, brilliance, or talent that stand in stark, markedly incongruous contrast to overall handicap. In some such persons the savant skills are remarkable, simply in contrast to the handicap (talented savants); in others, in a much rarer form of an already rare disorder, the ability would be spectacular in a normal person (prodigious savants) (Treffert 1989).

Savant syndrome is of special interest in autistic disorder, because as many as 10% of autistic persons have some savant skills (Rimland and Fein 1988). In Rimland's (1978) survey of 5400 autistic children, 531 cases (9.8%) were reported by parents to have special abilities. Among the subgroups of autistic children who fit the definition of classical early infantile autism, the incidence of savant skills was considerably higher than in the larger population of children who displayed autism. It is important to point out, however, that while savant syndrome is present in some persons with autistic disorder, particularly those with classic infantile autism, not all persons with autistic disorder are savants. Correspondingly, it is also important to point out that not all savants have autistic disorder. While much less common than in autistic disorder, savant syndrome occurs in persons with a variety of other forms of CNS dysfunction, including developmental disability or, in some cases, it occurs following brain injury or disease (Treffert 1989). Hill (1978) found the incidence of savant skills among an institutionalized mentally retarded population to be as low as 1:2000. Even though mental retardation is much more common than autistic disorder, approximately 50% of persons with savant syndrome are autistic, and approximately 50% are mentally retarded. A particularly intriguing new finding is the emergence of new or enhanced artistic talents in progressive frontotemporal dementia in older persons described by Miller et al. (1998), raising the question of what buried potential might reside in each of us.

The identical twin brothers, first reported by Horwitz and his coworkers (1965), are examples of savant syndrome occurring in autistic disorder. The brothers can identify on what day a given date fell or will fall over a time-span of 80,000 years, or can tell, for example, what date the third Thursday of March in the year 22420 will be, or identify what years, in the next 200, Easter will fall on March 23rd. They can also remember the weather for every day of their adult lives. Sacks (1987) describes these brothers swapping 20 digit prime numbers for amusement when they were hospitalized together; yet neither could multiply the simplest of numbers. They are both autistic and they are both savants—examples of savant syndrome in autistic disorder.

Leslie is blind with mental retardation and cerebral palsy (Treffert 1989). While he does display some autistic mannerisms, he does not have autistic disorder. He does, however, demonstrate a striking example of savant syndrome in a developmental disability other than autistic disorder. He has never had a music lesson in his life; yet, at about age 14, after hearing Tchaikovsky's Piano Concerto No. 1 for the first time as a television movie theme song one evening, he played the piece back completely, flawlessly, and without hesitation. Presently, his musical repertoire is prodigious. He can still repeat a lengthy and complex musical piece after a single hearing, but now he can also improvise and compose. He has perfect pitch and musicians who have observed Leslie indicate he has access to the rules of music intuitively and massively. His particular developmental disability is brain damage, apparently from a severe neonatal infection, as demonstrated by imaging studies (Treffert 1989).

The most well-known autistic savant, of course, is Raymond Babbitt, as portrayed by Dustin Hoffman in the award-winning movie Rain Man. The main character in the film, Raymond Babbitt, is a composite savant, not patterned after a specific individual, but created from a number of savant abilities derived from many such persons (Treffert 2000). What one sees in that remarkably accurate depiction are savant skills—memorization, eidetic imagery, lightning calculations—grafted on to basic autistic symptoms and behaviors—obsessive-compulsive rituals, echolalia, and wooden affect, gait, and diction. The movie was very well done. However, in addition to reminding audiences that not all autistic persons are savants, and not all savants are autistic, it is important to point out that, in the movie,

Raymond Babbitt is a high-functioning autistic person. Since autism is a spectrum disorder, some persons do function at a high level, but many others are severely disabled and do not reach the level of relatively independent functioning, as seen in that character. That movie, in addition to being a sensitive portrayal of a fascinating condition, performed a useful public education function and made autistic savant household words. This chapter explores that extraordinary condition in more depth.

SOME EARLY DESCRIPTIONS

In a series of lectures to the Medical Society of London in 1887, Dr. J. Landon Down (best known for having described Down syndrome) shared his 30-year experience as Superintendent of Earlswood Asylum during which time he had been struck by this extraordinary paradox of superiority and deficiency occurring in the same person (Down 1887). He described ten such cases. One individual built exquisite model ships from hand-fashioned parts and could recite complex texts verbatim, but could not understand a single word of what he had memorized. Music was a frequent skill. One boy in his care, after attending the opera, would come away with a perfect recollection of all the arias. Another boy could multiply many-digit figures in his head as quickly as they could be written on paper. Other cases showed the kinds of talents—art, music, lightning calculations, and mechanical genius—that have characterized all the "special faculties" (as Down termed them) since that time. In each instance, the special skill was coupled with a particular type of prodigious memory—verbal adhesion—a memory without consciousness as Down described it. One other observation has stood the test of time since that original description—females are conspicuously few among all savants. It is impossible to tell from Down's description how many of his cases were autistic disorder (there was no such condition defined as such in his day) and how many were other forms of developmental disability. Surely, some of his cases were autistic.

In 1887, the term idiot was a precise scientific term—IQ less than 25. It did not have the pejorative colloquial connotation that became attached to it in later years. So Dr. Down combined the term, an acceptable one at the time, with the word savant, derived from the French word savoir which means "to know" or "knowledgeable person," thus coining the term idiot savant to describe these fascinating persons. That term, for obvious reasons, has been largely discarded now and has been replaced by savant syndrome. Actually, idiot savant was a misnomer, since almost all of the reported cases have occurred in persons with IQs of 40 or above.

It was 27 years later that the next classic work on savants appeared. In his 1914 textbook *Mental Deficiency*, still available in revised editions today, Tredgold (1914) provides a colorful and complete description of savant syndrome. It is a trailblazing, classic, and insightful description. The usual, still-typical musical, artistic, mathematical, mechanical, and calendar calculating skills are described in colorful and eloquent detail. However, several additional skills are reported as well: the "gift of tongues"— a polyglot savant; a case of heightened "special senses"—olfactory and tactile abilities; and a case of "pronounced sense of locality"—spatial and directional skills. All of these special abilities remain hauntingly the same in the years that follow, and each case shows the prodigious memory so typical and uniform in all present-day cases, now a century after those first descriptions. Female savants, again, (and still) are conspicuously few.

Tredgold chronicles the case of The Genius of Earlswood Asylum in careful and elaborate detail. The Genius of Earlswood Asylum, James Pullen, was an extremely skillful *deaf and dumb* craftsman with remarkable drawing and memory abilities in whom even His Majesty King Edward took a tremendous interest. His masterpiece, "The Great Eastern," a 10-foot precisely scaled ship model took seven years to complete with the hand-fashioning of each plank, pin, rivet, and pulley. It gained worldwide attention when it won first prize in international competition. Two other clinicians studied Pullen's case in great detail (Sano 1918; Sequin 1866), including a post-autopsy brain map of each convolution and fissure, along with interesting speculation about a larger than normal corpus callosum and highly developed occipital lobes.

SAVANT SYNDROME TODAY—WHAT WE DO KNOW

After Tredgold's classic chapter, some anecdotal reports of individual savant cases continued to appear throughout world literature. But it was more than six decades later that Hill (1978) provided the next comprehensive review of savant syndrome along with some theories of causation. That same year, Rimland (1978) provided a very useful overview of savant syndrome based on a survey from parents and others on 5400 autistic children in the Institute for Child Behavior Research data bank. In 1988, Treffert provided the next comprehensive overview on savant syndrome in both autistic disorder and other forms of developmental disability in a journal review article and a book (1988;1989). Miller (1989) has provided a comprehensive overview of musical savants, with both autistic disorder and other developmental disabilities. Kehrer (1992) provided an overview article exploring the savant capabilities of autistic persons, specifically. The most recent comprehensive overview of savant syndrome, including an extensive bibliography, was published by Nettelbeck and Young (1999).

There are certain things we do know about savant syndrome, but they are mostly descriptive. There is much about this fascinating condition we do not know as yet, chiefly, how to explain it. No model of brain function or memory will be complete unless it can incorporate and explain this jarring juxtaposition of ability and disability. Let me begin with a summary of what we do know:

Incidence

Savant syndrome is rare. The approximate 9.8% incidence in autistic disorder and .06% (1:2000) incidence in mental retardation (mentioned earlier) remain good estimates of overall incidence.

Sex Ratio

Males outnumber females in an approximate 6:1 ratio. Part of the reason for the higher incidence in males is the fact that savant skills occur in as high as 10% of autistic persons and the sex ratio in that disorder itself is 4:1 males to females. However, others factors contribute as well, including the recent findings about testosterone and cerebral lateralization discussed below.

Congenital versus Acquired Etiology

Savant syndrome, in some cases, appears to be genetic or congenital, accompanying conditions such as autistic disorder or other developmental disabilities present from birth. In other cases of acquired disorders, it can occur from injury or disease to the central nervous system in infancy, childhood, or at a point later in life (Treffert 1988;1989; Miller et al. 1998). The special skills can appear suddenly, without explanation, or they can disappear just as suddenly or fade slowly over time. But they usually persist and develop more fully.

The Nature of the Special Skills

The ability or brilliance, while spectacular, occurs within a consistent and, intriguingly, narrow range considering all the skills in the human repertoire. It is generally limited to five areas: music, usually performance and usually piano playing, although complex composing, even in the absence of performance, has been reported as well (Cameron 1998); art, usually drawing or sculpting; mathematics, usually lightning calculating or facility with numbers such as calculating prime numbers; calendar calculating; and mechanical or spatial skills. Some observers list prodigious memory (mnemonism) as a separate special skill in some individuals, but, in my view, prodigious memory, usually in a very narrow range, is a uniform trait demonstrated by all savants, cutting across all the special skills or abilities as a shared, integral part of the syndrome itself.

In addition to these five typical or standard abilities, so markedly consistent in all reports, other skills have been reported less often. They include prodigious language facility—polyglot savant (O'Connor and Hermelin 1991; Smith and Tsimpli 1995); unusual sensory discrimination abilities in smell, touch, or vision (Rimland 1978); perfect appreciation of passing time without knowledge of a clock face; athletic or superior coordination and balance skills (Rimland 1978; Rimland and Fine 1988; Young 1995); and outstanding knowledge in specific fields such as neurophysiology, statistics, or navigation (Kehrer 1992; Rimland 1978).

Rimland and Fein (1988) looked at the frequency and type of savant skills in autistic persons only, as opposed to the broader sample of persons from a variety of developmental disabilities. In autistic savants, music was the most common skill, followed by memory which was listed as a special ability, then art, pseudoverbal abilities, mathematics, directions (spatial abilities), coordination, calendar calculating, and "extrasensory perception" in that order.

In most instances, a single special savant skill exists. In other cases, several skills exist simultaneously. Rimland and Fein (1988) observed that the incidence of multiple skills appeared higher in autistic savants than in savants with other developmental disabilities. The presence of several savant skills, even at prodigious levels, sometimes surfaces with the same surprise as with the original skill, such as a special ability to put jigsaw puzzles together rapidly, sometimes without reference to the puzzle picture. These skills, however, while noticeable, do not rise to the level of typical savant abilities in terms of scope or depth and are referred to as splinter skills (Young 1995).

Skills tend to be right hemisphere in type—nonsymbolic, artistic, concrete, directly perceived—in contrast to left hemisphere skills that are more sequential, logical, and symbolic, including language specialization. Whatever the special skills, they are always coupled with phenomenal memory within the skill area itself, and often vast stores of unrelated trivia (license numbers, dates, sports scores, zip codes) coexist as well. That memory, however, as discussed below, is of a special type—exceedingly deep but within very narrow confines.

The Extraordinary Memory of the Savant

Whatever the special skills in savant syndrome, remarkable memory of a unique and uniform type welds the condition together (Treffert

1989). Extraordinary skills plus exceptional memory, both within narrow but spectacular ranges, mark the savant syndrome. Terms such as automatic, mechanical, concrete, or habit-like have consistently appeared in descriptions by both clinicians and researchers throughout this past century. Down (1887) used the term verbal adhesion to describe the prodigious memory for facts or materials without comprehension of their meaning. Critchley (1979) described the savant "exultation of memory" as memory without reckoning. Tredgold (1914) described the phenomenal savant memory as "automatic" in form. Barr (1898) characterized his patient with prodigious memory "as an exaggerated form of habit."

Such unconscious memory—memory without reckoning—suggests the use of what Mishkin and Petri (1984) referred to as a noncognitive "habit" formation system, rather than a cognitive "memory" system. They proposed two different neural circuits for these different types of memory. The importance of the hippocampus and amygdala in differential memory functions—the hippocampus for simple recall and the amygdala for cataloguing and providing emotional tone to memory—suggests possible disturbances in neural circuitry in savants, given the uniform type of memory function they demonstrate. Rimland and Fein (1988) suggested that defects in amygdala function produced over-reliance on the hippocampus in memory function and retrieval, producing the stream of consciousness, supra-normal type of memory savants exhibit. In support of that hypothesis, Bauman and Kemper (1985) found histoanatomic abnormalities in the hippocampus, amygdala, cerebellum, and other areas of the forebrain in a postmortem examination of the brain of a 25-year-old autistic patient as compared to a control specimen. They concluded such pathology occurred early in the development (prenatally) and included neuron destruction in the affected areas. Those researchers further suggested that "although defects in memory have been little studied in autism, they may well underlie the pronounced difficulties in social interaction, language function, and learning that characterize these patients."

Blindness, Mental Handicap, and Musical Genius—A Recurrent Triad

Throughout the century-long literature on savant syndrome, there is a curious and conspicuous presence of blindness (usually linked to prematurity and retrolental fibroplasia), mental handicap (frequently from autism), and musical genius. Tredgold (1914) describes such a case dating back to 1861. Blind Tom, as he was known, reached international acclaim as a savant-pianist in the 1860s (Southall 1979). Treffert (1989) describes in detail two specific cases and reviews this recurrent triad in savants in considerable detail. Charness, Clifton, and McDonald (1988) describe comprehensive musical and psychological testing in another such blind, musical savant.

Rimland (1964) commented on the high incidence of premature children, some of whom developed retrolental fibroplasia. Keeler (1958) found that a large number of children with retrolental fibroplasia developed early infantile autism, while none of a control group of 18 patients with other types of blindness developed this disorder. Rimland (1964), and other investigators as well, have raised the question as to whether the same pathophysiology that harms the retina (which is brain tissue) might also harm other areas of the brain, such as the reticular activating system, producing the organic substrate for autism as well as blindness and savant capacity. This possibility is discussed in more detail by Treffert (1989).

SOME WELL KNOWN AUTISTIC SAVANTS

The bibliography on savant syndrome through this past century consists of several hundred articles and several books. In most of these accounts, no clear distinction exists between autistic disorder and other forms of developmental disability. Descriptions include a variety of disorders, such as mental retardation, organic brain syndrome of various etiologies, and, recently, a report of new artistic skills emerging in persons in the fifth or sixth decades of life with frontotemporal dementia (Miller et al. 1998). There are, however, some fairly extensive reports on a number of persons with savant skills in which the diagnosis of autistic disorder seems fairly well established and documented. I will list some of those and indicate what materials—written, film, or video—are available for those persons wanting more information about them.

In an historical overview of childhood psychosis, six of Kanner's (1971) original autistic cases had musical abilities specifically mentioned. Rimland's (1978) description of savant capabilities in children provided many examples of specific skills, with music being the most common. The identical twin brother calendar calculators have been extensively documented and described (Horwitz et al. 1965; Horwitz, Deming, and Winter 1969; Sacks 1987). Viscott (1970), after four years of psychotherapy with a female musical savant, described her case with unusual attention to the psychodynamic interactions with her personality traits and remarkable musical skills. Selfe (1977) wrote about Nadia, a child with all the signs and symptoms of early infantile autism, who, at age 3, had phenomenal drawing ability, but lost that astonishing ability at age 7 when she entered a school for language development. As her language skills improved, her special drawing ability vanished, raising the question as to whether her ability was simply a temporal coincidence, or whether there was in her, and perhaps in other savants, a tragic trade-off of the special skill for language. That dreaded trade-off, fortunately, does not usually occur and, indeed, to the contrary, in my experience and generally in the literature, the special skill can be used as a conduit toward normalization. As the special skill increases, so does language, socialization, and other daily living skills.

Stephen is an autistic artist living in London who has produced two tremendously successful art books built around his remarkable drawings (Wiltshire 1987; 1991). The President of the Royal Academy said: "Happily, every now and then, a rocket of young talent explodes and continues to shower us with his sparks. Stephen is one of those rockets . . . . I've never seen in all my competition drawing such a talent, such a natural and extraordinary talent this child seems to have . . . . [Stephen] is possibly the best child artist in Britain." Of particular interest is the almost incidental discovery of Stephen's rather extensive musical talents. This coexistence of several savant skills in the same individual is not unprecedented, but most savants tend to harbor skills only within their specialized areas.

Richard is a well-known Scottish artist who uses crayon as his medium (see Richard Wawro's drawing of *South Devon Coast, England,* on p. 84c). A 1983 videotape entitled *With Eyes Wide Open,* and a 1989 videotape entitled *A Real Rainman: Portrait of an Autistic Savant* document his outstanding talent. He is presently internationally recognized as an extremely talented artist.

Dustin Hoffman spent a great deal of time learning about autism and savant skills with Joseph. The movie, *Rain Man,* opened in Joseph's hometown with Dustin Hoffman paying tribute to Joseph and his family for the time they spent on the project. Joseph has lightning calculating skills and extensive memorization abilities. There have been two excellent documentaries about Joseph, a 1967 film called *The Invisible Wall* and an 1986 film entitled *Portrait of an Autistic Young Man,* both projects of the UCLA Behavioral Sciences Media Laboratory. Dustin Hoffman, in preparing for his role, carefully studied not only the films, but some 16 hours of outakes from the 1986 production as well.

Tony, blind and autistic, is an extremely talented pianist whose jazz (rare among musical savants) improvisations were sufficiently spectacular to cause him to be admitted to the prestigious Berklee College of Music in Boston from which he graduated magna cum laude. Films of Tony at age 6 provided evidence of his already burgeoning musical talent, and on March 2, 1997, the CBS Sunday Night Movie, *Journey of the Heart,* chronicled his remarkable story.

THEORIES TO EXPLAIN THE SAVANT

Since savant syndrome was first described, a number of theories have attempted to explain this remarkable condition. The results of all those theories can be summed up thus: To date no single theory has emerged that can explain all savants. Nevertheless, some of those are worthy of mention because they are rather wide reaching. Each of these theories is examined in greater detail by Treffert (1988; 1989).

Eidetic imagery is an intense, positively colored visual image that persists for a long time, generally for at least 40 seconds or longer, after scanning an object or stimulus. That term is sometimes used for a related but separate phenomenon generally referred to as photographic memory. While eidetic imagery may be present in some savants, it is not universal. Duckett (1976) and LaFontaine (1974) tested 30 savants specifically for eidetic imagery and concluded that while some savants did show such skills, it was not a uniform finding. Kehrer (1992) reviewed more recent findings on eidetic imagery and concluded that autistic savants do receive their memory material in a manner similar to eidetic imagery. However, the fact that eidetic imagery can be viewed as a marker of brain damage when it persists beyond childhood or adolescence (Giray and Barclay 1977), and the fact that such imagery is sometimes seen in certain types of brain injury (palinopsia) (Bender, Feldman, and Sobin 1968) may be, in the case of savants, indicative of brain damage or dysfunction rather than a unique savant characteristic.

Inherited skills, like eidetic imagery, are seen in some, but not all savants. Rife and Synder (1931) argued forcefully that their findings of some such genetic factors in 33 mentally retarded persons with special abilities refuted any behavioral explanation for the savant. Duckett (1976) found special skills in some of the relatives of 25 savants she studied, as did Young (1995) in her sample of 51 savants. Rimland (1978), commenting on autistic savants in particular, indicated that the tendency for these skills to run in families was present. LaFontaine (1974), however, found only one family member with special skills among the 23 relatives of five carefully studied savants. My own experience is that while some savants do have family members with similar special skills or abilities, it is not the case in most instances.

Sensory deprivation and social isolation are postulated by some as important contributors to savant skills. In these theories, sensory deprivation, from either defective sensory input channels or social isolation, leads to boredom which sensitizes the savant to minute changes in the environment and leads to the development of bizarre or trivial preoccupations, concentration, or rituals such as memorizing obscure facts or calendar calculating, for example (Tredgold 1914; Viscott 1970; Jaensch and Menhel 1928; Hoffman 1971; Nurcombe and Parker 1964). Rimland and Fine (1988) proposed that, in the autistic savant, attention is pathologically locked at the indistractable, super-intense end of the concentration scale, creating an inability to broaden sensory input. Kehrer (1992), likewise, commented on the faulty filtration of sensory impulses and its impact on the unusual memory processes seen in autistic savants.

A highly developed rote memory has been put forth by Hill (1978) and others as an explanation for savant abilities. However, Hermelin et al. (1989) demonstrated, with precise testing of a musical savant compared to a non-disabled professional musician, that the savant musical skills clearly went beyond memorization and extended to generative processing. O'Connor and Hermelin (1984) demonstrated that in calendar calculators special skills are based on rule-based applications of extensive expert knowledge. Nettelbeck and Young (1999) reviewed data with respect to memory ability and savant skills in great detail, and provided convincing proof that the entire range of savant abilities extended well beyond memorization. This innate access to the "rules of music" or "the rules of mathematics" has been commented upon by many researchers and argues for an explanation of the savant that includes enhanced memory skills but does not depend solely on them (Treffert 1989).

Compensation and reinforcement, to offset lack of more generalized skills, are postulated by others as important contributing forces in the acquisition, development, and honing of skills seen in savants. In this schema, praise rewards the savant for the unusual skill and adds to his self-esteem (LaFontaine 1974). The skill compensates for inferiority feelings (Jones 1926); serves as a defense for intellectual defects (Lindsley 1965); aids in the search for relationships with others (Nurcombe and Parker 1964); seeks to gain parental approval or love in the home (Viscott 1970); or to gain social reinforcement in the institutional setting (Duckett 1976; Hoffman 1971). Concrete thinking and impaired ability to think abstractly as a cause of savant syndrome was explored most extensively by Scheerer, Rothman, and Goldstein (1945) in a five-year study of an 11-year-old savant with multiple skills. In cases such as these, the researchers postulated that inability to think abstractly accounted for savants' channeling all their energies into the only outlet available to them for actualization—concrete mechanisms of expression. Steel, Gorman, and Flexman (1984) and Luszki (1966) found such impaired abstract thinking ability on formal psychological testing. The inability to think abstractly is common in many autistic and other developmentally disabled persons, but does not explain why some, and not all, acquire and demonstrate savant skills.

Left brain injury with right brain compensation as an organic cause of savant syndrome is an increasingly common explanation for savant syndrome, especially now with the easy availability of imaging studies to support those findings. Brink (1980) presented the case of a normal 9-year-old boy who was left mute, deaf, and paralyzed by a gunshot wound to the left hemisphere. Following that injury, unusual savant-like mechanical skill emerged, presumably from the undamaged right hemisphere. Tanguay (1973) pointed out that the skills most often seen in autistic savants are those associated with right hemispheric functioning, and the skills most lacking tend to be associated with the left hemisphere. Rimland (1978) also reported on the specialization of hemisphere functioning in the autistic savant, highlighting the simultaneous nature of right brain activities in contrast to the sequential nature of left brain activities. Steel, Gorman, and Flexman (1984), as well as Charness, Clifton, and MacDonald (1988), presented savant cases that showed evidence on imaging studies and on neuropsychological tests of left hemisphere damage. Treffert (1989) presented an additional case with a detailed description of left hemisphere damage as demonstrated on CAT scans. Hauser, DeLong, and Rosman (1975) found pneumoencephalographic abnormalities in the left temporal lobe and dilatation of the left temporal horn of the left ventricle in 15 out of 17 autistic patients. Four of these 17 patients had savant skills in music or mechanical areas. These researchers concluded motor and language functions in these patients were "taken over" by the right hemisphere because of disease on the left. The availability of PET scanning to assess not just brain structure, but also brain function, should provide much more data documenting left hemisphere/right hemisphere function and/or dysfunction.

Further studies in cerebral lateralization provide more evidence of left brain injury as an important factor in the development of savant syndrome, as well as providing an explanation for the disproportionately high male:female ratio not only in savant syndrome, but in autistic disorder itself. Geschwind and Galaburda (1987), citing a wide number of animal and human studies, have pointed out that the left hemisphere normally develops later than the right and is subjected to prenatal influences (some of them detrimental) for a longer period of time. In the male fetus, circulating testosterone can slow growth and impair neuronal migration in the more vulnerable left brain, with an actual enlargement and shift of dominance favoring talents associated with the right brain, the kind of skills seen in savants. The same marked male:female ratio is seen in dyslexia, delayed speech, autism, stuttering, and hyperactivity. It also accounts for the higher incidence of left-handedness in males. A "pathology of superiority" was postulated, with compensatory growth in the right brain as a result of poorer development or actual injury to the left brain. This hormonal influence on brain structure, particularly the cortex, provides a plausible explanation for the predominance of males with savant syndrome, and the predominance of right brain skills. Although a left brain injury/right brain compensation theory is not new, earlier theories could not explain why injury would occur so much more commonly in males. This finding accounts for that difference.

HOW DO THEY DO IT?

The most intriguing and engaging question, of course, is how do persons with savant syndrome, including autistic savants, accomplish their extraordinary feats given their equally extensive disabilities? No single theory or construct, as yet, can provide an explanation for all cases of this astonishing condition. Some of the contributing elements are listed in the section just above. My view, based on my own observations and review of literature to date, can be summarized thus: In the savant, there is disruption of typical left hemisphere functions as a result of prenatal influences, sometimes sex-linked (testosterone), or prenatal or subsequent CNS injury, even later in life, which, in turn, leads to a compensatory migration of neurons and dominance of right hemisphere function. A predilection for simultaneous, nonsymbolic, literal skills and functions results. Such cortical and/or corpus callosum abnormality is coupled with idiosyncratic hippocampal/amygdala/forebrain circuitry, probably arising from those same influences and injuries that produce the savant's characteristic cluster of symptoms, capabilities, and unique memory. In the talented savant, concreteness and impaired ability to think abstractly are locked in a very narrow band. Nevertheless, with constant repetition and practice, he can produce sufficient coding so that access to some unconscious algorithms can be automatically attained. In prodigious savants, some genetic factors may be operative as well, since practice alone cannot account for access to the vast rules of music, art, or mathematics innate in these individuals. Once established, intense concentration, practice, compensatory drives, and reinforcement play important roles in further developing and polishing the extraordinary mix of skill and memory made possible by unique and idiosyncratic brain functioning.

Young (1995) carried out the most recent and largest study on savants (51 persons) in which, in addition to obtaining family histories, each savant was interviewed. Standardized testing was carefully and systematically performed on each of the subjects. The results suggested that a savant is a neurologically impaired individual with idiosyncratic and divergent intellectual ability, along with language and intellectual impairments consistent with autism. He has intense interest and preoccupation with particular areas of ability. Skills are generally rule based, rigid, and highly structured, lacking critical aspects of creativity and cognitive flexibility. These circumstances, together with preserved neurological capacity to process information related to his skills, a well developed declarative memory, a familial predisposition toward high achievement and support, plus the opportunities for encouragement and reinforcement provide a climate in which savant skills develop.

In a more recent summary of observations, Nettelbeck and Young (1999) conclude that literal rote memory does not provide a basis for savant skills. Instead, skills are based on extensive, rule-based knowledge, are confined to defined activities, and are most commonly imitative and inflexible. Further, they conclude, savant skills do not represent forms of separate intelligences (outside the concept of overall general intelligence). Much of their paper explores why they reached that conclusion. Savant skills, they found, depend on modular processing, established by rehearsal on the basis of short- and/or long-term memory structures that have been spared damage. In essence, their conclusions regarding the presence of idiosyncratic cortical and memory circuitry in the savant are supportive and consistent with my conclusions and proposals outlined above. Instead of a "pathology of superiority" based on brain areas that are damaged, they propose that brain areas that are spared are most crucial in accounting for the special skills in the savant.

Kehrer (1992), applying his observations just to autistic savants, concluded: "Their perception and their perception processing function differently from those of normal people. The process of eidetic imagery, which also appears quite often in normal childhood, could explain one or the other savant ability. A further model of explanation would be a different structure and a different functioning of the memory store. Finally, emotions and experiences within the first months and years of life with their specific mechanisms of reinforcement are certainly important for the development and the possible diminishing of savant abilities."

WILLIAMS SYNDROME AND AUTISTIC DISORDER

Williams syndrome was first described in 1961, but only recently has it been the subject of considerable research and media attention. This syndrome overlaps savant syndrome in that a consistently significant number of individuals with this condition show savant-like musical talent, sometimes prodigiously so; it overlaps autistic disorder in that there are individuals who meet strict criteria for the diagnosis of autistic disorder as well (Gillberg and Rasmussen 1994). Williams syndrome is a genetic disorder in children with consistent findings of distinctive, facial features (often described as "elfin-like" or "pixie-like"); a variety of heart defects including aortic stenosis; elevated calcium levels associated with "colic-like" symptoms in infants; autistic-like behaviors such as inflexibility, ritualism, obsessiveness, and hyperacusis (Gillberg and Rasmussen 1994); and developmental delays coupled with attention deficits and cognitive disabilities, usually with IQs of less than 70. Many are reported to have well developed and sometimes prodigious, savant musical abilities, enough so that several music camps have grown up in the United States to help further the special talents of persons with Williams syndrome. One such camp is the Williams Syndrome Music and Arts Camp in Massachusetts.

What is unique to Williams syndrome, however, in contrast to other forms of developmental disabilities, including autistic disorder, is the presence of a rich, expansive, grammatically complex vocabulary with striking conversation and richly expressive story-telling skills in some persons. Equally striking, particularly in contrast to the usual behavioral handicaps of autism, is the extremely outgoing, friendly, polite, expressive social skills that these individuals possess. They are typically unafraid of strangers and are often drawn to adults. These distinctive, genetic physical features, coupled with what has been called a "cocktail party" personality and musical ability in persons with otherwise impaired cognition and autistic features, provide a most intriguing mix of ability and disability. This most unusual circumstance of impaired general cognition with precocious language abilities challenges theories about the ordinary link between language and cognition, and raises new possibilities and constructs regarding theories of language acquisition and brain function in autism, mental retardation, and other developmental disabilities.

Adding to the research interest in Williams syndrome is the fact that a specific genetic defect on chromosome 7 has been identified as the cause of this disorder. The genetic defect makes elastin production deficient in Williams syndrome, and it is this defect that is felt by many to account for the cardiovascular abnormalities. Gene defects on Chromosome 7 may also account for neurodevelopmental brain abnormalities, according to some researchers. Gillberg and Rasmussen (1994) report four cases of Williams syndrome concurrent with carefully diagnosed autistic disorder (as opposed to simply autistic-like behavior) and explore the research significance of the concurrence of the two disorders. The confluence of autistic disorder, mental retardation, and savant abilities in Williams syndrome, along with enhanced language so atypical of mental retardation, increased sociability and over-friendliness so atypical of autism, and conspicuous over-representation of savant musical skills, provide a most intriguing mix from a theoretical, research, clinical, and treatment point of view.

ELIMINATE THE DEFECT OR TRAIN THE TALENT

Etiologic controversies aside, what is the best approach to allow savants to have lives as productive and fulfilling as possible given their often severe mental handicaps? Phillips (1930) framed the question this way: "The problem of treatment comes next. The question that arises is one of method, whether it is better to try to eliminate the defects or train the talent . . . . Theoretically this question is unsettled. Some educators incline to the view that the child should be given what he does not like and be kept from doing what he does like. If he has artistic ability and does not like arithmetic, give him arithmetic." Phillips, a special education teacher, answered his own question with his pupil, Earl, who, because he did not like reading or arithmetic and had no ability to do either, and had no trainability in academic matters, was provided with "no alternative but to develop his special talent."

In the savant, the special skills are as much a force—obsessively propelled—as they are a gift. The musical savant must play, the artistic savant must sculpt, and the lightning calculator must compute. When the staff took Alonzo's clay away because they felt he was spending too much time sculpting at the expense of learning more important daily living skills, two weeks later, hidden under his bed, was a whole menagerie of little animals he had sculpted from tar he had scraped from the roof. He had to sculpt. Yet, it is important to learn daily living skills as well. So Phillips' question becomes not one of either training the talent or eliminating the defect; it is working on both. The special talent, in fact, can become a conduit toward normalization, using the unique ability to help toward more socialization, language acquisition, and independence, all without, in my experience, the dreaded trade-off of loss of special abilities for gains in those other areas. Nettelbeck and Young (1999) summarize recent thinking thusly: Interests of the savant are best served by a balanced educational approach that includes social skills training, counseling, and opportunities for interactions with others, together with encouraging savant skills but not letting them dominate the individual's life. Walker (1999) describes such an approach in her description of work with musical savants, including some autistic savants. She describes the evolution of a special education classroom, with emphasis on musical skills, up to the establishment of Hope University, an adult school of the arts, specifically for the mentally handicapped with special abilities. There the students' special talents serve as pathways to higher functioning, more independence, and more self-worth.

In Miller's (1989) book on musical savants, a music teacher chronicles her specific approach with a 6-year-old highly skilled musical savant over a three-year period, noting the positive, gratifying results of "training the talent" to increase socialization, language, and independence. Miller notes, that after three years of such an approach, there was musical growth but there was development in other areas as well, including reading, conversational language, and socialization.

He quotes the mother of the child describing her son before the piano was available as "spending hour after hour gazing out the window. His life is much different now and music has played a large role in his transformation." The teacher herself sums it up thus, "Our task is to help him express his uniqueness in more ordinary ways . . . it is increasingly difficult to recollect that he was, for a very long time, nonverbal and withdrawn. Now he engages people, takes direction, expresses courtesy and gives commands."

The goal of dealing with special skills in the savant—monotonous, impractical, and frivolous as they might sometimes seem—is not to eradicate them. It is rather to put them to good use, patiently and creatively, without fear they will disappear, consume, or overshadow everything else so that no other progress can occur. Such skills become modes of expression through which others can reach and interact with the savant. Such communication and mentoring can lead to the development of other related skills. Training the talent can diminish the defect.

Three savants, in particular, demonstrated this strategy convincingly. On October 23, 1983, *60 Minutes* aired a program on savant syndrome. George, an autistic savant, showed the ease with which he could calculate over a span of 40,000 years, as well as remember the weather for each day of his adult life. Leslie, blind and developmentally disabled with autistic features, reproduced fully and faithfully a complex classical musical piece that was played for him for the first time on that program. Alonzo, with acquired savant syndrome, secondary to a childhood head injury, sculpted a meticulously accurate and beautiful horse and colt from memory, using crystalline clay. He completed such a sculpture in about 20 minutes. The program demonstrated, in a very sensitive fashion, the astonishing skills and abilities of the savant contrasted with the disabilities of autistic disorder (George), other developmental disability (Leslie), and the acquired form of savant syndrome secondary to head injury (Alonzo). The program was informative and inspirational.

Even more inspiring, however, are the follow-up studies on those three individuals sixteen years later. George is no longer living in a supported apartment. He works as a bicycle messenger in New York City, where he lives independently in an apartment, takes the subway to work each day, and no longer requires a guardian. Alonzo has moved from the group home, now lives in his own condominium, and works part-time as a custodian at the local YMCA where he has become a loved and respected part of his community. Of course, he still sculpts. His works are internationally sought and some sell for five figure sums. Leslie can still reproduce whatever is played for him, but he has moved beyond that to improvise easily and marvelously. He now composes some of his own songs, and his repertoire consists of thousands of pieces. He has become more verbal and much more social. He interacts with his audiences now, showing considerable wit and creativity. George, Alonzo, and Leslie provide evidence of a hopeful scenario in which savant skills can be used as conduits for normalization and more independence, even in the face of still evident disabilities.

SUMMARY AND CONCLUSIONS

Since it was first described over a century ago, the phenomenon of savant syndrome—the juxtaposition of severe mental handicap and prodigious mental ability—has remained largely unexplained. Yet, no model of brain function and memory will be complete until it can account for this rare, but spectacular condition, with its islands of astonishing abilities in a sea of disability. The condition occurs in as many as 10% of persons with autistic disorder, a frequency much higher than in any other developmental disability. It is always linked to remarkable memory; yet considering all the skills in the human repertoire, the special abilities narrow to only five or six, with clinical presentations remarkably consistent and similar. The condition occurs in males six times more frequently than in females. Particularly intriguing is the conspicuously frequent triad of blindness, autism, or other developmental disability and musical genius. Research, thus far, points to an organic origin for the disorder, based on idiosyncratic and unique brain circuitry at the cortical and lower brain stem levels, resulting in memory circuits established from a variety of genetic, prenatal, or later CNS injury or disease.

There is more to savant syndrome than genetics, circuitry, or the brain's marvelous intricacy. Families, teachers, therapists, and caretakers are vitally important forces in accepting, nurturing, encouraging, and reinforcing the savants' abilities, rather than merely focusing on the disabilities. They have demonstrated, in so many cases, that handicaps need not necessarily blur hope, and that stereotyping and labeling only obscure and conceal, in a harmful manner, an individual's strengths. By "training the talent," instead of "eliminating the defect," not only do savant skills broaden, they progress and grow in other areas, without any regrettable trade-off of savant skills so often feared. Rather, the savant skills can be a conduit toward normalization for both higher- and lower-level functioning.

Many questions remain unanswered. But interest in this astonishing juxtapostition of ability and disability is accelerating now, and newer technology, including PET scans that look at brain function rather than just brain structure, will help provide insights not only into the savant syndrome, but into autistic disorder and other forms of developmental disability as well. Further, by using standardized testing and control samples, (rather than relying on anecdotal accounts that have characterized the literature to date), and then comparing those results with normal populations, including some prodigies in non-disabled populations, insights about skill acquisition and intelligence can be obtained. Such studies are already underway. Answers from those inquiries could provide important information about brain function, brain plasticity, intelligence, and, perhaps, even buried potential within us all. Meanwhile, the inspiration from these remarkable people, and their equally remarkable families, teachers, and caretakers will continue. A website through the Wisconsin State Medical Society Foundation is available to all interested readers at http://www.wismed.com/foundation/savant.htm.

CHAPTER SUMMARY

1. Savant syndrome is the presence of a spectacular (in the genius range) but narrow skill, combined with a similarly limited exceptional memory typically occurring in a person with autistic spectrum disorder and/or mental retardation.
2. The skill areas that are exaggerated in savant syndrome are usually restricted to functions typically associated with the right hemisphere of the brain: music, art, mathematics, calendrical calculations, and mechanical or spatial abilities.
3. Savant syndrome occurs in one in ten persons with autistic spectrum disorder and one in 2,000 persons with mental retardation.
4. Approximately half of persons with savant syndrome have autistic spectrum disorder, while a somewhat overlapping half have mental retardation.
5. Savant syndrome has a 6 to 1 male predominance.
6. Splinter skills in persons with autistic spectrum disorder and/or mental retardation are areas of relative or absolute strength that do not rise to the level of giftedness.
7. A recurrent pattern of savant syndrome involves the triad of blindness (usually secondary to Retinopathy of Prematurity (ROP), mental retardation (often associated with autistic spectrum disorder), and musical genius (most frequently involving the piano).
8. Williams syndrome is a chromosomal disorder (deletion 7q11) that presents with a distinctive facial appearance (elfin or pixie-like facies), congenital heart disease, elevated calcium level (with colic symptoms) in infancy, developmental delay with autistic symptoms, social extraversion with "cocktail party chatter" speech, and musical giftedness.

9. While there is no generally accepted explanation for the development/presence of savant skills, some kind of left brain injury (including fetal exposure to testosterone) with right hemispheric compensation appears to play a significant role.
10. With regard to therapy, the dichotomy of reinforcing the talent or emphasizing deficiencies is artificial and unjustified; a savant skill can be used as a conduit toward normalization without necessarily impairing or limiting the talent.

REFERENCES

Barr, M. W. 1989. Some notes on echolalia, with the report of an extraordinary case. *Journal of Nervous and Mental Diseases* 25:20–30.

Bauman, M., and Kemper, T. L. 1985. Histoanatomic observations of the brain in early infantile autism. *Neurology* 35:866–74.

Bender, M. B., Feldman, M., and Sobin, A. J. 1968. Palinopsia. *Brain* 91:321–38.

Brink, T. L. 1980. Idiot savant with unusual mechanical ability: An organic explanation. *American Journal of Psychiatry* 137:250–1.

Cameron, L. 1998. *The Music of Light: The Extraordinary Story of Hikari and Kenzaburo Oe.* New York: Free Press.

Charness, N., Clifton, J., and MacDonald, L. 1988. Case study of a musical "mono-savant": A cognitive-psychological focus. In *The Exceptional Brain*, eds. L. Obler and D. A. Fine. New York: Guilford.

Critchley, M. 1979. *The Divine Banquet of the Brain.* New York: Raven Press.

Down, J. L. 1887. *On Some of the Affections of Childhood and Youth.* London: Churchill.

Duckett, J. 1976. Idiot Savants: Super-specialization in mentally retarded persons. Doctoral Dissertation. University of Texas in Austin, Department of Special Education.

Geschwind N., and Galaburda A. M. 1987. *Cerebral Lateralization: Biological Mechanisms, Associations and Pathology.* Cambridge, MA: MIT Press.

Gillberg, C., and Rasmussen, P. 1994. Brief report: Four case histories and a literature review of Williams syndrome and autistic behavior. *Journal of Autism and Developmental Disorders.* 24:381–93.

Giray, E. F., and Barclay, A. G. 1977. Eidetic imagery: Longitudinal results in brain-damaged children. *American Journal of Mental Deficiency* 82:311–14.

Hauser, S. L., DeLong, G. R., and Rosman, N. P. 1975. Pneumographic findings in the infantile autism syndrome. *Brain* 98:667–88.

Hermelin, B., O'Connor, N., Lee, S., and Treffert, D. 1989. Intelligence and musical improvisation. *Psychological Medicine* 19:447–57.

Hill, A. L. 1978. Savants: Mentally retarded individuals with special skills. In *International Review of Research in Mental Retardation*, ed. N. Ellis. New York: Academic Press.

Hoffman, E. 1971. The idiot savant: A case report and review of explanations. *Mental Retardation* 9:18–21.

Horwitz, W. A., Kestenbaum, C., Person, E., and Jarvick, L. 1965. Identical twins—"idiot savants"—calendar calculators. *American Journal of Psychiatry* 121:1075–79.

Horwitz, W. A., Deming, W. E., and Winter, R. F. 1969. A further account of the idiot savants, experts with the calendar. *American Journal of Psychiatry* 126:412–15.

Jaensch, E. R., and Menhel, H. 1928. Gedachtnisleistung eines schwachsinnigen Eidetikers. *Psychiatrish Neurologische Wochenschrift* 30:101–03.

Jones, H. E. 1926. Phenomenal memorizing as a special ability. *Journal of Applied Psychology* 10:367–76.

Kanner, L. 1971. Childhood psychosis: A historical overview. *Journal of Autism and Childhood Schizophrenia* 1:14–19.

Kehrer, H. E. 1992. Savant capabilities of autistic persons. *Acta Paedopsychiatrica* 55:151–5.

Keeler, W. R. 1958. Autistic patterns and defective communication in blind children with retrolental fibroplasia. In *Psychopathology of Communication*, eds. P. Hoch and J. Zubin. New York: Grune and Stratton.

LaFontaine, L. 1974. Divergent abilities in the idiot savant. Doctoral Dissertation. Boston University in Boston, School of Education.

Lindsley, O. 1965. Can deficiency produce specific superiority: The challenge of the idiot savant. *Exceptional Children* 31:25–32.

Luszki, W. A. 1966. An idiot savant on the WAIS? *Psychological Reports* 19:603–9.

Miller, B. L., Cummings, J., Mishkin, F., Boone, K., Prince, F., Ponton, M., and Cotman, C. 1998. Emergence of artistic talent in frontotemporal dementia. *Neurology* 51:978–82.

Miller, L. 1989. *Musical Savants: Exceptional Skill in the Mentally Retarded.* Hillsdale, NJ: Lawrence Erlbaum Associates.

Mishkin, M., and Petri, H. L. 1984. Memories and habits: Some implications for the analysis of learning and retention. In *Neuropsychology of Memory*, eds. L. R. Squire and N. Butters. New York: Guilford Press.

Nettelbeck, T., and Young, R. 1999. Savant Syndrome. In *International Review of Research in Mental Retardation*, ed. C. M. Glidden. New York: Academic Press.

Nurcombe, M. D., and Parker, N. 1964. The idiot savant. *Journal of the American Academy of Child Psychiatry* 3:469–87.

O'Connor, N., and Hermelin, B. 1984. Idiot savant calendrical calculators: Math or memory? *Psychological Medicine* 14:801–6.

O'Connor, N., and Hermelin, B. 1991. A specific liguistic ability. *American Journal on Mental Retardation* 95:673–80.

Phillips, A. 1930. Talented imbeciles. *Psychological Clinics* 18:246–55.

Rife, D. C., and Snyder, L. H. 1931. Studies in human inheritance, VI: A genetic refutation of the principles of "behavioristic" psychology. *Human Biology* 3:347–487.

Rimland, B. 1964. *Infantile Autism: The syndrome and its implications for a neural theory of behavior.* New York: Appleton-Century-Crofts.

Rimland, B. 1978. Savant characteristics of autistic children and their cognitive implications. In *Cognitive Defects in the Development of Mental Illness*, ed. G. Serban. New York: Brunner/Mazel.

Rimland, B., and Fine, D. 1988. Special talents of autistic savants. In *The Exceptional Brain*, ed. L. Obler and D. A. Fein. New York: Guilford Press.

Sacks, O. 1987. The twins. *New York Review of Books* 32:16–20.

Sano, F. 1918. James Henry Pullen, the genius of Earlswood. *Journal of Mental Science* 64:251–67.

Scheerer, M., Rothman, E., and Goldstein, K. 1945. A case of "idiot savant": An experimental study of personality organization. *Psychological Monographs* 58:1–63.

Selfe, L. 1977. *Nadia: A Case of Extraordinary Drawing Ability in an Autistic Child.* London: Academic Press.

Sequin, E. 1866, 1971. *Idiocy and Its Treatment by the Physiological Method.* New York: Kelley.

Southall, G. 1979. *Blind Tom: The Post-Civil War Enslavement of a Black Musical Genius.* Minneapolis, Minnesota: Challenge Productions.
Smith, N., and Tsimpli, I. 1995. *The Mind of a Savant: Language, Learning and Modularity.* Oxford: Blackwell.
Steel, J. G., Gorman, R., and Flexman, J. E. 1984. Neuropsychiatric testing in an autistic mathematical idiot-savant: Evidence for nonverbal abstract capacity. *Journal of the American Academy of Child Psychiatry* 3:469–87.
Tanguay, P. E. 1973. A tentative hypothesis regarding the role of hemispheric specialization in early infantile autism. Paper presented at UCLA Conference on Cerebral Dominance, Los Angeles, CA.
Tredgold, A. F. 1914. *Mental Deficiency.* New York: William Wood.
Treffert, D. A. 1988. The idiot savant: A review of the syndrome. *American Journal of Psychiatry* 145:563–72.
Treffert, D. A. 1989. *Extraordinary People: Understanding "Idiot Savants."* New York: Harper and Row.
Treffert, D. A. 2000. *Extraordinary People: Understanding Savant Syndrome.* Backinprint.com.
Viscott, D. S. 1970. A musical idiot savant. *Psychiatry* 33:494–515.
Walker, D. 1999. *Journey to a Far Country: The Savants and Me.* Bryn Mawr, PA: Buy Books on the web.com.
Williams, J. C. P., Barratt-Boyes, B. G., and Lowe, J. G. 1961. Supravalvular aortic stenosis. *Circulation* 24:1311–18.
Wiltshire, S. 1987. *Drawings.* London: J. M. Dent and Sons.
Wiltshire, S. 1991. *Floating Cities.* New York: Summit Books.
Young, R. 1995. Savant syndrome: Processes underlying extraordinary abilities. Unpublished doctoral dissertation, University of Adelaide, South Australia.

Chapter • 10

The Broad Autism Phenotype

Joseph Piven

Autism is a behavioral syndrome defined by the co-occurrence of a set of particular behaviors and a characteristic course. Based on the results of twin and family studies it is now generally accepted that the etiology of autism is largely genetic. An important question for genetic studies of autism (as well as other complex neuropsychiatric disorders) is whether or not our current definitions of the behavioral syndrome of autism accurately reflect the underlying genetic substrates (or genotypes). Clearly, it has been the hope that the molecular genetics approaches developed over the last 15 years would help to refine more genetically meaningful nosological categories for complex neuropsychiatric disorders such as autism. However, to date, this approach has not yet produced the anticipated results.

In a recent review, Leboyer et al. (1998) suggested several strategies for determining biologically meaningful phenotypes. By identifying symptoms that occur most commonly or are most fundamental to the phenotype, by measuring which symptoms are concordant in twins or siblings, or by observing those symptoms that appear to follow recognizable patterns of inheritance, one can determine phenotypic subgroups. A second strategy is to identify, through family studies, pertinent (genetically related) phenotypes in relatives who do not meet full criteria for the disorder (i.e., to identify subclinical traits or endophenotypes that aggregate in family members not affected with the core phenotype). Progress using both these strategies has been made in understanding the genetically meaningful aspects of the autism phenotype. In this chapter, I concentrate primarily on outlining the gains that have been made in the second strategy, that of identifying genetically related aspects of the phenotype in non-autistic relatives of autistic probands, or what has more recently been referred to as the broad autism phenotype (BAP).

CHARACTERISTICS OF THE BROAD AUTISM PHENOTYPE

Although Kanner (1943) made the first references to the possibility that some relatives of autistic children seemed to have high rates of particular behavioral characteristics, it wasn't until the twin study by Folstein and Rutter (1977) that the first systematic evidence in support of this concept appeared. Extending these findings further, Bailey et al. (1995) recently reported that while concordance for autism was 60% in a set of monozygotic (MZ) twin pairs, versus 0% in dizygotic (DZ) pairs, concordance for a broader spectrum of cognitive deficits (i.e., reading, spelling, or language difficulties) or social abnormalities, was even higher (i.e., 92% as compared with a 10% rate in the DZ pairs). These results suggested that, in addition to causing autism, the genetic liability for this disorder may also be expressed in behavioral and cognitive characteristics which are milder but qualitatively similar to the defining features of autism.

Family history studies of three independent samples have now confirmed the existence of a broad or extended autism phenotype (BAP), demonstrating the familial aggregation of communication and social deficits and stereotyped behaviors in first- and second-degree relatives of individuals with autism (Bolton et al. 1994; Piven et al. 1997). Family interview studies have begun the important next step of beginning to define the range and pattern of characteristics which define this broader phenotype through more detailed and direct assessments of relatives. On the basis of evidence suggesting higher rates of the BAP in relatives of multiple-incidence versus single-incidence autistic probands (Palmer and Piven, submitted), Piven et al. (1997) directly examined parents from 25 multiple-incidence autism families (MIAFs) and compared them to parents of 30 Down syndrome (DS) probands on a number of direct measures of behavior and cognition. Parents and informants (usually spouses) were interviewed on a semi-structured personality interview, the *Modified Personality Assessment Schedule-Revised* (M,PAS-R), designed to examine personality features thought to comprise aspects of the BAP. Blind, best estimate ratings of these videotaped interviews were based on the subject and informant report of examples of particular behaviors, rather than on the interviewer's subjective judgment of the presence of these characteristics during the interview. On this personality instrument, MIAF parents were more frequently rated as having (1) little interest in or enjoyment from being with others (aloof); (2) little interest in and/or difficulty adjusting to change in routine (rigid); (3) nervousness or anxiety, not amounting to an anxiety disorder (anxious); and (4) excessive distress at the comments or behavior of others that were felt to be critical or insensitive (hypersensitive to criticism). Based on their conversations with the examiner during the M,PAS-R interview (and during an informal break in the interview session), parents were also rated on their pragmatic or social use of language and speech, using the *Pragmatic Rating Scale* (PRS) (Landa et al. 1992). On blind videotaped ratings of these interviews, parents of autistic children were rated more commonly than DS parents as having abnormalities of both pragmatic language and speech. Consistent with the suggestion that parents of autistic children often employ a rigid linguistic rule system (Landa et al. 1992), deficits observed in pragmatic language usually had more to do with a lack of relevance and clarity of message (e.g., being overly detailed), than on more social aspects of conversation (e.g., being too informal or failing to reciprocate during the conversation). Finally, parents were interviewed about the number and quality of friendships throughout their adult lives. These parents were noted to have significantly fewer quality friendships than DS parents. The results of this study replicated the findings from the Baltimore Autism Family Study where higher rates of deficits in the social aspects of personality (aloof, untactful, undemonstrative) and language (pragmatics), along with fewer quality friendships, were noted in a large sample of parents of autistic children (ascertained through a single autistic proband) in contrast to parents of DS individuals.

In order to determine which traits were most useful in distinguishing MIAF parents from DS parents in the study by Piven et al. (1997), the 11 variables examined in that study (eight personality variables from the M,PAS-R; total speech and pragmatic language scores from the PRS; and total friendship score from the *Friendship Interview*), were entered into a logistic regression analysis to predict case versus control status. The final model included four items—rigid and hypersensitivity to criticism (from the MPAS-R); total speech score (from the PRS); and friendship score (from the *Friendship Interview*)—and correctly classified 82% of the 101 subjects entered into this analysis. Three of the four items included in this model are qualitatively similar to the defining features of autism—social deficits (friendship), communication deficits (speech), and stereotyped behavior (rigid)—supporting the validity of these findings. A fourth characteristic, hypersensitivity to criticism, has been shown to be a measure of anxiety (i.e., it was highly correlated with neuroticism, N1, on the NEO-PI as well as anxiety on the M,PAS-R). And while anxiety is not a defining feature of autism, it is present in many individuals with autism and may be related to an additional genetic component contributing to the autism phenotype.

DEFINING THE BROAD AUTISM PHENOTYPE FOR USE IN GENETIC STUDIES

Although the genetic basis of autism is well established, the mechanisms of genetic transmission have not yet been determined. As a result of the absence of vertical transmission of the full syndrome of autism (i.e., autistic individuals rarely have children) and the possibility that reproductive stoppage rules may be operating (i.e., parents sometimes limit their plans for more children following the diagnosis of autism in their child), families with an autistic member are often small and usually contain only one individual affected with autism. In most families, the small number of individuals affected with autism limits the power of molecular genetic studies to locate genes underlying this disorder and affects our ability to observe for specific patterns of inheritance. Analysis of twin and family data have been most consistent with the possibility that autism could be the result of oligogenic inheritance with three or more interacting loci. However, when the broad autism phenotype (BAP) is considered, along with the diagnoses of autism and pervasive developmental disorder, (PDD, NOS), the examination of moderate size pedigrees (i.e., with two or more individuals affected with autism and others showing evidence of the BAP) is sometimes consistent with Mendelian mechanisms (figure 1). Inclusion of the genetically related BAP in genetic studies of autism may complement existing analytic approaches that are based on diagnosing only those meeting criteria for autism or PDD as affected, and, possibly, increase our ability to detect genes in this disorder.

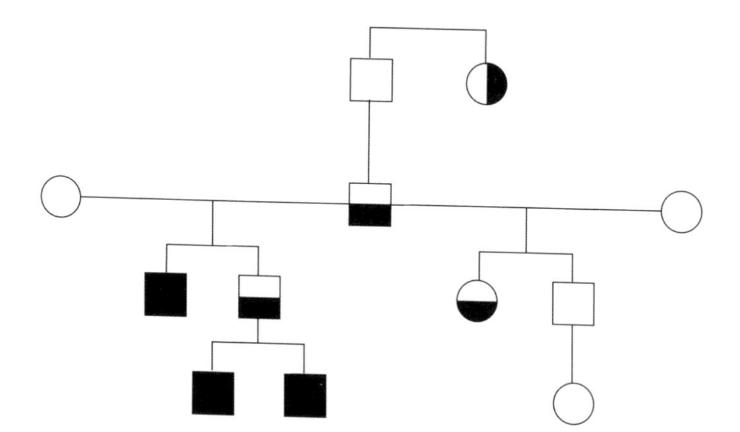

Figure 1. Moderate size pedigree with individuals affected with the autism (■), probable pervasive developmental disorder, not otherwise specified (PDD, NOS) (◑) and the broad autism phenotype (⬓, ◒)

While we do not yet know whether the genetic liability for the PDD/BAP phenotype is expressed continuously or discretely, the validity of the syndrome of autism is based on the co-occurrence of a set of qualitatively distinct behaviors, along with a characteristic course. Taking a similar syndromic or composite approach to defining the BAP is a reasonable first step for developing criteria for defining affected status for genetic studies. Using data from their study of MIAF and DS parents, Piven et al. (1997) constructed an equation whereby each of the four items retained in the logistic regression model described above was assigned one point if present (or, in the case of the speech and friendship scores, if their score was > 1.5 SD beyond the control mean) in an individual and zero points if absent (or if their score was < 1.5 SD beyond the control mean). Scores were summed to produce a composite score for the BAP (i.e., BAP = rigid + friends + speech + hypersensitive to criticism) with a range of zero to four. In order to maximize specificity without severely limiting sensitivity, a score for "affected" (i.e., the BAP was rated as present) was arbitrarily set at 2 or greater. Using this cutoff, 26/46 (58%) MIAF parents and only 2/55 (4%) DS parents were classified as affected, for a specificity and sensitivity of 96% and 56%, respectively. In 38% of the MIAF families, both parents had a BAP score of > 2, suggesting bilineal transmission of the genetic liability for autism in at least a subset of families. Figure 2 presents a case vignette, highlighting the personality characteristics from the M,PAS-R of one parent of two autistic children who met these criteria for the BAP.

> Mr. A is a 35-year-old male college professor of engineering and parent of an autistic child. He spends most of his free time reading. He describes himself as very organized, a very careful planner who writes out his lectures nearly verbatim before each class. His wife says he spends more time planning than any other professor she knows. Mr. A is most comfortable with routine in his life. He says he would be happy if he could have a life with no surprises. He requests that his courses be scheduled at the same time each semester. He feels "out of sorts" when his routine gets interrupted. His wife says he protests when asked to drop off a letter on his way to work because it disrupts his routine. He describes himself as fairly inflexible and says once his mind is made up, he won't change it. He gets into routines and sometimes does things in an illogical manner just because he has done them that way before. He prefers to go to the same restaurant every Saturday night.
>
> Mr. A related numerous examples of his discomfort in social situations. He says he spent more time with books than people during childhood. He doesn't see the point in "chit chat" or "small talk." He prefers there be a purpose to conversations. He also finds conversations to be difficult if roles are not firmly established. He has a set of rules for different interactions and when roles are clearly defined, he knows which rule to follow; otherwise he is very uncomfortable. He feels he has probably "fallen out of the loop" in his department because he tends to avoid social gatherings.

Figure 2. Vignette of an individual rated as having the broad autism phenotype on the basis of having evidence of rigid and aloof personality on the M,PAS-R.

OTHER CHARACTERISTICS AGGREGATING IN FAMILIES

Historically, cognitive deficits were the first characteristics to be considered as part of the broader expression of the underlying genetic liability to autism. Folstein and Rutter (1977) reported a higher concordance in MZ rather than in DZ twins for the presence of autism or a cognitive disorder (defined as severe language, speech or reading deficits, or mental retardation). While the data are now clear on showing that mental retardation does not aggregate at higher rates in autism families (Bolton et al. 1994), the question of whether additional cognitive deficits aggregate in families of autistic probands is less clear. Piven and Palmer (1997) found high rates of a number of cognitive deficits in MIAF parents in contrast to parents from DS families, including significantly different verbal-performance IQ scores, deficits on a measure of executive function (the four ring Tower of Hanoi), deficits in reading comprehension on the *Woodcock Johnson Battery*, and significantly worse performance on the *Rapid Automatized Naming Task*. Differences in verbal and performance IQ were largely due to significantly lower scores on performance IQ (pIQ), as measured by the *Wechsler Adult Intelligence Scale*. This result (i.e., lower pIQ) has been replicated in the Baltimore Autism Family Study (Folstein et al. 1999). Results from the London Family Study, while also revealing a significant difference between verbal-performance splits in autism and DS relatives, with a greater split among autism relatives, did not indicate significantly lower pIQ scores, but did show elevated verbal IQ scores in the autism relatives (Fombonne et al. 1997). In the area of executive function, somewhat more agreement that relatives (parents and siblings) of autistic probands do seem to have elevated rates of executive function deficits (Ozonoff et al. 1993; Hughes, Leboyer, and Bouvard 1997) exists across studies. The validity of this is supported by the frequent finding of impairment on tests of executive function in autistic individuals (Ozonoff et al. 1994). Finally, while the finding of reading comprehension deficits in MIAF parents requires replication, studies of individuals with autism indicate that reading deficits in autism are largely a result of deficits in comprehension and not decoding, unlike dyslexia (Rumsey and Hamburger 1990; Frith and Snowling 1983). The findings by Piven and Palmer (1997) showing no evidence of deficient performance in decoding words (the non-word reading task from the *Woodcock Johnson Battery*) are, therefore, consistent with findings in autistic individuals.

Four family studies, employing control groups and direct psychiatric assessments, have reported elevated rates of major depressive disorder in first- and second-degree relatives of autistic probands (Piven et al. 1991; Piven and Palmer 1999; Smalley, McCracken, and

Tanguay 1995; Bolton et al. 1998). In all four studies, most parents were noted to have had the onset of their depressive episodes prior to the birth of the autistic child (or children), suggesting that the high rate of depression was not the result of the stress of caring for a handicapped child. Piven and Palmer (1999) and Smalley, McCracken, and Tanguay (1995), using comparable instruments and diagnostic criteria, have also detected high rates of social phobia in relatives with autism. Two studies have examined the relationship of major depressive disorder to the BAP and found that those individuals showing social and communication deficits and stereotyped behaviors, consistent with a diagnosis of the BAP, did not have higher rates of major depressive disorder than those with no evidence of the BAP. The meaning of this finding must await further studies for clarification of the mechanisms underlying the relationship of the BAP to major depressive disorder.

THE SIGNIFICANCE OF THE BROAD AUTISM PHENOTYPE

Clarification of the boundaries of the phenotype in autism has several important potential implications for future research in autism, as well as implications for clinical practice. First, clarification of the range and characteristics of a broader autism phenotype may aid in genetic analysis by increasing sample size (and power) for genetic linkage studies and other genetic analyses (e.g. segregation analyses). Alternately, studies of the components of autism and the BAP may allow us to tease apart effects due to separate genes associated with distinct aspects of the phenotype (rather than employing syndromic-like definitions as we have proposed above, where a single algorithm includes a number of conceptually unrelated aspects that together define the BAP). In a disorder such as autism, which may be due to multiple, interacting genes, searching for a gene for a single aspect of the syndrome, such as rigidity, provides an alternative and potentially fruitful approach to looking for genes underlying this disorder. This same approach was successfully employed in a recent study of dyslexia where separate linkages to distinct reading tasks (e.g., phonological awareness and single word reading) were demonstrated (Grigorenko et al. 1996). Second, clarification of the broader autism phenotype provides important avenues for looking for brain-behavior relationships using neuroimaging of more mildly affected individuals. Relatives with the BAP provide a more cooperative subject pool than autistic subjects for imaging studies, and allow for the study of components of the phenotype (i.e., social abnormalities, language deficits, or stereotyped behaviors) to be examined separately in relation to brain structure and function. In a recent paper by Sears et al. (1999), caudate volume was significantly related to stereotyped behaviors but not to other symptoms of autism. Finally, the presence of the broader phenotype in families may index an important subgroup within this etiologically heterogeneous disorder. In the study by Bolton et al. (1994), verbal IQ in probands was associated with the familial aggregation of the BAP. This approach might be considered for other phenotypic markers in the proband (e.g., macrocephaly) or may even prove useful in defining homogeneous subgroups for linkage analysis.

Recognition of the BAP in parents and siblings also has potential importance in clinical practice. Early recognition of siblings who may be at elevated risks for cognitive, personality, or psychiatric deficits may lead to more effective intervention. Awareness of the existence of the BAP may also enable practitioners to be more tolerant and understanding of parental behaviors, and more insightful about relevant parental characteristics in formulating their recommendations for treatment. Finally, while it is still unclear as to how the presence of relatives with the BAP alters estimates for the recurrence of autism in families, eventually, accurate characterization of the BAP may have a role in genetic counseling of families at risk for having additional children with autism.

SUMMARY AND CONCLUSIONS

Clearly, there is now good evidence to indicate that a portion of the non-autistic relatives of autistic individuals have a set of behavioral and cognitive characteristics that are milder but qualitatively similar to the defining features of autism, including social and communication deficits and stereotyped behaviors. These behaviors are likely to be etiologically related to the genetic factors causing autism, although the final proof of this will come about only when genes for autism and the BAP are found. Initial efforts have begun to outline the range and pattern of behaviors that comprise this broad autism phenotype. Clarification of the boundaries and patterns of the BAP has important potential implications for furthering our understanding of the genetics of autism, as well as improving our clinical practice with families of autistic individuals.

CHAPTER SUMMARY

1. The Broad Autism Phenotype (BAP) is composed of characteristic behaviors, milder but qualitatively similar to the clinical features of autism found in relatives of persons with autism who do not have autism themselves.
2. Family studies have documented the presence of this extended autism phenotype, or BAP, by demonstrating familial

clustering of communication and social deficits and stereotyped behaviors in the relatives of persons with autism that are not severe enough for a diagnosis of autism.
3. Relatives of individuals with autism can exhibit rigidity, aloofness, anxiety, hypersensitivity to criticism, fewer friends, and deficits in pragmatic language.
4. The BAP may include cognitive deficits such as verbal-performance IQ differences (with verbal higher), executive function deficits, reading comprehension, and rapid naming.
5. The inheritance pattern of autism within families suggests multiple interacting genes contributing to the condition.
6. Although major depressive episodes are more common in family members of individuals with autism, they may be independent of the presence of the BAP.
7. Investigating the components of the BAP may contribute to the identification of genes for autism.

REFERENCES

Bailey, A., LeCouteur, A., Gottesman, I., Bolton, P., Simonoff, E., Yuzda, E., and Rutter, M. 1995. Autism as a strongly genetic disorder: Evidence from a British twin study. *Psychological Medicine* 25:63–77.

Bolton, P. F., MacDonald, H., Pickles, A., Rios, P., Goode, S., Crowson, M., Bailey, A., and Rutter, M. 1994. A case-control family history study of autism. *Journal of Child Psychology and Psychiatry* 35:877–900.

Bolton, P. F., Pickles, A., Murphy, M., and Rutter, M. 1998. Autism affective and other psychiatric disorder: Patterns of familial aggregation. *Psychological Medicine* 28:385–95.

Folstein, S. E., Santangelo, S. L., Gilman, S. E., Piven, J., Landa, R., Lainhart, J., Hein, J., and Wzorek, M. 1999 submitted. Predictors of cognitive test patterns in autism families.

Folstein, S. E., and Rutter, M. 1977. Infantile autism: A genetic study of 21 twin pairs. *Journal of Child Psychology and Psychiatry* 18:297–321.

Fombonne, E., Bolton, P., Prior, J., Jordan, H., and Rutter, M. 1997. A family study of autism: Cognitive patterns and levels in parents and siblings. *Journal of Child Psychology and Psychiatry* 38(6):667–84.

Frith, U., and Snowling, M. 1983. Reading for meaning and reading for sound in autistic and dyslexic children. *British Journal of Developmental Psychology* 1:329–42.

Grigorenko, E. L., Wood, F. B., Meyer, M. S., Hart, L. A., Speed, W. C., Shuster, A., and Pauls, D. L. 1996. Susceptibility loci for distinct components of developmental dyslexia on chromosomes 6 and 15. *American Journal of Human Genetics* 60:27–39.

Hughes, C., Leboyer, M., and Bouvard, M. 1997. Executive function in parents of children with autism. *Psychological Medicine* 27:209–20.

Kanner, L. 1943. Autistic disturbances of affective contact. *Nervous Child* 2:217–50.

Landa, R., Piven, J., Wzorek, M. M., Gayle, J. O., Chase, G. A., and Folstein, S. E. 1992. Social language use in parents of autistic individuals. *Psychological Medicine* 22(1):245–54.

Leboyer, M., Bellivier, F., Nosten-Bertrand, M., Jouvent, R., Pauls, D., and Mallet, J. 1998. Psychiatric genetics: Search for phenotypes. *Trends in Neurosciences* 21(3):102–05.

Ozonoff, S., Rogers, S., Farnham, J., and Pennington, B. 1993. Can standard measures identify subclinical markers of autism? *Journal of Autism and Developmental Disorders* 23:429–44.

Ozonoff, S., Strayer, D., McMahon, W., and Filloux, F. 1994. Executive function abilities in autism and Tourette syndrome: An information processing approach. *Journal of Child Psychology and Psychiatry* 35:1015–32.

Palmer, P., and Piven, J. Submitted. Comparison of multiple and single incidence autism families on rates of the broader autism phenotype and perinatal optimality.

Piven, J., Chase, G. A., Landa, R., Wzorek, M., Gayle, J., Cloud, D., and Folstein, S. 1991. Psychiatric disorders in the parents of autistic individuals. *Journal of the American Academy of Child and Adolescent Psychiatry* 30(3):471–8.

Piven, J., Gayle, J., Chase, G. A., Fink, B., Landa, R., Wzorek, M., and Folstein, S. 1990. A family history study of neuropsychiatric disorders in the adult siblings of autistic individuals. *Journal of the American Academy of Child and Adolescent Psychiatry* 29:177–83.

Piven, J., and Palmer, P. 1999. Psychiatric disorder and the broad autism phenotype: Evidence from a family study of multiple-incidence autism families. *American Journal of Psychiatry* 156:557–63.

Piven, J., Palmer, P., Landa, R., Santangelo, S., Jacobi, D., and Childress, D. 1997. Personality and language characteristics in parents from multiple-incidence autism families. *American Journal of Medical Genetics and Neuropsychiatric Genetics* 74(4):398–411.

Piven, J., and Palmer, P. 1997. Cognitive deficits in parents from multiple-incidence autism families. *Journal of Child Psychology and Psychiatry* 38(8):1011–22.

Piven, J., Palmer, P., Jacobi, D., Childress, D., and Arndt, S. 1997. The broader autism phenotype: Evidence from a family study of multiple-incidence autism families. *American Journal of Psychiatry* 154:185–90.

Rumsey, J. M., and Hamburger, S. D. 1990. Neuropsychological divergence of high-level autism and severe dyslexia. *Journal of Autism and Developmental Disorders* 20:155–67.

Sears, L. L., Vest, C., Mohamed, S., Bailey, J., Ranson, B. J., and Piven, J. 1999. An MRI study of the basal ganglia in autism. *Progress in Neuro-Psychopharmacology and Biological Psychiatric* 23:613–24.

Smalley, S., McCracken, J., and Tanguay, P. 1995. Autism, affective disorders, and social phobia. *American Journal of Medical Genetics* 60:19–26.

Chapter • 11

Seizures, Landau-Kleffner Syndrome, and Autistic Regression: Differential Diagnosis and Treatment

John F. Mantovani

The autistic spectrum/pervasive developmental disorders (termed autism in this chapter) are now recognized as neurobiological conditions of the developing brain, which are frequently associated with other symptoms of neurological dysfunction (Gillberg and Coleman 1992; Rapin 1998). Abnormal electroencephalograms (EEGs) and/or clinical seizures are among the most common associations with autism, occurring in at least fifty percent of affected individuals (Volkmar and Nelson 1990; Tuchman, Rapin, and Shinnar 1991; Tuchman et al. 1998). A specific subgroup of children with autism who experience loss of social, cognitive, and language abilities following initially normal development is of particular interest in this respect (Kurita 1985; Rogers and DiLalla 1990).

This "autistic regression" group appears to have a significantly increased incidence of severely abnormal EEGs, compared to autistic children without a history of regression (Deonna et al. 1993; Tuchman and Rapin 1997). Severely abnormal EEGs are also characteristic of Landau-Kleffner Syndrome, a rare neurological disorder in which previously normal children have progressive loss of language abilities (Landau and Kleffner 1957). Recognition of overlapping clinical and electrophysiological features in these conditions has led to speculation that there may be a pathophysiological relationship between them (Gillberg 1991; Tuchman et al. 1998). This chapter discusses the diagnosis and treatment of seizures, Landau-Kleffner syndrome, and autistic regression in order to provide a clinical perspective on their complex interrelationships.

SEIZURES IN AUTISM

Seizures are episodic alterations of consciousness and/or motor and perceptual functions caused by abnormal paroxysmal discharges of cerebral neurons. The neuronal disturbances, due to abnormal electrophysiological processes, can be evaluated by an EEG to provide a visual record of cerebral electrical patterns, including those predisposing to clinical seizures. The clinical syndrome of recurrent seizures is termed epilepsy. Several specific EEG abnormalities (spikes and sharp waves) have been termed "epileptiform" because of their significant association with clinical seizures (figure 1).

Electroencephalograms (EEGs) can provide only circumstantial evidence for epilepsy unless an actual seizure is recorded because of

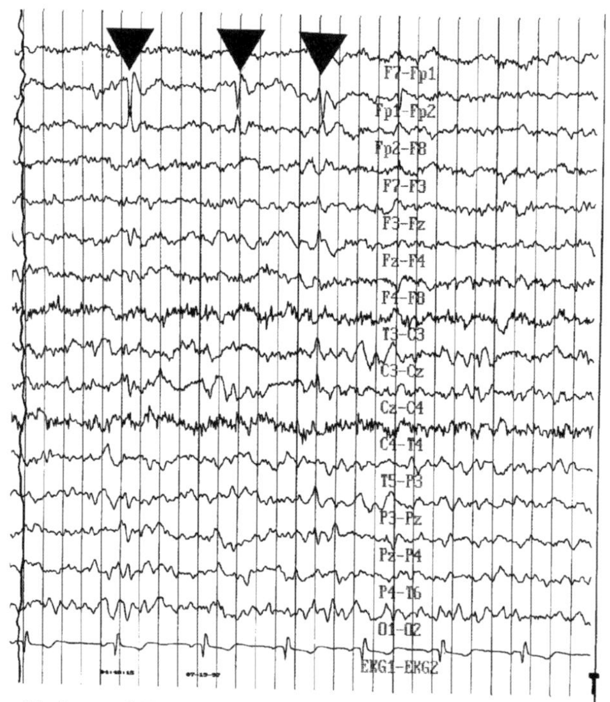

Figure 1. 16-channel EEG performed on a six-year-old neurologically well girl during light sleep. Focal spike and sharp wave (epileptiform) discharges are indicated by the arrows and occur over the left frontal lobe.

the occurrence of epileptiform abnormalities in children without clinical seizures. Approximately three percent of neurodevelopmentally normal children (Cavazutti, Cappella, and Nalin 1980) and eight to fifteen percent of autistic children without seizures (Rapin 1995; Tuchman and Rapin 1997) have epileptiform EEGs.

Seizures are classified by their clinical manifestations and EEG patterns as generalized, partial, or partial with secondary generalization. Initial treatment approaches are also based on this classification because certain anticonvulsants are more effective with specific seizure types. The incidence of seizures in children with autism ranges from thirty to forty percent, and the usual ages of onset are before the age of five or during the teenage years. Partial-complex and partial seizures with secondary generalization are the most commonly diagnosed forms, but no seizure type is specific for children with autism.

Associated features predisposing to seizures include female gender, severe mental retardation, motor deficits, and a specific pattern of language disability termed verbal auditory agnosia (Rapin et al. 1977; Tuchman et al. 1998). The factors accounting for these predispositions are unknown, but appear to correlate with the severity of the underlying autism.

Although clinical seizures are often obvious with episodic loss of consciousness and rhythmical, convulsive motor activity, they can be subtle and particularly difficult to diagnose in autistic children. Abrupt behavioral changes, including aggressive outbursts, repetitive motor automotisms, and staring spells are common in autistic children without epilepsy. In view of the lack of specificity of EEG findings, a practical determination of which children are experiencing seizures can be difficult. Often a detailed history regarding preceding circumstances and a description of the child's behavior during the episode will be of more value than an EEG in distinguishing clinical seizures from paroxysmal behaviors.

Seizures are generally unprovoked by circumstances and have a sudden onset. They usually consist of very similar motor and behavioral features with each occurrence, and they are typically followed by postictal somnolence, lethargy, or agitation. In general, seizures occur infrequently and only rarely do they occur on a daily basis.

Absence (petit mal) seizures are a notable exception since they may occur many times a day. Absence seizures generally consist of ten to thirty-second episodes of staring unresponsiveness that interrupt on-going activities, but which are not followed by any postictal effects. Nonetheless, absence seizures are uncommon in autistic individuals and almost invariably demonstrate a characteristic epileptiform pattern of generalized spike and wave complexes on routine EEGs (figure 2).

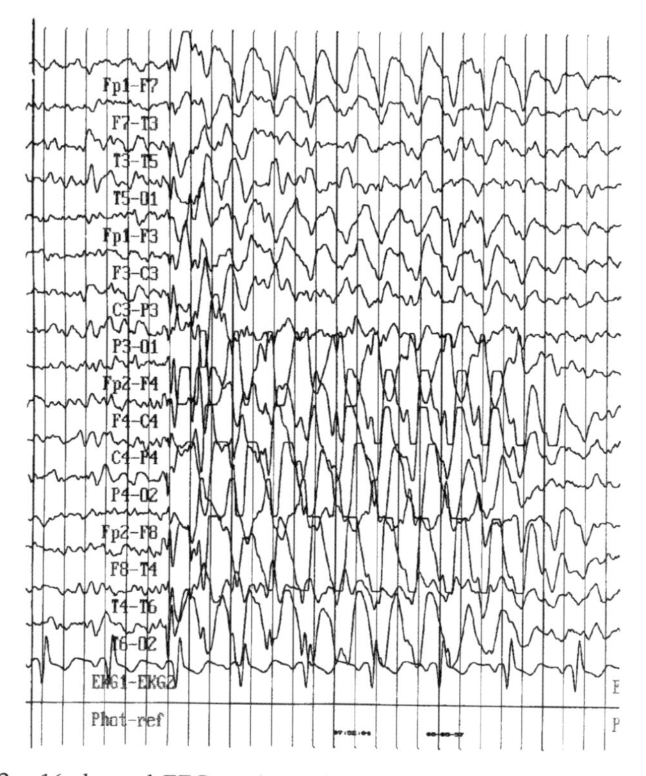

Figure 2. 16-channel EEG performed on a ten-year-old boy with absence seizures. Prominent 3.5 Hz spike and wave discharges are seen over both hemispheres with a right hemisphere predominance.

Unlike absence seizures, however, partial complex seizures are more common in those with autism and may have less specific EEG abnormalities. Partial complex seizures are notorious for their clinical variability and more subtle symptoms, including episodic confusion associated with repetitive mannerisms or altered responsiveness with lip smacking and mild changes in facial expression. Electroencephalograms in partial complex seizure disorders are often only mildly abnormal and non-epileptiform, particularly if sleep is not recorded. As a result of variability in clinical manifestations and inconsistent EEG findings, the diagnosis of partial-complex seizures can be elusive in any patient and is even more difficult in children with autism.

In cases involving recurrent paroxysmal behaviors or episodic alteration of awareness suggesting the presence of clinical seizures, home videos of spells, sleep EEGs with prolonged recording times, or simultaneous video-EEG studies in specialized telemetry units may be helpful. Unfortunately, such prolonged sleep recordings are also more likely to disclose epileptiform discharges in autistic children without clinical seizures (Villalobos et al. 1996). In some cases, only temporal correlation of a clinical event with a simultaneous EEG can resolve this issue.

LANDAU-KLEFFNER SYNDROME

Landau-Kleffner syndrome (LKS), acquired epileptic aphasia, is a condition that was described more than forty years ago in six children attending a school for the hearing impaired. Although they had normal hearing and previously normal language development, these children, with severely abnormal EEGs, had lost their ability to understand and produce oral language. In their original paper, Landau and Kleffner (1957) suggested that the children's language regression might be due to "persistent convulsive discharge in brain tissue largely concerned with linguistic communication, resulting in the functional ablation of these areas for normal linguistic behavior." Subsequently, a follow-up study of these patients and three additional cases noted a variable prognosis and questioned whether recovery might depend on anticonvulsant treatment and/or compensatory neuropsychological processes involving nonlinguistic abilities (Mantovani and Landau 1980).

Although quite rare, LKS has attracted worldwide attention, as a result of its unusual pathophysiology. Studies have centered on the relationship between the severe electrophysiological abnormalities noted on EEGs and the associated loss of linguistic abilities, as well as various treatment approaches (Deonna 1991; Roulet 1995; Tuchman 1997). The original hypothesis that the language deficits are caused by clinically unapparent epileptiform abnormalities (subclinical seizures) which interfere with linguistic processing has received considerable support, stimulating interest in other conditions with similar features (Deonna 1995; Aicardi 1996).

The usual age of onset of LKS is between four and seven years, although atypical cases beginning before the age of three or after nine years of age have also been described. The prognosis is variable but generally better in those with fluctuating aphasia; worse in those with onset before age five (Mantovani and Landau 1980; Bishop 1985; Paquier, VanDongen, and Loonen 1992). Affected children often appear to have become deaf as seen in their failure to respond to verbal language (verbal auditory agnosia). They also frequently exhibit serious behavioral abnormalities including hyperactivity. Most importantly, these children maintain their social awareness, use of gestures, and measured cognitive abilities on standardized tests of nonverbal skills (Landau and Kleffner 1957; Mantovani and Landau 1980; Rapin 1995). Additionally, children with LKS maintain their prior interest in toys, interactive games, and imaginative play. It is their older age of onset and preserved developmental abilities in nonverbal areas that clinically serve to distinguish children with LKS from those with autistic regression.

In addition to their aphasia, children with LKS have dramatically epileptiform EEGs (figure 3), and, in seventy percent of cases, clinical seizures. Common seizure types include staring spells with excessive drooling (atypical absence) and generalized tonic-clonic episodes. Despite the ease of clinical seizure control in most of these children and the absence of seizures in a significant minority, their EEGs are often resistant to the effects of anticonvulsant medications. Electroenceph-

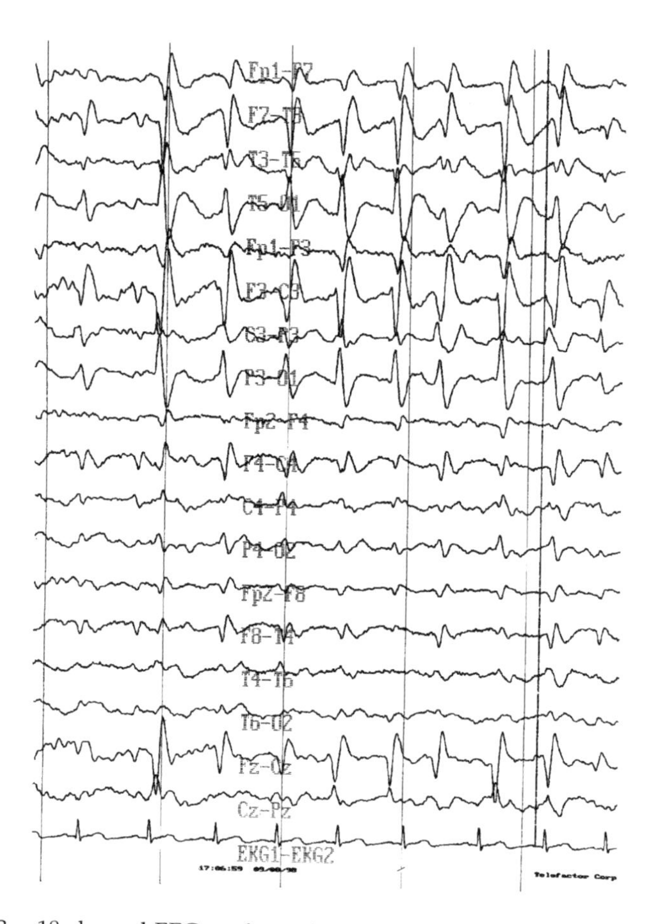

Figure 3. 18-channel EEG performed on a seven-year-old boy with Landau-Kleffner syndrome during deep sleep. Constant spike and sharp wave complexes are seen over the entire left hemisphere and the right frontal, temporal, and parietal lobes.

alogram findings, including spikes, sharp waves, and spike wave complexes, are typically found over bilateral centro-temporal brain regions that subserve language and auditory processing functions (Nakano, Okuno, and Mikawa 1989; Stefanatos 1993; Morrell et al. 1995).

Although awake EEGs, obtained in the early stages of LKS, may occasionally show unilateral temporal spike discharges, sleep studies invariably show severely epileptiform activity. In most cases, a sleep EEG shows extremely frequent or even constant electrocerebral seizure activity, even though the child has no visible signs of clinical seizures. This condition is termed continuous spike wave syndrome of slow sleep (CSWS) and occurs in several clinical forms, including one that overlaps with LKS (Jayakar and Seshia 1991; Rintahaka, Chugani, and Sandar 1995; Roulet 1995).

Although the relationship of EEG findings to the cause of LKS is still debated, fluctuation in the aphasia has been temporally correlated to EEG changes. Clinical improvement has typically occurred following suppression of epileptiform activity by anticonvulsants or corticosteroids or surgical elimination of epileptogenic discharge by subpial cortical transection (Lerman, Lerman-Sagie, and Kivity 1991; Zardini et al. 1995; Morrell et al. 1995).

Additional support for the concept of a causal relationship between the EEG abnormalities and functional impairments has also come from recognition of other subclinical, *nonparoxysmal* epilepsies (Deonna 1995; Aicardi 1996). Children with severely epileptiform EEGs, but few or no clinical seizures, have been found to have a variety of intermittent or progressive neuropsychological deficits. Transient cognitive impairments during *subclinical* epileptiform EEG discharges have been documented repeatedly over the years (Aarts et al. 1984; Binnie et al. 1987; Kasteleijn-Nolst Trenite 1995).

Other studies have emphasized the importance of frequent subclinical seizures in producing permanent cognitive deficits (Roulet Perez et al. 1993; Roulet 1995; Deonna 1995). Furthermore, negative effects on reaction time and short-term memory tests, as well as school performance tasks, have been shown to improve in affected patients when epileptiform discharges were suppressed by valproic acid (Plioplys 1994; Kasteleijn-Nolst Trenite 1995).

Additional syndromes, including the previously mentioned continuous spike wave syndrome of slow sleep (CSWS), Rolandic epilepsy with speech dyspraxia, acquired epileptiform opercular syndrome, and several disorders with occipital spikes on EEG and cognitive deficits have been added to this group of subclinical epilepsies (Roulet, Deonna, and Despland 1989; Deonna, Roulet, and Fantan 1993; Shafrir and Prensky 1995; Nass, Gross, and Devinsky 1998b). A full review of this challenging and evolving subject is beyond the scope of this chapter, but the hypothesis that severe electrophysiological abnormalities disrupt normal developmental processes has gained wide acceptance. Nonetheless, the acceptance of a causal relationship between EEG findings and neuropsychological deficits does little to explain the underlying cause of the epileptiform activity itself, which remains completely unknown at this time.

In LKS, standard brain imaging with computerized axial tomography (CAT) or magnetic resonance imaging (MRI) is usually normal, although there have been rare cases of abnormalities caused by localized infections, demyelination, and tumors (Perniola et al. 1993; Otero, Cordova, and Diaz 1989; Nass, Heier, and Walker 1993). Further studies of children with LKS using positron emission tomography (PET) and single photon emission computer tomography (SPECT) have shown the expected abnormalities of glucose uptake and cerebral perfusion in the temporal lobes (Maquet et al. 1990; O'Tuama et al. 1992; Guerreiro, Camargo, and Kato 1996; DaSilva et al. 1997; O'Regan et al. 1998). The pathophysiology of these abnormalities and their relationships to EEG findings and clinical manifestations of LKS remain under investigation.

AUTISTIC REGRESSION

Despite incomplete understanding of the significance of subclinical epileptiform discharges in children with LKS, similar EEG abnormalities in children with autism have recently received considerable attention. Among autistic children, the subgroup that undergoes autistic regression (AR) after a period of more appropriate development comprises at least thirty percent of cases (Rogers and DiLalla 1990). Affected children have normal or nearly normal development during the first year or two of life and then lose developmental skills.

Importantly, their regression is not limited to language loss. It also includes dramatic deterioration of social interaction and cognitive abilities. Affected children lose previously acquired words and verbal understanding, withdraw from social contact, and lose interest in their toys. The process can occur acutely or insidiously, usually beginning between eighteen and twenty-four months of age (Tuchman and Rapin 1997). In rare situations when cognitive, behavioral, and language regression occur in children above the age of thirty months, the diagnostic term disintegrative disorder (DD) is preferred (Volkmar and Cohen 1989; Rapin 1995).

Whether AR and DD are truly distinct disorders is not known. Autistic regression is difficult to recognize initially and, in many cases, it is only identified when the child is later referred for developmental evaluation. Typically, children with AR have the more severe forms of autism and generally poor prognoses. In the vast majority of cases, no cause of the children's regression can be identified, since the pathophysiology of this disorder is completely unknown. Sleep EEGs and functional neuroimaging with SPECT have identified abnormalities over the temporal and parietal lobes in some children with AR that are similar, but not necessarily identical, to those in children with LKS (Chez 1996; Nass, Gross, and Devinsky 1998a; O'Regan et al. 1998; Tuchman 1997).

Despite the clinical distinctions noted previously, the functional imaging and electrophysiological similarities between LKS and AR have led to speculation on a possible pathophysiological overlap between these syndromes. In this regard, Tuchman and Rapin (1997) studied a large cohort of over 500 children with autism and correlated the incidence of prior autistic regression with the presence of clinical seizures and epileptiform EEGs. Statistical analysis, following removal of data on the children with clinical seizures, identified a significant correlation between those with AR and epileptiform EEGs.

In the 335 children without epilepsy, the percentage of children with AR who had had epileptiform sleep EEGs was nearly twice as high as those without regression (nineteen percent versus ten percent). Although this represents a significant increase in such EEG abnormalities in the children with AR, a majority of children who had suffered regression had neither epileptiform EEGs nor clinical seizures. This was, however, a retrospective study, and the timing, as well as the setting and duration of the EEGs, was quite variable among patients. For example, the population with regression and no seizures, studied with overnight EEGs, had a forty-six percent incidence of epileptiform activity, compared to a fourteen percent incidence in those with a one-hour sleep study (Tuchman et al. 1998). Such a discrepancy clearly illustrates the potential importance of such factors and the need for a prospective study to further evaluate these issues.

In summary, current clinical criteria permit distinctions among children with autism and clinical seizures, those with autistic epileptiform regression, and non-autistic children with Landau-Kleffner syndrome. In the interest of standardizing terminology, Tuchman (1997) has suggested a classification employing the umbrella term, *acquired epileptiform aphasias* to include LKS, (*acquired epileptiform aphasia*), autistic regression with epileptiform EEG (*autistic epileptiform regression*), and disintegrative disorder with epileptiform EEGs (*disintegrative epileptiform regression*). This descriptive approach should improve diagnostic classification and encourage better communication among those investigating relationships between acquired developmental disabilities and severely abnormal EEG patterns.

TREATMENT APPROACHES

Appropriate treatment recommendations vary depending on the diagnosis. The treatment of seizure disorders is relatively straight forward while medical therapy of children with LKS is poorly standardized, and beneficial medical therapy for those with autistic regression is still speculative.

Treatment of seizures in children with autism is nearly identical to that in others with epilepsy (Volkmar and Nelson 1990; Gillberg 1991). The goals of medication are clinical control of seizures and absence of significant side effects. Treatment of seizures is generally recommended when the episodes are recurrent and when clinical seizures affect the functioning or safety of the child. Despite the fact that the vast majority of seizures last only minutes and are very rarely associated with brain injury or other complications, the unpredictability of their occurrence, the strong emotional reactions of caregivers, and safety concerns often justify treatment. Therapy usually relies on anticonvulsant medications such as carbamazepine and sodium valproate. Although an increasing number of medications are available for use, none has been evaluated prospectively in this population.

Optimal treatment recommendations for LKS are less clear. Affected children are usually treated with anticonvulsant medications that are effective in controlling clinical seizures, but have inconsistent effects on language recovery (Mantovani and Landau 1980; Deonna 1991). *Spike suppressing* medications, such as valproic acid, ethosuximide, and benzodiazepines are often preferred since carbamazepine, phenytoin, and phenobarbital are generally less effective in this disorder (Marescaux et al. 1990; Tuchman 1997). Both seizure control and language improvement have been reported in some children with LKS following treatment with valproic acid, ethosuximide, calcium channel blockers, ACTH, corticosteroids, pulse-methylprednisolone, and intravenous gammaglobulin (Marescaux et al. 1990; Deonna 1991; Lerman, Lerman-Sagie, and Kivity 1991; Chez et al. 1998; Fayad, Choueiri, and Mikati 1997). A small number of patients have also been treated with the ketogenic diet with positive results (Bergqvist and Brooke-Kayal 1997).

Most recently, an increasing number of children with LKS have been treated with a specific neurosurgical approach, multiple subpial transection. Initially introduced by Morrell and co-workers (1989), this technique has been used in a number of centers and reported to produce gradual and encouraging levels of linguistic improvement in over fifty percent of children who had been resistant to medical treatments (Morrell et al. 1995; Sawhney et al. 1995). Unfortunately, no prospective controlled studies have been performed to permit any firm recommendations for a specific treatment approach. Additionally, there is lack of consensus regarding the goals of treatment in LKS.

Whether successful treatment is defined as control of clinical seizures alone, reduction of EEG epileptiform activity, normalization of the EEG, or clinical improvement in language abilities remains an open and critically important question.

Based on reported case series and personal experience, I continue to favor attempts to normalize the EEG as we suggested in our original study (Mantovani and Landau 1980). Although this approach has yet to be validated in a controlled prospective study, similar treatment goals and approaches have been advocated by others as well (Deonna 1991; Lerman, Lerman-Sagie, and Kivity 1991; Marescaux et al. 1990; Aicardi 1996). It is hoped that prospective studies comparing various treatments in patients with LKS will guide our therapeutic recommendations in the future. However, the small number of patients seen at any one institution clearly requires the multicenter approach recommended by Landau (1992, 1998).

There are even less data regarding the advisability of medical treatment for children with autistic regression and epileptiform EEGs. Only a few prolonged EEG studies have been completed, and no prospective series with a significant number of patients having EEGs near the onset of their symptoms has been published. Furthermore, no controlled prospective treatment studies have been reported in this group. Consequently, there is no scientific validation of medical therapy with anticonvulsant medications, steroids, or other means at the present time.

Case studies and small series have reported mixed results in children with autistic regression subjected to various therapeutic approaches, including anticonvulsant medications, steroids, and MST surgery (Stefanatos, Grover, and Geller 1995; Chez et al. 1998; Neville, Harkness, and Cross 1997; Nass, Gross, and Devinsky 1998b; Nass et al. 1998). Until further analysis leads to documenting the safety and efficacy of specific treatments in children with autistic epileptiform regression, families and physicians should exercise caution as they evaluate each child's situation. Additional studies are strongly needed on this condition, which has a significantly greater incidence than LKS.

Definitive understanding of these varied neurobiological conditions and their optimal therapy have not yet been achieved. These are important disorders considering the severe and often permanent neurodevelopmental disabilities that result from autism, LKS, and related syndromes. Additional studies to define the pathophysiology and role of epilepsy, as well as effective treatment in these disorders will be of great interest. All of us agree that the hope of identifying effective therapy for children with autism and for those with epilepsies affecting intellectual and linguistic functions mandates our continued interest and investigation.

CONCLUSIONS AND RECOMMENDATIONS

Despite the lack of consensus and scientific understanding of the central issues, several provisional recommendations can be made. These clinical approaches are framed as answers to specific questions.

1. Which children with autism or developmental regression should have an EEG?
   - children with clinical seizures
   - children with acquired aphasia
   - children with cognitive and behavioral regression
   - children with autistic regression
2. What kind of EEG is best?
   - an EEG performed as close as possible to the time of the linguistic, autistic, or cognitive regression
   - an EEG recording sleep for an extended period (at least six hours to eight hours)
   - an EEG using video-telemetry for simultaneous recording of behavioral responses and electrocerebral activity (in some cases)
3. Who needs therapy?
   - children with clinical seizures affecting their functioning or safety (to control seizures)
   - children with Landau-Kleffner syndrome (to normalize their EEG?)
   - children with autistic regression and epileptiform EEGs (possibly similar to LKS group in some cases)
4. What types of therapy may be beneficial?
   - anticonvulsants that suppress epileptiform activity such as sodium valproate, ethosuximide, or benzodiazepines
   - other measures like corticosteroids or the ketogenic diet to suppress epileptiform activity
   - neurosurgical treatment with multiple subpial transection in highly selected and resistant cases (possibly)

CHAPTER SUMMARY

1. Approximately one third of children with autism have seizures which typically start either before age five or after the onset of puberty.

2. Approximately half of children with autism have epileptiform (abnormal) electrocephalograms (EEGs) with or without seizures.
3. A detailed clinical history is more important than the EEG in determining whether a child with autism is having seizures.
4. Autistic regression (AR) is a loss of previously acquired language, play, and social skills usually occurring between 18 and 24 months of age.
5. Children with autism who exhibit AR may have an increased incidence of abnormal EEGs.
6. Children with autism who exhibit AR are often those who are more severely involved and who have generally worse prognoses.
7. In Landau-Kleffner syndrome (LKS), the seizure focus causes a functional interruption of brain activity necessary for normal linguistic behavior and thus produces a clinical picture of aphasia (*acquired epileptiform aphasia*).
8. Landau-Kleffner syndrome has a typical age of onset between ages four and seven years, somewhat later than classical autism.
9. Children with LKS tend to maintain their social awareness and their non-verbal communicative and play skills; their regression is limited to language.

REFERENCES

Aarts, J. H. P., Binnie, C. D., Smit, A. M., and Wilkins, A. J. 1984. Selective cognitive impairment during focal and generalized epileptiform EEG activity. *Brain* 107:293–308.

Aicardi, J. 1996. Epilepsy as a non-paroxysmal disorder. *Acta Neuropediatrica* 2:248–57.

Bergqvist, A. G. C., and Brooks-Kayal, A. R. 1997. Ketogenic diet in the treatment of acquired epileptic aphasia. *Annals of Neurology* 42:504.

Binnie, C. D., Kasteleijn-Nolst Trenite, D. A. G., and Smit, A. M. 1987. Interactions of epileptiform EEG discharge and cognition. *Epilepsy Research* 1:239–45.

Bishop, D. V. 1985. Age of onset and outcome in acquired aphasia with convulsive disorder (Landau-Kleffner syndrome). *Developmental Medicine and Child Neurology* 27:705–12.

Cavazutti, G. B., Cappella, L., and Nalin, A. 1980. Longitudinal study of epileptiform EEG patterns in normal children. *Epilepsia* 21:43–55.

Chez, M. G., Loeffel, M., Buchanan, C. P., and Field-Chez, M. 1998. Pulse high dose steroids in combination therapy with valproic acid in epileptic aphasia patients with PPD or autism. *Annals of Neurology* 44:539.

Chez, M. 1996. Clinical spectrum of patients referred for Landau-Kleffner syndrome previously diagnosed with PDD or autism. *Annals of Neurology* 40:A114.

DaSilva, E. A., Chugani, D., Muzik, O., and Chugani, H. 1997. Landau-Kleffner syndrome: Metabolic abnormalities in temporal lobe are a common feature. *Journal of Child Neurology* 12:489–95.

Deonna, T. 1995. Cognitive and behavioral disturbances as epileptic manifestations in children: An overview. *Seminars in Pediatric Neurology* 2:254–59.

Deonna, T., Ziegler, A. L., Moura-Serra, J., and Innocenti, G. 1993. Autistic regression in relation to limbic pathology and epilepsy: Report of two cases. *Developmental Medicine and Child Neurology* 35:166–76.

Deonna, T., Roulet, F., and Fantan, D. 1993. Speech and oral-motor deficits of epileptic origin in BPERS. *Neuropediatrics* 24:83–7.

Deonna, T. 1991. Acquired epileptiform aphasia in children (Landau-Kleffner syndrome). *Journal of Clinical Neurophysiology* 8:288–98.

Fayad, M. N., Choueiri, R., and Mikati, M. 1997. Landau-Kleffner syndrome: Consistent response to repeated intravenous gammaglobulin doses: A case report. *Epilepsia* 38:489–94.

Gillberg, C., and Coleman, M. 1992. *The Biology of the Autistic Syndromes*, 2nd ed. London: McKeith Press.

Gillberg, C. 1991. The treatment of epilepsy in autism. *Autism and Developmental Disorders* 21:61–77.

Guerreiro, M. M., Camargo, E. E., and Kato, M. 1996. Brain single photon emission computer tomography imaging in Landau-Kleffner syndrome. *Epilepsia* 37:60–7.

Jayakar, P., and Seshia, S. 1991. Electrical status epilepticus during slow-wave sleep: A review. *Journal of Clinical Neurophysiology* 8:299–311.

Kasteleijn-Nolst Trenite, D. A. G. 1995. Transient cognitive impairment during subclinical epileptiform EEG discharges. *Seminars in Pediatric Neurology* 2:246–53.

Kurita, H. 1985. Infantile autism with speech loss before the age of thirty months. *Journal of the American Academy of Child Psychiatry* 24:191–96.

Landau, W. M. 1998. Syndrome of acquired aphasia with convulsive disorder in children: Commentary. *Neurology* 51:1241.

Landau, W. M. 1992. Landau-Kleffner syndrome. An eponymic badge of ignorance. *Archives of Neurology* 49:353.

Landau, W. M., and Kleffner, F. R. 1957. Syndrome of acquired aphasia with convulsive disorder in children. *Neurology* 7:523–30.

Lerman, P., Lerman-Sagie, T., and Kivity, S. 1991. Effect of early corticosteroid therapy for Landau-Kleffner syndrome. *Developmental Medicine and Child Neurology* 33:257–60.

Mantovani, J. F., and Landau, W. M. 1980. Acquired aphasia with convulsive disorder: Course and prognosis. *Neurology* 30:524–29.

Maquet, P., Hirsch, B., Dive, D., Salmon, E., Marescaux, C., and Franck, G. 1990. Cerebral glucose utilization during sleep in Landau-Kleffner syndrome: A PET study. *Epilepsia* 31:778–83

Marescaux, C., Hirsch, E., Finck, S., Maquet, P., Schlumberger, E., and Sellal, F. 1990. Landau-Kleffner syndrome: A pharmacologic study of five cases. *Epilepsia* 31:768–77.

Morrell, F., Whisler, W. W., Smith, M. C., Hoeppner, T. J., deToledo-Morrell, L., Pierre-Louis, S. J. C., Kanner, A. M., Buelow, J. M., Ristanovic, R., Berger, D., Chez, M., and Hasegawa, H. 1995. Landau Kleffner syndrome: Treatment with subpial intracortical transection. *Brain* 118:1529–46.

Morrell, F., Whisler, W. W., and Bleck, T. P. 1989. Multiple subpial transection: A new approach to the surgical treatment of focal epilepsy. *Journal of NeuroSurgery* 70:231–39.

Nakano, S., Okuno, T., and Mikawa, H. 1989. Landau-Kleffner syndrome: EEG topographic studies. *Brain Development* 11:43–50.

Nass, R., Gross, A., and Devinsky, O. 1998a. Patterns of EEG abnormalities in autistic spectrum disorder: Correlation with clinical status and outcome. *Annals of Neurology* 44:578.

Nass, R., Gross, A., and Devinsky, O. 1998b. Autism and autistic epileptiform regression with occipital spikes. *Developmental Medicine and Child Neurology* 40:453–58.

Nass, R., Gross, A., Wisoff, J., and Devinsky, O. 1998. Autistic epileptiform regression: Response to multiple subpial resections. *Annals of Neurology* 44:554.

Nass, R., Heier, L., and Walker, R. 1993. Landau-Kleffner syndrome: Temporal lobe tumor vesection results in good outcome. *Pediatric Neurology* 9:303–05.

Neville, R. G., Harkness, W. F., and Cross, J. H. 1997. Surgical treatment of severe autistic regression in childhood epilepsy. *Pediatric Neurology* 16:137–40.

O'Regan, M. E., Braun, J. K., Goodwin, G. M., and Clarke, M. 1998. Epileptic aphasia: Consequence of regional hypometabolic encephalopathy. *Developmental Medicine and Child Neurology* 40:508–16.

Otero, B., Cordova, S., and Diaz, F. 1989. Acquired epileptic aphasia (Landau-Kleffner syndrome) due to neurocysticercosis. *Epilepsia* 30:569–72.

O'Tuama, L. A., Urion, D. K., Janicek, M. J., Treves, S. J., Bjornfon, B., and Moriarity, J. M. 1992. Regional cerebral perfusion in Landau-Kleffner syndrome and related childhood aphasias. *Journal of Nuclear Medicine* 33:1758–65.

Paquier, P. F., VanDongen, H. R., and Loonen, C. B. 1992. The Landau-Kleffner syndrome or "acquired aphasia with convulsive disorder": Long-term follow-up of six children and a review of the recent literature. *Archives of Neurology* 49:354–59.

Perniola T., Margari, L., Buttiglione, M., Andreula, C., Simone, I. L., and Santostasi, R. 1993. A case of Landau-Kleffner syndrome secondary to inflammatory demyelinating disease. *Epilepsia* 34:551–56.

Plioplys, A. V. 1994. Autism: EEG abnormalities and clinical improvement with valproic acid. *Archives of Pediatric and Adolescent Medicine* 148:220–22.

Rapin, I., and Katzman, R. 1998. Neurobiology of autism. *Annals of Neurology* 43:7–14.

Rapin, I. 1995. Autistic regression and disintegrative disorder: How important the role of epilepsy. *Seminars in Pediatric Neurology* 2:278–85.

Rapin, I., Mattis, S., and Rowan, J. A. 1977. Verbal auditory agnosia in children. *Developmental Medicine and Child Neurology* 19:192–207.

Rintahaka, P. J., Chugani, H. T., and Sandar, R. 1995. Landau-Kleffner syndrome with continuous spikes and waves during slow-wave sleep. *Child Neurology* 10:127–33.

Rogers, S. J., and DiLalla, D. L. 1990. Age of symptom onset in young children with pervasive developmental disorders. *Journal of the American Academy of Child and Adolescent Psychiatry* 29:863–72.

Roulet, E. 1995. Syndromes of acquired epileptic aphasia and epilepsy with continuous spike waves during sleep: Models for prolonged cognitive impairment of epileptic origin. *Seminars in Pediatric Neurology* 2:269–77.

Roulet, E., Deonna T., and Despland, P. 1989. Prolonged intermittent drooling and oromotor dyspraxia in benign childhood epilepsy with centrotemporal spikes. *Epilepsia* 30:564–68.

Roulet-Perez, E., Davidoff, V., Despland, P., and Deonna, T. 1993. Mental and behavioral deterioration of children with epilepsy and CSWS: Acquired epileptic frontal syndrome. *Developmental Medicine and Child Neurology* 35:661–74.

Sawhney, I. M., Robertson, I. J., Polkey, C. E., Binnie, C. D., and Elwes, R. D. 1995. Multiple subpial transections: A review of 21 cases. *Journal of Neurology, Neurosurgery, and Psychiatry* 58:344–49.
Shafrir, Y., and Prensky, A. L. 1995. Acquired epileptiform opercular syndrome: A second case report, review of the literature, and comparison to the Landau-Kleffner syndrome. *Epilepsia* 36:1050–57.
Stefanatos, G. A., Grover, W., and Geller, B. 1995. Case study: Corticosteroid treatment of language regression in pervasive developmental disorder. *Journal of American Academy of Child and Adolescent Psychiatry* 34:1107–11.
Stefanatos, G. A. 1993. Frequency modulation analysis in children with Landau-Kleffner syndrome. *Annals of the New York Academy of Sciences* 682:412–14.
Tuchman, R., Jayakar, P., Yaylali, I., and Villalobos, R. 1998. Seizures and EEG findings in children with autism spectrum disorder. *CNS Spectrums* 3(3): 61–70.
Tuchman, R. 1997. Acquired epileptiform aphasia. *Seminars in Pediatric Neurology* 4(2):93–101.
Tuchman, R., and Rapin, I. 1997. Regression in pervasive developmental disorders: Seizures and EEG correlates. *Pediatrics* 99:560–6.
Tuchman, R., Rapin, I., and Shinnar, S. 1991. Autistic and dysphasic children: II Epilepsy. *Pediatrics* 6:1219–25.
Villalobos, R., Tuchman, R., and Jayakar, P. 1996. Prolonged EEG monitoring findings in children with pervasive developmental disorder and regression. *Annals of Neurology* 40:311.
Volkmar, F. R., and Nelson, D. S. 1990. Seizure disorders in autism. *American Academy of Child and Adolescent Psychiatry* 29:127–9.
Volkmar, F., and Cohen, D. 1989. Disintegrative disorder as "late onset" autism. *The Journal of Child Psychology and Psychiatry* 30:717–24.
Zardini, O., Molteni, B., Nardocci, N., Sarti, D., Avanzini, G., and Granata, T. 1995. Linguistic development in a patient with Landau-Kleffner syndrome: Nine-year follow-up. *Neuropediatrics* 26:19–25.

Chapter • 12

Neuropharmacological Therapy in Autism

Andrew W. Zimmerman
Brian Bonfardin
Scott M. Myers

We now have promising drug treatments for patients with autistic spectrum disorders and are gaining new insights into the basic mechanisms that underlie these disorders. Although most drugs in current use are limited to modifying behavioral symptoms in autism, increasingly specific drug actions, combined with newly emerging data on the neurobiology of autism, are leading to effective treatments with the potential to improve patients' long-term outcomes. In Part I, this chapter reviews the background of drug treatment in autism. We discuss the "art" of pharmacology in autism in Part II and suggest general guidelines for drug therapy. In Part III we present emerging concepts and new directions.

PART I. REVIEW OF THE LITERATURE

Reports of pharmacologic manipulation of the neurochemistry of patients with autism first appeared in the literature over 40 years ago. A wide variety of agents that act at serotonergic, dopaminergic, noradrenergic, opioid, and other neurotransmitter systems have been studied (for reviews, see McDougle 1997; Campbell et al. 1996; Cook and Leventhal 1995; Gilman and Tuchman 1995; Sloman 1991). However, despite significant improvements in recent years, there has been a general deficiency of well-designed, controlled studies with adequate sample size and statistical power. Much of the literature available to guide clinical practice consists of small, open-label studies and case reports.

This body of literature can be difficult to interpret because it reflects many of the problems inherent in studies of autistic spectrum disorders and pediatric psychopharmacology in general. Problems with syndrome definition, clinical heterogeneity, and comorbidity are basic to autism research (Volkmar and Cohen 1997). Increasing use of the *Diagnostic and Statistical Manual of Mental Disorders* (DSM-IV) and *International Classification of Diseases* (ICD-10) criteria together with diagnostic instruments such as the *Autism Diagnostic Interview* (ADI) (Lord 1997) in clinical trials will help to ensure that subjects are comparable, at least in terms of diagnosis. Published studies address a variety of target behaviors and symptoms, including "core" autistic symptoms, such as social interaction and communication, associated maladaptive behaviors, and aspects of cognitive function. Interpretation of behavioral responses is problematic, and a wide variety of outcome measures have been used.

Some of the most common measures are listed in table I. This list is far from complete, because over 40 specific measurement instruments have been used in pharmacologic trials in autism in the last 10 years alone. Direct observation of frequencies of various target symptoms (such as maladaptive behaviors), individualized parent- or clinician-rated Likert scales, and non-quantified, subjective data are also commonly reported. Although there has been little systematic study of the placebo response in autistic children, significant positive effects have been reported (Ernst et al. 1990; Belsito et al. 1998). The natural temporal variability of behavior in many patients with autism may contribute to these findings, and it certainly can confound short-term studies. Many published studies include patients who were taking other psychotropic medications concomitantly.

Despite these limitations, much useful information is available. The purpose of this portion of the chapter is to review the literature briefly. This body of literature, in combination with clinical experience, as well as theoretical considerations based on current knowledge of the neurochemistry of autism and associated behaviors, and inferences from re-

Table I. Examples of Outcome Measures Commonly Utilized in Pharmacological Trials in Autism

Aberrant Behavior Checklist (AbBC)
Abnormal Involuntary Movement Scale (AIMS)
Autism Behavior Checklist (AuBC)
Children's Global Assessment Scale (CGAS)
Children's Psychiatric Rating Scale (CPRS)
Clinical Global Impression Scale (CGI)
Conners Parent-Teacher Questionnaire (PTQ)
Ritvo-Freeman Real Life Rating Scale
Timed Stereotypies Rating Scale (TSRS)
Vineland Adaptive Behavior Scale, Maladaptive Behavior Subscales
Yale-Brown Obsessive Compulsive Scale (Y-BOCS)

search pertaining to conditions with similar symptoms (and possibly similar neurobiology), will, we hope, allow the clinician to devise a rational approach to medical management of an individual patient. A thorough discussion of the neurochemical disturbances that have been implicated in the pathophysiology of autism is beyond the scope of this chapter, and this topic has recently been reviewed elsewhere (Anderson and Hoshino 1997; Potenza and McDougle 1997; Cook and Leventhal 1996; Cook 1990).

Early Attempts To Modulate Serotonin: Tryptophan, SD, Methysergide, L-dopa

The psychomimetic effects of the serotonergic hallucinogen lysergic acid diethylamide (LSD) stimulated speculation about the role of serotonin in a variety of disorders, including autism. Early metabolic studies involving administration of the serotonin precursor tryptophan to autistic children yielded mixed results (Sutton, Read, and Arbor 1958; Shaw, Lucas, and Rabinovitch 1959; Schain and Freedman 1961). However, tryptophan supplementation has been used successfully in combination with the serotonergic drugs trazodone (O'Neil, Page, and Adkins 1986) and buspirone (Gedye 1991a) to reduce aggressive behavior. Recently, short-term tryptophan depletion has been shown to exacerbate behavioral symptoms including stereotypy and self-injury (McDougle et al. 1993; McDougle et al. 1996).

The discovery of elevated whole blood serotonin in autistic children (Schain and Freedman 1961), which has been replicated extensively (Anderson et al. 1987) and seems to involve 30% to 50% of patients, led to attempts at pharmacological reduction. Lysergic acid diethylamide (LSD) was initially administered because of the potential to "break through autistic defenses" and because of theoretical interest in serotonin inhibition (Freedman, Ebin, and Wilson 1962; Bender, Goldschmidt, and Siva Sankar 1962; Bender, Faretra, and Cobrinik 1963; Simmons et al. 1966). The results were mixed. Bender and colleagues (1962;1963) and Simmons et al. (1966) reported increased social interaction, decreased stereotypy, and improved affect. Freedman, Ebin, and Wilson (1962) found increased anxiety and hallucinations to be problematic.

Fish and colleagues (1969) reported the use of the serotonin antagonist methysergide to lower blood serotonin levels in 11 young, hospitalized autistic children. Six children experienced worsening of their symptoms; three showed no change; and the two most cognitively impaired subjects showed some improvement in alertness, affective responsiveness, and goal-directed activity. L-dopa, which lowers serotonin as well as increases dopamine, has also been studied in autistic patients. Ritvo et al. (1971) found no improvement, whereas

Campbell et al. (1976), in a double-blind, crossover study of L-dopa and L-amphetamine found improved activity in hypoactive children, as well as modest increases in communication and affective responsiveness with L-dopa. A recent study revealed no significant positive response to 0.5 mg/kg/day of L-dopa (Sugiyama et al. 1998).

Fenfluramine

Fenfluramine, an amphetamine analogue that promotes release of serotonin from granules and prevents synaptic reuptake is effective in reducing blood serotonin levels (for review, see Aman and Kern 1989). Since the initial report of improvement in three autistic boys on fenfluramine (Geller et al. 1982), this drug has been studied extensively. Twenty-seven studies published prior to 1989 have been thoroughly reviewed by Aman and Kern (1989) (also see reviews by Campbell 1988; du Verglas, Banks, and Guyer 1988). They concluded that reports of improvement in IQ are not substantiated by balanced studies and that some studies suggested impaired discrimination learning. However, many studies did suggest that treatment with fenfluramine was associated with improvement in social adjustment, stereotypic behavior, activity level, and attention (Aman and Kern 1989). Subsequently, a number of studies, many of them double-blind and placebo-controlled, have failed to demonstrate significant clinical benefits of fenfluramine despite marked reduction of whole blood serotonin (Sherman et al. 1989; Ekman et al. 1989; Stern et al. 1990; Duker et al. 1991; Leventhal et al. 1993). Long-term treatment has not been well tolerated (Varley and Holm 1990) and concerns about toxicity have been raised and debated in the literature (Gualtieri 1986; Schuster, Lewis, and Seiden 1986; Ritvo et al. 1987; Gualtieri 1987). Most authors do not support the clinical use of fenfluramine in children with autism (Campbell 1988; Leventhal et al. 1993; McDougle 1997).

Clomipramine

Clomipramine is a tricyclic antidepressant that is a potent but nonselective serotonin reuptake inhibitor. It is nonselective because it also inhibits, to some extent, norepinephrine and dopamine transporters. Seven trials involving two or more patients are summarized in table II. These studies suggest that some adults and children with autism benefit from treatment with clomipramine. Decreased stereotypy, self-injury, obsessive-compulsive behavior, and dyskinesias, as well as improved social interaction, have been reported (table II). In the largest and most recent open-label trial, 18 of 35 autistic adults responded positively to treatment with 75 to 200 mg per day of clomipramine (Brodkin et al. 1997). Two double-blind, crossover studies included a total of 28 patients with autism (Lewis et al. 1995; Gordon et al. 1993). Clomipramine was shown to be superior to placebo (Lewis et al. 1995; Gordon et al. 1993) and desipramine (Gordon et al. 1993). Because of the beneficial effects, three of four autistic patients in the Lewis et al. study and 19 of 24 in the Gordon et al. study were continued on clomipramine after the trial was completed. One study involving young children (3 to 8 years of age) found overall worsening in seven of eight patients initially enrolled (Sanchez et al. 1996). Side effects including seizures, behavioral deterioration, weight changes, constipation, sedation, and cardiac symptoms or ECG changes (table II) were commonly reported in the clomipramine trials. Clomipramine has also been reported to be an effective adjunct to behavioral management of trichotillomania in an autistic girl (Holttum, Lubetsky, and Eastman 1994).

Buspirone

Buspirone is an anxiolytic agent that binds with high affinity to serotonin 1A (5-HT1A) receptors and acts as a partial agonist. Dopamine (D2) and 5-HT2 effects may also be important; down-regulation of 5-HT2 receptors occurs with chronic administration (Jann 1988). Reports describing the use of buspirone in patients with autism are summarized in table III. Only two of the studies, involving a total of two patients, included placebo controls and some type of masking (Ratey et al. 1991; McCormick 1997). Another involved an open-label trial with blind comparison to either methylphenidate or fenfluramine (Realmuto, August, and Garfinkel 1989). The largest study (22 patients) employed an open label design and utilized the CGI subscales for global severity and global improvement as outcome measures. Improvements in target behaviors including anxiety, aggression, irritability, temper outbursts, self-injury, hyperactivity, and stereotypy or ritualistic behavior have been described (table III). However, King and Davanzo (1996) reported an 81% increase in aggression in adults with autism and/or severe or profound mental retardation who were treated with buspirone.

Buspirone is generally not associated with sedation, cognitive impairment, withdrawal reactions, or interactions with other medications commonly prescribed for patients with disabilities. The only significant side effects reported in buspirone trials involving autistic patients were the increased aggression noted by King and Davanzo (1996) and involuntary movements of the mouth in one patient studied by Buitelaar, van der Gaag, and van der Hoeven (1998). However, it should be noted that the emergence of psychosis in two children treated with buspirone for anxiety has been reported (Soni and Weintraub 1992).

Table II. Clomipramine Trials in Autism/DD (N>1)

Reference	Study Design	N (with autism)	Age Range (yrs)	Dosage	Duration (wks)	Results	Adverse Effects
Brodkin et al. 1997	open-label	35	18–44	75–250 mg/day	12	18/35 responders by CGI; dec repetitive thoughts and behavior, agrression, SIB; improved social relatedness	13/35 including seizures, constipation, weight gain, sedation, anorgasmia
Sanchez et al. 1996	open-label	8 (7 completed study)	3.5–8.7	50–175 mg/day	5	by CGCR 1/7 improved, 6/7 worsened; by CGI, 0/7 improved, 2/7 worsened; stereotypies dec in 4/7, inc in 2/7	8/8 at least 1, 5/8 3 or more; urinary retention, insomnia, sedation, SIB, crying, aggression, tantrums, irritability
Lewis et al. 1995	double-blind, placebo-controlled crossover	4 (of 10 with MR)	18–42	titrated to max of 3 mg/kg	8	3/4>50% dec in stereotypy relative to placebo levels; 3/3 dec SIB; 3/4 returned to CMI after study; group dec in requirement for staff intervention for behavior during CMI phase (17% of days) vs placebo (70% of days)	1/4 autistic patients had seizure; for whole group, change in appetite, constipation, inc salivation, dizziness, palpitations, tiredness, sweating (none severe)
Brasic et al. 1994; Brasic et al. 1997	open-label	5	6.9–12.3	titrated to 200 mg/day	8–72+	mod to marked dec in general dyskinesias (5/5), akathisia (4/5), tics (5/5); dec compulsions	3/5 extreme agitation; 1/5 tremors, diarrhea, insomnia, anorexia

Reference	Study Design	N (with autism)	Age Range (yrs)	Dosage	Duration (wks)	Results	Adverse Effects
Gordon et al. 1993; Gordon et al. 1992	double-blind crossover	12 vs desipramine and 12 vs placebo	6–23	titrated to 250 mg/day or 5 mg/kg/day	5	superior to placebo and to desipramine by multiple measures; parents of 19/24 elected to continue clomipramine; autistic behavior 25% improved, compulsive behavior 33% improved	seizure (1), prolonged QT (1), tachycardia (1), insomnia, sedation, GI symptoms; 8/12 inc irritability, outbursts, aggression on desipramine
Garber et al. 1992	open-label	4 (of 11 studied)	10–20	25–125 mg/day, max 3 mg/kg	4–52	2/4 showed >75% dec in target behaviors (stereotypy and SIB); 1/4>50% dec; 1/4 worse after 8 days	aggression, rash, constipation, enuresis
McDougle et al. 1992	open-label	5	13–33	75–250 mg/day	12	4/5 improved social relatedness, dec obsessive-compulsive behavior and aggression	mild dry mouth

dec decreased, **inc** increased, **CGI** Clinical Global Impression Scale, **CGCR** Clinical Global Concensus Rating, **CMI** clomipramine, **MR** mental retardation, **SIB** self-injurious behavior

Table III. Buspirone Trials In Autism/PPD

Reference	Study Design	N (with autism)	Age Range (yrs)	Dosage	Duration (wks)	Results	Adverse Effects
Buitelaar, van der Gaag, and van der Hoeven 1998	open-label	22	6–17	15–45 mg/day	6–8	9/22 marked response and 7/22 moderate response (CGI)- dec anxiety, irritability, outbursts	abnormal involuntary movements (1), minimal sedation (2), slight agitation (2), initial nausea (1)
McCormick 1997	double-blind, placebo-controlled, crossover	1	4	10 mg/day	3	dec hyperactivity, inc compliance in school	none reported
Frischauf 1997	open-label	1	12	40 mg/day	?	dec aggression, dec depression, inc speaking and attention	none reported
King and Davanzo 1996	open-label	10 (of 26 with MR)	28–63	30–60 mg/day	8–59	aggression inc by 81%; no significant effect on SIB	none reported (other than the inc aggression)
Hillbrand 1995	open-label	1	41	80 mg/day	104	dec aggression	none reported
Ricketts et al. 1994	open-label	3 (of a group of 5 with MR and SIB)	27–34	30–60 mg/day	118–145	dec SIB by 13–72%, allowed dec in neuroleptic dose	none reported

Reference	Study Design	N (with autism)	Age Range (yrs)	Dosage	Duration (wks)	Results	Adverse Effects
Ratey et al. 1991	multiple-baseline placebo lead-in with blinded treatment phase, ABA design	1 (of a group of 6 with MR)	29	15–45 mg/day	11	dec SIB, dec anxiety	none in autistic subjects, 1 other had inc anxiety and minor inc aggression
Ratey et al. 1989	open-label	3 (of a group of 14 with DD)	25–38	20–30 mg/day	26 in one case, others not reported	dec tantrums, aggression, SIB, inc social behavior, coping with transition; 5 nonresponders - not clear whether any were autistic	heightened activity in 2 cases - unclear whether they were autistic
Realmuto, August, and Garfinkel 1989	open-label with blinded comparision to methyl-phenidate or fenflur-amine	4	9–10	15 mg/day	4	dec hyperactivity (2/4), dec stereotypy (2/4), dec aggression (2/4)	none reported

dec decreased, **inc** increased, **DD** developmental disabilities, **MR** mental retardation, **PDD** pervasive developmental disorders, **SIB** self-injurious behavior

Trazodone

Trazodone, like buspirone, has both serotonin agonist and antagonist properties. Efficacy in the treatment of aggressive and self-injurious behavior in individual autistic patients has been reported (Gedye 1991b; Benjamin et al. 1995). Use in combination with tryptophan supplementation in two patients with other developmental disabilities has been mentioned previously (O'Neill, Page, and Adkins 1986; Gedye 1991a).

Selective Serotonin Reuptake Inhibitors (SSRIs)

Fluoxetine has been used to treat a variety of symptoms in patients with autism, and studies involving two or more patients are described in table IV. Improvements in social interaction, depressive symptoms, lethargy, stereotypic and compulsive behaviors, irritability, and tantrums have been reported in open-label studies (table IV). In the largest of these open-label trials, DeLong and colleagues (1998) described positive responses in 22 of 37 children. Responses to fluoxetine were strongly correlated with family history of the major affective disorders. Cook et al. (1992) found improvement in overall clinical severity and severity of perseverative or compulsive behavior in 15 of 23 children and adults with autism. Significant side effects occurred in 5 of 23 children and included activation, anorexia, and insomnia. Individual case reports have also described efficacy of fluoxetine in the treatment of autistic patients with trichotillomania (Hamdan-Allen 1991); depression (Ghaziuddin, Tsai, and Ghaziuddin 1991); and self-injury, restlessness, agitation, and self-stimulation (Markowitz 1992). Mehlinger et al. (1990) described improved mood, decreased ritualistic behaviors, and resolution of enuresis in a 26-year-old autistic woman.

In a double-blind, placebo-controlled trial, fluvoxamine was found to be superior to placebo in decreasing maladaptive behaviors and improving social relatedness and communication with minimal side effects (McDougle et al. 1996) (table V). Eight of 15 patients were positive responders to fluvoxamine, whereas none of the patients randomized to placebo responded. McDougle and colleagues (1990) and Harvey and Cooray (1995) had previously described excellent responses to fluvoxamine in two patients with autism and disabling repetitive behaviors.

Sertraline has also been studied in patients with autism (table V). Most of the autistic patients studied experienced clinical improvement in target behaviors including repetitive behaviors, self-injury, and outbursts or aggressive behaviors (table V). McDougle et al. (1998) reported improvement in repetitive and aggressive behavior, but not social relatedness, in 24 of 42 (57%) adult patients with pervasive developmental

Table IV. SSRI Trials in Autism/PDD: Fluoxetine (N>1)

Reference	Study Design	N (with autism)	Age Range (yrs)	Dosage	Duration (wks)	Results	Adverse Effects
DeLong et al. 1998	open -label	37	2–7	0.2–1.4 mg/kg/day	56–144	22/37 positive response; 11 excellent response; improved behavior, language, affect, social interaction	Hyperactivity, agitation, aggression
Fatemi et al. 1998	open-label	7	9–20	20–80 mg/day	5–136	dec irritability, lethargy, stereotypy, and inappropriate speech (ABC)	appetite suppression, vivid dreams, hyperactivity
Koshes 1997	open-label	2	26,42	20 mg/day	?	improved social interaction; dec rituals; dec depressive symptoms (including hypersomnia); inc frustration tolerance	none reported
Cook et al. 1992	open-label	23	7.0–28.8	20 mg QOD - 80 mg/day	1.5–60	15/23 improved by CGI rating of overall clinical severity and severity of perseverative or compulsive behavior	significant in 5/23; restlessness, hyperactivity, agitation, anorexia, insomnia, "elated affect," inc screaming

Reference	Study Design	N (with autism)	Age Range (yrs)	Dosage	Duration (wks)	Results	Adverse Effects
Todd 1991	open-label	4	8-19	20-30 mg/day	56–64 in 3 responders	3/4 marked improvements; 2/4 dec rituals and stereotypies; 2/3 dec tantrums, outbursts; no improvement in language or cognitive or social functions	none reported
Ghaziuddin, Tsai, and Ghaziuddin 1991	open-label	4	13–21	20–40 mg/day	up to 32, not specified for all cases	3/4 dec depression - improved mood/affect, dec irritability; no change in stereotypies or compulsions	agitation, irritability, increased compulsive behavior

dec decreased, **inc** increased, **ABC** Aberrant Behavior Checklist, **CGI** Clinical Global Impression Scale, **PDD** pervasive developmental disorders, **SSRI** Selective Serotonin Reuptake Inhibitors disorders, including 15 of 22 (68%) with autistic disorder. Uncommon adverse effects included agitation, headaches, anorexia, sedation, tinnitus and weight gain. Buck (1995) described a decrease in aggressive outbursts in a 33-year-old man with pervasive developmental disorder not otherwise specified (PDD NOS) when sertraline was added to his medical regimen of perphenazine and lorazepam.

A case report by Snead, Boon, and Presberg (1994) described resolution of self-injurious behavior in a high functioning 15-year-old male with autism treated with paroxetine. More recently, the use of paroxetine in institutionalized patients with mental retardation has been assessed (Davanzo et al. 1998). Seven of these patients also had PDD diagnoses. Severity, but not frequency, of aggression was statistically significantly reduced over a four-month period with an apparent diminution of effectiveness after four weeks of treatment (Davanzo et al. 1998; table V).

Inositol

Inositol is a precursor of the second messenger for some serotonin receptors which has been reported to decrease symptoms in patients with obsessive-compulsive disorder. However, in a recent study, it was found to be ineffective in nine children with autism (Levine et al. 1997).

Lithium

Although the exact biological basis for the clinical efficacy of lithium is unknown, it has been an important antimanic, antidepressant, and mood-stabilizing agent for many years. There is evidence that lithium enhances net serotonin neurotransmission and gamma-aminobutyric acid (GABA) neurotransmission, as well as attenuating dopamine function and enhancing or stabilizing acetylcholine function (Price and Heninger 1994). Inhibition of neurotransmitter-coupled adenylate cyclase activity, receptor-G-protein coupling, and phosphatidylinositol cell signalling pathways may be important mechanisms (Price and Heninger 1994).

Campbell et al. (1972) compared lithium to chlorpromazine in a controlled crossover study of ten children with hyperactivity, most of whom were autistic. They found no significant differences between lithium and chlorpromazine, and concluded that neither was particularly efficacious in this group of patients. However, they did note a trend toward decreased explosiveness, aggressiveness, hyperactivity, and "psychotic speech" with lithium and suggested that it deserved further study (Campbell et al. 1972). Epperson et al. (1994) reported

Table V. SSRI Trials in Autism/PDD: Fluvoxamine, Sertraline, and Paroxetine (N>1)

Reference	Study Design	N (with autism)	Age Range (yrs)	Dosage	Duration (wks)	Results	Adverse Effects
McDougle et al. 1996 (fluvoxamine)	double-blind, placebo-controlled	30 (15 in fluvoxamine group)	18–53	200–300 mg/day	12	8/15 fluvoxamine responders, 0/15 placebo responders; dec repetitive thoughts and behavior, maladaptive behavior, aggression; inc social relatedness and language	nausea, moderate sedation
Steingard et al. 1997 (sertraline)	open-label	9	6–12	25–100 mg/day	2–52+	8/9 clinically significant improvement at dose 25–50 mg/day; dec behavioral reactions with transitions or environmental changes; 3 responders showed less effect after 3–7 mo.	behavioral worsening (2) at 75 mg/day; stomach aches
Hellings et al. 1996 (sertraline)	open-label	5 (of 9 with MR)	20–47	25–150 mg/day	4–30	8/9 total patients improved by CGI (dec SIB and/or aggression) - unclear whether the nonresponder was autistic	worsening of skin picking in 1 patient with Prader-Willi syndrome
McDougle et al. 1998 (sertraline)	open-label	42	18–39	50–200 mg/day	12	24/42 improved by CGI; dec repetitive and aggressive symptoms; no improvement in social relatedness	agitation, headaches, reduced appetite, sedation, weight gain, tinnitus

Reference	Study Design	N (with autism)	Age Range (yrs)	Dosage	Duration (wks)	Results	Adverse Effects
Davanzo et al. 1998 (paroxetine)	open-label	7 (of 15 with MR)	30–56	10–50 mg/day	3–25	dec severity (8/13), but not frequency of aggression over 4-month period; no significant dec in SIB severity or frequency; no difference between autistic and non-autistic patients	agitation requiring discontinuation (1)

dec decreased, **inc** increased, **CGI** Clinical Global Impression Scale, **MR** mental retardation, **PDD** pervasive developmental disorders, **SIB** self-injurious behavior, **SSRI** Selective Serotonin Reuptake Inhibitors successful augmentation of fluvoxamine therapy with lithium resulting in improved social relatedness and marked reduction in aggressive and impulsive behavior in a 27-year-old man with autism.

Comorbid mania and bipolar disorder have been reported in patients with autism (Komoto, Seigo, and Hirata 1984; Steingard and Biederman 1987; Kerbeshian, Burd, and Fisher 1987; DeLong 1994; Wozniak et al. 1997). Wozniak et al. (1997) reported that 21% of referred children with PDD also had mania, but their diagnostic criteria for mania have been challenged (Tanguay 1997). Several case reports describe children and adolescents with autism and atypical bipolar disorder or mania who responded well to treatment with lithium (Steingard and Biederman 1987; Kerbeshian, Burd, and Fisher 1987; Cook and Leventhal 1995). Most of these patients had family histories of bipolar disorder. DeLong (1994) described successful long-term results in 6 of 23 patients with pervasive developmental disorders who had been treated with lithium. More mild involvement (Asperger's syndrome or PDD NOS) and positive family history seemed to be associated with positive responses.

Neuroleptics

The "typical" neuroleptics are dopamine (D2) receptor antagonists which also interact with histamine (H1), norepinephrine (alpha-1-adrenergic), and acetylcholine (muscarinic) receptors. They have been used in the treatment of autism for over 50 years. Early controlled studies evaluated the efficacy of neuroleptics such as trifluoperazine (Fish, Shapiro, and Campbell 1996), haloperidol and fluphenazine (Faretra, Dooher, and Dowling 1970; Engelhardt et al. 1973), thiothixene (Campbell et al. 1970), molindone (Campbell et al. 1971a), and chlorpromazine (Campbell et al. 1972), with modest positive results reported.

Campbell and colleagues have subsequently published a series of papers describing double-blind, placebo-controlled studies which document the efficacy of haloperidol in reducing target behaviors such as stereotypy, hyperactivity, inattention, withdrawal, tantrums, and negative or labile affect (Campbell et al. 1978; Cohen et al. 1980; Anderson et al. 1984; Anderson et al. 1989). They initially reported that haloperidol administration was associated with improved discrimination learning (Anderson et al. 1984). However, a subsequent study showed neither an advantageous nor deleterious effect on learning (Anderson et al. 1989). Aspects of social relatedness were also found to improve with use of haloperidol in each of these studies. Locascio et al. (1991) found that older children responded better to haloperidol than younger children, and that higher functioning children responded better in general (to both haloperidol and placebo) when compared to those with more intellectual impairment.

The same group of investigators showed that clinical responders continued to benefit from treatment, with 71.5% improved after six months, and that a discontinuous (5 days per week) treatment schedule did not diminish efficacy (Perry et al. 1989). Best results were usually obtained at low doses (Joshi, Capozolli, and Coyle 1988; Campbell et al. 1978; Anderson et al. 1984; Anderson et al. 1989).

Haloperidol-related dyskinesias, including withdrawal dyskinesias, are significant problems that have been shown to occur in 33.9% of autistic children and adolescents enrolled in a large, prospective, longitudinal study (Campbell et al. 1997). Female sex and pre- and perinatal complications may be associated with increased susceptibility to dyskinesias, and cumulative dose and/or length of exposure to the medication may be important (Campbell et al. 1997; Armenteros et al. 1995).

The use of pimozide to treat children with autism has also been reported. One double-blind, crossover study included 34 autistic children and a significant reduction in aggressive and destructive behavior was described (Naruse et al. 1982). Ernst et al. (1992) conducted an open-label pilot study and found behavioral improvement in seven of eight low-functioning, hospitalized, autistic boys. Side effects were mild and transient. In a recent survey of caregivers of patients with autism, thioridazine was found to be the most commonly prescribed neuroleptic medication (Aman et al. 1995); yet we are unaware of any published trials investigating its use in this population.

Atypical Neuroleptics

Atypical neuroleptics are usually classified as such because of their ability to produce antipsychotic effects in a majority of patients without inducing significant extrapyramidal symptoms and because of their enhanced efficacy in treating negative symptoms (Potenza and McDougle 1997).

Risperidone is a potent serotonin (5-HT2) and dopamine (D2) antagonist. A number of case reports and small series support the efficacy of risperidone in decreasing target symptoms such as hyperactivity, aggressiveness, repetitive behaviors, and self-injury, as well as, in some cases, improving social relatedness in patients with autism (Purdon et al. 1994; Simeon et al. 1995; McDougle et al. 1995; Demb 1996; Rubin 1997). Larger open-label trials are described in table VI. The majority (83%) of the 90 autistic patients described in these studies were considered to be responders (table VI), although the effect of publication bias may be significant. Hyperactivity, aggressive and impulsive behavior, lability of affect, explosivity, self-injurious behavior, irritability, and oppositionality have commonly been reported to decrease significantly with risperidone treatment at relatively low doses (table VI). In addition, improvement in some aspects of social relatedness has been described (Fishman and Steele 1996; McDougle et al. 1997). Recently, McDougle and colleagues (1998) conducted a 12-week double-blind, placebo-controlled trial of risperidone in adults with autism. Of those completing the study, 57% in the risperidone group were positive responders as compared to 6% of the placebo group. Aggression, repetitive behavior, and overall scores on the *Ritvo-Freeman Real-Life Rating Scale* improved significantly. Nine of the 15 who were treated in an open-label fashion following completion of the controlled trial were categorized as responders.

Significant weight gain was commonly reported as a side effect in these studies (table VI). For example, McDougle et al. (1997) reported a mean weight gain of 8 kg in 12 weeks; Perry et al. (1997) 5.4 kg in 7 weeks; and Nicholson, Awad, and Sloman (1998) 3.5 kg in 12 weeks. Extrapyramidal symptoms were very uncommon, and sedation was usually mild and transient (table VI).

Large, controlled trials of risperidone in patients with autism are currently underway, and much more information regarding the efficacy and safety of this agent in this population will soon be available. Case reports describing the successful use of clozapine (Zuddas et al. 1996; Rubin 1997) and olanzapine (Horrigan, Barnhill, and Courvoisie 1997; Rubin 1997) in patients with autism are beginning to appear in the literature. Potenza et al. (1999) recently published the results of a 12-week, open-label pilot trial of olanzapine in eight patients with autism. Six of seven who completed the trial were considered to be clinical responders. Increased appetite and weight gain were prominent side effects. Further study of both agents is warranted; however, it is unlikely that large trials involving the use of clozapine in autistic children will be forthcoming because of the risk of agranulocytosis and the need for weekly monitoring of blood counts in order to attempt to prevent it.

Other Modulators Of Dopaminergic Neurotransmission

The equivocal positive effects of the dopamine precursor L-dopa were discussed previously because of the ability of this agent to lower serotonin levels. Dollfus et al. (1992) compared the effects of the dopamine agonist bromocriptine to those of amisulpride, which is a dopamine antagonist. Bromocriptine administration was associated with improvement in hyperactivity and inattention, whereas the use of amisulpride was associated with decreased behavioral inhibition and withdrawal.

Table VI. Risperidone Trials in Autism/PDD (N>5)

Reference	Study Design	N (with autism)	Age Range (yrs)	Dosage	Duration (wks)	Results	Adverse Effects
McDougle et al. 1998	Double-blind, placebo-controlled	31	21–35	1–10 mg/day	12	8/14 risperidone responders, 1/16 placebo responders; dec aggression, repetitive behavior, overall symptoms of autism	sedation, weight gain, agitation, GI symptoms
Nicolson, Awad, and Sloman 1998	open-label	10	4.5–10.8	1–2.5 mg/day	12	8/10 responders by CGI; dec hyperactivity, aggression; dec total CPRS and autism factor scores; dec mean total CARS and PTQ scores	weight gain (common); transient sedation, constipation, sialorrhea, urinary incontinence
Perry et al. 1997	open-label	6	7.3–14.8	1–6 mg/day	4–34	5/6 responders by CGI and CPRS; dec angry affect, lability of affect, hyperactivity	weight gain in 5/6; sedation; hepatotoxicity (on 6 mg/day) withdrawal dyskinesia; sialorrhea; inc stereotypy
McDougle et al. 1997	open-label	18	5–18	1–4 mg/day	12	12/18 responders by CGI; dec repetitive behavior, aggression and impulsivity; inc social relatedness (eye contact, affectual reactions subscale of RFRLRS)	weight gain in 12/18; sedation 6/18; nocturnal enuresis, sialorrhea, blunted affect, agitation, motor incoordination

Reference	Study Design	N (with autism)	Age Range (yrs)	Dosage	Duration (wks)	Results	Adverse Effects
Horrigan and Barnhill 1997	open-label	11	6–34	0.5–2 mg/day	4	11/11 marked clinical improvement, dec mean PTQ; dec aggression, self-injury, explosivity, overactivity; inc sleep	weight gain in 8/11; mild sedation; inc hepatic enzymes (1); new onset seizures (1)
Findling et al. 1997	open-label	6	5.0–9.5	0.75–1.5 mg/day	8	6/6 responders by CGI, CPRS, OCS; dec tantrums, irritability, restlessness, aggression, fearfulness	weight gain; sedation; transient dyspepsia and tearfulness (1)
Fishman and Steele 1996	open-label	14	9–17	0.75–1.5	8–60	13/14 responders by CGAS; dec disruptive behaviors, agitation, anxiety, aggression, hyperactivity, obsessionality, inattention, perceptual sensitivity; inc social relatedness and communication	transient sedation (5/14); sleep-onset insomnia, transient headache
Hardan et al. 1996	open-label	11 (of 20 with DD)	8–17	1–4.5 mg/day	8–65	8/11 improved and tolerated drug; dec hyperactivity, aggression, oppositionality, SIB, impulsivity	3/11 intolerable; weight gain, sedation, drooling, mild tremor; lethargy, vomiting, staring spells; galactorrhea, amenorrhea

Reference	Study Design	N (with autism)	Age Range (yrs)	Dosage	Duration (wks)	Results	Adverse Effects
Lott, Kerrick, and Cohen 1996	open-label	14 (of 33 with MR)	25–49	2–8 mg/day	at least 26 weeks	12/14 improved overall, 2 no change; dec aggression, SIB, property destruction	akathisia, insomnia, sedation, weight gain, pseudoparkinsonism

dec decreased, **inc** increased, **DD** developmental disabilities, **MR** mental retardation, **PDD** pervasive developmental disorders, **SIB** self-injurious behavior, **CARS** Childhood Autism Rating Scale, **CGAS** Children's Global Assessment Scale, **CGI** Clinical Global Impressions Scale, **CPRS** Children's Psychiatric Rating Scale, **OCS** Obsessive Compulsive Scale, **PTQ** Conners Parent-Teacher Questionnaire, **RFRLRS** Ritvo-Freeman Real-Life Rating Scale

Amantadine is an antiviral agent which also acts presynaptically and possibly postsynaptically to enhance dopaminergic neurotransmission. It is also a glutamate N-methyl-D-aspartate (NMDA) receptor antagonist (Kornhuber et al. 1994). Chandler, Barnhill, and Gualtieri (1991) reported the use of amantadine in 28 patients, 12 of whom had autism, PDD, or *autistic features*. Of these 12, 4 were considered responders and 5 had partial responses but experienced side effects. Decreased tantrums, aggression, self-injury, and agitation were reported. Improved social relatedness, concentration, cooperation, school performance, and energy levels were also noted in some patients. Two patients experienced exacerbation of symptoms, including self-injurious behavior, tearfulness, agitation, irritability, and tantrums. Other side effects included anorexia, weight loss, and insomnia. A recent, double-blind, placebo-controlled trial of amantadine resulted in modest improvements in behavior (King et al. 2000, in press). A substantial number of children in this study showed behavioral improvement when treated with placebo.

CNS Stimulants

Stimulants, such as methylphenidate and dextroamphetamine, enhance noradrenergic and dopaminergic neurotransmission by increasing presynaptic release and inhibiting reuptake of these transmitters. Early trials of dextroamphetamine and levoamphetamine in autistic children suggested that the decrease in hyperactivity often noted was outweighed by negative effects such as increased irritability and stereotypy (Campbell et al., Response to triiodothyronine, 1972; Campbell et al., Acute responses, 1972). Hoshino et al. (1977) reported improvement in autistic behavior, hyperactivity, and impulsive behavior in some autistic children on methylphenidate; however, the methodology has been criticized (Aman 1988).

These early studies led many authors to conclude that stimulants are contraindicated in patients with autism (Aman 1982; Volkmar, Hoder, and Cohen 1985). However, several subsequent publications have suggested that some autistic children respond favorably (Geller, Guttmacher, and Bleeg 1981; Vitriol and Farber 1981; Schmidt 1982; Strayhorn et al. 1988; Birmaher, Quintana, and Greenhill 1988; Quintana et al. 1995). Birmaher, Quintana, and Greenhill (1988) conducted an open-label trial of methylphenidate and found improvement in hyperactivity, impulsivity, and attentiveness in eight of nine autistic children without an associated increase in stereotypy or irritability. In a double-blind, placebo-controlled crossover study, Quintana et al. (1995) showed modest but statistically significant improvement in hyperactivity in ten children with autism using outcome measures such as the *Conners Abbreviated Parent Questionnaire*, the hyperactivity factor of the *Conners Teacher Questionnaire*, and the *Aberrant Behavior Checklist*. No worsening of behavior or stereotypic movements were evident. At present, the role of stimulants in the management of hyperactivity, impulsivity, and inattentiveness in patients with autism is unclear. Large, controlled studies seem to be warranted.

Beta-Blockers

Beta-blockers are postsynaptic norepinephrine receptor antagonists. Several preliminary studies that included one or more patients with autism showed efficacy of beta-blockers in reducing aggressive outbursts (Williams et al. 1982; Kuperman and Stewart 1987; Ratey et al., Autism, 1987). Ratey and colleagues have described improvements in target behaviors such as aggressiveness, irritability, self-injury, property destruction, inattentiveness, and speech and socialization in autistic adults treated with propranolol or nadolol (Ratey et al., Autism, 1987; Ratey et al., Brief report, 1987; Ratey and Lindem 1991). Luchins and Dojka (1989) studied a group of mentally retarded adults that included one autistic man who exhibited decreased aggression and self-injury on propranolol. Decreased stereotypy and aggressive outbursts have been reported in a man with PDD and Fragile X Syndrome, who was treated with long-acting propranolol in a double-blind, placebo-controlled fashion (Cohen, Tsiouris, and Pfadt 1991). Connor (1994) demonstrated that nadolol was more efficacious than propranolol in reducing aggression, irritability, self-injury, inattention, and hyperkinesis in an 11-year-old boy with PDD and mental retardation.

Tricyclic Antidepressants (Excluding Clomipramine)

The nonselective tricyclics, such as imipramine and desipramine, predominantly block presynaptic reuptake of norepinephrine, although serotonin reuptake is inhibited as well. Campbell et al. (1971b) studied the use of imipramine in ten young autistic children and concluded that the infrequent beneficial effects were outweighed by the toxic effects. Only two of the ten patients were rated improved by the clinician. Desipramine has been shown to be ineffective and inferior to clomipramine in treating autistic symptoms (including stereotypies), anger, and compulsive, ritualized behaviors (Gordon et al. 1993).

Clonidine

Clonidine is an alpha-2 adrenergic receptor agonist that acts at presynaptic autoreceptors to decrease release of norepinephrine. Jaselskis et al. (1992) conducted a double-blind, placebo-controlled trial of oral clonidine in eight autistic children with excessive inattention, hyperactivity, and impulsivity. Clonidine was found to be modestly effective in the short-term treatment of irritability and hyperactivity as measured by teacher ratings on the *Aberrant Behavior Checklist* (ABC) and parent ratings on the *Conners Abbreviated Parent-Teacher Questionnaire*. Six patients continued in an open study, and it was found that after 6 to 8 weeks of good response, tolerance to therapeutic effects developed in four.

Fankhauser et al. (1992) administered transdermal clonidine to nine patients with autism in a double-blind, placebo-controlled crossover study. Clinician ratings on the *Clinical Global Impressions Scale* (CGI) and on the social relationships to people, affectual responses, and sensory responses subscales of the *Ritvo-Freeman Real Life Rating Scale* demonstrated that clonidine was superior to placebo in reducing hyperarousal behaviors. Koshes and Rock (1994) also used transdermal clonidine successfully to manage explosive, aggressive outbursts in a young autistic woman.

Drowsiness and hypotension were common side effects, especially in the first few weeks of treatment with clonidine and at higher doses (Jaselskis et al. 1992; Fankhauser et al. 1992). McCracken and Martin (1997) reported depressive symptoms and behavioral deterioration associated with clonidine treatment in an autistic boy. Electrocardiographic changes may also be problematic in children treated with this medication (Kumarachandran 1994). Guanfacine may have less sedating and hypotensive effects but, to our knowledge, trials in patients with autism have not yet been published.

Opiate Antagonists

Naloxone and naltrexone are opiate antagonists that have been studied in patients with autism and in others with self-injurious behavior (SIB). These studies are based on the theory that overactivity of brain opioids plays a role in the pathogenesis of these problems. Naloxone has a relatively short half-life and must be administered parenterally, which decreases its clinical usefulness. Also, in a double-blind, placebo-controlled trial in an autistic girl, SIB was found to increase on naloxone and decrease on naltrexone (Barrett, Feinstein, and Hole 1989).

Naltrexone has been reported to be efficacious in reducing target behaviors such as SIB, hyperactivity, and aggression as well as improving social interaction in small open and double-blind studies and case reports (Herman et al. 1986; Leboyer, Bouvard, and Dugas 1988; Lienemann and Walker 1989; Barrett, Feinstein, and Hole 1989;

Walters et al. 1990; Panksepp and Lensing 1991; Taylor et al. 1991; Leboyer et al. 1992). Other investigators, however, demonstrated no reduction in SIB or other maladaptive behaviors in autistic patients treated with naltrexone (Zingarelli et al. 1992). Studies involving ten or more patients with autism are reviewed in table VII. Most of these studies showed some beneficial effect on hyperactivity, but no improvement in core symptoms of autism (Kolmen et al. 1997; Kolmen et al. 1995; Campbell et al. 1993; Willemsen-Swinkels, Buitelaar, and van Engeland 1996). No improvement in learning was detected (Kolmen et al. 1997; Kolmen et al. 1995; Campbell et al. 1993; Gonzalez et al. 1994). Improvement in SIB in this population has not been clearly established, and both transient and non-transient exacerbation has been reported (Knabe, Schultz, and Richard 1990; Willemsen-Swinkels et al. 1995; Benjamin et al. 1995). Naltrexone has a bitter taste and can be difficult to administer, but the side effects are quite mild (table VII).

Adrenocorticotrophic Hormone (ACTH) Analog: ORG 2766

ORG 2766 is a synthetic ACTH (4-9) analog that lacks substantial steroidogenic activity and can be administered orally. It has been shown to modulate disturbed social behavior in rats (Niesink and van Ree 1983). The normalizing effect of ORG 2766 on environmentally induced disturbed social behavior in rats is completely antagonized by naltrexone, suggesting that these behaviors may be due to altered activity of brain opioid systems (Niesink and van Ree 1983).

Buitelaar and colleagues have studied the effects of ORG 2766 in patients with autism. In a 4-week double-blind, placebo-controlled crossover study involving 14 autistic children, the administration of 20 mg per day of ORG 2766 was found to be associated with an increase in aspects of social interaction and a decrease in stereotypic behavior during playroom observation (Buitelaar et al. 1990; Buitelaar et al. 1992a). In a second controlled crossover trial, 40 mg per day of ORG 2766 was given for eight weeks to 20 children with autism (Buitelaar et al. 1992b). Improvement was noted on the *Aberrent Behavior Checklist* social withdrawal subscale and in social interaction and play behavior in the playroom setting. However, in a recent double-blind, placebo-controlled parallel trial in which 30 autistic children with performance IQs greater than 60 received ORG 2766, and 20 received placebo, no significant group differences in social or communicative behavior were demonstrated (Buitelaar et al. 1996). There was not a significant difference between the number of individual responders in the ORG 2766 group (10/30) and the placebo group (4/20).

Table VII. Naltrexone Trials in Autism/PDD (N>9)

Reference	Study Design	N (with autism)	Age Range (yrs)	Dosage	Duration (wks)	Results	Adverse Effects
Kolmen et al. 1997; Kolmen et al. 1995	double-blind, placebo-controlled crossover	24	3.0–8.3	1 mg/kg/day	2 on naltrexone, 6–7 total	significant improvement on parent measures (CGI, Conners Imp-Hyp Factor, restlessness item on side effects rating scale) but not on teacher ratings or clinician CGI or CPRS; no improvement on learning measures	difficult to administer because of bitter taste; mild side effects including drowsiness, dec appetite, rhinorrhea
Willemsen-Swinkels, Buitelaar, and van Engeland 1996	double-blind, placebo-controlled crossover	23 (20 completed study)	3–7	20–40 mg/day; 0.74–1.18 mg/kg/day	4 on naltrexone, 10 total	improved teacher ratings of hyperactivity and irritability (ABC, target behavior checklists, CGI); no difference from placebo on parent CGI; no difference in playroom assessment (including social reciprocity); concluded that naltrexone could not be recommended for clinical use in autism	2 dropped out because of bitter taste; no serious untoward effects reported

Reference	Study Design	N (with autism)	Age Range (yrs)	Dosage	Duration (wks)	Results	Adverse Effects
Willemsen-Swinkels, Buitelaar, and van Engeland 1996	double-blind, placebo-controlled crossover	24 (of 32 with MR)	18–46	single 100 mg dose then 50–150 mg/day	4	single dose no effect; daily treatment no beneficial effects; inc stereotypy on ABC subscale; placebo more effective	inc self-injury (1), nausea, tiredness, sedation
Bouvard et al. 1995	double-blind, placebo-controlled crossover	10	5–14	0.5 mg/kg/day	4	modest clinical improvements in hyperactivity, hostility, restraint, sociability, communication, object relations, and attention (naltrexone marginally greater effects than placebo); 4 strong responders	none
Campbell et al. 1993; Gonzales et al. 1994; Campbell et al. 1990	double-blind, placebo-controlled parallel groups	41 (23 received naltrexone)	2.9–7.8	0.5–1.0 mg/kg/day	3	dec hyperactivity (on 3 measures); no effect on discrimination learning or core symptoms of autism	sedation, dec appetite, vomiting
Campbell et al. 1989; Campbell et al. 1988	open-label	10	3.4–6.5	0.5, 1.0, 2.0 mg/kg single dose weekly	3	dec withdrawl inc verbal production; dec stereotypies	mild sedation

dec dereased, **inc** increased, **ABC** Aberrant Behavior Checklist, **CGI** Clinical Global Impression Scale, **CPRS** Children's Psychiatric Rating Scale, **MR** mental retardation

Anticonvulsants

In addition to their roles in seizure management, anticonvulsants such as carbamazepine and valproic acid have been shown to have positive behavioral effects in some patients with developmental disabilities (see Sovner 1991). Many of these patients did not have epilepsy but did have comorbid psychiatric diagnoses such as mania or bipolar disorder. Both carbamazepine and valproic acid are established alternatives to lithium for mood stabilization in adults, and their use in children and adolescents is commonly advocated (Geller and Luby 1997; Botteron and Geller 1995).

Plioplys (1994) described three young children with autism and epileptiform findings on an electroencephalogram (EEG) during sleep who improved markedly with valproic acid therapy. In fact, such a dramatic improvement in language and social skills took place that within one month none of the three children qualified for the diagnosis of autism by DSM-III-R criteria any longer, and there was no clinical suggestion of seizures in any of these children. In a recent retrospective study, Bardenstein et al. (1998) found that valproic acid monotherapy resulted in significant improvement in both EEG recordings and clinical status in 29 of 42 patients with PDD. Thirty-two showed subjective clinical improvement in eye contact, attention, self-stimulation, and language. Several case reports have also described marked positive effects of valproic acid on bipolar symptoms in autistic adults (Sovner 1989) and language and social skills in autistic children (Childs and Blair 1997).

Carbamazepine has antidepressant and antimanic properties, and has been used to treat mania, rapid cycling, aggression, self-injury, impulsivity, irritability, episodic dyscontrol, and other target symptoms in epileptic and nonepileptic patients with developmental disorders (for review, see Sovner 1991). Sovner (1991) reviewed a case of carbamazepine-responsive depression in a 25-year-old woman with autism and mild mental retardation. Other reviewers have also referred to personal experience with carbamazepine in patients with autism and clinical evidence of partial seizures (Cook and Leventhal 1995). We are not aware of any larger clinical trials of carbamazepine in patients with autism. Like many other drugs with antidepressant properties, carbamazepine has been reported to induce mania (Reiss and O'Donnell 1984; Pleak et al. 1988).

Lamotrigine is a newer anticonvulsant that has been studied in patients with autism. Uvebrant and Bauziene (1994) reported a decrease in autistic symptoms in eight of thirteen autistic patients treated for intractable epilepsy, regardless of efficacy in controlling the seizures. However, Belsito et al. (1998) studied the behavioral effects of this drug in 35 children with autism and did not find significant differences between lamotrigine and placebo. In another recent trial, lamotrigine was found to be associated with increased aggressive behavior in a group of older adolescents and adults with epilepsy and intellectual deficits (Beran and Gibson 1998).

There is clinical overlap between the phenomena of autistic regression and classic acquired epileptic aphasia (Landau-Kleffner syndrome), a condition which may respond to steroid treatment. Stefanatos, Grover, and Geller (1995) described significant prednisone-associated improvement in language and social relatedness in a young child with PDD, a history of regression, and a normal EEG. Mott et al. (1996) conducted an open-label trial of prednisone in 12 children with autistic disorder or PDD NOS and found improvement in language, attention, purposeful directed behavior, and receptive emotional abilities in about half of the children. They suggested that a trial of oral prednisone should be considered in patients with autism because they might actually have a steroid-responsive encephalopathy (possibly an overlapping subtype of Landau-Kleffner syndrome).

Immune Modulators

Intravenous immunoglobulin (IVIG) is commonly used to treat patients with immunodeficiencies, autoimmune disorders, and immunoinflammatory disorders. Gupta, Aggarwal, and Heads (1996) treated ten autistic children with 400 mg/kg of IVIG every 4 weeks for at least 6 months. According to clinical observation, improvement in social behavior, eye contact, and response to commands were reported. Decreased echolalia, improved articulation, and increased vocabulary were also noted. Two patients showed dramatic improvement in speech, but, in the others, there was little effect on spontaneous meaningful speech. Plioplys (1998) studied the effects of IVIG in ten autistic children and found marked improvement in one, mild improvement attributed to placebo effect in four, and no improvement in five. The single clear responder deteriorated to baseline over the five months following completion of four infusions given over 18 weeks of the study. Lagae et al. (1998) recently described the efficacy of IVIG in a patient with Landau-Kleffner syndrome. In another open-label pilot study of seven patients using systematic behavioral assessments, no benefits were detected (DelGiudice-Asch et al. 1999).

Pentoxifylline, a phosphodiesterase inhibitor with immunomodulatory effects, has been shown by Japanese investigators to have beneficial effects in autistic patients (for review, see DelGiudice-Asch and Hollander 1997). In addition to behavioral improvement, the use of pentoxifylline is often associated with EEG improvement. Corticosteroids, previously discussed, may also exert their effects through immune modulation. A recent abstract suggests that improvement in hyperactivity, attention, and interpersonal relatedness was associated with open-label administration of oral vancomycin to a small group of autistic children with a history of chronic diarrhea preceding the onset of autistic features (Sandler et al. 1998).

Vitamins and Minerals

Over a dozen published studies have reported improvements in autistic patients treated with high-dose Vitamin B6 (pyridoxine) and magnesium (for reviews, see Pfeiffer et al. 1995; Singh et al. 1998; Aman and Singh 1988; Rimland 1987). These studies have been challenged because of methodological problems such as imprecise outcome measures, small sample sizes, use of the same subjects in multiple studies, lack of long-term follow-up data, lack of adjustment for regression effects in measuring improvements, and questionable clinical significance of improvements (Pfeiffer et al. 1995; Aman and Singh 1988). However, the data suggest that some patients with autism may benefit from this treatment, although additional studies that address the methodological concerns are needed. Recently, in a 10-week double-blind, placebo-controlled crossover trial involving ten autistic patients, Findling, Maxwell, and Wiznitzer (1997) found that the combination of pyridoxine and magnesium was ineffective in ameliorating autistic behaviors according to parent, teacher, and clinician ratings. There were no individual responders.

Rimland (1988) conducted a large survey and found that parents of children with autism gave vitamin B6 and magnesium the highest satisfaction rating of any pharmacologic intervention. In contrast, Aman et al. (1995) found that vitamins were the least satisfying agents to the parents they surveyed. Toxicity has been reported with high doses of pyridoxine (Schaumburg et al. 1983; Berger and Schaumburg 1984), but Rimland argues that most adverse effects can be avoided with co-administration of magnesium and low to moderate doses of other B vitamins (Rimland 1988).

Dolske et al. (1993) conducted a 30-week, double-blind, placebo-controlled trial of vitamin C (ascorbic acid) in 18 autistic children in residential treatment and found improvement in the total and sensory motor scores on the *Ritvo-Freeman Real Life Rating Scale*. The tyrosine hydroxylase cofactor, tetrahydrobiopterin, was recently shown to have beneficial effects on social functioning and communication in six autistic children who had relatively low CSF levels of this compound at baseline (Fernell et al. 1997), consistent with earlier findings in

Japan (Naruse et al. 1987). Zinc deficiency has been described as an etiologic factor in pica in patients with developmental disabilities, and replacement therapy may reduce or eliminate the behavior (Bhalla et al. 1983; Lofts, Schroeder, and Maier 1990).

Miscellaneous Hormones and Other Agents

Triiodothyronine (T3) has been administered to euthyroid patients with autism and found to have beneficial effects, including decreased withdrawal, increased affective responsiveness and communication, and improved motor initiation (Sherwin, Flach, and Stokes 1958; Campbell et al., Lithium and chlorpromazine,1972; Campbell et al., A controlled crossover study, 1978). Administration of thyrotropin-releasing hormone (TRH) was associated with transient decreases in hyperactivity and increases in affective responsiveness, spontaneous speech, focusing, and euphoria (Campbell et al., Response to thyrotropin, 1978). Melatonin has been used successfully to regulate sleep in children with developmental disabilities, some of whom had autism (Jan and O'Donnell 1996). Recently, three autistic children were reported to have developed improvements in behavior and communication, as well as gastrointestinal symptoms after secretin administration during endoscopy (Horvath et al. 1998). A number of controlled trials were underway or had been completed but not published at the time of this chapter's revision. The only published double-blind placebo-controlled trial at the time of revision showed that treatment with a single dose of synthetic human secretin was not associated with significant improvements on any of the outcome measures (Sandler et al. 1999). Rossi et al. (1999) recently reported beneficial effects of the histamine H1-receptor antagonist niaprazine in 52% of 25 patients with autism and associated behavior and sleep problems. Administration of this sedating antihistamine, which is not available in the United States, at a dose of 1 mg/kg/day divided into 3 doses, resulted in decreased hyperkinesis, inattention, frustration, resistance to change, anxiety, aggressiveness, and sleep disturbance.

Part II. The "Art" of Neuropsychopharmacology in Autism

This section attempts to describe the "nonscientific" aspect of placing individuals with developmental disabilities, especially those with autistic symptoms (DSM-IV), on medications. Some of these suggestions capture the clinical "art" of pharmacology in autism.

First, each individual diagnosed as having autism or PDD may respond unpredictably to medications—only showing effect to large doses or having significant response to very low doses, such as 2 mg. of fluoxetine every other day. Secondly, the time needed to conclude effectiveness may be prolonged, such as 6 or 7 months for fluoxetine. Homeopathic principles of using very small doses for long periods of time may apply; on the other hand, relatively benign medications often require megadosing, such as the use of 80 to 100 mg. of buspirone or 25 mg. of folic acid (Gillberg et al. 1986). Thirdly, clarifying expectations or defining a "response" to medication can be difficult. Adding a DSM-IV diagnosis and objectively redefining the diagnostic criteria for that disorder with time samples, frequency, and intensity of behavioral episodes, or standardized behavioral checklists (see table I) make defining a response a reasonable task. Relying on caregivers' verbal reports of "She's better." allows greater room for error. Lastly, ruling out medical causes for behavior in autistic children and adults requires lengthy and aggressive work-ups. For example, medical conditions can cause self-injurious behavior (SIB) (Bosch et al. 1997).

One solution to this inherent complicating nature of treating behavior with medication is to practice good medicine with patience. Multiple visits or reviewing reports from a variety of settings is a first step. Helping caregivers tolerate difficult behavior and teaching them self-protection can buy time. Finding professionals in a medical community comfortable with developmental disabilities who advocate medical work-ups for seizure disorders, gastrointestinal disease, dental, and infectious diseases, allows for more time to see individuals prior to prescribing medications for them. It also clarifies causes.

This approach engenders an intuitive feel for an autistic child or adult and gives the prescriber a sense of the patient's depression, anxiety, or psychosis. A logical warning against prescribing occurs if the physician senses that a caregiver needs the medication more than the client being examined. Stressful roommates, overtired parents, or a recent move can all cause behavioral problems that appear as a psychiatric disorder. Waiting often "heals" the syndrome. In short, objectifying problem behaviors, using DSM-IV diagnosis and objective measurements of behaviors, and ruling out medical and environmental causes are the first two steps. The third step—being patient—can be just as difficult.

The act of prescribing medications for problem behaviors has a seductive quality: the physician heals or changes a person and "saves the day." Not to prescribe quickly frustrates families, and some physicians may be tempted to respond to this allure, producing a "stick-on effect," in which each visit to the physician produces a new medication, a new attempt to "save the day." As a result, more medications are added to the patient's regimen. Autistic individuals may eventually be prescribed five or six drugs, often two or more in the same class. This practice is undesirable, since it often leads to unnecessary complex drug interactions or toxicity.

Case Example #1

M. B. is a 20-year-old autistic adult who was discharged to a community group home from an institution for the disabled after having lived in the institution for over a decade. She was prescribed 20 mg. t.i.d. of buspirone for anxiety, secondary to obsessive compulsive disorder. She tolerated her group home for two years, but then moved. Her new routine was inconsistent; she became violent. Multiple mental health center visits resulted in additional prescriptions of haloperidol and lithium. During her third hospitalization, her medications included haloperidol, risperidone, loxitane, and propanolol. Fluoxetine was added. She was then diagnosed with schizophrenia due to "earplugging" and asocial behaviors. A clinician, experienced in the care of autistic persons, advised tapering off all neuroleptics and propanolol, but continuing fluoxetine, elevated to 40 to 80 mg. (obsessive compulsive disorder doses in adults). Her daily routines were structured, and a change in diagnosis to obsessive compulsive disorder and autism was made, disregarding the concept of schizophrenia.

Level I Medications: Buspirone, Trazodone, Naltrexone, Vitamins

Once the decision to medicate is made and baseline data is in place, low risk medications are often the safest approach (table VIII). The present neurochemical theories of autism strongly support serotonergic interventions (McDougle et al., A double-blind placebo-controlled study, 1996; Cook and Leventhal 1996; Potenza and McDougle 1997). Buspirone and trazodone mainly affect serotonin, are relatively safe, and allow for flexible dosing schedules. These two medications offer a response 25 to 30% of the time. However, buspirone often requires higher dosing than expected, 80 to 100 mg., divided two or three times daily. Both drugs show some immediate side-effects: buspirone causes alterations in energy level and trazodone causes orthostasis, leg swelling, or pain. Starting with low doses and slowly increasing the dosage decreases the risks of side effects and helps with anxiety symptoms and mild depression. Both drugs decrease aggression and violence (Gedye 1991a, 1991b; Realmuto, August, and Garfinkel 1989; Ratey et al. 1989; Ratey and Lindem 1991). Due to the high frequency of seizure disorders in this population, buspirone has proven particularly helpful in individuals with irritability and anxiety-depressive symptoms as related to chronic seizures (Ricketts et al. 1994; Blumer 1997).

Table VIII. Drug Selection in Autism

Level	I. Low Yield: Low Risk	IIa. Moderate Yield: Moderate Risk	IIb.	III. Moderate Yield: High Risk		IV. High Risk: Low Yield
Drugs		SSRIs	ADD drugs	Atypical Antipsychotics	Mood Stabilizers	Typical Antipsychotics
	Buspirone Trazodone Naltrexone	Fluoxetine Paroxetine Sertraline Fluvoxamine Clomipramine	Methylphenidate Dextroamphet-amine Adderall® Guanfacine Clonidine	Risperidone Olanzapine Quetiapine Clozapine	Lithium Carbamazepine Valproic acid New Antiepileptic Drugs (AED) Lamotrigine Topiramate Tiagabine Gabapentin	Thioridazine Chlorpromazine Mesoridazine Loxapine Thiothixene Haloperidol Fluphenazine
Results	Decreased:	Decreased:	Decreased:	Decreased:	Decreased:	Decreased:
	SIB Aggression Violence Stereotypy	SIB Sexual Aggression Violence Stereotypy OCD Depression Social withdrawal	Aggression Hyperactivity Stereotypy Depression	Violence Aggression SIB Psychosis Activity	Mania-Bipolar Aggression SIB Activity	Aggression Violence SIB Psychosis

Level	I. Low Yield: Low Risk	IIa. Moderate Yield: Moderate Risk	IIb.	III. Moderate Yield: High Risk		IV. High Risk: Low Yield
	Increased:	Increased:	Increased:	Increased:	Increased:	Increased:
	Mood Psychological Development	Energy Mood	Attention Activity Mood	Mood	Mood	
Risks		SSRIs	ADD Meds	Atypical Antipsychotics	Mood Stabilizers	Typical Antipsychotics
	Buspirone Dizziness Agitation Trazodone Dizziness Blood pooling Sedation Naltrexone Skin rash Liver injury	Mania Weight changes Stomach problems Seizures Movement disorders Drug-drug interactions Serotonin syndrome Serotonin depletion Withdrawal syndrome	Cardiovascular Weight changes Arousal Tics Tolerance Polypharmacy Clonidine Sedation Weight gain Psychosis Mania Dysphoria	Movement Disorders Chemical restraint Weight changes Mania Dizziness Enuresis Tolerance Delayed onset WBC Seizures Sedation	Lithium Weight gain Thyroid/renal Cognitive loss Carbamazepine and Valproic acid Electrolytes Liver functions CBC Drug-drug Interactions Hair loss Newer AED Mania Rash	Tardive dyskinesia Akathisia Chemical restraint Sexual loss Prolactin increase Visual loss Bladder problems Tolerance Rebound Cognitive loss

Naltrexone

Another drug with a good safety profile that may offer resounding benefits is naltrexone. Again, the dosing is idiosyncratic: one case may respond to 25 mg., another to 200 mg. Recent case reports suggest the need for a one- to two-year trial. Some clinicians choose an opioid antagonist for high-frequency or high-intensity self-injurious behavior (SIB). Individuals who self abuse to the point of seeing blood, or who do it secretly at night and seem driven to SIB due to irritability, may respond to naltrexone. Mild side effects do occur (rash, unsteady gait). Sometimes no benefits are clear. Initial worsening on naltrexone may require starting with clonidine to combat withdrawal (Thompson et al. 1994). Response to naltrexone and remission of chronic SIB may engender acquisition of new skills or psychological development (Taylor et al. 1991). A trial of naltrexone for SIB appears to have low risk and potential for great benefits.

Level IIa: Selective Serotonin Reuptake Inhibitors (SSRIs)

At the next level of intervention, with more potential for benefits and risks of side-effects, are the selective serotonin reuptake inhibitors (fluoxetine, paroxetine, fluvoxamine, and sertraline). These antidepressants are effective for anxiety, depression, and eating disorders, and may decrease sexually compulsive behavior through modulation of serotonin. Based on our current knowledge of autism, SSRIs may address a basic neurochemical defect. Much of the research surrounds clomipramine, found to decrease the frequency and intensity of obsessive compulsive disorder behaviors and the violence associated with them. But its high side-effect profile has relegated clomipramine to an agent for augmenting SSRIs (Leonard 1997). Adding low doses of clomipramine to SSRIs requires monitoring blood levels, particularly when it is added to fluoxetine. Buspirone also holds this capacity as an augmenting agent for SSRIs. Bedtime dosing of trazodone with SSRIs offers a syngeristic effect on serotonin systems.

Beginning with buspirone or trazodone and adding an SSRI appears logical, given the present emphasis on serotonin in autism. This may be an effective treatment for associated depression and anxiety disorders. A review of the catchment area studies shows these two groups of disorders to be prevalent in the general population and provides a good starting point or initial theory when treating autistic behaviors; for example, SIB is a function of obsessive compulsive disorder or dysthymia (Hales, Yudofsky, and Talbot 1994).

Populations with active or chronic seizure disorders accompanied by chronic irritability, violence, self-abuse, or depressive symptoms respond well to SSRIs. The addition of low dose tricyclics may augment the antidepressant effects (Blumer 1997). Some clinicians resort to tricyclics only after trying SSRIs and low risk augmenting agents (buspirone, trazodone). As is the case with clomipramine, tricyclics appear relegated to the role of augmenting agents due to their high-risk profiles. Monitoring blood levels and EKGs can help avoid significant drug-drug interactions and elevations (Leonard 1997).

A significant risk of SSRIs is their mood elevating effects, especially for children who have no mood problems. Starting SSRIs with very low doses given every other day usually helps to avoid typical initial side effects (gastrointestinal distress, increased energy), but once higher doses are attained, the risk for mood elevation increases. New onset violence or irritability may point to developing hypomania. The typical symptoms of hypomania—decreased need for sleep and food, increased energy, increased pleasurable activities (masturbation, securing toys), hyperactivity—if left untreated, may lead to psychosis. Solutions to this relatively common problem include: (1) addition of mood stabilizers; (2) changing SSRIs; (3) emergency short-term use of clonazepam; and (4) stopping the SSRI. Recently, some clinicians have discussed using atypical antipsychotics, although risperidone itself may stimulate increased mood. Selective Serotonin Reuptake Inhibitors also carry significant risk of drug-drug interactions; monitoring for these is difficult. Using low doses for long periods minimizes significant or abrupt onset of drug-drug side effects. On discontinuation, SSRIs need to be tapered (Rosenbaum 1998); they show little rebound or inherent side effects when tapered slowly. The risk of movement disorders is more of a clinical curiosity, but when SSRIs are added to typical antipsychotics, the risk of drug-drug interactions is very real. With the present variety of SSRIs, a clinician can choose a drug with side effect profiles suited to the individual's need: stimulating versus sedating. The two biggest long-term problems appear to be mood elevation and drug-drug interactions. If a medical or environmental solution or behavioral solution is found, these groups of medications are easily tapered, an added benefit.

A typical progression of treatment for an individual with, say, aggression, SIB, and insomnia, may start with buspirone, aggressively increasing the dosage, and then adding trazodone. If behavioral data shows that a response has not been attained, either buspirone or trazodone is tapered, the dosage increased, and naltrexone added. If the response is still below the criteria established prior to starting medications, the first medication is tapered and discontinued, naltrexone is continued, and a very low dose SSRI is added and slowly increased. Decisions for further increasing dosages or ascertaining when maximal improvement has been reached should be based on objective measures of SIB, sleep data, and frequency and intensity of irritability.

Level IIb: Stimulants and Clonidine

A third group of medications known to be effective in autistic children, but carrying clear risks of side effects, are "ADD-medications," stimulants (Campbell et al., Neuroleptic-related dyskinesias, 1997), and clonidine (Jaselskis et al. 1992). With the present overemphasis on ADD diagnosis and the ease of response to the stimulants, the need for baseline behavioral data and clear objective data to determine a response in follow-up, cannot be overemphasized (Volkmar, Hoder, and Cohen 1985). In the nonverbal and developmentally disabled population, psychiatric disorders such as depression, anxiety, and adjustment disorders, as well as distress due to medical problems overlap with symptoms of ADD. Akathisia due to neuroleptics can appear as ADD as well. Clinical patience helps to illuminate these differences.

The immediate side effects of stimulants usually resolve when low doses are started and slowly increased. Over time, however, a tolerance to stimulants may take hold and a "stick-on effect" to dosing becomes possible; each new behavioral problem equals a dose increase. Decreasing or tapering dosages of stimulants carries a risk of rebound, possibly related to dopamine overactivity. With each decrease, problematic behaviors may recur and become more intense. Stimulants are sometimes considered short-term solutions, but are continued after new medications are added, particularly SSRIs, often leading to polypharmacy. The combined effects of stimulants with the mood elevating effects of the SSRIs may cause mania or hypomania.

Although the benefits of stimulants can be remarkable, caution should be exercised with multiple dose increases, additions of other stimulating medications (particularly SSRIs), and the addition of second agents, such as clonidine, to control side effects from stimulants.

Clonidine has been used extensively with autistic children (Jaselskis et al. 1992; Fankhauser et al. 1992), despite the potential for decreasing central norepinephrine (Kemph 1993), resulting in sedation or "chemical restraint." With the quick fix of clonidine, many parents appear relieved from not having to deal with the complicated behavioral problems, but others are concerned with the "dullness" of their children. (Clonidine is often added to stimulants to control afternoon or evening rebound.) Tapering off clonidine can be difficult for autistic children because of the "awakening" or rebound effect of dosage decreases. With each decrease, problematic behaviors may recur and become more intense. Minimizing dose increases by constantly attempting to make small decreases when behavioral data are stable may help placate parents' fears and avoid complicated issues of chemical restraint. Because of the appearance of dullness, decreased activity and speech, and sustained changes in vital signs (Campbell et al.

1972), many clinicians have moved away from propanolol as a treatment for autistic individuals, and some avoid it completely. With lower risk alternatives available, the use of propanolol may be antiquated. The same may be true of clonidine in the next decade.

Level III: Mood Stabilizers And Atypical Antipsychotics ("Atypicals")

Lithium and anticonvulsants (carbamazepine and valproic acid) are frequently used for bipolar disorder in the autistic population. The research in adult pharmacology strongly supports the use of mood stabilizers for the following: bipolar disorder, depression, obsessive compulsive disorder, and post traumatic stress disorder, as well as dementia. Aggressive behaviors also respond to lithium and valproic acid (Rao et al. 1998). However, the need to monitor blood and the potential side effects place this group of medications in a second line of treatment, except for clear-cut bipolar disorders.

Levels I and II

Clinicians who treat aggressive behaviors with mood stabilizers first, may bypass interventions that have lower risks and are as potentially beneficial. Low doses of mood stabilizers are frequently ineffective (which may not be the case with less risky medicines) and may still carry the risk of side effects. Mood stabilizers may need extended trial times to clarify their effects. It is also essential to taper off mood stabilizers slowly, to avoid adverse effects (seizures). These combined factors and the paucity of research in children with autism mitigate against their frequent use.

Many clinicians, however, who use SSRIs and prescribe mood stabilizers in response to SSRI-induced mania and subtherapeutic blood levels may control drug-induced mania. Clear cases of bipolar disorder or difficult-to-treat depression deserve this level of intervention. A logical course of treatment for behavioral problems may graduate to the use of mood stabilizers after there has been no objective response to lower level, lower risk medications, particularly serotonin-based interventions.

Early research has shown that the new generation of seizure medications—lamotrigine, gabapentin, topiramate, and tiagabine—stabilize mood as well as decrease violence, irritability, and aggression. Also, with these medications, one is free from the need to monitor blood. Present studies are clarifying which of these new seizure medications will prove most beneficial and least risky.

The *older* mood stabilizers, particularly lithium, bring up the issue of chemical restraint, cognitive dulling, and the appearance of sedation. Valproic acid and carbamazepine can induce hepatotoxicity or leukopenia and both carry risks of drug-drug interactions (see Leonard 1997 for review). Many clinicians voice concern over long-term use of these agents and look forward to freer use of the "newer" mood stabilizers after conclusive research is done.

Case Example #2

T. S., a five-year-old boy with autism and moderate mental retardation, presented with a two-month history of increasing hyperactivity, aggression, and insomnia. His teachers had noted that he was sometimes "sad" and intermittently ate large amounts of food. The family history was notable for bipolar disorder in the maternal grandfather and a maternal uncle had committed suicide. After the diagnosis of mania and bipolar disorder was made and treatment with valproic acid was started, the child's sleep and behaviors improved within one week. Six months later, his symptoms reappeared and he had a valproic acid level of 37 mg/liter (therapeutic, 50–100). The dose was increased and his behavior and sleep patterns improved again, coincident with a return of the valproate level to 60.

Another group of drugs often used solely for mood stabilizing effects are the atypical antipsychotics (risperidone, olanzapine, quetiapine, and clozapine). Risperidone has been studied heavily and used with great intensity in the autistic population (see table VI). It is an unusual atypical, from a clinical perspective, in that it seems to bridge atypical agents and *typical* antipsychotics (Perry et al. 1997). The frequency of extrapyramidal side effects, akathisia, and changes in prolactin at higher doses make risperidone look clinically identical to high potency agents. However, low doses (0.5–1.0 mg. b.i.d.) have many "atypical" effects on negative symptoms, mood stabilization, and decreased impulsivity. The *switch* from atypical to typical effects appears to be related to dose. This switch occurs in populations of the elderly, children, and developmentally disabled faster and at lower strengths. The use of liquid risperidone at very low doses may give access to good clinical response with a low risk for side effects. Clinicians who use higher doses may have to deal with more side effects.

Risperidone at higher doses also raises questions of chemical restraint: drooling, dull appearance, loss of skills, and enuresis. Case reports also point to the antidepressant action of risperidone on the serotonin system and hypomania or mania due to its sustained use (Simon, Blubaugh, and Pippidis 1996). Risperidone's clearest benefit, when compared to other atypicals, is the quick onset of action for psychotic symptoms and significant response for violence, aggression, and SIB. Avoiding high doses helps eliminate rebound when the dose is tapered. Clinicians may also see tolerance to risperidone's benefits over sustained trial times (one to two years). It seems to respond to replacement with alternative atypicals, such as olanzapine, quetiapine, and clozapine.

Quetiapine and olanzapine are under present study (Fava 1997). Clinicians may find these two agents excellent replacements for older, higher risk neuroleptics (chlorpromazine, thioridazine, loxapine, mesoridazine). These atypicals do carry significant risk for weight gain, especially with olanzapine and risperidone, but parents' concerns with *chemical restraint* seem rare with olanzapine or quetiapine. The onset of action may be delayed with olanzapine or quetiapine and some clinicians will start with risperidone at low doses. If a trial concludes as a failure, olanzapine or quetiapine may be added, then risperidone tapered off.

Case Example #3

A 14-year-old nonverbal girl with autism, generalized tonic-clonic seizures, and severe mental retardation was treated for eight years with multiple successive medication regimens for marked anxiety, frequent agitation, aggression, and self-injurious behavior (SIB). Responses to Levels I, II, and III agents were short-lived or inconsistent. On risperidone and lamotrigine, seizures came under control and there were decreased agitation and SIB. However, she continued to have disrupted sleep. After risperidone was changed to olanzapine, she became calmer and her sleep improved. With the replacement of lamotrigine with topiramate, her mood stabilized further and she has become her *best ever*, now responsive to training for augmentative communication.

Clozapine carries the highest risk of the atypicals due to the need for blood work, significant side effects of start-up doses, and long-term risk of seizures. Agranulocytosis is worrisome as well. Clozapine seems the atypical of last resort if risperidone, olanzapine, and quetiapine treatments fail. Yet, clozapine is very effective in treating tardive dystonic and dyskinetic disorders from exposure to typical neuroleptics. If lower level treatment strategies have failed and other atypicals have not produced a response, the high risk of clozapine may be justified.

Level IV: Neuroleptics (*Typical* Antipsychotics)

Once the most common drugs prescribed for persons with developmental disabilities, low potency neuroleptics—loxapine, thioridazine, chlorpromazine, and mesoridazine—may no longer be needed (Aman et al. 1995). Due to patients' dramatic initial responses to treatment with these drugs, they were not just the only options available for a number of years, they were seductive because their sedating and dulling effects offered quick relief from adverse behaviors. After treating a number of cases of disabling extrapyramidal syndrome, tardive dyskinesia, and tardive akathisia (EPS/TDK), many clinicians have grown disenchanted with this class of drugs. Tapering them is difficult as well, due to rebound and withdrawal dyskinesia. Very slow tapering schedules (decreases of 5% to 10% of the total weekly dose once or twice a month) may be required. Withdrawal dyskinesias may respond to atypical agents or valproic acid. Clozapine may be needed for certain periods or lifelong to treat TDK using these agents. Some clinicians state that with so many lower risk levels available for intervention, low potency neuroleptics are never needed. Some of the behavioral or movement disorder worsening seen with slow tapering schedules may respond well to low level interventions with Vitamin E, buspirone, or trazodone, but it can take years to discontinue low potency neuroleptics. The concept of chemical restraint clearly has its origins in the use of these medications.

High potency neuroleptics—haloperidol, pimozide, and thiothixene—have fewer side effects, but an equivalent risk of movement disorders. Their faster onsets and clear effects in psychotic disorders make them needed agents. Yet, as more atypical agents are developed, these may fade away as well. The effectiveness of risperidone and the low risk of EPS/TDK at lower doses also make them less appealing. Again, for individuals with autism, tapering off these agents may require significant patience to avoid withdrawal dyskinesia and rebound behaviors. Adding lower risk interventions—vitamin E, buspirone, trazodone, or atypicals—may allow for faster tapering and less discomfort for the patients. Haloperidol's parkinsonian effects define part of the clinical syndrome of chemical restraint.

General Guidelines for Drug Therapy

The following general guidelines deserve consideration in the drug treatment of children and adults with autistic spectrum disorders.

1. General: After establishing the diagnosis of autism and completing the medical evaluation, define areas of problem behaviors for treatment. Rule out medical conditions or environmental factors that may be aggravating the patient. Practice patience. Evaluate for comorbid diagnoses, such as OCD, bipolar disorder, or seizures. Consider drug therapy in the context

of the patient's total treatment plan. Drug therapy is an adjunct to behavioral, speech, and occupational therapies and the patient's educational plan. Outline a method for monitoring drug effects (e.g., autism rating scales, table I; parent and teacher reports and videotapes; and direct observations at follow-up visits). Keep a flow sheet record of drug trials, doses, and side effects. Communicate with parents and caregivers regarding aims of treatment, regimen, and potential side effects.

2. Agents: Select a single agent with low or moderate risk (Level I or II) that is most likely to produce benefit (with the fewest side effects) related to the symptom or diagnosis of greatest concern. Start at low doses (or lower than usual, as for SSRIs) and increase in increments to recommended doses or until toxic effects appear. Use each agent long enough to be certain that it is (or is not) effective (e.g., at least 6 weeks or up to 6 months for SSRIs). Try to estimate compliance by the patient and caregivers.
3. Successive Trials: If there has been partial (although not optimal) response within the category under treatment, proceed to another drug designated for treatment of the same diagnosis or symptoms (e.g., methylphenidate→clonidine→guanfacine for inattention, hyperactivity, and impulsivity). Move to drugs with higher risks (Levels III or IV) as required by knowledge of the patient's history. Avoid the use of two agents simultaneously until the first is well established and drug interactions and side effects of the second drug can be anticipated. Consider drug costs, frequency, and mode of administration.
4. Avoid: Sedatives as well as sedative effect of medications in patients with autism. Avoid long-term side effects, such as tardive dyskinesia secondary to neuroleptics. Avoid the "stick-on effect" (the temptation to treat each symptom with another drug). Reassess drug efficacy with drug holidays after 6 to 12 months of therapy. Re-establish treatment objectives and outcomes regularly. Require regular follow up and monitoring of patients, and avoid long-term prescriptions.

PART III. EMERGING CONCEPTS AND NEW DIRECTIONS

We are now on the threshold of important new findings that will help define the pathogenesis and develop new treatments for autism. Over the next several years, we may anticipate that one or more genetic loci will be confirmed in autism through family studies and new molecular genetic techniques, such as the analysis of differential gene expression in neural tissues (Liang and Pardee 1992). Morphological studies using advanced techniques are likely to help us discover some of the abnormalities in dynamic network connectivity that occur during early development of the neuropil (see chapter on neural mechanisms). Clues from these areas, combined with our increasing knowledge of drug actions in autism, will facilitate new clinical trials using existing drugs as well as new ones under development.

Increasing numbers of necessary clinical drug trials are now taking place in autism, supported by private foundations, drug companies, and public funds. The National Institute of Mental Health has provided funding for Research Units on Pediatric Psychopharmacology (RUPP) for multi-site studies to compare the relative efficacy and safety of commonly used (if incompletely tested) drugs for treating children, adolescents, and young adults with autistic disorders. Current studies should emphasize statistically valid designs, with adequate controls and safety. Most rely on behavioral measures and do not yet define the heterogeneous subgroups within autism, such as that associated with early onset bipolar disorder (DeLong 1994). We know that autism is a heterogeneous and multigenic disorder that may also have multiple additional triggers and modifiers. In order to sort out this complexity and define biological markers, it would be helpful to have validated subgroup classifications, similar to the International Classification of Epilepsy (ICE) (International League Against Epilepsy 1981). The ICE was based primarily on clinical descriptions of seizures and has guided basic as well as clinical research in epilepsy for nearly 20 years. Such groupings should be possible in autism, from large group analyses of clinical data and measures such as the *Autism Diagnostic Interview* (ADI) (Lord 1997). From these clinically based guidelines, we should be able to conduct research that will establish or modify the subgroups when definitive biological measures, drug, or clinical treatment responses are found.

In order to move from treating symptoms to the ideal of modifying the neural substrate of the autistic spectrum disorders, we will need to develop safe *in vivo* methods for following neurobiological parameters in patients during drug trials. In addition to PET, SPECT, and functional MRI brain imaging techniques, it may become possible to follow the differential expression of those approximately 20,000 genes (20% of the entire genome) that are expressed exclusively in the central nervous system, with the use of new molecular techniques (Briley 1997). Until specific genes and their products are identified in autism, candidates for useful biological markers include neural cell adhesion molecule (NCAM) (Plioplys 1990), hormones and growth factors, cell signalling molecules or DNA transcription factors in serum, CSF, or cell cultures (Zimmerman, Jinnah, and Lockhart 1998).

The culture of olfactory neuroblasts from patients is a promising technique for the study of cellular mechanisms as well as drug effects *in vitro* (Wolozin et al. 1992; Naidu, Leopold, and Ronnet 1997).

The relationship of epilepsy to autism, and the relevance of epileptic aphasia (Landau-Kleffner syndrome) to autistic regression has been a fruitful area of research (see chapter on epilepsy). Similar questions in autism can also be raised for childhood epilepsy, with respect to mechanisms for normal (or abnormal) development of the neuropil. While the best type of EEG methodology for optimal detection of seizure discharges in patients with autism remains to be defined, it is likely that treatment with anticonvulsants and corticosteroids can be beneficial in some patients (Plioplys 1994; Mott et al. 1996). The relationships of these drug treatments to age, biological measures, and clinical outcomes need further study. For example, Slotkin et al. (1996) have demonstrated an important relationship between prenatal corticosteroids and serotonin transporter development in rats' brains. Positive responses of patients to treatment with corticosteroids have raised important questions about possible interactions of neurochemical, neuroendocrinological, and neuroimmunological factors in the development of the fine cortical architecture (neuropil) in autism. They also imply that abnormalities in neuropil development might be modified by corticosteroids, as well as by hormones, cytokines, and growth factors during sensitive developmental periods.

Our current emphasis on altering neurotransmitters, especially serotonin, for only the symptomatic treatment of behavior in autism deserves further examination. We might consider the possibility that early (ages 2 to 4 years) treatment of autism with SSRIs, for example, could improve the short- as well as the long-term outcomes of children with autistic disorder. In rats' brains, serotonin and its receptors have important trophic effects during specific prenatal and neonatal periods that later result in effects on behavior (Borella, Bindra, and Whitaker-Azmitia 1997). Because serotonin is essential for normal neuronal growth and differentiation, early treatment with SSRIs may enhance development during critical periods or *windows of opportunity*, that are unresponsive at later times (Blue et al. 1996; Osterheld-Haas and Hornung 1996).

Serotonin has important interactions with other transmitters as well that may be affected in autism, such as glutamate, GABA, dopamine, and acetylcholine. Glutamate and its receptors, the excitatory neurotransmitter system, are especially important for normal cortical development. They are responsible for long-term potentiation (LTP), the neurophysiological basis of learning and memory (Conti and Hicks 1996). Insufficient growth and development of the neuropil could result from too little glutamate activity. Conversely, *excitotoxity* may result from excess glutamate or abnormal expression of its receptors or their subunits, which undergo dynamic changes during development (Bittigau and Ikonomidou 1997). Glutamate receptors (e.g., NMDA) are especially concentrated in the limbic system and cerebellum areas in which Bauman and Kemper (1994) have identified cellular abnormalities in autism. Overactivity in glutamate systems may be coupled with decreased activity in serotonin-containing cells, and, thereby, result in excitotoxic suppression of neuronal development (especially in limbic and cerebellar circuitry). In Rett syndrome, which has many similarities to autism, up-regulation of glutamate receptors may occur in response to decreased serotonin, a result of deficient cholinergic innervation (Blue et al. 1996). Expected shifts of glutamate receptor subtypes during development may also fail to occur, because of genetic or environmental factors such as infections. An example of this is the persistence of the NR2D glutamate receptor subtype, normally an embryonic form, whose abnormal persistence may alter the frequency of synaptic responses leading to decreased synaptic plasticity (Okabe et al. 1998; Vicini et al. 1998). New drugs for epilepsy and other disorders that act at glutamate receptors (e.g., topiramate) may, therefore, benefit treatment (both short- and long-term) in autism (Herrling 1997).

For many years, magnesium has been advocated for the treatment of autism (Rimland 1988), although its mechanism of action is unknown. It is notable that magnesium blocks NMDA receptor channels in a voltage-dependent manner (Wollmuth, Kuner, and Sakmann 1998). However, it can also potentiate (voltage-independent) NMDA responses at saturating glycine concentrations. This response is *permitted* or prevented, depending on the receptor's subunit composition. (Paoletti, Neyton, and Ascher 1995). Should altered NMDA receptors be important in autism, magnesium could be neuroprotective. It may also be possible to model this and other effects *in vitro* (e.g., in olfactory neuroblast cultures). We should consider the efficacy and modes of action of magnesium, as well as other *natural therapies* (pyridoxine, dimethylglycine, and folic acid, among others) that physicians and families have found over the years to improve their autistic children's behavior and cognition.

CONCLUSION

From an extensive literature of drug treatments in autism, we are currently treating this heterogeneous group of patients we term *autistic*, each as an individual, using principles from the art of neuropsychopharmacology. We will enhance our growing experience from systematic drug trials in autism by defining and validating subgroups of patients by means of genetic and neurobiological markers. One may envision that applying this art to increased scientific scrutiny will lead to new understanding of the basic science, further magnifying the clinical art and improving the lives of persons with autism.

Acknowledgements

We thank Valerie Ames and Charlotte McCurry for assistance in preparation of the manuscript. This work was supported by a grant from the East Tennessee Chapter of the Autism Society of America.

CHAPTER SUMMARY

1. Neuropharmacological therapy may be an important adjunct to educational and behavioral interventions in many patients with autism.
2. Clinicians utilize data from clinical trials in autistic patients, knowledge of the neurobiology of autism, and clinical experience with treating autism and other neurobehavioral disorders to devise rational approaches to medical management of individual patients, based on particular target behaviors and comorbid diagnoses.
3. When considering the use of medication for behavioral symptoms in children with autism, it must be remembered that some patients will be extremely sensitive to even very low (homeopathic) doses while, conversely, others will only respond to extremely high doses.
4. Some medications that will be effective in treating behavioral symptoms in children with autism may need very prolonged periods of observation before demonstrating their efficacy.
5. Behavioral deterioration in a child with autism requires that physical (medical) and environmental causes be considered prior to initiating a course of drug intervention.
6. Medications with a low risk profile (fewer, milder, and more transient side effects) should be given precedence over those with higher risk profiles when initiating drug therapy for behavioral symptoms in children with autism.
7. Sedation is not an appropriate goal of medication when used in children with autism.
8. A variety of lines of evidence have implicated serotonergic dysfunction in the pathogenesis of autism, and selective serotonin reuptake inhibitors (SSRIs) may be an effective and relatively safe class of drugs for modifying maladaptive behaviors in children with autism.

9. The use of certain agents, such as SSRIs, during critical periods of brain development may have impact on ultimate structure and function.

REFERENCES

Aman, M. G. 1982. Stimulant drug effects in developmental disroders and hyperactivity—toward a resolution of disparate findings. *Journal of Autism and Developmental Disorders* 12:385–98.

Aman, M. G. 1988. The use of methylphenidate in autism. *Journal of the American Academy of Child and Adolescent Psychiatry* 27:821–2.

Aman, M. G., and Singh, N. N. 1988. Vitamin, mineral, and dietary treatments. In *Psychopharmacology of the Developmental Disabilities*, ed. M. G. Aman and N. N. Singh. New York: Springer-Verlag.

Aman, M. G., and Kern, R. A. 1989. Review of fenfluramine in the treatment of the developmental disabilities. *Journal of the American Academy of Child and Adolescent Psychiatry* 28:549–65.

Aman, M. G., van Bourgondien, M. E., Wolford, P. L., and Sarphare, G. 1995. Psychotropic and anticonvulsant drugs in subjects with autism: Prevalence and patterns of use. *Journal of the American Academy of Child and Adolescent Psychiatry* 34:1672–81.

Anderson, G. M., Freedman, D. X., Cohen, D. J., Volkmar, F. R., Hoder, E. L., McPhedran, P., Minderaa, R. B., Hansen, C. R., and Young, J. G. 1987. Whole blood serotonin in autistic and normal subjects. *Journal of Child Psychology and Psychiatry* 28:885–900.

Anderson, G. M., and Hoshino, Y. 1997. Neurochemical studies of autism. In *Handbook of Autism and Pervasive Developmental Disorders*, 2nd ed., ed. D. J. Cohen and F. R. Volkmar. New York: Wiley.

Anderson, L. T., Campbell, M., Grega, D. M., Perry, R., Small, A. M., and Green, W. H. 1984. Haloperidol in the treatment of infantile autism: Effects on learning and behavioral symptoms. *American Journal of Psychiatry* 141:1195–202.

Anderson, L. T., Campbell, M., Adams, P., Small, A. M, Perry, R., and Shell, J. 1989. The effects of haloperidol on discrimination learning and behavioral symptoms in autistic children. *Journal of Autism and Developmental Disorders* 19:227–39.

Armenteros, J. L., Adams, P. B., Campbell, M., and Eisenberg, Z. W. 1995. Haloperidol-related dyskinesias and pre-and perinatal complications in autistic children. *Psychopharmacology Bulletin* 31:363–9.

Bardenstein, R., Chez, M. G., Helfand, B. T., Buchanan, C., and Zucker, M. 1998. Improvement in EEG and clinical function in pervasive developmental delay (PPD): Effect of valproic acid. *Neurology* 50:A86.

Barrett, R. P., Feinstein, C., and Hole, W. T. 1989. Effects of naloxone on self-injury: A double-blind, placebo analysis. *American Journal on Mental Retardation* 93:644–51.

Bauman, M., and Kemper, T. L. 1994. Neuroanatomic observations of the brain in autism. In *The Neurobiology of Autism*, ed. M. L. Bauman and T. L. Kemper. Baltimore, MD: Johns Hopkins University Press.

Belsito, K. M., Kirk, K. S, Landa, R. J., Law, P. A., and Zimmerman, A. W. 1998. Lamotrigine therapy for childhood autism: A randomized, double-blind, placebo-controlled trial. *Neurology* 50:A85.

Bender, L., Goldschmidt, L. and Siva Sankar, D. V. 1962. Treatment of autistic schizophrenic children with LSD-25 and UML-491. *Recent Advances in Biological Psychiatry* 4:170–7.
Bender, L., Faretra, G., and Cobrinik, L. 1963. LSD and UML treatment of hospitalized disturbed children. *Recent Advances in Biological Psychiatry* 5:84–92.
Benjamin, S., Seek, A., Tresise, L., Price, E., and Gagnon, M. 1995. Case study: Paradoxical response to naltrexone treatment of self-injurious behavior. *Journal of the American Academy of Child and Adolescent Psychiatry* 34:238–42.
Beran, R. G., and Gibson, R. J. 1998. Aggressive behavior in intellectually challenged patients with epilepsy treated with lamotrigine. *Epilepsia* 39:280–2.
Berger, A., and Schaumburg, H. H. 1984. More on neuropathy from pyridoxine abuse. *New England Journal of Medicine* 311:986–7.
Bhalla, J. N., Khanna, P. K., Srivastava, J. R., Sur, B. K., and Bhalla, M. 1983. Serum zinc levels and pica. *Indian Pediatrics* 20:667–70.
Birmaher, B., Quintana, H., and Greenhill, L. L. 1988. Methylphenidate treatment of hyperactive autistic children. *Journal of the American Academy of Child and Adolescent Psychiatry* 27:248–51.
Bittigau, P., and Ikonomidou, C. 1997. Glutamate in neurologic diseases. *Journal of Child Neurology* 12:471–85.
Blue, M. E., Hohmann, C. F., Wallace, S. A., Naidu, S., and Johnston, M. V. 1996. Excitatory and inhibitory neurotransmitter receptor expression is altered in Rett syndrome and in a mouse model for Rett syndrome. *Journal of Neuroscience* 22:460.
Blumer, D. 1997. Antidepressant and double antidepressant treatment for the affective disorder of epilepsy. *The Journal of Clinical Psychiatry* 58:3–15.
Borella, A., Bindra, M., and Whitaker-Azmitia, P. M. 1997. Role of the 5-HT1A receptor in development of the neonatal rat brain: Preliminary behavioral studies. *Neuropharmacology* 36:445–50.
Bosch, J., Van Dyke, D., Smith, S. M., and Poulton, S. 1997. Role of medical conditions in the exacerbation of self-injurious behavior: An exploratory study. *Mental Retardation* 35:124–30.
Botteron, K. N., and Geller, B. 1995. Pharmacologic treatment of child and adolescent mania. *Child and Adolescent Psychiatric Clinics of North America* 4:283–304.
Bouvard, M. P., Leboyer, M., Launay, J. M., Recasens, C., Plumet, M. H., Waller-Perotte, D., Tabuteau, F., Bondoux, D., Dugas, M., Lensing, P., and Panksepp, J. 1995. Low-dose naltrexone effects on plasma chemistries and clinical symptoms in autism: A double-blind, placebo-controlled study. *Psychiatry Research* 58:191–201.
Brasic, J. R., Barnett, J. Y., Kaplan, D., Sheitman, B. B., Aisemberg, P., LaFargue, R. F., Kowalik, S., Clark, A., Tsaltas, M. O., and Young, J. G. 1994. Clomipramine ameliorates adventitious movements and compulsions in prepubertal boys with autistic disorder and severe mental retardation. *Neurology* 44:1309–12.
Brasic, J. R., Barnett, J. Y., Sheitman, B. B., and Tsaltas, M. O. 1997. Adverse effects of clomipramine. *Journal of the American Academy of Child and Adolescent Psychiatry* 36:1165–6.
Briley, M. 1997. From dirty drugs to hyperselectivity and part way back again. *Human Psychopharmacology* 12:121–5.
Brodkin, E. S., McDougle, C. J., Naylor, S. T., Cohen, D. J., and Price, L. H. 1997. Clomipramine in adults with pervasive developmental disorders: A prospective open-label investigation. *Journal of Child and Adolescent Psychopharmacology* 7:109–121.

Buck, O. D. 1995. Sertraline for reduction of violent behavior. *American Journal of Psychiatry* 152:953.

Buitelaar, J. K., van Engeland, H., van Ree, J. M., and de Wied, D. 1990. Behavioral effects of Org 2766, a synthetic analog of the adrenocorticotrophic hormone (4–9), in 14 outpatient autistic children. *Journal of Autism and Developmental Disorders* 20:467–8.

Buitelaar, J. K., van Engeland, H., de Kogel, K., de Vries, H., van Hooff, J., and van Ree, J. M. 1992a. The use of adrenocorticotrophic hormone (4–9) analog ORG 2766 in autistic children: Effects on the organization of behavior. *Biological Psychiatry* 31:1119–29.

Buitelaar, J. K., van Engeland, H., de Kogel, K., de Vries, H., van Hooff, J., and van Ree, J. M. 1992b. The adrenocorticotrophic hormone (4–9) analog ORG 2766 benefits autistic children: Report on a second controlled clinical trial. *Journal of the American Academy of Child and Adolescent Psychiatry* 31:1149–56.

Buitelaar, J. K., Dekker, M. E., van Ree, J. M., and van Engeland, H. 1996. A controlled trial with ORG 2766, and ACTH-(4–9) analog, in 50 relatively able children with autism. *European Neuropsychopharmacology* 6:13–9.

Buitelaar, J. K., van der Gaag, R. J., and van der Hoeven, J. 1998. Buspirone in the management of anxiety and irritability in children with prevasive developmental disorder: Results of an open-label study. *Journal of Clinical Psychiatry* 59:56–9.

Campbell, M., Fish, B., Shapiro, T., and Floyd, A. 1970. Thiothixene in young disturbed children: A pilot study. *Archives of General Psychiatry* 23:70–2.

Campbell, M., Fish, B., Shapiro T, and Floyd, A. 1971a. Study of molindone in disturbed preschool children. *Current Therapeutic Research* 13:28–33.

Campbell, M., Fish, B., Shapiro, T., and Floyd, A. 1971b. Imipramine in preschool autistic and schizophrenic children. *Journal of Autism and Childhood Schizophrenia* 1:267–82.

Campbell, M., Fish, B., Korein, J., Shapiro, T., Collins, P., and Koh, C. 1972. Lithium and chlorpromazine: A controlled crossover study of hyperactive severely disturbed young childen. *Journal of Autism and Childhood Schizophrenia* 2:234–63.

Campbell, M., Fish, B., David, R., Shapiro, T., Collins, P., and Koh, C. 1972. Response to triiodothyronine and dextroamphetamine: A study of preschool schizophrenic children. *Journal of Autism and Childhood Schizophrenia* 2:343–58.

Campbell, M., Fish, B., Shapiro, T., and Floyd, A. 1972. Acute responses of schizophrenic children to a sedative and a "stimilating" neuroleptic: A pharmacologic yardstick. *Current Therapeutic Research* 14:759–66.

Campbell, M., Small, A. M., Collins, P. J., Friedman, E., David, R., and Genieser, N. 1976. Levodopa and levoamphetamine: A crossover study in young schizophrenic children. *Current Therapeutic Research* 19:70–83.

Campbell, M., Anderson, L. T., Meier, M., Cohen, I. L., Small, A. M., Samit, C., and Sachar, E. J. 1978. A comparison of haloperidol and behavior therapy and their interaction in autistic children. *Journal of the American Academy of Child Psychiatry* 17:640–55.

Campbell, M., Small, A. M., Hollander, C. S., Korein, J., Cohen, I. L., Kalmijn, M., and Ferris, S. 1978. A controlled crossover study of triiodothyronine in autistic children. *Journal of Autism and Childhood Schizophrenia* 8:371–81.

Campbell, M., Hollander, C. S., Ferris, S., and Greene, L. W. 1978. Response to thyrotropin releasing hormone stimulation in young psychotic children: A pilot study. *Psychoneuroendocrinology* 3:195–201.

Campbell, M. 1988. Annotation: Fenfluramine treatment of autism. *Journal of Child Psychology and Psychiatry* 29:1–10.
Campbell, M., Adams, P., Small, A. M., Tesch, L. M., and Curren, E. L. 1988. Naltrexone in infantile autism. *Psychopharmacology Bulletin* 24:135–9.
Campbell, M., Overall, J. E., Small, A. M., Sokol, M. S., Spencer, E. K., Adams, P., Foltz, R. L., Monti, K. M., Perry, R., Nobler, M., and Roberts, E. 1989. Naltrexone in autistic children: An acute open dose range tolerance trial. *Journal of the American Academy of Child and Adolescent Psychiatry* 28:200–6.
Campbell, M., Anderson, L. T., Small, A. M., Locascio, J. J., Lynch, N. S., and Choroco, M. C. 1990. Naltrexone in autistic children: A double-blind and placebo-controlled study. *Psychopharmacology Bulletin* 26:130–5.
Campbell, M., Anderson, L. T., Small, A. M., Adams, P., Gonzalez, N. M., and Ernst, M. 1993. Naltrexone in autistic children: Behavioral symptoms and attentional learning. *Journal of the American Academy of Child and Adolescent Psychiatry* 32:1283–91.
Campbell, M., Schopler, E., Cueva, J. E., and Hallin, A. 1996. Treatment of autistic disorder. *Journal of the American Academy of Child and Adolescent Psychiatry* 35:134–43.
Campbell, M., Armenteros, J. L., Malone, R. P., Adams, P. B., Eisenberg, Z. W., and Overall, J. E. 1997. Neuroleptic-related dyskinesias in autistic children: A prospective, longitudinal study. *Journal of the American Academy of Child and Adolescent Psychiatry* 36:835–43.
Chandler, M., Barnhill, L., and Gualtieri, C. T. 1991. Amantadine: Profile of use in the developmentally disabled. In *Mental Retardation: Developing Pharmacotherapies*, ed. J. J. Ratey. Washington, DC: American Psychiatric Press.
Childs, J. A., and Blair, J. L. 1997. Valproic acid treatment of epilepsy in autistic twins. *Journal of Neuroscience Nursing* 29:244–8.
Cohen, I. L., Campbell, M., Posner, D., Small, A. M., Triebel, D., and Anderson, L. T. 1980. Behavioral effects of haloperidol in young autistic children. *Journal of the American Academy of Child Psychiatry* 19:665–7.
Cohen, I. L., Tsiouris, J., and Pfadt, A. 1991. Effects of long-acting propranolol on agonistic and stereotyped behaviors in a man with pervasive developmental disorder and Fragile X Syndrome. *Journal of Clinical Psychopharmacology* 11:398–9.
Connor, D. F. 1994. Nadolol for self-injury, overactivity, inattention, and aggression in a child with pervasive developmental disorder. *Journal of Child and Adolescent Psychopharmacology* 4:101–11.
Conti, F. and Hicks, T. P. 1996. *Excitatory Amino Acids and the Cerebral Cortex*. Cambridge, MA: MIT Press.
Cook, E. H. 1990. Autism: Review of neurochemical investigation. *Synapse* 6:292–308.
Cook, E. H., Rowlett, R., Jaselskis, C., and Leventhal, B. 1992. Fluoxetine treatment of children and adults with autistic disorder and mental retardation. *Journal of the American Academy of Child and Adolescent Psychiatry* 31:739–45.
Cook, E. H., and Leventhal, B. L. 1995. Autistic disorder and other pervasive developmental disorders. *Child and Adolescent Psychiatry Clinics of North America* 4:381–99.
Cook, E. H., and Leventhal, B. L. 1996. The serotonin system in autism. *Current Opinion in Pediatrics* 8:348–54.
Davanzo, P. A., Belin, T. R., Widawski, M. H., and King, B. H. 1998. Paroxetine treatment of aggression and self-injury in persons with mental retardation. *American Journal on Mental Retardation* 102:427–37.

DelGiudice-Asch, G., and Hollander, E. 1997. Altered immune function in autism. *CNS Spectrums* 2:61–8.

DelGiudice-Asch, G., Simon, L., Schmeidler, J., Cunningham-Rundles, C., and Hollander, E. 1999. Brief report: A pilot open clinical trial of intravenous immunoglobulin in childhood autism. *Journal of Autism and Developmental Disorders* 29:157–60.

DeLong, G. R. 1994. Children with autistic spectrum disorder and a family history of affective disorder. *Developmental Medicine and Child Neurology* 36:674–88.

Delong, G. R., Teague, L. A., and McSwain Kamran, M. 1998. Effects of fluoxetine treatment on young children with idiopathic autism. *Developmental Medicine and Child Neurology* 40:551–62.

Demb, H. B. 1996. Risperidone in young children with pervasive developmental disorders and other developmental disabilities. *Journal of Child and Adolescent Psychopharmacology* 6:79–80.

Dollfus, S., Petit, M., Menard, J. F., and Lesieur, P. 1992. Amisulpride versus bromocriptine in infantile autism: A controlled crossover comparative study of two drugs with opposite effects on dopaminergic function. *Journal of Autism and Developmental Disorders* 22:47–60.

Dolske, M. C., Spollen, J., McKay, S., Lancashire, E., and Tolbert, L. 1993. A preliminary trial of ascorbic acid as supplemental therapy for autism. *Progress in Neuropsychopharmacology and Biological Psychiatry* 17:765–74.

Duker, P. C., Welles, K., Seys, D., Rensen, H., Vis, A., and van den Berg, G. 1991. Brief report: Effects of fenfluramine on communicative, stereotypic, and inappropriate behaviors of autistic-type mentally handicapped individuals. *Journal of Autism and Developmental Disorders* 21:355–63.

duVerglas, G., Banks, S. R., and Guyer, K. E. 1988. Clinical effects of fenfluramine on children with autism: A review of the research. *Journal of Autism and Developmental Disorders* 18:297–308.

Ekman, G., Miranda-Linné, F., Gillberg, C., Garle, M., and Wetterberg, L. 1989. Fenfluramine treatment of twenty children with autism. *Journal of Autism and Developmental Disorders* 19:511–32.

Engelhardt, D. M., Polizos, P., Waizer, J., and Hoffman, S. P. 1973. A double-blind comparison of fluphenazine and haloperidol. *Journal of Autism and Childhood Schizophrenia* 3:128–37.

Epperson, C. N., McDougle, C. J., Anand, A., Marek, G. J., Naylor, S. T., Volkmar, F. R., Cohen, D. J., and Price, L. H. 1994. Lithium augmentation of fluvoxamine in autistic disorder: A case report. *Journal of Child and Adolescent Psychopharmacology* 4:201–7.

Ernst, M., Locascio, J. J., Small, A. M., Lynch, N., and Campbell, M. 1990. Placebo response in autistic children. Scientific Proceedings of the Annual Meeting, *American Academy of Child and Adolescent Psychiatry* 6:47.

Ernst, M., Magee, H. J., Gonzalez, N. M., Locascio J. J., Rosenberg, C. R., and Campbell, M. 1992. Pimozide in autistic children. *Psychopharmacology Bulletin* 28:187–91.

Fankhauser, M. P., Karumanchi, V. C., German, M. L., Yates, A., and Karumanchi, S. D. 1992. A double-blind, placebo-controlled study of the efficacy of transdermal clonidine in autism. *Journal of Clinical Psychiatry* 53:77–82.

Faretra, G., Dooher, L., and Dowling, J. 1970. Comparison of haloperidol and fluphenazine in disturbed children. *American Journal of Psychiatry* 126:1670–3.

Fatemi, S. H., Realmuto, G. M., Khan, L., and Thuras, P. 1998. Fluoxetine in treatment of adolescent patients with autism: A longitudinal open trial. *Journal of Autism and Developmental Disorders* 28:303–7.

Fava, M. 1997. Psychopharmacologic treatment of pathologic aggression. *Psychiatric Clinics of North America* 20:427–51.
Fernell, E., Watanabe, Y., Adolfsson, I., Tani, Y., Bergstrom, M., Hartvig, P., Lilja, A., von Knorring, A., Gillberg, C., and Langstrom, B. 1997. Possible effects of tetrahydrobiopterin treatment in six children with autism—clinical and position emission tomography data: A pilot study. *Developmental Medicine and Child Neurology* 39:313–18.
Findling, A. L., Maxwell, K., Scotese-Wojtila, L., Huang, J., Yamashita, T., and Wiznitzer, M. 1997. High-dose pyridoxine and magnesium administration in children with autistic disorder: An absence of salutary effects in a double-blind, placebo-controlled study. *Journal of Autism and Developmental Disorders* 27:467–78.
Findling, A. L., Maxwell, K., and Wiznitzer, M. 1997. An open clinical trial of risperidone monotherapy in young children with autistic disorder. *Psychopharmacology Bulletin* 33:155–9.
Fish, B., Campbell, M., Shapiro, T., and Floyd, A. J. 1969. Schizophrenic children treated with methysergide (Sansert). *Diseases of the Nervous System* 30:534–40.
Fish, B., Shapiro, T., and Campbell, M. 1996. Long-term prognosis and the response of schizophrenic children to drug therapy: A controlled study of trifluoperazine. *American Journal of Psychiatry* 123:32–9.
Fishman, S., and Steele, M. 1996. Use of risperidone in pervasive developmental disorders: A case series. *Journal of Child and Adolescent Psychopharmacology* 6:177–90.
Freedman, A. M., Ebin, E. V., and Wilson, E. A. 1962. Autistic schizophrenic children: An experiment in the use of D-lysergic acid diethylamide (LSD-25). *Archives of General Psychiatry* 6:35–45.
Frischauf, E. 1997. Drug therapy in autism. *Journal of the American Academy of Child and Adolescent Psychiatry* 36:577.
Garber, H. J., McGonigle, J. J., Slomka, G. T., and Monteverde, E. 1992. Clomipramine treatment of stereotypic behaviors and self-injury in patients with developmental disabilities. *Journal of the American Academy of Child and Adolescent Psychiatry* 31:1157–60.
Gedye, A. 1991a. Buspirone alone or with serotonergic diet reduced aggression in a developmentally disabled adult. *Biological Psychiatry* 30:88–91.
Gedye, A. 1991b. Trazodone reduced aggressive and self-injurious movements in a mentally handicapped male patient with autism. *Journal of Clinical Psychopharmacology* 11:275–6.
Geller, B., Guttmacher, L., and Bleeg, M. 1981. Coexistence of childhood onset pervasive developmental disorder and attention deficit disorder with hyperactivity. *American Journal of Psychiatry* 138:388–9.
Geller, B., and Luby, J. 1997. Child and adolescent bipolar disorder: A review of the past 10 years. *Journal of the American Academy of Child and Adolescent Psychiatry* 36:1168–76.
Geller, E., Ritvo, E., Freeman, B., and Yuwiler, A. 1982. Preliminary observations on the effect of fenfluramine on blood serotonin and symptoms in three autistic boys. *New England Journal of Medicine* 307:165–9.
Ghaziuddin, M., and Tsai, L. 1991. Depression in autistic disorder. *British Journal of Psychiatry* 159:721–3.
Ghaziuddin, M., Tsai, L., and Ghaziuddin, N. 1991. Fluoxetine in autism with depression. *Journal of the American Academy of Child and Adolescent Psychiatry* 30:508–9.

Gianutos G., Stewart, C., and Dunn, J. P. 1985. Pharmacological changes in dopaminergic systems induced by long-term administration of amantadine. *European Journal of Pharmacology* 110:357–61.

Gillberg, C., Wahlström, J., Johansson, R., Törnblom, M., and Albertsson-Wikland, K. 1986. Folic acid as an adjunct in the treatment of children with the autism Fragile-X syndrome (Afrax). *Developmental Medicine and Child Neurology* 28:624–7.

Gilman, J. T., and Tuchman, R. F. 1995. Autism and associated behavioral disorders: Pharmacotherapeutic intervention. *Annals of Pharmacotherapy* 29:47–56.

Gonzalez, N. M., Campbell, M., Small, A. M., Shay, J., Bluhm, L. D., Adams, B. P., and Foltz, R. L. 1994. Naltrexone plasma levels, clinical response and effect on weight in autistic children. *Psychopharmacology Bulletin* 30:203–08.

Gordon, C. T., Rapoport, J. J., Hamburger, S. D., State, R. C., and Mannheim, G. B. 1992. Differential response of seven subjects with autistic disorder to clomipramine and desipramine. *American Journal of Psychiatry* 149:363–6.

Gordon, C. T., State, R. C., Nelson, J. E., Hamburger, S. D., and Rapoport, J. L. 1993. A double-blind comparison of clomipramine, desipramine, and placebo in the treatment of autistic disorder. *Archives of General Psychiatry* 50:441–7.

Gualtieri, C. T. 1986. Fenfluramine and autism: Careful reappraisal is in order. *Journal of Pediatrics* 108:417–9.

Gualtieri, C. T. 1987. Reply. *Journal of Pediatrics* 110:159–61.

Gupta, S., Aggarwal, S., and Heads, C. 1996. Brief report: Dysregulated immune system in children with autism: Beneficial effects of intravenous immune globulin on autistic characteristics. *Journal of Autism and Developmental Disorders* 26:439–52.

Hales, R. E., Yudofsky, S. C., and Talbott, J. A. 1994. Epidemiology. *Textbook of Psychiatry*, 2nd ed. Washington, DC: American Psychiatric Press.

Hamdan-Allen, G. 1991. Brief report: Trichotillomania in an autistic male. *Journal of Autism and Developmental Disorders* 21:79–82.

Hardan, A., Johnson, K., Johnson, C., and Hrecznyj, B. 1996. Case study: Risperidone treatment of children and adolescents with developmental disorders. *Journal of the American Academy of Child and Adolescent Psychiatry* 35:1551–6.

Harvey, R. J., and Cooray, S. E. 1995. The effective treatment of severe repetitive behavior with fluvoxamine in a 20-year-old autistic female. *International Clinical Psychopharmacology* 10:201–03.

Hellings, J. A., Kelley, L. A., Gabrielli, W. F., Kilgore, E., and Shah, P. 1996. Sertraline response in adults with mental retardation and autistic disorder. *Journal of Clinical Psychiatry* 57:333–6.

Herman, B. H., Hammock, M., Arthur-Smith, A., Egan, J., Chatoor, I., Zelnik, N., Corradine, M., and Rosenquist, J. 1986. Role of opioid peptides in autism: Effects of acute administration of naltrexone. *Society for Neurosciences Abstracts* 12:1172.

Herrling, P. L. 1997. *Excitatory Amino Acids: Clinical Results with Antagonists.* San Diego: Academic Press.

Hillbrand, M. 1995. The use of buspirone with aggressive behavior. *Journal of Autism and Developmental Disorders* 25:663–4.

Holttum, J. R., Lubetsky, M. J., and Eastman, L. E. 1994. Comprehensive management of trichotillomania in a young autistic girl. *Journal of the American Academy of Child and Adolescent Psychiatry* 33:577–81.

Horrigan, J. P., and Barnhill, L. J. 1997. Risperidone and explosive aggressive autism. *Journal of Autism and Developmental Disorders* 27:313–23.

Horrigan, J. P., Barnhill, L., and Courvoisie, H. E. 1997. Olanzapine in PDD. *Journal of the American Academy of Child and Adolescent Psychiatry* 36:1166–7.

Horvath, K., Stefanatos, G., Sokolski, K. N., Wachtel, R., Nabors, L., and Tildon, J. T. 1998. Improved social and language skills after secretin administration in patients with autistic spectrum disorders. *Journal of the Association of Academic Minority Physicians* 9:9–15.

Hoshino, Y., Kumashiro, H., Keneko, M., and Takahashi, Y. 1977. The effects of methylphenidate on early infantile autism and its relation to serum serotonin levels. *Folia Psychiatrica et Neurologica Japonica* 31:605–14.

International League Against Epilepsy, Commission on Classification and Terminology. 1981. Proposal for revised clinical and electroencephalographic classification of epileptic seizures. *Epilepsia* 22:489–501.

Jan, J. E., and O'Donnell, M. E. 1996. Use of melatonin in the treatment of pediatric sleep disorders. *Journal of Pineal Research* 21:193–9.

Jann, M. W. 1988. Buspirone: An update on a unique anxiolytic agent. *Pharmacotherapy* 8:100–16.

Jaselskis, C. A., Cook, E. H., Fletcher, K. E., and Leventhal, B. L. 1992. Clonidine treatment of hyperactive and impulsive children with autistic disorder. *Journal of Clinical Psychopharmacology* 12:322–7.

Joshi, P. T., Capozolli, J. A., and Coyle, J. T. 1988. Low-dose neuroleptic therapy for children with childhood-onset pervasive developmental disorder. *American Journal of Psychiatry* 145:335–8.

Kemph, J. 1993. Treatment of aggressive children with clonidine: Results of an open pilot study. *Journal of the American Academy of Child and Adolescent Psychiatry* 32:577–81.

Kerbeshian, J., Burd, L., and Fisher, W. 1987. Lithium carbonate in the treatment of two patients with infantile autism and atypical bipolar symptomatology. *Journal of Clinical Psychopharmacology* 7:401–05.

King, B. H., and Davanzo, P. 1996. Buspirone treatment of aggression and self-injury in autistic and nonautistic persons with severe mental retardation. *Developmental Brain Dysfunction* 9:22–31.

King, B. H., Wright, D. M., Handen, B. L., Sikich, L., Zimmerman, A. W., McMahon, W., Cantwell, E., Davanzo, P. A., Dourish, C., Dykens, E. M., Jaselskis, C. A., Leventhal, B. L., Lord, C., Lubetsky, M. J., Myers, S. M., Ozonoff, S., Shah, B. G., Leavitt, J., Snape, M., Steele, E. W., Williamson, K., and Cook, E. H. 2000 (in press). A double-blind, placebo-controlled study of amantadine hydrochloride in the treatment of children with autistic disorder. *Journal of the American Academy of Child and Adolescent Psychiatry.*

Knabe, R., Schultz, P., and Richard, J. 1990. Initial aggravation of self-injurious behavior in autistic patients receiving naltrexone treatment. *Journal of Autism and Developmental Disorders* 20:591–2.

Kolmen, B. K., Feldman, H. M., Handen, B. L., and Janosky, J. E. 1995. Naltrexone in young autistic children: A double-blind, placebo-controlled crossover study. *Journal of the American Academy of Child and Adolescent Psychiatry* 34:223–31.

Kolmen, B. K., Feldman, H. M., Handen, B. L., and Janosky J. E. 1997. Naltrexone in young autistic children: Replication study and learning measures. *Journal of the American Academy of Child and Adolescent Psychiatry* 36:1570–8.

Komoto, J., Seigo, U., and Hirata, J. 1984. Infantile autism and affective disorder. *Journal of Autism and Developmental Disorders* 14:81–4.

Kornhuber, J., Weller, M., Schoppmeyer, K., and Riederer, P. 1994. Amantadine and memantine are NMDA receptor antagonists with neuroprotective properties. *Journal of Neural Transmission Supplement* 43:91–104.

Koshes, R. J., and Rock, N. 1994. Use of clonidine for behavioral control in an adult patient with autism. *American Journal of Psychiatry* 151:1714.
Koshes, R. J. 1997. Use of fluoxetine for obsessive-compulsive behavior in adults with autism. *American Journal of Psychiatry* 154:578.
Kumarachandran, K. 1994. ECG and clonidine. *Journal of the American Academy of Child and Adolescent Psychiatry* 33:1351–2.
Kuperman, S. and Stewart, M. 1987. Use of propranolol to decrease aggressive outbursts in younger patients. *Psychosomatics* 28:315–9.
Lagae, L. G., Silberstein, J., Gillis, P. L., and Caesar, P. J. 1998. Successful use of intravenous immunoglobulins in Landau-Kleffner syndrome. *Pediatric Neurology* 18:165–8.
Leboyer, M., Bouvard, M., and Dugas, M. 1988. Effects of naltrexone on infantile autism. *Lancet* 26:715.
Leboyer, M., Bouvard, M. P., Launay, J. M., Tabuteau, F., Waller, D., Dugas, M., Kerdelhue, B., Lensing, P., and Panksepp, J. 1992. Brief report: A double-blind study of naltrexone in infantile autism. *Journal of Autism and Developmental Disorders* 22:309–19.
Leonard, H. 1997. Pharmacology of the selective serotonin reuptake inhibitors in children and adolescents. *Journal of the American Academy of Child and Adolescent Psychiatry* 36:725–35.
Leventhal, B. L., Cook, E. H., Morford, M., Ravitz, A. J., Heller, W., and Freedman, D. X. 1993. Clinical and neurochemical effects of fenfluramine in children with autism. *Journal of Neuropsychiatry and Clinical Neurosciences* 5:307–15.
Levine, J., Aviram, A., Holan, A., Ring, A., Barak, Y., and Belmaker, R. H. 1997. Inositol treatment of autism. *Journal of Neural Transmission* 104:307–10.
Lewis, M. H., Bodfish, J. W., Powell, S. B., and Golden, R. N. 1995. Clomipramine treatment for stereotypy and related repetitive movement disorders associated with mental retardation. *American Journal on Mental Retardation* 100:299–312.
Li, W. H. 1997. *Molecular Evolution*. Sunderland, MA: Sinauer Associates, Inc.
Liang, P., and Pardee, A. B. 1992. Differential display of eukaryotic messenger RNA by means of the polymerase chain reaction. *Science* 257:967–71.
Lienemann, J., and Walker, F. 1989. Nalrexone for treatment of self-injury. *American Journal of Psychiatry* 146:1639–40.
Locascio, J. L., Malone, R. P., Small, A. M., Kafantaris, V., Ernst, M., Lynch, N. S., Overall, J. E., and Campbell, M. 1991. Factors related to haloperidol response and dyskinesias in autistic children. *Psychopharmacology Bulletin* 27:119–26.
Lofts, R. H., Schroeder, S. R., and Maier, R. H. 1990. Effects of serum zinc supplementation on pica behavior of persons with mental retardation. *American Journal of Mental Retardation* 95:103–9.
Lord, C. 1997. Diagnostic instruments in autism spectrum disorders. In *Handbook of Autism and Pervasive Developmental Disorders*, 2nd ed., ed. D. J. Cohen and F. R. Volkmar. New York: Wiley.
Lott, R. S., Kerrick, J. M., and Cohen, S. A. 1996. Clinical and economic aspects of risperidone treatment in adults with mental retardation and behavioral disturbance. *Psychopharmacology Bulletin* 32:721–9.
Luchins, D. J., and Dojka, D. 1989. Lithium and propranolol in aggression and self-injurious behavior in the mentally retarded. *Psychopharmacology Bulletin* 25:372–5.
Markowitz, P. I. 1992. Effect of fluoxetine on self-injurious behavior in the developmentally disabled: A preliminary study. *Journal of Clinical Psychopharmacology* 12:27–31.

McCormick, L. H. 1997. Treatment with buspirone in a patient with autism. *Archives of Family Medicine* 6:368–70.
McCracken, J. T., and Martin, W. 1997. Clonidine side effect. *Journal of the American Academy of Child and Adolescent Psychiatry* 36:160–1.
McDougle, C. J. 1997. Psychopharmacology. In *Handbook of Autism and Pervasive Developmental Disorders*, 2nd ed., ed. D. J. Cohen and F. R. Volkmar. New York: Wiley.
McDougle, C. J., Naylor, S. T., Goodman, W. K., Volkmar, F. R., Cohen, D. J., and Price, L. H. 1993. Acute tryptophan depletion in autistic disorder: A controlled case study. *Biological Psychiatry* 33:547–50.
McDougle, C. J., Price, L. H., and Goodman, W. K. 1990. Fluvoxamine treatment of coincident autistic disorder and obsessive-compulsive disorder: A case report. *Journal of Autism and Developmental Disorders* 20:537–43.
McDougle, C. J., Price L. H., Volkmar, F. R., Goodman, W. K., Ward-O'Brien, D., Nielsen, J., Bregman, J., and Cohen, D. J. 1992. Clomipramine in autism: Preliminary evidence of efficacy. *Journal of the American Academy of Child and Adolescent Psychiatry* 31:746–50.
McDougle, C. J., Brodkin, E. S., Yeung, P. P., Naylor, S. T., Cohen, D. J., and Price, L. H. 1995. Risperidone in adults with autism or pervasive developmental disorder. *Journal of Child and Adolescent Psychopharmacology* 5:273–82.
McDougle, C. J., Naylor, S. T., Cohen, D. J., Aghajanian, G. K., Heninger G. R., and Price, L. H. 1996. Effects of tryptophan depletion in drug-free adults with autistic disorder. *Archives of General Psychiatry* 53:993–1000.
McDougle, C. J., Naylor, S. T., Cohen, D. J., Volkmar, F. R., Heninger, G. R., and Price, L. H. 1996. A double-blind, placebo-controlled study of fluvoxamine in adults with autistic disorder. *Archives of General Psychiatry* 53:1001–08.
McDougle, C. J., Holmes, J. P., Bronson, M. R., Anderson, G. M., Volkmar, F. R., Price, L. H., and Cohen, D. J. 1997. Risperidone treatment of children and adolescents with pervasive developmental disorders: A prospective, open-label study. *Journal of the American Academy of Child and Adolescent Psychiatry* 36:685–93.
McDougle, C. J., Brodkin, E. S., Naylor, S. T., Carlson, D. C., Cohen, D. J., and Price, L. H. 1998. Sertraline in adults with pervasive developmental disorders: A prospective open-label investigation. *Journal of Clinical Psychopharmacology* 18:62–6.
McDougle, C. J., Holmes, J. P., Carlson, D. C., Pelton, G. H., Cohen, D. J., and Price, L. H. 1998. A double-blind, placebo-controlled study of risperidone in adults with autistic disorder and other pervasive developmental disorders. *Archives of General Psychiatry* 55:633–41.
Mehlinger, R., Scheftner, W. A., and Poznanski, E. 1990. Fluoxetine and autism. *Journal of the American Academy of Child and Adolescent Psychiatry* 29:985.
Mott, S. H., Weinstein, S. L., Conry, J. A., Kenworthy, L. E., Lockwood, S., Wagner, A., and Packer, R. J. 1996. Pervasive developmental disorder/autism versus Landau-Kleffner syndrome: Steroid-responsive encephalopathy characterized by language and social interactive impairment. *Annals of Neurology* 40:332.
Naidu, S., Leopold, D. A., and Ronnet, G. V. 1997. Abnormal olfactory receptor neuronal development in Rett syndrome. *Annals of Neurology* 42:513.
Naruse, H., Nagahata, M., Nakane, Y., Shirachahi, K., Takesada, M., and Yamazaki, K. 1982. A multi-center double-blind trial of pimozide (Orap),

haloperidol and placebo in children with behavior disorders, using cross-over design. *Acta Paedopsychiatrica* 48:173–84.
Naruse, H., Hayashi, T., Takesada, M., Nakane, Y., Yamazaki, K., Noguchi T., Watanabe, Y., and Hayaishi, O. 1987. Therapeutic effect of tetrahydrobioterin in infantile autism. *Proceedings of the Japan Academy* 63:231–3.
Nicholson, R., Awad, G., and Sloman, L. 1998. An open trial of risperidone in young autistic children. *Journal of the American Academy of Child and Adolescent Psychiatry* 37:372– 6.
Niesink, R. J. M., and van Ree, J. M. 1983. Normalizing effect of an adrenocorticotropic hormone (4–9) analog ORG 2766 on disturbed social behavior in rats. *Science* 221:960–2.
Okabe, S., Collin, C., Auerbach, J. M., Meiri, N., Bengzon, J., Kennedy, M. B., Segal, M., and McKay, R. D. G. 1998. Hippocampal synaptic plasticity in mice overexpressing an embryonic subunit of the NMDA receptor. *The Journal of Neuroscience* 18:4177–88.
O'Neil, M., Page, N., and Adkins, W. N. 1986. Trytophan-trazodone treatment of aggressive behavior. *Lancet* 2:859–60.
Osterheld-Haas, M. C., and Hornung, J. P. 1996. Laminar development of the mouse barrel cortex: Effects of neurotoxins against monoamines. *Experimental Brain Research* 110:183–95.
Panksepp, J., and Lensing, P. 1991. Brief report: A synopsis of an open-trial of naltrexone treatment of autism with four children. *Journal of Autism and Developmental Disorders* 21:243–9.
Paoletti, P., Neyton, J., and Ascher, P. 1995. Glycine-independent and subunit-specific potentiation of NMDA responses by extracellular Mg2+. *Neuron* 15:1109–20.
Perry, R., Campbell, M., Adams, P., Lynch, N., Spencer, E. K., Curren, E. L., and Overall, J. E. 1989. Long-term efficacy of haloperidol in autistic children: Continuous versus discontinuous drug administration. *Journal of the American Academy of Child and Adolescent Psychiatry* 28:87–92.
Perry, R., Pataki, C., Munoz-Silva, D. M., Armenteros, J., and Silva, R. R. 1997. Risperidone in children and adolescents with pervasive developmental disorder: Pilot trial and follow-up. *Jounal of Child and Adolescent Psychopharmacology* 7:167–79.
Pfeiffer, S. I., Norton, J., Nelson, L., and Shott, S. 1995. Efficacy of vitamin B6 and magnesium in the treatment of autism: A methodology review and summary of outcomes. *Journal of Autism and Developmental Disorders* 25:481–93.
Pleak, R. R., Birmaher, B., Gavrilescu, A., Abichandani, C., and Williams, D. T. 1988. Mania and neuropsychiatric excitation following carbamazepine. *Journal of the American Academy of Child and Adolescent Psychiatry* 27:500–3.
Plioplys, A. 1998. Intravenous immunoglobulin treatment of children with autism. *Journal of Child Neurology* 13:79–82.
Plioplys, A. V. 1994. Autism: Electroencephalogram abnormalities and clinical improvement with valproic acid. *Archives of Pediatrics and Adolescent Medicine* 148:220–2.
Plioplys, A. V., Hemmens, S. E., and Regan, C. M. 1990. Expression of a neural cell adhesion molecule serum fragment is depressed in autism. *Journal of Neuropsychiatry and Clinical Neurosciences* 2:413–7.
Potenza, M. N., Holmes, J. P., Kanes, S. J., and McDougle, C. J. 1999. Olanzepine treatment of children, adolescents, and adults with pervasive developmental disorders: An open-label pilot study. *Journal of Clinical Psychopharmacology* 19:37–44.

Potenza, M. N., and McDougle, C. J. 1997. The role of serotonin in autism-spectrum disorders. *CNS Spectrums* 2:25–41.
Price, L. H., and Heninger, G. R. 1994. Lithium in the treatment of mood disorders. *New England Journal of Medicine* 331:591–8.
Purdon, S. E., Lit, W., Labelle, A., and Jones, B. D. 1994. Risperidone in the treatment of pervasive developmental disorder. *Canadian Journal of Psychiatry* 39:400–5.
Quintana, H., Birmaher, B., Stedge, D., Lennon, S., Freed, J., Bridge, J., and Greenhill, L. 1995. Use of methylphenidate in the treatment of children with autistic disorder. *Journal of Autism and Developmental Disorders* 25:283–94.
Rao, P., Shuja, I., El-Asyouty, E., El-Mallakh, R., and Lippmann, S. 1998. Divalproex for impulse-control disorders in comorbid mental retardation. *Primary Psychiatry* 5:68–70.
Ratey, J. J., Bemporad, J., Sorgi, P., Bick, P., Polakoff, S., O'Driscoll, G., and Mikkelsen, E. 1987. Brief report: Open trial effects of beta-blockers on speech and social behaviors in 8 autistic adults. *Journal of Autism and Developmental Disorders* 17:439–46.
Ratey, J. J., Mikkelsen, E., Sorgi, P., Zuckerman, H. S., Polakoff, S., Bemporad, J., Bick, P., and Kadish, W. 1987. Autism: The treatment of aggressive behaviors. *Journal of Clinical Psychopharmacology* 7:35–41.
Ratey, J. J., Sovner, R., Mikkelsen, E., and Chmielinski, H. E. 1989. Buspirone therapy for maladaptive behavior and anxiety in developmentally disabled persons. *Journal of Clinical Psychiatry* 50:382–84.
Ratey, J. J., and Lindem, K. J. 1991. Beta-blockers as primary treatment for aggression and self-injury in the developmentally disabled. In *Mental Retardation: Developing Pharmacotherapies*, ed. J. J. Ratey. Washington, DC: American Psychiatric Press.
Ratey, J. J., Sovner, R., Parks, A., and Rogentine, K. 1991. Buspirone treatment of aggression and anxiety in mentally retarded patients: A multiple-baseline, placebo lead-in study. *Journal of Clinical Psychiatry* 52:159–62.
Realmuto, G. M., August, G. J., and Garfinkel, B. D. 1989. Clinical effect of buspirone in autistic children. *Journal of Clinical Psychopharmacology* 9:122–5.
Reiss, A. L., and O'Donnell, D. J. 1984. Carbamazepine-induced mania in two children: Case report. *Journal of Clinical Psychiatry* 45:272–4.
Ricketts, R. W., Goza, A. B., Ellis, C. R., Singh, Y. N., Chambers, S., Singh, N. N., and Cooke, J. C. 1994. Clinical effects of buspirone on interactable self-injury in adults with mental retardation. *Journal of the American Academy of Child and Adolescent Psychiatry* 33:270–6.
Rimland, B. 1987. Megavitamin B6 and magnesium in the treatment of autistic children and adults. In *Neurobiological Issues in Autism*, ed. E. Schopler and G. Mesibov. New York: Plenum.
Rimland, B. 1988. Controversies in the treatment of autistic children: Vitamin and drug therapy. *Journal of Child Neurology* 3:568–72.
Ritvo, E. R., Yuwiler, A., Geller, E., Kales, A., Rashkis, S., Schicor, A., Plotkin, S., Axelrod R., and Howard, C. 1971. Effects of L-dopa in autism. *Journal of Autism and Childhood Schizophrenia* 1:190–205.
Ritvo, E. R., Yuwiler, A., Freeman, B. J., Geller, E., Realmuto, G., Killoran, S. M., Piggott, L. R., Gdowski, C. L., and Fischhoff, J. 1987. Reappraisal of Fenfluramine and autism: Careful reappraisal is in order. *Journal of Pediatrics* 110:158–9.
Rosenbaum, J. F. 1998. Selective serotonin reuptake inhibitor discontinuation syndrome: A randomized clinical trial. *Society of Biological Psychiatry* 44:77–87.

Rossi P. G., Posar, A., Parmeggiani, A., Pipitone, D. S., and D'Agata, M. 1999. Niaprazine in the treatment of autistic disorder. *Journal of Child Neurology* 14:547–50.

Rubin, M. 1997. Use of atypical antipsychotics in children with mental retardation, autism, and other developmental disabilities. *Psychiatric Annals* 27:219–21.

Sanchez, L. E., Campbell, M., Small, A. M., Cueva, J. E., Armenteros, J. L., and Adams, P. B. 1996. A pilot study of clomipramine in young autistic children. *Journal of the American Academy of Child and Adolescent Psychiatry* 35:537–44.

Sandler, A. D., Sutton, K. A., DeWeese, J., Girardi, M. A., Sheppard, V., and Bodfish, J. W. 1999. Lack of benefit of a single dose of synthetic human secretin in the treatment of autism and pervasive developmental disorder. *New England Journal of Medicine* 341:1801–6.

Sandler, R. H., Bolte, E. R., Buchanan, C. P., Maxwell, A. P., and Chez, M. G. 1998. Antibiotic intervention trial for the treatment of children with delayed onset autism. *Pediatric Research* 43:105A.

Schain, R. J., and Freedman, D. X. 1961. Studies on 5-hydroxyindole metabolism in autistic and other mentally retarded children. *Journal of Pediatrics* 58:315–20.

Schaumburg, H., Kaplan, J., Windebank, A., Vick, N., Rasmus, S., Pleasure, D., and Brown, M. J. 1983. Sensory neuropathy from pyridoxine abuse. *New England Journal of Medicine* 309:445–8.

Schmidt, K. 1982. The effect of stimulant medication in childhood-onset pervasive developmental disorder: A case report. *Journal of Developmental and Behavioral Pediatrics* 3:244–6.

Schuster, C. R., Lewis, M., and Seiden, L. S. 1986. Fenfluramine: Neurotoxicity. *Psychopharmacology Bulletin* 22:148–51.

Shaw, C. R., Lucas, J., and Rabinovitch, R. D. 1959. Metabolic studies in childhood schizophrenia. *Archives of General Psychiatry* 1:366–71.

Shaziuddin, M. T. L. 1991. Depression in autistic disorder. *British Journal of Psychiatry* 159:721–3.

Sherman, J., Factor, D. C., Swinson, R., and Darjes, R. W. 1989. The effects of fenfluramine (hydrochloride) on the behaviors of fifteen autistic children. *Journal of Autism and Developmental Disorders* 19:533–43.

Sherwin, A. C., Flach, F. F., and Stokes, P. E. 1958. Treatment of psychoses in early childhood with triiodothyronine. *American Journal of Psychiatry* 115:166–7.

Simeon, J. G., Carrey, N. J., Wiggins, D. M., Milin, R. P., and Hosenbocus, S. N. 1995. Risperidone effects in treatment-resistant adolescents: Preliminary case reports. *Journal of Child and Adolescent Psychopharmacology* 5:69–79.

Simmons, J. Q., Leiken, S. J., Lovaas, O. I., Schaeffer, B., and Perloff, B. 1966. Modification of autistic behavior with LSD-25. *The American Journal of Psychiatry* 123:1201–11.

Simon, E. W., Blubaugh, K. M., and Pippidis, M. 1996. Substituting traditional antipsychotics with risperidone for individuals with mental retardation. *Mental Retardation* 34:359–66.

Singh, N. N., Ellis, C. R., Mulick, J. A., and Poling, A. 1998. Vitamin, mineral, and dietary treatments. In *Psychotropic Medications and Developmental Disabilities,* eds. S. Reiss and M. G. Aman. Columbus, OH: The Ohio State University.

Sloman, L. 1991. Use of medication in pervasive developmental disorders. *Psychiatric Clinics of North America* 14:165–82.

Slotkin, T. A., Barnes, G. A., McCook, E. C., and Seidler, F. J. 1996. Programming of brainstem serotonin transporter development by prenatal glucocorticoids. *Developmental Brain Research* 93:155–61.

Snead, R. W., Boon, F., and Presberg, J. 1994. Paroxetine for self-injurious behavior. *Journal of the American Academy of Child and Adolescent Psychiatry* 33:909–10.

Soni, P., and Weintraub, A. L. 1992. Buspirone-associated mental status changes. *Journal of the American Academy of Child and Adolescent Psychiatry* 31:1098–9.

Sovner, R. 1989. Developments in the use of psychotropic drugs. *Current Opinion in Psychiatry* 2:636–40.

Sovner, R. 1991. Use of anticonvulsant agents for treatment of neuropsychiatric disorders in the developmentally disabled. In *Mental Retardation: Developing Pharmacotherapies*, ed. J. J. Ratey. Washington, D.C.: American Psychiatric Press.

Stefanatos, G. A., Grover, W., and Geller, E. 1995. Case study: Corticosteroid treatment of language regression in pervasive developmental disorder. *Journal of the American Academy of Child and Adolescent Psychiatry* 34:1107–11.

Steingard, R., and Biederman, J. 1987. Lithium responsive manic-like symptoms in two individuals with autism and mental retardation. *Journal of the American Academy of Child and Adolescent Psychiatry* 26:932–5.

Steingard, R. J., Ziminitzky, B., DeMaso, D. R., Bauman, M. L., and Bucci, J. P. 1997. Sertraline treatment of transition-associated anxiety and agitation in children with autistic disorder. *Journal of Child and Adolescent Psychopharmacology* 7:9–15.

Stern, L. M., Walker, M. K., Sawyer, M. G., Oades, R. D., Badcock, N. R., and Spence, J. G. 1990. A controlled crossover trial of fenfluramine in autism. *Journal of Child Psychology and Psychiatry* 31:569–85.

Strayhorn, J. M., Rapp, N., Donina, W., and Strain, P. S. 1988. Randomized trial of methylphenidate for an autistic child. *Journal of the American Academy of Child and Adolescent Psychiatry* 27:244–7.

Sugiyama, N. S. H., Igarashi, Y., Ito, M., and Fukuda, T. 1998. Low-dose levodopa therapy of autistic disorder: Evaluation of clinical effectiveness. *No to Hattatsu* 30:51–5.

Sutton, H. E., Read, J. H., and Arbor, A. 1958. Abnormal amino acid metabolism in a case suggesting autism. *American Journal of Diseases of Children* 96:23–8.

Tanguay, P. E. 1997. Discussion of: Mania in children with pervasive developmental disorder revisted. *Journal of the American Academy of Child and Adolescent Psychiatry* 36:1559–60.

Taylor, D. V., Hetrick, W. P., Neri, C. L., Touchette, P., Barron, J. L., and Sandman, C. A. 1991. Effect of naltrexone upon self-injurious behavior, learning, and activity: A case study. *Pharmacology, Biochemistry, and Behavior* 40:79–82.

Thompson, T., Hackenberg, T., Cerutti, D., Baker, D., and Axtell, S. 1994. Opioid antagonist effects on self-injury in adults with mental retardation: Response form and location as determinants of medication effects. *American Journal of Mental Retardation* 99:85–102.

Todd, R. D. 1991. Fluoxetine in autism. *American Journal of Psychiatry* 148:1089.

Uvebrant, P., and Bauziene, R. 1994. Intractable epilepsy in children. The efficacy of lamotrigine treatment, including non-seizure-related benefits. *Neuropediatrics* 25:284–9.

Varley, C. K., and Holm, V. A. 1990. A two-year follow-up of autistic children treated with fenfluramine. *Journal of the American Academy of Child and Adolescent Psychiatry* 29:137–40.

Vicini, S., Wang, J. F., Li, J. H., Zhu, W. J., Wang, Y. H., Luo, J. H., Wolfe, B. B., and Grayson, D. R. 1998. Functional and pharmacological differences between recombinant N-methyl-D-aspartate receptors. *Journal of Neurophysiology* 79:555–66.

Vitriol, C., and Farber, B. 1981. Stimulant medication in certain childhood disorders. *American Journal of Psychiatry* 138:1517–8.

Volkmar, F. R., Hoder, E. L., and Cohen, D. J. 1985. Inappropriate uses of stimulant medications. *Clinical Pediatrics* 24:127–30.

Volkmar, F. R., and Cohen, D. J. 1997. Diagnosis and classification of autism and related conditions: Consensus and issues. In *Handbook of Autism and Pervasive Developmental Disorders*, 2nd ed., ed. D. J. Cohen and F. R. Volkmar. New York: Wiley.

Walters, A. S., Barrett, R. P., Feinstein, C., Mercurio, A., and Hole, W. T. 1990. A case report of naltrexone treatment of self-injury and social withdrawal in autism. *Journal of Autism and Developmental Disorders* 20:169–76.

Willemsen-Swinkels, S. H. N., Buitelaar, J. K., Nijhof, G. J., and van Engeland, H. 1995. Failure of naltrexone hydrochloride to reduce self-injurious and autistic behavior in mentally retarded adults. *Archives of General Psychiatry* 52:766–73.

Willemsen-Swinkels, S. H. N., Buitelaar, J. K., and van Engeland, H. 1996. The effects of chronic naltrexone treatment in young autistic children: A double-blind placebo-controlled crossover study. *Biological Psychiatry* 39:1023–31.

Williams, D. T., Mehl, R., Yudofsky, S., Adams, D., and Roseman, B. 1982. The effect of propranolol on uncontrolled rage outbursts in children and adolescents with organic brain dysfunction. *Journal of the American Academy of Child Psychiatry* 21:129–35.

Wollmuth, L. P., Kuner, T., and Sakmann, B. 1998. Adjacent asparagines in the NR2-subunit of the NMDA receptor channel control the voltage-dependent block by extracellular Mg2+. *Journal of Physiology* 506 (Pt 1):13–32.

Wolozin, B., Sunderland, T., Zheng, B. B., Resau, J., Dufy, B., Barker, J., Swerdlow, R., and Coon, H. 1992. Continuous culture of neuronal cells from adult human olfactory epithelium. *Journal of Molecular Neuroscience* 3:137–46.

Wozniak, J., Biederman, J., Faraone, S. V., Frazier, J., Kim, J., Millstein, R., Gershon, J., Thornell, A., Cha, K., and Snyder, J. B. 1997. Mania in children with pervasive developmental disorder revisited. *Journal of the American Academy of Child and Adolescent Psychiatry* 36:1552–9.

Zimmerman, A. W., Jinnah, H. A., and Lockhart, P. J. 1998. Behavioral neuropharmacology. *Mental Retardation and Developmental Disabilities Research Reviews* 4:26–35.

Zingarelli, G., Ellman, G., Hom, A., Wymore, M., Heidorn, S., and Chicz-DeMet, A. 1992. Clinical effects of naltrexone on autistic behavior. *American Journal on Mental Retardation* 97:57–63.

Zuddas, A., Ledda, M. G., Fratta, A., Muglia, P., and Cianchetti, C. 1996. Clinical effects of clozapine on autistic disorder. *American Journal of Psychiatry* 153:738.

Chapter • 13

Parent and Family Issues: *Stress and Knowledge*

Martin A. Kozloff and John S. Rice

GENERAL STATEMENTS ABOUT FAMILIES

We can make three general statements about families of children with autism. First, families face many challenges, including the following:

1. The unexpectedness of a child's developing and being diagnosed with autism.
2. A child's behavioral excesses (e.g., tantrums, mess making) and behavioral deficits (e.g., communication, self-care).
3. Families' difficulties determining what is wrong or what went wrong in their child's development, leading to uncertainty about the past and future, and leaving some families with nagging questions about their culpability and adequacy.
4. The difficulty many families face finding and sustaining timely and effective evaluations and treatment.
5. Parents' confusion stemming from competing claims among professionals about the best treatments for autism and the nature of their child's subjectivity. At one extreme, parents are told that their child is a person with typical self-consciousness trapped in a body that does not move as the child wills. At the other extreme, parents are told that their child has a diminished capacity for self-awareness and reflective thought in general.
6. Strained interaction with extended family and strangers (e.g., when parents take their child to public places where quiet behavior is expected) which transforms some families into outsiders or objects of pity.

7. The difficulties many families have satisfying their child's medical, recreational, educational, and social needs within the ordinary round of family life.

A second general statement is that parents' participation in their children's education (assessment, program planning, instruction, program evaluation, and revision) is largely peripheral (Boyle and Offord 1988; Hertweck 1986; Mehan 1986, 1993; Turnbull and Turnbull 1990; Zahner et al. 1992). For example, the detailed insider knowledge parents and siblings have of a child's learning characteristics is not asked for, is not included, is trivialized, or re-interpreted in typical educational practices, which are often governed by professional-territorial, economic, and ideological interests rather than by child- and family-centered interests.

Third, except for a dozen or so programs around the country (e.g., as described by Anderson et al. 1987; Fenske et al. 1985; Fox, Dunlap, and Philbrick 1997; Harris et al. 1990; Holmes 1998; Howlin and Rutter 1987; Koegel and Johnson 1989; Lord, Bristol, and Schopler 1993; Lovaas 1988; Maurice, Green, and Luce 1996; Prizant and Wetherby 1993; Rogers and DiLalla 1991), most educational programs are tragically deficient with respect to staff skills; the scope of the curriculum; the training, support and participation of families; and the quality and outcomes of instruction. We say tragically deficient because of the great discrepancy between what could be (from information readily available in books and journals and at conferences) and what typically is the quality of education for children with autism (as a result of poor teacher training, schools refusing to use certain well-tested forms of instruction, and educational fads).

Taken together, the conditions and events identified above foster undesirable changes in some families:

1. There is increasing strain on family resources—time, energy, finances, and coping skills.
2. Many families are vulnerable to individuals, such as service providers, sitters, neighbors, and relatives who cannot be counted on for emotional support and hands-on assistance; to groups, such as those making inflated claims for explanations and treatments of autism; and to the economic system, which may or may not enable a family to remain or relocate to communities offering needed services.
3. The likelihood of marital conflict, anxiety, and depression increases.
4. There is interference with work and career advancement.
5. As energy is depleted, unproductive interactions with the child with autism develop, as other family members try to

stop disruptive behavior in ways that reinforce the behavior (Brotherson and Goldstein 1992; Cutler 1991; Cutler and Kozloff 1987; Fogon and Schor 1993; Patterson 1982; Weiss 1991).

Since knowledge helps families work productively to meet challenges, the remainder of this chapter will suggest the kinds of knowledge families may find useful. This includes: (1) areas and benefits of family participation; (2) psychosocial development; (3) productive interaction with children; (4) phases of learning and instruction; (5) settings for instruction; and (6) educational programs.

AREAS AND BENEFITS OF FAMILY PARTICIPATION

Family is often the only group children can depend on over the long haul. Laws, regulations, and sources of funding change; excellent teachers burn out from paperwork and politics; innovative directors of special education are stymied by foot-dragging school boards; enlightened principals are replaced by ideologues who believe autistic children learn best via "child-centered" and "developmentally appropriate" approaches rather than direct instruction and precision teaching. Knowing how to evaluate a child's progress and educational program (curriculum and instruction) and discovering how to teach are more than things parents might do— they are things parents often must do.

The early assessment of a child's development and behavioral repertoire will be more comprehensive, more detailed, and more reliable when parents are involved. Parents can provide information on their child's competencies, deficits, likes, and dislikes for activities, places, persons, and times of day. This information is important in making decisions about tasks to teach, settings for instruction, signals, prompts, and reinforcers. If teachers have to discover through trial and error whether, for example, a child learns best with manual prompts using a least-to-most strategy, it will take much valuable time; and, in the meantime, the child will learn the errors. Parents can collect assessment information by observing their child during activities in the round of daily life, conducting short teaching sessions, and by keeping a journal that helps them recall their child's learning under different conditions. This information assists in the development of an individualized curriculum and in planning details of instruction for specific tasks.

Ongoing evaluations of a child's progress are more comprehensive, detailed, and reliable when families are involved. For example, parents can help determine how much the skills worked on at school are generalizing to the home. In addition, parents may notice changes in a child that are not part of the school's evaluation. Parents may identify undesirable changes in a child's behavior when certain methods are used at school; for example, parents may find that when a child's undesirable behaviors are no longer reinforced at school, the child whines more and more at home. Teachers must know of these changes—not just that they are happening, but precisely when, where, and how often—to help families reduce problem behaviors.

When parents and siblings conduct teaching programs in the home and in other settings, they often find the following changes:

1. Their child learns more in less time.
2. Family members are able to help the child generalize skills learned at school to the home and from the home to school.
3. Parents and teachers more easily collaborate in adjusting a child's program. For example, they might decide to begin working on increasing a child's verbal requests, or to switch from full manual prompts to partial prompts. In addition to a more fluent program evaluation and revision process, collaboration reduces or prevents mutual suspicions and dissatisfactions that often occur in stressful situations.

PSYCHOSOCIAL DEVELOPMENT

The education of autistic children should be guided by a model of children's psychosocial development. Such a model can assist parents and teachers to (1) identify behaviors and environments for assessing children's strengths and needs; (2) use assessment information to plan curricula (know sequence of concepts and skills to teach) and instruction (child-caregiver communication); and (3) identify behaviors and environments for evaluating a child's progress. An adequate model of psychosocial development would depict (1) the ways in which elemental behaviors emerge and are assembled into complex, compound tasks and activities as children interact with their environments; and (2) how children are provided with different social positions, roles, and identities as they become increasingly competent participants in social systems, such as family and school. The following is a brief description of a model of psychosocial development discussed in Kozloff (1994a, 1994b).

The model of psychosocial development focuses on six competency areas. Each competency area includes specific tasks grouped by the functions they serve. Notice that tasks learned in earlier competency areas contribute to a child's capacities for learning in other competency areas; that is, the model depicts psychosocial development as a cumulative process.

Area A: Interest in, Attention, and Orientation to the Environment

This competency area is essential to children's further psychosocial development; that is, the items in this area are necessary if a child is to participate competently in social interaction/instruction. Items in this area include (1) visually tracking movements of hands, objects, and persons; (2) looking at objects and parts of the body spontaneously and on request; (3) turning to locate the source of sounds; and (4) attending and orienting to the speech of others.

Area B: Participation in Elementary and Early Forms of Social Interaction

This area identifies fundamental competencies in social interaction, the pervasive context in which children learn to take turns and perform expected actions during their turns. Elementary social exchanges, such as greetings and goodbyes, questions and answers, and requests for assistance are usually assembled into longer social sequences at meals, play, or lessons. Therefore, an early objective in the education of autistic children must be to teach them how to participate in social exchanges. Items in this area include (1) responding to one's own name and to requests, such as "Look"; (2) making eye contact (spontaneously and on request) to produce natural reinforcers, such as at play; (3) approaching other persons spontaneously and on request; (4) showing and giving objects (i.e., initiating interaction or taking a turn); (5) expressing needs, wants, or preferences by vocalizing, reaching, pointing, shaking the head, or placing an adult's hand on a desired object; (6) imitating an adult's movements, sounds, words, and actions; and (7) enacting greetings, goodbyes, thanks, questions, answers, and descriptions.

Area C: Body Coordination and Locomotion

Items in this area bring a child into contact with objects and activities from which the child can learn about time, space, movement, cause and effect, and social norms. These include (1) fluency at moving and using (extending, flexing, rotating) hands, arms, and legs; (2) bending and standing; (3) carrying objects; (4) throwing, kicking, and catching a ball; (5) hopping, jumping, running, and many more.

Area D: Simple Actions and Interactions With Objects

Items in this area build on tasks from previous areas. Examples of items in this area include (1) component actions such as reaching, grasping, picking up, releasing, placing, switching hand-to-hand, pushing away, turning over, rotating, fitting, and squeezing; and (2) composite activities such as putting objects into containers, wrapping/covering and unwrapping/uncovering, stacking, stirring, stringing, screwing/unscrewing, turning pages, winding/unwinding, scribbling, tracing, coloring, spreading, placing (e.g., utensils on a mat), inserting (e.g., utensils into a drawer), rolling, folding, cutting, and assembling.

Area E: Common-sense Knowledge of How the World Works and of the Cultural Configuration

As children pay attention to their own behaviors and to the activities around them, they acquire knowledge in the form of concepts, propositions, and strategies. Examples include knowledge (1) that some events signal later events (e.g., the sound of a car signals the arrival of a person at the front door); (2) that causal relationships exist (e.g., if a handle is turned counter-clockwise, the water flow stops); (3) that there are associations among objects, activities, persons, places, words/names (e.g., some kinds of food are eaten only in the kitchen; other foods may be eaten outside the house); (4) that there are characteristics by which one can describe and group objects and events (e.g., color, shape, use, speed, number, distance, position); (5) that there are actors (I, you, we); and (6) that there are recipes and strategies (e.g., how to get dressed).

Area F: Increasingly Competent Participation in More Complex Forms of Social Organization

As a child becomes more competent, others may begin to see the child as increasingly attuned to what is going on and more capable of taking part. Others may then provide the child with opportunities to perform more complex tasks in more complex forms of social organization, e.g., helping to prepare meals or participating more in conversations. These changes further increase a child's competent participation in lessons, play, chores, stories, shopping, and conversations.

In addition to identifying competency areas and behaviors, the model of psychosocial development above suggests the following:

1. It makes sense to begin a child's education with items in the earlier areas, i.e., interest in, attention, and orientation to the environment and participation in elementary and early forms of social interaction. A child's progress in other areas depends on competence in these areas.

2. Increasing competence in one area facilitates beneficial change in other areas. For example, as children learn to move their bodies from one place to another (area C) and to interact with objects (area D), they acquire common-sense knowledge of how the world works. This increases their competence with items in area F.
3. Therefore, we should keep track of change in all of the competency areas, including the ones that are not yet the focus of a child's educaton.
4. If a child is not making much progress in an area, we should assess the child's skills in the earlier areas. It is likely that these earlier tasks are tools skills or components of behaviors in the harder areas which must be strengthened before the child can progress.

PRODUCTIVE AND COUNTER-PRODUCTIVE EXCHANGES

All forms of social organization—families, classrooms, schools, economic systems, nation states—boil down to interpersonal exchanges by which members accomplish routine activities: greetings, buying and selling, asking and answering questions, getting across new concepts, sharing meals, or playing games. As shown in the section on psychosocial development, competent participation in interpersonal exchanges is necessary for children's psychosocial development, e.g., learning to speak, having conversations, and taking part in lessons. However, not all interpersonal exchanges are conducive to psychosocial development.

There are two sorts of exchanges. Counter-productive exchanges involve conflict or incongruity. One or both persons engage in behaviors that are aversive to the other person; or one person engages in desirable behavior but receives little or nothing in return. In general, counter-productive exchanges teach participants how to engage in conflict. In productive exchanges, however, each person performs behaviors that are reinforcers for the other person and teaches cooperation. From the standpoint of the participant, each person's behavior is desirable. This section describes exchanges in pairs—a productive exchange followed by a counter-productive alternative. This information may help parents and other caregivers identify counter-productive exchanges that need to be replaced and productive exchanges that need to be strengthened. More complete descriptions are found in Kozloff (1988, 1994a, 1994b).

1a. Rewarded Coercion

In this exchange, a child does something that is aversive to a caregiver; for example, the child makes one more weird noise, makes a mess, or bangs his or her head. The caregiver tries to stop the behavior by expressing shock or anger, asking questions ("Are we supposed to scream?"); stating rules ("We don't scream."); trying to distract the child (e.g., turning on music); or removing events (e.g., difficult tasks) that may evoke the child's coercive behavior. These reactions often reinforce the aversive/coercive behavior. Temporarily distracted by the reinforcing events, the child stops the behavior, which, then, negatively reinforces the caregiver for reacting as he or she did, i.e., for accidentally reinforcing the coercive behavior.

The reader can see the vicious cycle. Each person is negatively reinforced for his or her actions in the exchange. Therefore, the exchange is likely to occur more often, and the participants become more skillful at coercing and giving in to coercion. Gradually, the child is seen as an adversary with whom family members, caregivers, and peers may avoid interacting. These changes degrade the child's identity and place in social systems and further decrease the child's opportunities for learning alternative desirable behaviors.

1b. Unrewarded Coercion

In this alternative to the rewarded coercion exchange, a caregiver remains outwardly calm and does not give in to a child's coercive behavior. Instead, the caregiver provides opportunities for desirable alternative behavior and reinforces those behaviors. For example, Sally typically throws intense and lengthy tantrums. Instead of giving her candy or turning on the TV to "get her to stop" (as they used to do), her parents leave the room. Whenever Sally ends a tantrum in less time than usual, her parents come back into the room and interact with her in a way that Sally likes. Jerry tells his parents that he wants something by taking them by the hand, yelling, and leading them to the item. His parents realize that this interferes with Jerry learning to talk. After spending several months teaching Jerry to imitate basic sounds, when Jerry takes them by the hand, they require that he imitate sounds that are close to words used in a request, e.g., "kuh me" (for "Come with me") (Carr et al. 1994).

2a. Rewarded Threat

This exchange can develop out of the rewarded coercion exchange. For example, caregivers soon learn that a child's screaming precedes worse behavior (e.g., self-injury), or that coercive behavior is more likely in certain settings. As a result, when presented with these cues (threats), caregivers may become afraid or angry, try to soothe or distract the child, allow the child to receive reinforcers for inadequate performances, or remove tasks or requests that upset the child. These reactions probably reinforce the threatening behavior. Distracted by the reinforcers, the child stops the threatening behavior and does not go on to perform the really coercive behavior. The caregiver feels relieved and is, therefore, negatively reinforced for having reinforced the child's threats. With repetitions of these kinds of exchanges, the child's threat behaviors increase in frequency and skill. The child comes to command much reinforcement through threats; the child loses opportunities to learn alternative behaviors; and caregivers feel increasingly tense about what he or she will do next (hypervigilance).

2b. Unrewarded Threat

Instead of inadvertently reinforcing threatening behavior, caregivers remain outwardly calm, ignore milder problem behaviors, and set up a mutual reward exchange with the child; that is, the child must perform some small desirable behavior before receiving reinforcing objects, activities, or choices. The more this alternative exchange is repeated, the more children learn that threatening does not work and they become more skillful at performing desirable behaviors. Caregivers develop tolerance of milder problem behaviors and become more skilled at teaching desirable behaviors. For example, when Tammy was bored, she would begin to whine. This whining would escalate to screaming. To avoid the escalation, her parents gave her snacks when she whined. This taught Tammy to whine both out of boredom and to get snacks.

Now, her parents have a list of simple tasks for Tammy to do during the day. Tammy has learned that when she does three tasks in a short period of time (cooperates with three simple requests), she may choose a toy from a special toy box, or her parents will play with her. Tammy's whining decreased. Now when she is bored, she goes to her parents to initiate their asking her to do something; or she begins to do some of the simple tasks that they have been teaching her to do.

3a. Rewarded Noncompliance (Nagging)

In this exchange, a child does not cooperate with a caregiver's initiations, e.g., requests or questions, so the caregiver repeats the initiations louder and/or with extra signals, such as livid facial expressions. These repetitions probably strengthen the child's uncooperative responses. When the child finally cooperates, it reinforces the caregiver for nagging on a variable ratio schedule, which sustains nagging at a steady rate.

At some point, a caregiver may decrease making requests at all. ("What's the point? She hardly ever does what you ask.") When this happens, the child has fewer chances to learn prosocial behavior, valuable in family or school. On the other hand, some caregivers find a child's worsening noncompliance highly provocative and begin punishing the child. This sets the stage for the child to use counter-aggression (Schindler and Arkowitz 1986).

3b. Single Cues or Cooperation Training

Instead of repeating requests over and over, a caregiver makes sure a child pays attention before presenting signals, gives clear simple signals, immediately reinforces improvements in cooperation, and responds to noncompliance by ignoring it, or if necessary (e.g., crossing a street) manually prompting the child through the motions (Engelmann and Colvin 1983).

4a. Aversive Methods

In this exchange, a child does something that is aversive to a caregiver, e.g., noncompliance or hitting. The caregiver reacts by delivering aversive consequences, such as spanking or taking away positive reinforcers, such as toys. Sometimes this exchange is a single episode—the child reacts to the punishment by expressing fear or pain and temporarily stops the behavior. This reinforces the caregiver for punishing. Sometimes, however, one punishment exchange evokes another, and instead of stopping his or her aversive behavior, the child escalates (hits harder) or adds another aversive behavior (screaming). The caregiver punishes the child again, and the fight continues. In time, each person learns new and more skillful aversive/aggressive ways to punish the other person. In addition, both child and caregiver become anxious, depressed, and withdrawn.

4b. Mutual Reward Alternatives to Aversive Methods

Instead of trying to punish a child's undesirable behavior, a caregiver remains outwardly calm and encourages or waits for desirable behaviors to reinforce (e.g., milder forms of a problem behavior; performance of an undesirable behavior in a more desirable place; or performance of a desirable alternative behavior). For example, Jackie used to scribble on the walls with crayons. This would make his mother so angry that she would yell at him and roughly put him in his room. This did not teach Jackie not to color on the walls; it only made Jackie fearful of his mother moving quickly toward him. It also made his mother feel frustrated at herself. Now, Jackie's mother has set up a special table where Jackie colors on large pieces of paper, but he has to perform a few simple chores in order to earn the crayons. Jackie's mother gives him the crayons and walks with him right past the walls where he used to color. She tells him the rule: "No coloring on walls. Color on paper." She has Jackie repeat the rule; then he sits at his table and colors all he wants, with occasional praise and participation from his mother.

5a. Lack of Opportunities for Desirable Behavior

In this exchange a child would benefit from an opportunity to respond (e.g., helping to prepare a meal), but the caregiver does not notice opportunities, or notices but does not signal the child to respond. In effect, the child's interest and proximity to activities is on extinction and weakens. As the child's competencies fail to improve, caregivers regard the child as incapable of learning more skills and spend even less time and effort in finding opportunities to improve skills. This stabilizes the child's role as "incompetent."

5b. Plenty of Opportunities for Desirable Behavior

In this exchange, a caregiver notices learning opportunities and gives a child clear signals to respond. As the child's interest and competence increase, caregivers are reinforced for their efforts to provide learning opportunities. This completes a productive cycle of caregivers providing even more opportunities while the child's psychosocial development advances.

6a. Improper Prompting

In this exchange, a child makes, or is about to make, an incorrect or inadequate response, but the caregiver either gives no prompts or prompts ineffectively. Consequently, the child learns to make errors. The child's competencies increase slowly, if at all, and the caregiver is minimally reinforced for teaching efforts that weaken. Thus, the child is seen as less capable than he or she really is.

6b. Proper Prompting

In this alternative exchange, a child makes, or is about to make, an incorrect or inadequate response, but the caregiver provides an adequate prompt. Both the child and the caregiver become more competent at teaching and learning. Their estimations of the child's capacities increase.

7a. Lack of Rewards for Desirable Behavior

Here, a child performs a desirable behavior—either a new one or an improved one. However, the caregiver does not notice the desirable behavior or does not provide adequate reinforcement. Consequently, the child's desirable behaviors weaken or fail to increase. This decreases the child's opportunities for participation and reinforcement, which (as an establishing operation) then increases the value of reinforcing consequences the child receives for disruptive behavior—as in the rewarded coercion, reward threat, and nagging exchanges.

7b. Plenty of Rewards for Desirable Behavior

When a child performs a desirable behavior, a caregiver notices and properly reinforces the behavior. The child's desirable behaviors increase, as does the caregiver's attention and reinforcement of desirable behaviors.

It is important to understand that one kind of exchange may alter the rates of other exchanges. For example, as rewarded coercion increases, caregivers become more sensitive to aversive events and are more likely to reinforce their child's threatening behavior ("Anything to stop her screaming!"). As aversive behaviors increase, these caregivers may eventually use punishment or interact less often with their child.

However, introducing a mutally rewarding exchange (e.g., increasing the reinforcement of a child's desirable behavior) can start a productive spiral. As a child's desirable behaviors (e.g., cooperation) increase, caregivers have more opportunities to reinforce desirable behavior. As desirable behaviors increase still more, caregivers form more positive conceptions of their child. This further increases the rate of reinforcement and decreases the rate of aversive behavior.

EIGHT PHASES OF INSTRUCTION AND LEARNING

Behavior can change in eight important ways. If parents or teachers work on only a few of these changes, they have not helped their children become as competent and independent as they could become. The eight phases are acquisition, fluency-building, endurance, behavioral momentum, generalization and discrimination, adaptation, retention, and maintenance. Definitions of these terms and brief descriptions of instructional methods that foster these changes follow.

Acquisition

Acquisition is the earliest phase of learning; that is, when a person learns the components of a composite task (e.g., the concepts, strategies, and operations [movements] involved in setting a table or reading) and learns to assemble the components into accurate and/or successful composite performances.

Fluency-building

Fluency-building generally follows acquisition. Fluency-building occurs when a person learns not only to perform a task accurately, but to use concepts, strategies, and operations smoothly and quickly (Dougherty and Johnston 1996; Johnson and Layng 1996). For example, in reading, fluency means that a person pronounces words clearly, moves quickly from one word to the next, moves quickly from the end of one line to the start of the next, and modulates stress and tone in response to punctuation marks. Fluency-building is essential to the education of children with autism because when children are fluent:

1. They enjoy performing tasks at which they are skilled.
2. They remain proficient at the task over time with less practice.
3. They are more likely to reassemble different component skills (e.g., reaching, manipulating objects, naming objects, following directions) automatically into new or creative combinations (e.g., cooperative play). This is called "response adduction" (Binder 1996; Binder and Watkins 1990; Binder, Haughton, and Van Eyk 1990; Dougherty and Johnston 1996; Haughton 1980; Johnson and Layng 1992, 1996; Jordon and Robbins 1971; Lindsley 1990, 1996).
4. They can perform successfully in the face of distractions, and for longer periods of time without fatigue.

Fluency is fostered by providing students with frequent practice sessions (typically very short sessions) on components skills with much initial prompting to help students move through routines faster for a smooth behavioral flow. This is in contrast to the frequently interrupted sequences found in discrete trial instruction.

Endurance

Endurance is the ability a student has to engage in an activity for an extended period of time. Unfortunately, teachers seldom work on endurance; they focus more on students' making the right response or finishing the task at hand. However, if students are not able to sustain skillful activity, their skill will be of little use outside the classroom, where endurance is needed.

Endurance is fostered by continually practicing and improving component skills (as in fluency-building); gradually increasing the length of practice sessions; and moving from practice environments to more naturalistic ones.

Behavioral Momentum

Behavioral momentum (Plaud and Gaither 1996) is that ability a student has to remain fluent in such activities as reading or problem solving despite distractions, e.g., ambient noise. Most teachers focus on correct answers or on having students finish their lessons, and seldom help these students learn to continue working despite noise, fatigue, or frustration. Students' skills are fragile; yet, they must learn to sustain them in the outside world.

Momentum is fostered by practicing to the point of fluency and beyond, practicing in the presence of increasingly intrusive distractors, and introducing events that have been associated with students' success (e.g., music).

Generalization

Generalization (sometimes called "application" or "transfer") is the ability a student has to use skills or concepts acquired in one environment in other environments. For example, a student applies skills learned with one soda machine to other soda machines (Mundschenk and Sasso 1995). Unfortunately, most teachers take generalization for granted, or fail to think about it at all. What their students learn in class is largely wasted. However, behaviorally-sophisticated teachers thoughtfully facilitate generalization in several ways. They do this by:

1. Helping students practice to the point of fluency.
2. Teaching in a way that increases the chances of generalization, for example:
   a. Giving students learning opportunities in a variety of settings, e.g., reading different type faces from different materials.
   b. Using natural signals, prompts, and consequences.
   c. Teaching skills that are functional, valued, expected, and for which frequent opportunities and models in other settings exist.
3. Providing specific instruction on generalization by using general case instruction (Albin and Horner 1988; Horner, McDonnell, and Bellamy 1986) or sequential modification (Haring 1988).
   a. In general case instruction, a teacher helps students understand the similarities and differences among a wide range

of juxtaposed examples, e.g., different eating utensils. This prepares students for handling novel situations outside the classroom.

b. In sequential modification, the teacher works with students in one setting or with one kind of problem. When students are skilled with that one type (exemplar), the teacher probes the extent of students' generalization to a second situation. If there is little generalization, the teacher helps students apply the skill acquired in the first setting to the second setting. The process of assessing skill generalization in a new setting and then teaching in the new setting continues until a wide range of settings is covered.

Adaptation

Adaptation is not the same as generalization. Adaptation means that a person alters (does not simply transfer) a concept, strategy, or operation to suit the circumstances. For example, a child modifies his or her way of operating a soda machine that has buttons rather than square panels to push. Behaviorally informed teachers foster students' capacities to adapt skills to new situations by ensuring that their students' tool skills (components or basics) are broad and fluent (firm and fast).

Retention

Retention is the ability of a student to be skillful despite the passage of time between practice or performance. Unfortunately, few teachers foster retention. When a unit is finished, it is over, and they go on to the next. Consequently, their students do not retain what they learned, and the hard work was for nothing. Teachers can foster retention by working on fluency, endurance, and adaptation, and by strategically integrating earlier skills and knowledge with new ones being taught.

Maintenance

Maintenance is the ability of a student to be skillful in the absence of instruction or assistance. In other words, the student is independent. Few teachers think about maintenance, so skills weaken when students are on their own. This is another example of wasted education. Teachers can ensure maintenance by:

1. Providing earlier instruction to a high degree of skill and fluency.
2. Slowly fading instruction and assistance.

3. Teaching students to evaluate their own performances and follow a problem-solving sequence, such as using a guideline to "try another way" or by reciting rules of procedure.

Settings of Instruction

The education of many children with autism occurs during sit-down sessions in a special place and time. This may be necessary for certain skills and at certain (e.g., early) stages. However, the success of early instruction in this setting inadvertently trains many teachers to teach almost solely in this setting, inhibiting fluency, generalization, endurance, retention, and maintenance. This section examines three complementary settings for instruction that cover a wide sample of a child's environments. The three settings are routine tasks and activities, incidental-engineered opportunities, and special sessions.

Routine Tasks and Activities

The round of daily life is a recurring sequence of tasks (setting the table, eating, cleaning up) and larger activities (meals). Routine tasks and activities are an important instructional setting because:

1. They provide regular and frequent opportunities to participate in social life.
2. A child's participation can vary from partial (handing someone a spoon) to lengthier contributions (stirring soup).
3. A child learns about (a) means-end relations (to accomplish Z, first do X, and Y), (b) parts and wholes (a sandwich consists of bread, filling, and condiment), and (c) social conventions (e.g., for meals and games).
4. A child's participation is likely to be noticed, reinforced, or supported by available models to enhance estimation of the child's competence.
5. The signals, prompts, and reinforcers are normative, "natural," and reliably there; therefore generalization of skill to other settings is easier.

Incidental-Engineered Opportunities

There are four kinds of incidental-engineered opportunities: incidental teaching, the mand-model technique, the delay procedure, and chain interruption. These can be used when teaching routine tasks and activities as well.

Incidental Teaching. Here, a caregiver waits for or engineers the setting to encourage a particular response. For example, a parent opens the refrigerator door, exposing a child's favorie juice. The child pulls the door open. The parent prompts, reinforces, and/or encourages the child to expand the performance.

The Mand-Model Technique. Here, a caregiver inserts a request into a child's ongoing activity, and then prompts and/or reinforces the child's response (Goetz and Sailor 1988). For example, while a child is playing with toy cars, his mother asks what he is doing, or asks him to show her a red car. This brings the child into contact with possibly unnoticed events and helps him generalize into the play setting behaviors he acquired elsewhere (e.g., color naming and the question-answer format). In contrast to incidental teaching, the mand-model technique involves more initiation by a caregiver.

The Delay Procedure. In the delay procedure, a caregiver identifies spots in a task or interaction where a child could make a request (Halle, Baer, and Spradlin 1981). The caregiver participates in the interaction as usual, but at the pre-selected spot interrupts the flow for a few seconds and waits for the child's request. If a request is not forthcoming, the caregiver models one.

Chain Interruption. In chain interruption, a caregiver interrupts the child engaged in a sequence and makes a request requiring the child to insert another behavior into the sequence, thus enriching it (Hunt and Goetz 1988).

Special Teaching Sessions

Special sessions (i.e., massed practice with a discrete trial format) are very useful and, perhaps, essential under certain conditions for:

1. Initially strengthening responsiveness and turn-taking during simple collaborative tasks, i.e., bringing a child into the social world.
2. Improving child-caregiver exchanges.
3. Helping caregivers increase teaching competence and giving children with a history of slow progress the experience of success.
4. Practicing weak behaviors for generalizing routine tasks and activities.

Even so, it is essential that caregivers move a child's instruction away from these sessions and into routine activities.

EVALUATING A CHILD'S EDUCATIONAL PROGRAM

The following are items and questions parents might use to guide observations and make judgments about their children's education.

A. Assessment and Program Planning
   1. Is the sample of behavior large? Is the sample obtained at school, home, and other settings? Is information precise (Exactly how many times or for how long did a child perform a behavior?) and rich (Is there a running record of how a child perfomed a behavior so that strong and weak components can be identified?) Is information collected at different times and by different persons in order to get a big picture and to assess reliability?
   2. Are parents' additions and interpretations included?
   3. Are there long-term program (curriculum) plans? Do they follow reasonable sequences; e.g., one area (e.g., motor imitation) later contributing to the next (e.g., imitating how to play); component ("tool") skills (such as reaching, grasping, fitting, watching what you are doing) later assembled into functional composite tasks (e.g., opening and closing containers, putting things away)?
   4. Do teaching plans identify specific behavior changes or do plans merely list abstractions, such as probabilities or psychological dispositions? Statements such as "She will want to . . ." or "He will demonstrate competence at washing his face" are unacceptable. If educators do not know how to be more concrete, they should not be in the business.
   5. Do teaching program plans discuss all eight phases of learning: acquisition (accuracy); fluency-building (accuracy plus smooth and fast performance, fostered by practice); generalization (same behavior, different conditions); endurance (fluency for extended time); behavioral momentum (fluency despite distractions); adaptation (altering behavior to suit circumstances); retention (fluency over time between practices); maintenance (fluency in the absence of instruction)?

B. Child-Caregiver Interaction
   1. Are most exchanges of the mutual reward variety?
   2. Do caregivers quickly notice that they have engaged in a counterproductive exchange (e.g., nagging) and correct it?

C. Instruction
   1. Is communication "faultless" (Engelmann and Carnine 1991)?
      a. Is it clear to the child what the child is to do?
      b. Is the information unambiguous, or is it possible for a child to arrive at more than one interpretation? For example, is the child shown a red circle and a blue

square and told "This is red." as the caregiver points to the red circle? (This is ambiguous. Is the child learning red or circle?)

2. Does the caregiver count it as a correct response ("Good" or mark off a task on a recording sheet) even though she told the child to look three times, and manually prompted the correct response twice after two earlier errors? (This is one example of confusing words [correct] and things [behavior]).
3. Does the caregiver unnecessarily break up what could be a fluent stream of actions into discrete trials? For example, even though a child may be able (or could learn) to put in several puzzle pieces in a row, or imitate many models in a row, or read many words in a row, the caregiver does one response at a time, i.e., requires that the child pause for several seconds before the next "trial." This, of course, not only inhibits fluency; it gives a child time to engage in problematic behavior.
4. Does the caregiver use "Good, ""Good job," in a mechanical, indiscriminate way? (This is another example of confusing words [reinforcement] and things [effects of consequences]).
5. Are behaviors learned in one lesson or area clearly generalized to other lessons and areas? (If not, a caregiver may be operating on the false assumption that learning is stored somewhere and carried from place to place.)
6. Does the caregiver frequently ask nonquestions: "Will you cooperate?"
7. Is group instruction really one-at-a-time-while-sitting-in-a-row instruction?
8. Has kindness been replaced by rough treatment?

D. Evaluation
    1. See A. 1 and 2.
    2. Are weak tool skills (component behaviors such as reaching, grasping, fitting, and concept knowledge) identified for future practice?
    3. Are strong components identified for future assembly into complex, functional composites?

It is important for parents to use a list such as the above to help them be mindful of the quality of their child's education. So often, parents struggle just to get schools to have a class for autistic children or to find a class for their child. After all their labor, they expect (hope?) that teachers will do a good job—will read current literature and are expert in the use of instructional techniques. Sometimes, the name of the approach that is allegedly used in a class (applied behavior analysis, for example) lulls parents into a false sense of security (Rice 1996). However, just as parents would not give their child a drug simply because a physician called it medicine, without making sure it was what their child needed and would not cause harm, so parents must not take it for granted that their child is receiving an excellent education. It is a good idea for parents to observe in class to determine if teacher-child exchanges are of the productive variety; to observe instruction to determine whether teachers are technically proficient (e.g., communicating faultlessly, reinforcing in a timely fashion, skillfully correcting errors); and to examine data and lesson plans over time to see if their child is actually becoming more proficient and if the different phases of learning are incorporated (acquisition, fluency, generalization). These observations will provide a credible basis for any later discussions with teachers and administrators about the quality of their child's education.

CHAPTER SUMMARY

1. The challenges that autism presents to families are intensified by programs that simultaneously exhibit marginal competence while minimizing interactions with the families themselves.
2. The family stresses unique to autism can then be magnified further by the stresses of family interactions with the systems intended to treat the autism.
3. Knowledge offers the best opportunity to meet the challenges and minimize the familial stresses of working with a child with autism.
4. Parent knowledge and parent involvement are better guarantors of optimal progress than professional judgment.
5. Families need to be involved in teaching their children with autism in the home setting, but cannot be expected to assume the major portion of the burden for such instruction.
6. A model of children's psychosocial development divided into specific competency areas is a useful, if not necessary, framework for both understanding and providing intervention for the child with autism.
7. Productive exchanges that teach participants cooperation can be helpful and reduce stress for parents and children with autism and for professionals.

8. In planning and evaluating instructional interventions, it is important to be aware of the many different ways in which behavior can change.
9. Instruction and intervention for children with autism need to occur across a variety of settings besides the classroom.

REFERENCES

Albin, R. W., and Horner, R. H. 1988. Generalization with precision. In *Generalization and Maintenance: Life-style Changes in Applied Settings*, eds. R. H. Horner, G. Dunlap, and R. L. Koegel. Baltimore, MD: Paul H. Brookes Publishing Co.

Anderson, S. R., Avery, D. L., DiPietro, E. K., Edwards, G. L., and Christian, W. P. 1987. Intensive home-based early intervention with autistic children. *Education and Treatment of Children* 10:352–66.

Binder, C. 1996. Behavioral fluency: Evolution of a new paradigm. *The Behavior Analyst* 19:163–97.

Binder, C., Haughton, E., and Van Eyk, D. 1990. Precision teaching attention span. *Teaching Exceptional Children* Spring:24–7.

Binder, C., and Watkins, C. L. 1990. Precision teaching and direct instruction: Measurably superior instructional technology in schools. *Performance Improvement Quarterly* 3:74–95.

Boyle, M. H., and Offord, D. R. 1988. Prevalence of childhood disorder, perceived need for help, family dysfunction, and resource allocation for child welfare and children's mental health services in Ontario. *Canadian Journal of Behavioural Science* 20:374–88.

Brotherson, M. J., and Goldstein, B. L. 1992. Time as a resource and constraint for parents of young children with disabilities: Implications for early intervention services. *Topics in Early Childhood Special Education* 12(4):508–27.

Carr, E. G., Levin, L., McConnachie, G., Carlson, J. I., Kemp, D. C., and Smith, C. E. 1994. *Communication-based Intervention for Problem Behavior.* Baltimore, MD: Paul H. Brookes Publishing Co.

Cutler, B. C. 1991. Families and Services in Autism: Promises to Keep. Unpublished doctoral dissertation. Boston University School of Education: Boston.

Cutler, B. C., and Kozloff, M. K. 1987. Living with autism: Effects on families and family needs. In *Handbook of Autism and Pervasive Developmental Disorders*, eds. D. J. Cohen, A. Donnellan, and R. Paul. New York: John Wiley and Sons.

Dougherty, K. M., and Johnston, J. M. 1996. Overlearning, fluency, and automaticity. *The Behavior Analyst* 19:289–92.

Engelmann, S., and Carnine, D. 1991. Theory of Instruction: Principles and Applications (revised edition). Eugene, OR: ADI Press.

Engelmann, S., and Colvin, G. 1983. *Generalized Compliance Training.* Austin, TX: PRO-ED.

Fenske, E. C., Zalenski, S., Krantz, P. J., and McClannahan, L. E. 1985. Age at intervention and treatment outcome for autistic children in a comprehensive intervention program. *Analysis and Intervention in Developmental Disabilities* 7:7–31.

Fogon, J., and Schor, D. 1993. Mothers of children with spina bifida: Factors related to maternal psychosocial functioning. *American Journal of Orthopsychiatry* 63(1):146–52.

Fox, L., Dunlap, G., and Philbrick, L. A. 1997. Providing individual supports to young children with autism and their families. *Journal of Early Intervention* 21(1):1–14.

Goetz, L., and Sailor, W. 1988. New directions: Communication development in persons with severe disabilities. *Topics in Language Disorders* 8(4):41–54.

Halle, J. W., Baer, D. M., and Spradlin, J. E. 1981. An analysis of caregivers' generalized use of delay in helping children: A stimulus control procedure to increase language use in handicapped children. *Journal of Applied Behavior Analysis* 14:389–409.

Haring, N. G. 1988. *Generalization for Students with Severe Handicaps: Strategies and Solutions.* Seattle, WA: University of Washington Press.

Harris, S., Handleman, J. S., Kristoff, B., Bass, L., and Gordon, R. 1990. Changes in language development among autistic and peer children in segregated and integrated preschool settings. *Journal of Autism and Developmental Disorders* 20:23–32.

Haughton, E. C. 1980. Practicing practices: Learning by activity. *The Behavior Analyst* 1:3–20.

Hertweck, A. 1986. The language of attribution: Constructing rationales for educational placement. In *Discourse and Institutional Authority*, eds. S. Fisher and A. D. Todd. Norwood, NJ: Ablex.

Holmes, D. L. 1998. *Autism through the Lifespan: The Eden Model.* Bethesda, MD: Woodbine House.

Horner, R. H., McDonnell, J. J., and Bellamy, G. T. 1986. Teaching generalized skills: General case instruction in simulation and community settings. In *Education of Learners With Severe Handicaps: Exemplary Service Strategies*, eds. R. H. Horner, L. H. Meyer, and H. D. Fredericks. Baltimore, MD: Paul H. Brookes Publishing Co.

Howlin, P., and Rutter, M. 1987. *Treatment of Autistic Children.* Chichester, England: Wiley.

Hunt, P., and Goetz, L. 1988. Teaching spontaneous communication in natural settings through interrupted behavior chains. *Topics in Language Development* 9(1):58–71.

Johnson, K. R., and Layng, T. V. J. 1992. Breaking the structuralist barrier: Literacy and numeracy with fluency. *American Psychologist* 47:1475–90.

Johnson, K. R., and Layng, T. V. J. 1996. On terms and procedures: Fluency. *The Behavior Analyst* 19:281–88.

Jordon, J. B., and Robbins, L. S. 1971. *Let's Try Doing Something Else Kind of Thing.* Arlington, VA: Council for Exceptional Children.

Koegel, R. L., and Johnson, J. 1989. Motivating language use in autistic children. In *Autism: Nature, Diagnosis, and Treatment*, ed. G. Dawson. New York: Guilford Press.

Kozloff, M. A. 1988. *Productive Interaction With Students, Children, and Clients.* Springfield, IL: Charles C Thomas.

Kozloff, M. A. 1994a. *Improving Educational Outcomes for Children With Disabilities: Principles of Assessment, Program Planning, and Evaluation.* Baltimore, MD: Paul H. Brookes Publishing Co.

Kozloff, M. A. 1994b. *Improving Educational Outcomes for Children With Disabilities: Guidelines and Protocols for Practice.* Baltimore, MD: Paul H. Brookes Publishing Co.

Lindsley, O. R. 1990. Precision teaching: By teachers for children. *Teaching Exceptional Children* Spring:10–15.

Lindsley, O. R. 1996. Is fluency free-operant response-response chaining? *The Behavior Analyst* 19:211-24.

Lord, C., Bristol, M., and Schopler, E. 1993. Early intervention for children with autism and related developmental disorders. In *Preschool Issues in Autism*, eds. E. Schopler, M. E. Van Bourgondien, and M. M. Bristol. New York: Plenum Press.
Lovaas, O. I. 1988. Behavioral treatment and normal educational and intellectual functioning of young autistic children. *Journal of Consulting and Clinical Psychology* 55:3–9.
Maurice, C., Green, G., and Luce, S. C. 1996. *Behavioral Intervention for Young Children with Autism*. Austin, TX: PRO-ED.
Mehan, H. 1986. The role of language and the language of role in institutional decision making. In *Discourse and Institutional Authority*, eds. S. Fisher and A. D. Todd. Norwood, NJ: Ablex.
Mehan, H. 1993. Beneath the skin and between the ears: A case study in the politics of representation. In *Understanding Practice: Perspectives on Activity and Context*, eds. S. Chaiklin and J. Lave. Cambridge: Cambridge University Press.
Mundschenk, N. A., and Sasso, G. M. 1995. Assessing sufficient social exemplars for students with autism. *Behavioral Disorders* 21:62–78.
Patterson, G. R. 1982. Coercive Family Processes. Eugene, OR: Castaglia.
Plaud, J. J., and Gaither, G. A. 1996. Behavioral momentum: Implications and development from reinforcement theories. *Behavior Modification* 2:183–201.
Prizant, B. M., and Wetherby, A. M. 1993. Communication in preschool autistic children. In *Preschool Issues in Autism*, eds. E. Schopler, M. E. Van Bourgondien, and M. M. Bristol. New York: Plenum Press.
Rice, J. S. 1996. *A Disease of One's Own*. New Brunswick, NJ: Transaction.
Rogers, S. J., and DiLalla, D. L. 1991. A comparative study of the effects of a developmentally based preschool curriculum on young children with autism and young children with other disorders of behavior development. *Topics in Early Childhood Special Education* 11:29–47.
Schindler, F., and Arkowitz, H. 1986. The assessment of mother-child interactions in physically abusive and nonabusive families. *Journal of Family Violence* 1(3):247–57.
Turnbull, A. P., and Turnbull, J. A. 1990. *Families, Professionals, and Exceptionality: A Special Partnership*. Columbus, OH: Merrill.
Weiss, S. J. 1991. Stressors experienced by family caregivers of children with pervasive developmental disorders. *Child Psychiatry and Human Development* 21(3):203–16.
Zahner, G. E. P., Pawelkiewicz, J., DeFrancesco, J. J., and Adnopoz, J. 1992. Children's mental health service needs and utilization patterns in an urban community: An epidemiological assessment. *Journal of the American Academy of Child and Adolescent Psychiatry* 31:951–60.

Chapter • 14

Autism: Summary of Selected Decisions

Brooke R. Whitted

- **Students With Autism and Educational Placement**

A. *Least Restrictive Environment (LRE)*

The Individuals with Disabilities Education Act (IDEA) provides that each state must establish procedures to assure that, to the maximum extent appropriate, children with disabilities are educated with children who are not disabled, and that separate classes, separate schooling, or other removal of children with disabilities from the regular educational environment occurs only when the nature or severity of the disability is such that education in regular classes with the use of supplementary aides and services cannot be achieved satisfactorily (20 U.S.C. 1412) (a) (5) (A)).

In addition, the IDEA regulations require schools to educate children with disabilities, together with children who do not have disabilities (34 C.F.R. 300.550). According to this regulation, when selecting a placement, school authorities may only remove children with disabilities from the regular educational environment if "the nature or severity of the disability is such that education in regular classes with the use of supplemental aids and services cannot be achieved satisfactorily." (34 C. F. R. 300.550 (b) (2)). In all cases, the determination of what constitutes the LRE must be made on an individual, case-by-case basis.

A number of LRE tests have been developed by the courts to determine whether a school district has met its burden under IDEA. The three most widely applied, however, are the *Roncker* test, the *Daniel RR* test, and the *Holland* test. The *Roncker* test was devised by the sixth Circuit in *Roncker v. Walter*, 100 F.2d 1058 (6th Cir. 1983). When determining the LRE for a particular student, the *Roncker* test examines three elements:

1. Comparison of educational benefits in the restricted setting with educational benefits in a regular setting;
2. Degree to which the student will disrupt the regular classroom; and
3. Cost of the regular classroom placement.

The *Roncker* test was also adopted by the Eighth Circuit in *A.W. v. Northwest R-1 School District*, 813 F.2d 158 (8th Cir. 1987) and the Fourth Circuit in *DeVries v. Fairfax County School Board*, 882 F.2d 876 (4th Cir. 1989). The second LRE test was devised by the Fifth Circuit in *Daniel RR v. State Board of Education*, 874 F.2d 1036 (5th Cir. 1989), and was also adopted by the Third and Eleventh Circuits. *Daniel RR* starts its LRE inquiry by examining whether the school district has "taken steps to accommodate the handicapped child in regular education." Because the IDEA requires school districts to provide supplementary aids and services, and to modify the mainstream program when they mainstream children with disabilities, the question of whether education in a regular classroom with the use of supplemental aids and services is appropriate for a given child, under *Daniel RR*, involves the following three-part inquiry:

1. Will the child receive an educational benefit, both non-academic and academic, from the regular education placement?
2. What is the child's overall educational experience in the mainstreamed environment, balancing the benefits of regular and special education?
3. What effect does the special education child's presence have on the regular classroom environment and the education that the other students are receiving?

Finally, the Ninth Circuit developed a hybrid of the *Roncker* and *Daniel RR* tests in the *Holland* case. *Sacramento v. Rachel Holland.*, 14 F.3d 1398, 1404 (9th Cir. 1994). The *Holland* test, essentially a balancing test, examines four elements:

1. The educational benefits of full time regular education;
2. Non-academic benefits;
3. The effect of the child on the teacher and the children; and
4. The costs of mainstreaming the child.

By endorsing such tests, the circuit courts have emphasized that the LRE requirement of IDEA creates a presumption in favor of educating children with disabilities alongside their mainstream peers. In response, the notion of full inclusion for students with disabilities, including those with autism, has become a fundamental feature of many special education reform initiatives, even though the term full inclusion does not appear anywhere in IDEA. Although many believe that full inclusion is the next logical step in securing appropriate and legally required services for children and youth with disabilities, others disagree. Kauffman and Hallahan described full inclusion as "special education's largest bandwagon ever, one having gathered such great mass and momentum that it seems to many unstoppable." Simpson, Richard L. 1995. Children and youth with autism in an age of reform: A perspective on current issues. *Behavioral Disorders* 21(1):7-20, citing Kauffman, J. M., and Hallahan, D. P. 1994. *The Illusion of Full Inclusion*, Preface. Austin, TX: PRO-ED.

While recent case law has generally *supported* inclusive placements for students with disabilities, (e.g. *Board of Education, Sacramento City Unified School District v. Holland*, 1992; *Greer v. Rome City School District*, 1991; *Oberti v. Board of Education*, 1992), a contradictory trend appears to be unfolding concerning students with autism. Courts across the country have upheld more restrictive placements for students with autism. Boomer, L. W. 1995. Legal issues concerning children with autism and pervasive developmental disabilities. *Behavioral Disorders* 21(1):53-61. See also *Oberti v. Board of Education: A Rational View* by Whitted and Davis, *Clearinghouse Review*, July-August, 1997, p.132.

B. *Case Law*

1. **More Restrictive Placement Upheld**

a. *Residential Placement Upheld as LRE for Student with Autism*

(1) ***In re Drew P. v. Clarke County School District***, 877 F.2d 927 (11th Cir. 1989).

(a) *Facts:* Drew P., a sixteen-year-old student in Georgia, was diagnosed at an early age as both autistic and severely mentally retarded. As Drew matured, his behaviors became increasingly aggressive at home and school. In 1985, Drew's parents placed him at Parkwood, a residential center for students with mental retardation. While at Parkwood, an evaluation was conducted, which determined that Drew required placement in a residential center with facilities for students with autism. Drew's local school district, however, also conducted an evaluation and determined that a residential placement was unnecessary. After the local school district refused to pay for the proposed residential placement, Drew's parents requested an administrative review. The hearing officer determined that Drew did not require residential placement in a facility for autistic children. On appeal, the state hearing officer sustained the regional officer's holding. Following this decision, Drew's parents filed suit in federal court.

(b) While the federal suit was pending, Drew's placement was changed to a residential center for autistic children in Tokyo, Japan, and later changed again to another residential school in Boston. In 1987, the federal district court determined that Drew's educational needs could not be met by the programs available in the Georgia school district. Furthermore, it held that the school district must provide a residential placement for Drew at a center specializing in autism until his 21st birthday. It also awarded Drew's parents partial reimbursement for the autistic school placement, but denied reimbursement for Drew's original placement at Parkwood. The school district appealed this decision.

(c) *Held:* **Affirmed, for the parents. The 10th circuit, using the preponderance of the evidence**

standard, determined that the evidence presented at the district court level properly concluded that a residential treatment center for autistic children was necessary in order for Drew to receive an educational benefit.

(d) *Reasoning:* The appeals court rejected the school district's argument that a placement at his home school was sufficient to provide Drew with an appropriate education. The court found that the parents' expert overwhelmingly proved that residential placement was necessary for Drew to receive any educational benefit, because Drew must be educated by teachers specially trained in working with autistic children. **The court also held that the evidence at trial demonstrated that autistic children require "constant, round the clock, expert educational supervision in order to progress."**

(2) ***Ash v. Lake Oswego School District,*** No. 7J, 980 F.2d 585 (9th Cir. 1992).

(a) *Facts:* In *Ash*, the parents of Christopher Ash, a 10-year-old child with autism, unilaterally placed him in a private residential setting.[1] Christopher's parents subsequently demanded reimbursement from the school, even before they asked the district to evaluate him and develop an IEP. Relying on the psychiatrist's recommendation, the Ashes chose to place Christopher at the residential facility because his behavior had begun to severely deteriorate, with severe tantrums occurring on a daily basis. Christopher attended this placement for 4 years before his parents requested an evaluation from the district. When the school district denied residential reimbursement as too restrictive, the parents filed for due process.

[1]*Under the newly amended IDEA, parents lose their right to seek retroactive reimbursement if they fail to notify the district at least 10 days in advance of their intention to place children privately and seek funding.*

(b) The hearing officer found the district's IEP to be appropriate, and noted that even though Christopher could maintain better harmony with his family through the residential placement, he did not require the placement to provide him with educational benefit. The hearing officer also reasoned that autistic children do not require residential placements unless they present a physical threat to themselves or others, and Christopher did not in this case. Based on this finding, Christopher's parents sought relief in federal court.

(c) The federal district court reversed the hearing officer's decision and supported the parents as to reimbursement at the time of the IEP, but not before that time. In determining whether residential placement was necessary, the court found that the focus must be on whether the placement is required for educational purposes apart from the medical, social, or emotional problems that are severable from learning. Both parties appealed this decision. The school district appealed the award of residential placement and the parents appealed the denial of residential reimbursement for the time before an IEP was developed.

(d) ***Held:* Affirmed, Christopher was not capable of deriving educational benefit without a residential placement.**

(e) *Reasoning:* The 9th circuit rejected the school district's assertion that the district judge lost sight of the "educational benefit" when assessing the sufficiency of the IEP for Christopher and, instead, measured the IEP in terms of whether Christopher would be successful outside of a classroom setting. The 10th circuit determined that the district court did examine whether Christopher would derive an educational benefit, and came to the conclusion that the school district could not demonstrate that their IEP would provide the type and amount of consistency necessary for Christopher to obtain some educational benefit from its implementation.

(f) One of the reasons the court supported the residential placement is that it believed the school district's IEP did not adequately address daily living skills, such as toilet training, eating, and dressing, and determined that even if these skills were taught, they would be better learned in a residential setting.[2]

b. *Segregated Program Determined LRE for Student With Autism*

(1) ***Student v. Somerset County Board,*** 24 IDELR 743(D. Md. 1996).

(a) *Facts:* The district proposed to place a 10-year-old with severe autism and mental retardation at Sarah Peyton School, a school 50 miles from the student's home. The student is among the 10 to 15% most severely autistic children. He has a mental age of under 2 years for most functions, and is at a language age of 10 months. In addition, he requires constant supervision for behavior and is not toilet trained. Sarah Peyton School has a staff/student ratio of 3:11, with 5 students per class. It is also attached to a regular school and would provide the student with some interaction opportunities. The student's parents opposed this placement, arguing for a regular class placement at the student's neighborhood school, with supplemental aids and services. After losing at due process, the parents appealed to the district court.

[2]*Now, IDEA's purpose has been slightly elevated - at 20 U.S. 1400(c)(5)(E)(ii), part of its goal should be to prepare students to lead "independent adult lives to the* maximum *extent possible (emphasis added), "and at §1400(d)(1)(A), to prepare students for employment and independent living.*

(b) ***Held:*** **For the district. The court upheld the IEP team's recommendation of continued placement at Peyton.**

(c) *Reasoning:* Although the parents argued that the IEP team had "automatically" recommended placement at Peyton based upon the level of services the student needed, the court found otherwise. Following the analysis of *Roncker v. Walker* (infra.), the court determined: 1) Without considering the supplementary aids and services that can be implemented at the neighborhood school, Peyton provided an education superior to full inclusion at the neighborhood school. 2) The services that make Peyton superior cannot feasibly be provided at the neighborhood school. The regular class would be a 4th grade class and there was no indication that the student would benefit in any way from being treated as a regular student in a regular classroom. There would be no attempt to teach the student the regular fourth grade curriculum, and because of his distractibility, he could not be educated in a large group. He would require a full-time aide and would have to be placed in a section of the classroom where he would receive full-time instruction from the aide. Peyton offers substantial benefits to the student because of its structure and smaller class size. 3) The placement at Peyton, with daily interaction with non-disabled students for activities such as lunch, P.E., and assemblies is the appropriate placement.

(2) ***DeVries v. Fairfax County School Board*** 882 F.2d 876 (4th Cir. 1989).

(a) *Facts:* The mother of Michael DeVries, a 17-year-old boy with autism contested the district's proposed placement in a vocational center 13 miles from his home, because she wanted him educated in the local public high school. Michael had depressed cognitive functioning, exhibited immature behavior, and needed a predictable environment. Both the due process hearing officer and district court judge found that Michael was properly placed at the vocational center. The mother appealed this decision to the 4th appellate circuit, arguing that Michael's IEP did not provide the appropriate public education he is entitled to receive and that the district court failed to consider IDEA's mainstreaming component.

(b) ***Held:*** **For the District. Although DeVries has a desire to be placed at the local high school, the facts do not demonstrate that he would receive an "appropriate public education" at that institution.**

(c) *Reasoning:* The court of appeals noted that they were fully persuaded the district court correctly concluded that Michael could not be satisfactorily educated in regular classes, even with the use of supplementary aids and services. The disparity was so great between the cognitive levels of the 17-year-old student and his non-disabled peers that the court was concerned that the student would be simply "monitoring" the regular class.

2. **Less Restrictive Placement Upheld**

a. *Residential Placement* Rejected in *Favor of Private Day Placement; Child Properly Identified as Neurologically Impaired, Not Autistic*

(1) ***Schreiber v. Ridgewood Board of Education,*** 25 IDELR 421 (D. N.J. 1997).

(a) *Facts:* R. S. was an emotionally disabled child who began exhibiting emotional problems in the first grade. Although R. S.'s parents initially rejected a special education evaluation from the school district, they agreed to the evaluation three years after it was originally proposed. The school district's child study team examined R. S. and determined she was classified as neurologically impaired (NI). After this evaluation, R. S. was educated in a regular classroom for two years. At the beginning of the 1994-1995 school year, R. S.'s parents requested that she be identified as autistic and placed in a residential program. However, the school district proposed a private day program instead. R. S.'s parents requested a due process hearing to determine her appropriate placement.

(b) The hearing officer found that the weight of the evidence indicated that R. S. had been properly identified as NI, not autistic, and did not require residential treatment. The school district's experts proved that while R. S. did exhibit some autistic-like behaviors, she had an ability to think and express herself coherently—not a common characteristic of children with autism. The parents' own expert admitted that while R. S. required an intensive program, such treatment was available in settings other than a residential program. The parents appealed this decision to a federal district court.

(c) *Held:* **For the district. The parents failed to prove by a preponderance of the evidence that R. S. is autistic or that a residential placement was appropriate.**

(d) *Reasoning:* The court, while expressing sympathy for the parents' dilemma in finding the ideal surroundings for R. S., could not accept the argument that R. S. was autistic and required residential care. The court stated, "The Court appreciates the concerns of R. S.'s parents and their desire to provide her with the best opportunities available. Their search for the most beneficial program for R. S. will most likely be never-ending. The hard work of parents of a disabled child is never done.

After careful evaluation of the evidence, however, the court concludes that plaintiffs have failed to show by a preponderance of the evidence that R. S. is autistic or that residential placement is required." The court also noted that they have given great deference to the findings of the administrative judge, as is required by the statutory standard, and found from the testimony that the parents only presented two doctors who found R. S. as autistic, while the district had four doctors who diagnosed her as NI.

b. *Parents' Request For Residential Placement Denied, Hearing Officer Supports Less Restrictive Placement At a District High School*

(1) ***In re: Scott M.,*** 24 IDELR 1229 (SEA N. H. 1996).

(a) *Facts*: Scott M. was a 17-year-old student with multiple disabilities, including severe mental retardation, minimal speech, a seizure disorder, and cerebral palsy. His parents challenged the district's IEP which called for four hours a day of regular education with modifications and a one-to-one aide, 10 hours a week of special education classes and prevocational work settings, speech therapy, occupational therapy, and physical therapy. Scott's parents requested a residential placement that focused on language development and challenged the district's classification, arguing that autism should be added to the current classification.

(b) *Held:* **For the district. Although Scott did display some "autistic-like behaviors," his classification was properly designated as mental retardation. Furthermore, the hearing officer found that the district's IEP was appropriate for Scott's educational needs.**

(c) *Reasoning:* The hearing officer seemed to concentrate his examination of the facts on the various experts each of the parties presented at the hearing. The parents' expert, an advocate for children with disabilities, argued that Scott should be labeled as autistic and, therefore, required a residential program that focused on his language needs. On the other hand, the district's experts, both trained professionals in the field of autism, argued that while Scott's profile was consistent with a diagnosis of PDD/Autism, these features were also consistent with severe mental retardation. Moreover, **whatever "label" attaches to Scott should not dictate educational programming.** The hearing officer found the district's experts to be much more credible than the parents' and determined that the district demonstrated Scott's primary disability should be mental retardation. Finally, the hearing officer examined Scott's progress in his public school and found that the district "has amply demonstrated its unfailing commitment to providing an appropriate education to this youngster which is functional in nature, appropriate to his level of development, and clearly focused on the transition from the world of school to post high-school, including community living.

c. *Self Contained Classroom Too Restrictive, Regular Classroom Placement Upheld*

(1) ***Hartman v. Loudoun County Board of Education***, 24 IDELR 1171 (E.D. Va. 1996).

(a) *Facts:* The parents of Mark, an 11-year-old non-verbal student with autism, contested the school district's decision to change his educational placement from the regular classroom to a self-contained classroom for autistic students. The parents argued that the regular classroom would expose him to a full range of academic subjects and allow him to be educated with non-disabled peers. The district's self-contained placement was upheld in due process. The hearing officer applied the LRE test from *Daniel RR* and determined that the self-contained classroom was the appropriate placement because it was located in a regular education school and would provide mainstreaming opportunities, while offering Mark academic instruction and related services from which he could benefit.

(b) *Held:* **For the parents. The district court reversed the decision of the hearing officer, finding that while the LRE test from *Daniel RR* was the proper analysis, the outcome of the case at due process was improper because the evidence supported the conclusion that Mark could derive educational benefit in a regular education classroom with supplementary aids and services.**

(c) *Reasoning:* The court looked at the supplementary aids and services that could be delivered in the regular classroom, specifically, a one-to-one aide and a "properly adapted" curriculum, as well as the district's inadequate attempts to accommodate Mark in the mainstream. Such failed attempts included insufficient staff training, lack of individuals experienced with autism on the student's IEP team, and failure to follow the advice of those individuals who were properly trained. Personnel changes and the discontinuation of supplementary consulting services by inclusion experts were cited by the court as indications that the district's inclusion efforts decreased during the time Mark was included in the regular classroom. Additional evidence was presented that Mark was not mentally retarded; rather his disability primarily affected his ability to communicate. Sufficient weight was given to testimony by Mark's private tutor that Mark was capable of educational progress.

C. *Analysis and Discussion of Trends*

1. While there appears to be a trend toward more inclusive placements for most students with disabilities, the opposite seems to hold true for students with autism. Whether it is a child's parents or the school district advocating for a less restrictive placement, the courts tend to find in favor of more restrictive settings. An exception is found in cases such as re: *Scott M.* and *Schreiber v. Ridgewood Board of Education*, where autism eligibility was rejected and the school district was found to provide a comprehensive IEP; or *Hartman v. Loudoun County Board of Education*, where the court focused on the school district's inadequate and insufficient attempts at inclusion.

2. As Richard Simpson points out in his article cited on page 335, one can only guess at the reasoning for such a paradox regarding autism and the LRE requirement. Simpson theorizes that autism is viewed as an enigma. Children with autism exhibit unique characteristics that often set them apart from their peers with special needs, and it is perceived by many parents and professionals as so unique that students with autism should receive completely separate specialized interventions and placements.

   In analyzing the case law dealing with placements for children with autism, it becomes apparent that the courts may also see autism as an enigma. This would explain the difference in LRE decisions for children with autism.

- **<u>Specific Educational Methods</u>**

D. *Introduction*

1. The selection of specific educational methods has traditionally been an area in which the courts will give much deference to the judgment of state and local public education officials. The leading case in this area is *Lachman v. Illinois State Board of Education*, 852 F.2d 290 (7th Cir. 1988). The *Lachman* court articulated a position regarding the provision of a method based on the concept of a free and appropriate public education (FAPE) analysis set out in *Board of Education v. Rowley*, 458 U.S. 176 (1982). Based

on *Rowley*, the *Lachman* court held that as long as a school district is providing a procedurally and substantively correct IEP, parents do not have a right to compel school districts to provide a specific method. The *Lachman* court emphasized the high degree of deference that is properly due to the educational policy judgments of state and local public education officials.

2. However, even in the light of the *Lachman* decision, the 1990s have witnessed an influx of cases where the main issue concerns the selection of educational methods. "Parents who have discovered a 'cure' for their child's disability are demanding specific, often expensive, programs which are not normally available or utilized in public school districts." Weatherly, Charles L. and Melinda H. Maloney, Burgeoning Issues in Special Education, *School Law in Review* 1997, 10(6). As the following cases illustrate, parents of children with autism have been quite successful in persuading the courts to accept their choice of educational method over the school district's. These decisions are not inconsistent with *Lachman*, but rather find that the school district has failed in its responsibility to provide appropriate services. This failure, in effect, opens the door for the parents to propose their own choice of appropriate method, and for them to be reimbursed retroactively.

E. *Provision of Specific Educational Method Upheld By Court*

1. ***Highbridge Board of Education***, 24 IDELR 589 (SEA 1995). (Lovaas)

a. *Facts:* The parents of J. S., a 5-year-old child with autism, sought reimbursement for expenses associated with an in-home Lovaas training program, the Bancroft School Young Autism Project, and the continuation of this training with a view towards eventual mainstreaming. The school district had previously provided J. S. with a placement that implemented the Lovaas technique for 10 hours daily at a private school for children with autism. However, J. S.'s parents supplemented the district's placement with 30 hours of home-based Lovaas training. When the private placement was no longer available, the district proposed a kindergarten placement in a regular classroom, with a full-time trained special education teacher as his personal aide, and a few hours of Lovaas home instruction. J. S.'s parents felt that J. S., who engaged in severe self-injurious and aggressive behavior, required intensive home-based Lovaas training in order to benefit from special education.

b. *Holding:* **For the parents. The administrative law judge determined that the least restrictive environment, where J. S. could obtain a free and appropriate education offering some educational benefit, is at home with Bancroft-program instruction.**

c. *Reasoning:* The judge determined that the district had not shown that J. S. has been able to generalize the information learned at school to his home environment. Therefore, J. S. was far from prepared for the "disorienting" experience of a regular classroom, even with the assistance of a full-time special education teacher. Furthermore, mainstreaming, while a notable goal, should be explored "gingerly," without harming J. S.'s progress in the home program. The home instruction itself should be 7 days a week, 10 hours a day, through the intensive structured, Lovaas method provided by the Bancroft program.

2. ***Delaware County Intermediate Unit #25 v. Martin and Melinda K.***, 831 F. Supp. 1206 (E. D. Penn. 1993). (Lovaas)

   a. *Facts:* Paul, a 2-year-old boy diagnosed with PDD, was enrolled at a private special needs center by the county mental health and mental retardation agency. When Paul turned 3 years old, the educational costs became the responsibility of the local educational agency (LEA). The agency proposed continuing Paul's placement at the special needs center with partial funding provided by the school district. At this time, however, Paul's parents became interested in obtaining Lovaas-based training, and withdrew him from the special-needs program in order to educate Paul through the Lovaas program.

   b. When the educational agencies failed to develop an IEP more than halfway through the school year,

Paul's parents requested a due process hearing, seeking approval of the placement they had selected. Soon thereafter, the agencies proposed a placement at another special-needs center, based on the principles of the Treatment and Education of Autistic and Related Communication, Handicapped Children (TEACCH) program. Paul's parents rejected this placement and obtained a due process hearing.

c. The hearing officer ruled in favor of the district, finding that the proposed placement in the TEACCH program was appropriate, but did award the parents compensatory education for the delay in preparing the IEP. The parents appealed this decision.

d. ***Holding:*** **For the parents. The educational agencies failed to offer Paul an appropriate placement; therefore, Paul was entitled to Lovaas training at public expense.**

e. *Reasoning:* The court found many inadequacies with the proposed placement for Paul, including not enough time in the TEACCH program, failure to develop a timely, adequate IEP, and failure to identify a satisfactory mainstreaming component. The court also determined that Paul would "suffer significant regression if removed from the Lovaas program at this point." Therefore, the proposed educational program was not reasonably calculated to provide an appropriate education for Paul.

3. ***Capistrano Unified School District***, 23 IDELR 1209 (SEA CA. 1995) (Lovaas)

   a. *Facts:* A 4-year-old student with autism and developmental delays in language, motor, cognitive, and social skills was placed, by the school district, in a special day class for children with severe disabilities. Although the student's parents initially agreed to the placement, they contested the school district's refusal to include behavioral therapy in the student's IEP. The student had begun to receive private, outside, one-to-one, Lovaas behavior modification therapy, at the parents' expense, and was making progress.

Eventually, the parents began to find fault with the education the student was receiving as well, claiming that the program was too challenging and did not provide the student with educational benefit. Finally, the parents requested a due process hearing, arguing that the student required the one-to-one Lovaas behavior therapy in order for him to benefit from his education. The parents further asserted that they were entitled to reimbursement for the costs they incurred for the private Lovaas behavior therapy.

b. ***Held:*** **For the parents. The school district was ordered to reimburse the parents for the cost of the therapy and to provide 25 hours of one-to-one, *in-home therapy* per week to the student throughout the school year.**

c. *Reasoning:* First, the hearing officer rejected the school district's argument that the student did not exhibit autistic-like behaviors, and, therefore, did not require behavioral therapy. The hearing officer determined from the evidence presented that the student did exhibit autistic-like behaviors, and that these behaviors must be taken into account in determining his unique and individual needs. Next, after examining his individual needs, the officer found that the student required one-to-one instruction in a structured environment, extensive language therapy, and instruction in social skills. Given these needs, the officer concluded that the district's placement was entirely inappropriate. All of the children in the class received the same level of instruction, regardless of their needs, and this level exceeded the student's abilities. Furthermore, the program lacked one-to-one instruction and appropriate instruction in language skills. In contrast, the officer determined that the student was receiving educational benefit from his appropriate, in-home Lovaas therapy, and this program was designed to meet his unique and individual needs. Finally, the hearing officer found that, since the district was not able to provide an appropriate program from which the student could derive educational benefit, the parents were entitled to the Lovaas therapy they requested.

4. ***T. H. v. Board of Education of Palatine Community Consolidated School Distict 15***, 55 F. Supp.2d 830, 137 Ed.Law Rep. 555 (N.D.Ill. 1999) (Lovaas)

   a. *Facts:* The parents of T. H., a five-year-old child with autism, filed an action in federal district court to enforce two administrative hearing decisions requiring the school district to pay for the child's home-based Lovaas program. The dispute involved the district's initial placement recommendation following T. H.'s initial case study evaluation in 1997. Although both parents and the school district agreed that T. H. was eligible for special education as a child with autism, and agreed on his IEP goals, the two parties disputed placement. The district proposed its "early childhood program," which consisted of attendance in a cross categorical classroom for 2.5 hours per day, four days a week. This classroom time was to include 90 minutes per week (mpw) of speech and language therapy, 60 mpw of social work services, and 60 mpw of occupational therapy. The parents rejected this placement and requested that the district consider an intensive ABA/DTT Lovaas program that T. H. was already receiving at private cost for 35 to 40 hours per week. Th district rejected this request and the parties went to two levels of due process hearings, with the parent prevailing at both levels. Notably, the Level I hearing officer concluded, and the Level II officer agreed, that the district's program was inadequate since it was not based on the recommendations of autism experts who testified on behalf of T. H. at the hearings. The district appealed to federal court.

   b. *Holding:* **For the parents. The district court held that the school district's IEP violated the IDEA; that the parent's placement of T. H. in the home-based Lovaas program was reasonably calculated to enable T. H. to receive educational benefits; and the parents were entitled to full reimbursement associated with the costs of the Lovaas program as well as their attorneys' fees for both due process hearings and the present district court action.**

   c. *Reasoning:* In a lengthy opinion, the court reviewed the extensive hearing evidence regarding both T. H.'s "unique needs and capacities" as a child with autism, as well as the evidence regarding the inappropriateness of the district's proposed placement. The court determined that the IEP process had been dysfunctional, that the IEP was not individualized to meet T. H.'s needs, and that the proposed program would not provide T. H. with an educational benefit. Moreover, the court rejected the district's assertion that a school district has the right, pursuant to the Lachman decision, to dictate educational methods. The court determined that Lachman was "irrelevant" in situations such as this where the school district's IEP was not "substantially appropriate."

- **Related Issues Dealing With Students With Autism**

F. *Specific Staff Requirements*

1. **Staff Training Not a Related Service Under IDEA**

a. ***Sioux Falls School District v. Koupal***, 526 N.W. 2d. 248 (S.D. 1994)

(1) *Facts:* The mother of Brett Koupal, a 6-year-old boy with severe autism, appealed the circuit court's judgement rejecting her IDEA challenge of the school district's refusal to include specific teacher training in her child's IEP. Brett received special education from the Sioux Falls School District, which included instruction through the TEACCH method, a program specifically designed for children with autism. In both of Brett's past IEPs, his mother attached typed pages identified as "Other Related Services," establishing a requirement that any teacher working with Brett receive comprehensive training in the TEACCH method. In the summer following his second year in school, Brett's mother became aware that his summer school teacher had not received TEACCH instruction. Although the school district did subsequently arrange for this teacher to receive TEACCH training, they also announced their intent to exclude from Brett's IEP language specifically requiring the TEACCH course for his teachers.

(2) At the hearing initiated by Brett's mother, the hearing officer determined that teacher training could be included in an IEP as a related service, and it was inappropriate for the school district to remove the requirement from Brett's current IEP. The school district appealed, and, on independent review, the circuit court reversed the decision. Brett's mother appealed to the South Dakota Supreme Court asserting that the district court erred in holding that specific teacher training could not be mandated in Brett's IEP as a related service, and in finding immaterial the teacher training language in the two previous IEPs. The mother also appealed the denial of attorney's fees.

(3) *Holding:* **The South Dakota Supreme Court affirmed the decision of the circuit court based upon an examination of IDEA's definition of related services. The court acknowledged that under IDEA an IEP must meet the child's identified special education and related services needs.** ***However, upon close examination of what constitutes a related service, it determined that the definition does not include teacher training.***

(4) *Reasoning:* The court reasoned that while the list of services identified as related services may not be all inclusive, the scope of the listed services clearly fails to encompass specific teacher training. Therefore, because teacher training is not a related service under federal law, it cannot be required in an IEP. Addressing the mother's argument that inadequately trained teachers may deprive her disabled son of a chance for maximum progress, the court noted that although providing capable teachers may be implicit in IDEA, Congress left teacher competency in the control of school administrators. Next, the court determined that the district court did not err in finding the contents of the prior IEPs irrelevant in determining what should be included in his present IEP. The court stated that it could find no requirement in

IDEA which binds school authorities or parents indefinitely to the terms of an IEP.

2. **Teacher Assistant Not Required To Have Specific Training In Particular Type Of Behavior Management**

   a. ***Conejo Valley Unified School District***, 23 IDELR 1081 (SEA 1995) (Lovaas Training Rejection)

      (1) *Facts:* A 7-year-old student diagnosed with autism was mainstreamed into a regular first-grade class with the assistance of a full-time instructional assistant. A daily communication journal shared between school and home detailed numerous incidents of the student's misbehaving at school, including incidents of pinching and hitting other students, spitting, and throwing objects. The student's parents noted that the student ceased exhibiting such behaviors at home when the family began intensive Lovaas training with him. They subsequently requested a due process hearing to determine whether the student's current instructional assistant required training in Lovaas behavior management in order to meet the student's needs.

      (2) ***Held:* For the district.**

      (3) *Reasoning:* While the student's assistant must have knowledge of autism, appropriate and inappropriate behavior, and appropriate behavioral modification techniques, she was not required to obtain training in a particular type of behavioral management. The district provided evidence that the student's current instructional assistant had been sufficiently trained to work with him. Furthermore, the district also provided evidence from the student's teachers that his behavior had improved and he had made progress since entering the first grade class. Therefore, the hearing officer concluded that the instructional assistant had sufficient training to meet the student's needs.

G. *Facilitated Communication*

1. **School District Ordered To Investigate Facilitated Communication Techniques For Student With Autism**

a. ***LeMars Community School District***, 19 IDELR 284 (SEA 1992)

(1) *Facts:* Andy, a 16-year-old boy diagnosed with autism, was first identified as in need of special education at the age of 3, and began receiving services in a self-contained classroom. In 1992, Andy's parents began to find dissatisfaction with the services Andy was receiving from the LeMars School District. In addition to concerns that Andy's IEP did not afford him appropriate integration opportunities, his parents also argued that the school should implement facilitated communication strategies in order for Andy to fully benefit from the integration experiences he was receiving. When the district refused, the parents requested due process.

(2) *Held:* **For the parents, in part. The hearing officer found that Andy's current placement was appropriate, but ordered the district to incorporate facilitated communication strategies into Andy's program.**

(3) *Reasoning:* The hearing officer closely examined the benefits of providing facilitated communication to Andy. He noted that Andy had been evaluated regarding the potential for benefiting from facilitated communication in 1992, and it was determined that this strategy had potential for adding to Andy's ability to communicate. Furthermore, the officer found that the equipment needed for facilitated communication would probably qualify under the category of assistive technology, and, thus, must be evaluated on a case-by-case basis.

2. **School District Not Obligated To Accept Independent Education Evaluation (IEE) Conducted Using Facilitated Communication**

a. ***Jackson Public Schools***, 23 IDELR 756 (SEA 1995)

(1) *Facts:* John, a 13-year-old boy with autism began receiving special education services at the age of 3. At the start of his fifth grade year, John was placed in a regular elementary school, with his time divided between a regular fifth grade classroom and a self-contained special education classroom. John had the support of a teaching assistant in the regular grade placements and had used facilitated communication. During this year, the school district conducted two diagnostic evaluations, placing John's functioning in the moderately retarded range. The evaluations also determined that John's academic performance, self-help skills, language skills, and social skills were at the pre-school level. Dissatisfied with these results, John's parents obtained an independent education evaluation (IEE). While the school district's evaluation was based partially on facilitated communication, the IEE was based entirely on facilitated communication. The IEE concluded that John was functioning in the range of normal intelligence with academic skills in reading and arithmetic appropriate for his age. Disagreeing with the district's evaluation, in light of their IEE, the parents requested due process.

(2) *Held:* **For the District. The school district's evaluations accurately identified John as mentally retarded and functioning at a pre-school level, even with facilitation.**

(3) *Reasoning:* The hearing officer found that the only indication of cognitive functioning above the mentally retarded level was the IEE obtained by the parents. All other psychological testing, from the past and present, placed John in the mentally retarded range. The hearing officer did acknowledge the amount of controversy regarding facilitated communication, and noted that its validity was supported based on the source. The officer then concluded that federal and state law mandated the use of a variety of sources, and that, in

this situation, the school district's determination was based on overwhelming evidence from multiple sources. This was in sharp contrast to the parents' IEE, based on only a single test. Furthermore, the IEE evaluator both administered the test and facilitated the responses, possibly creating evaluator bias.

H. *Specific Behavior Interventions*

1. **Use of Time-out Room Appropriate For Student With Autism**

a. ***Boerne Independent School District***, 25 IDELR 102 (SEA 1996)

(1) *Facts:* Lauren was a 13-year-old girl who received special education, as a mentally retarded, speech-impaired, and autistic child in a self-contained classroom. Lauren's seventh grade IEP included a behavior management plan that called for the use of time-out procedures, including the use of a time-out room. The time-out room used for Lauren was immediately adjacent to her classroom. A teacher or teacher's aide was stationed at the door leading in and out of the time-out room, and any student placed in the room was always visible from a window in each of the doors. Only 5 days into her seventh grade school year, Lauren's parents withdrew her from school after Lauren injured herself while trying to climb out a window in the time-out room. At a due process hearing regarding this issue, Lauren's parents argued that the use of the time-out room was inappropriate and unsafe, and, therefore, Lauren's behavior management plan was inappropriate.

(2) ***Held:*** **For the district. The hearing officer determined that the behavior management plan incorporated into Lauren's IEP, which included the use of these time-out procedures, was appropriate.**

(3) *Reasoning:* The hearing officer noted that the evidence did not support the parents' contentions

that the use of the time-out room was entirely inappropriate for Lauren. The evidence presented at the hearing demonstrated that the behavior management plan was working in the few short days that Lauren attended school. Therefore, Lauren's parents failed to meet the burden of proof to demonstrate that the implementation of Lauren's IEP by the district was inappropriate or that procedural violations occurred.

2. **Use Of Blanket Wrapping Technique Upheld**

a. ***Heidemann v. Rother***, 84 F.3d 1021 (8th Cir. 1996)

(1) *Facts:* Cherry Heidemann was a 9-year-old nonverbal, mentally, and physically disabled girl at the time of this action. Cherry's disabilities included severe mental retardation, visual and hearing impediments, epilepsy, and learning disabilities. At times, Cherry's teachers would utilize a behavior management technique known as "blanket wrapping" on Cherry. Blanket wrapping involved binding her body with a blanket in order to immobilize Cherry's arms, legs, and hands. This technique was recommended by the school's physical therapist in order to provide Cherry with "security and comfort," and because the use of this treatment would also provide her with "warmth and stability and would have a calming effect on her." In 1993, Cherry's parents withdrew her from school due to the use of blanket wrapping, and subsequently filed a 1983 claim against the school district, its employees, board members, and the physical therapist who recommended the technique. Cherry's parents argued that the blanket wrapping technique was used as a means of physical restraint. They alleged that Cherry was "wrapped against her will for periods of one and a half hours or more," and that on the day prior to her withdrawal from school, Mrs. Heidemann allegedly found Cherry "blanket wrapped on the floor, with flies crawling in and around her mouth and nose." Although the Heidemanns had initially approved the use of the blanket wrapping,

they argued that they were unaware it was being used in this manner.

(2) ***Holding:*** **The circuit court held for the school district.**

(3) *Reasoning:* First, the court found that the blanket wrapping technique was not an unreasonable bodily restraint that violated Cherry's constitutional rights. Next, the court found that even if the technique was a "substantial departure" from professional norms, which the court determined it was not, the district employees would not have known so, and, therefore, would have qualified immunity. Similarly, the parents could not maintain a Rehabilitation Act claim because the defendants "did not depart grossly from acceptable standards among qualified professionals." Finally, the parents could not maintain an IDEA claim, because they were seeking monetary damages, and under IDEA the prevailing party is precluded from receiving monetary damages. Thus, the circuit court found that the defendants were entitled to qualified immunity on all of the parents' claims.

3. **Use Of Aversive Stimulation**

a. *Possible Use Of Aversive Stimulation Endorsed by Hearing Officer*

(1) ***Phelan v. Bell,*** 8 F.3d 369 (6th Cir. 1993)

(a) *Facts:* The mother of Terry Phelan, a severely disabled 18-year-old boy, brought an action under IDEA to contest the school district's refusal to use a controversial form of electric shock therapy to control Terry's behavior.

(b) Terry Phelan engages in severe Self-Injurious Behavior (SIB), by striking his head up to 120 times per minute. In 1989, Terry's mother, frustrated that the school district was not sufficiently addressing Terry's SIB, began to investigate alternative methods to control the SIB. Eventually, she discovered the Self-Injurious Behavior Inhibiting System (SIBIS), an electronic device that straps to the head and generates a mild, brief electrical shock in response to each instance of SIB. At Terry's IEP meeting, after the school district proposed an IEP that would have continued the use of prior ineffective programs, Terry's mother proposed the use of SIBIS. After the school district refused to consider SIBIS, Terry's mother brought this IDEA action.

(c) Although the administrative hearing officer did not order the school district to use the SIBIS program on Terry, the officer did find that its use would not violate state or federal law, and added that the device should only be used after "all reasonable alternatives had failed." Later that year, Terry's mother filed a motion for attorney's fees under IDEA. The district court granted her motion, but awarded her only 25% of the fees, finding that she only prevailed on one of the four issues presented at the hearing. Both parties now appeal the award of attorneys' fees.

(d) *Held:* **For the parent. The court held that as the prevailing party at the hearing, she is entitled to 100% of attorney's fees.**

(e) *Reasoning:* Upon examination of the outcome of the hearing, the court determined that the parent's action resulted in a marked change in the legal relationship between the parties in a number of ways. First, the parent succeeded in obtaining a determination that SIBIS was a viable option for Terry, both legally and in actuality. Although the SIBIS is not presently "required" for Terry, it is one of the options that should be considered. Second, the parent's persistence brought about a definite change in Terry's legal relationship with the defendant school district.

Before the due process hearings, the defendants proposed merely to continue an IEP that was unable to address, let alone reduce, Terry's SIB. Now, the defendants are required to implement a new IEP with new approaches to Terry's SIB. "Based on [the parent's] success on the possible use of SIBIS and her role as a catalyst for the new IEP for Terry, we hold that [the parent] is a prevailing party." Therefore, Terry's mother was entitled to 100% of her attorney's fees.

b. *School District Not Required To Consider The Use Of Aversive Stimulation*

(1) ***Salinas Union High School District***, 22 IDELR 301 (SEA 1995)

(a) *Facts:* The parents of a 17-year-old deaf and autistic student proposed the use of an aversive stimulation device, the Self Injurious Behavior Inhibiting System (SIBIS), to reduce his self-injurious behaviors. Specifically, the student engaged in "flapping" at his ears with his hands and biting his hands. Both of these behaviors were known to bruise, redden, and/or break the skin, at times to the point of drawing blood. After receiving education in the home for awhile, the student was gradually moved into a program for the hearing impaired at a district high school. When the district rejected the use of SIBIS for this student, his parents sought a determination that the use of SIBIS was a necessary related service in order to ensure that the student received a free and appropriate education (FAPE).

(b) ***Held:* For the district. The district is not required to use the SIBIS as part of the student's school program in order to provide him with FAPE.**

(c) *Reasoning:* The hearing officer noted that the evidence presented at the hearing indicated the student was making significant academic and social progress in the district's behavior plan. The school was successfully utilizing a technique called Professional Assault Response Training (PART) that involved temporarily restraining the student's hands and legs. Furthermore, the evidence was clear that the student was not inflicting significant injury on himself, but was sucessfully achieving educational benefit. Therefore, the SIBIS device was not a necessary related service for the student to receive FAPE.

- **Facilitated Communication and the Criminal Justice System**

I. *Fraud Charges Not Maintained Against Supporters Of Facilitated Communication Following Dismissed Child Abuse Charges*

1. ***Storch v. Syracuse***, 629 N.Y.S.2d 958 (1995)

a. *Facts:* Jenny Storch is autistic and non-verbal. In 1991, an aide at Jenny's school reported that Jenny had claimed to be sexually assaulted by her father. Jenny was alleged to have communicated this information through the facilitated communication used at the school. Upon learning of this information, the school reported the accusation to the authorities, and a petition was later raised against Jenny's father for child abuse. At the Family Court hearing, the judge determined that facilitated communication was not generally accepted as reliable in the scientific community and refused to accept the testimony elicited by the facilitated communication. Following this determination, the petition was withdrawn and the proceeding discontinued. Thereafter, Jenny's parents filed a claim in federal district court, essentially arguing that facilitated communication was a hoax. They filed claims against a number of parties, including the teacher's aide who reported the abuse, a professor who was a leading advocate of facilitated communication, and the university where he taught. After this claim was dismissed for lack of subject matter jurisdiction, the parents refiled in state court raising essentially the same claims. The university and the professor moved for a summary judgment.

b. ***Held:*** **For the professor and the university.**

c. *Reasoning:* The court concluded that although the professor was an avid supporter of facilitated communication (FC), and admitted that FC is still not a proven method, his statements concerning FC did not amount to fraud, nor did any of the defendants owe the parents any duty. Thus, the parents failed to state a claim against the defendants under any of the theories asserted. The defendants' motion for summary judgment was granted, dismissing the claims against them.

J. *Use of Testimony Elicited By Facilitated Communication Upheld by Court in Child Abuse Case*

1. ***State v. Warden***, 22 IDELR 436 (KS. Sup.Ct. 1995)

a. *Facts:* Through the use of facilitated communication, a 12-year-old student with autism and severe or profound mental retardation alleged that he had been sexually abused by an employee at the residential school he attended. Although the employee confessed the crime to the police and admitted it to a co-worker, he denied both statements at the trial. At the trial, the student again used facilitated communication to testify against the employee. After the jury found the employee guilty of indecent liberties with a child, the employee appealed, raising objections to the use of facilitated communication (FC) during the trial.

b. ***Held:*** **For the state.**

c. *Reasoning:* Although the court initially rejected that the statements elicited through the use of FC were scientific evidence, it reasoned that the FC testimony was valid regardless. Because FC is just a method of communication, it requires no scientific interpretation, and lay jurors may be relied upon to interpret its results. Therefore, the test of whether FC is scientific evidence and accepted in the scientific community is inapplicable. Furthermore, the jury was able to observe the student's use of FC and could decide what weight, if any, to accord the FC testimony.

Requests For LOVAAS-Based Programs Awarded:

1. *Allamakee Community School District*, 24 IDELR 516 (IA 1996)
2. *Board of Education of the Ann Arbor Public Schools*, 24 IDELR 621 (MI 1996)
3. *Delaware County Intermediate Unit #25 v. Martin and Melinda K.*, 831 F.Supp. 1206 (E.D. Penn. 1993)
4. *Highbridge Board of Education*, 24 IDELR 589 (NJ 1995)
5. *Independent School District No. 318*, 24 IDELR 1096 (MN 1996)
6. *Rose v. Chester County Intermediate Unit*, 24 IDELR 61 (E.D. Penn. 1996)
7. *Watertown Public Schools*, 24 IDELR 92 (MA 1996)
8. *T. H. v. Board of Education of Palatine Community Consolidated School District 15*, 55 F. Supp. 2d 830 (N.D. Ill. 1999)

Private Placements For Students With Autism Awarded:

1. *Ash v. Lake Oswego School District*, 980 F.2d 585 (9th Cir. 1992)
2. *Corbett v. Regional Center For East Bay*, 699 F.Supp. 230 (N.D. CA 1988)
3. *Delaware County Intermediate Unit #25 v. Martin and Melinda K.*, 831 F.Supp. 1206 (E.D. Penn. 1993)
4. *In re: Drew P. v. Clarke County School District*, 877 F.2d 927 (11th Cir. 1989)
5. *Robertson County School System v. King*, 24 IDELR 1036 (6th Cir. 1996)
6. *Rose v. Chester County Intermediate Unit*, 24 IDELR 61 (E.D. Penn. 1996)

CHAPTER SUMMARY

1. Recent case law tends to support both less restrictive and more restrictive placements for students with disabilities,

from full mainstreaming, which some authors call "inclusion," to residential placements funded by the local school system.

2. In determining whether residential placement should be funded by a school district, the courts are focusing on whether the residential placement is required for educational purposes, not on the diagnosis in and of itself.
3. When there is disagreement over whether a child is primarily autistic, mentally retarded, or has a pervasive developmental disorder, the diagnostic label does not dictate the educational placement, but rather the individual child's needs.
4. Generally, as long as a school district is providing a procedurally and substantively correct IEP, parents do not have a right to compel the school to adopt a specific teaching method. The school is required to provide appropriate services, and not what the parents might consider optimal services.
5. A court has ruled that specific teacher training is not included under "Other Related Services"; teacher competency remains within the providence of the school administration.
6. Court decisions allow the continued investigation of Facilitated Communication (FC) for use with students with autism; however, the unrestrained use of this unproved method is risky at best.
7. Time-out, blanket wrapping, and aversive stimulation can be considered legitimate intervention strategies for students with autism, to be used on a case-by-case basis and tied to individual needs.
8. Court testimony through the use of Facilitated Communication has been accepted on a case-by-case basis, but has usually been rejected by the courts.

Subject Index

(Page numbers in italics indicate material in figures or tables.)